Advanced Grammar in Use

A self-study reference and practice book for advanced learners of English

Third Edition

with answers

Martin Hewings

CAMBRIDGE
UNIVERSITY PRESS

CAMBRIDGE
UNIVERSITY PRESS

University Printing House, Cambridge CB2 8BS, United Kingdom

One Liberty Plaza, 20th Floor, New York, NY 10006, USA

477 Williamstown Road, Port Melbourne, VIC 3207, Australia

4843/24, 2nd Floor, Ansari Road, Daryaganj, Delhi – 110002, India

79 Anson Road, #06–04/06, Singapore 079906

Cambridge University Press is part of the University of Cambridge.

It furthers the University's mission by disseminating knowledge in the pursuit of education, learning and research at the highest international levels of excellence.

www.cambridge.org
Information on this title: www.cambridge.org/9781108430463

First published 2013
Fahasa edition 2017

20 19 18 17 16 15 14 13 12 11 10 9 8 7 6 5 4 3 2 1

Printed in Vietnam by Fahasa

A catalogue record for this publication is available from the British Library

ISBN 978-1-108-43046-3 Paperback with answers and CD-ROM for Windows XP, Vista or 7 and Mac OSX 10.6, 10.7
ISBN 978-1-107-69738-6 Paperback with answers
ISBN 978-1-107-61378-2 Paperback without answers

Contents

If you are not sure which units you need to study, use the **Study planner** on page 210.

If you are not sure which units you need to study, use the **Study planner** on page 210.

If you are not sure which units you need to study, use the **Study planner** on page 210.

If you are not sure which units you need to study, use the **Study planner** on page 210.

Thanks

I would like to thank all those who worked with me on the first two editions of *Advanced Grammar in Use*, in particular Jeanne McCarten and Alison Sharpe for their encouragement. Thanks also to my former colleagues and students in the English for International Students Unit at the University of Birmingham for their help and interest.

For this third edition I am grateful to Colin McIntosh, Nora McDonald, Annabel Marriott, Sabina Sahni, Kevin Doherty, Andy George, Claire Cole and Janet Weller. Claire and Janet in particular have given me tremendous support in preparing the book and the accompanying CDROM.

Thanks to Sophie Joyce, Sandy Nichols, Katie Mac, Ian Mitchell and David Whamond for the illustrations and to Kamae Design for their work on the finished product. I would also like to thank Cambridge University Press for allowing me access to the Cambridge International Corpus.

Many students and teachers sent me comments on the 2nd edition, and these have been very helpful in writing this new edition. Thank you all for taking the trouble to contact me.

Finally, my thanks, as ever, to Suzanne, David and Ann.

The authors and publishers acknowledge the following sources of photographs and are grateful for the permissions granted.

p. 6: WithGod/Shutterstock; p. 11: Comstock Images/Thinkstock; p. 17: Thinkstock; p. 33: Image Source/Glowimages; p. 39: Thinkstock; p. 109: Thinkstock; p. 114: Bildagentur RM/Glowimages.

To the student

Who the book is for

Advanced Grammar in Use is for advanced students of English. It was written mainly as a self-study book, but might also be used in class with a teacher.

How the book is organised

There are 100 units in the book, each looking at a particular area of grammar. Some sections within each unit focus on the particular use of a grammatical pattern, such as *will be* + *-ing* (as in *will be travelling*); others explore grammatical contrasts, such as whether to use *would* or *used to* in reporting past events, or when we use *except* or *except for*. The 100 units are grouped under a number of headings such as *Tenses* and *The future*, and you can find details of this in the *Contents*. Each unit consists of two pages. On the left-hand page are explanations and examples; on the right-hand page are practice exercises. The letters next to each exercise show you which section(s) of the left-hand page you need to understand to do that exercise.

At the back of the book you will find a number of further sections.

- *Appendices* (pages 202 and 204) Two appendices provide further information about irregular verbs and passive verb forms.
- *Glossary* (page 205) Although terms to describe grammar have been kept to a minimum, some have been included, and you can find explanations of these terms in the *Glossary*.
- *Study planner* (page 210) You can use the *Study planner* to help you decide which units you should study, or which parts of the *Grammar reminder* you should read first.
- *Grammar reminder* (page 222) This presents examples and explanations of areas of grammar that you are likely to have studied already at earlier stages of learning English. References on the left-hand page of each unit point you to the sections of the *Grammar reminder* relevant to that unit. Read these sections to refresh your understanding before you start work on the more advanced grammar points in the unit.
- *Additional exercises* (page 240) If you want further practice of grammar points, follow the references at the bottom of the right-hand page of a unit. These will tell you which of the *Additional exercises* to do next.
- *Keys* (page 251, 277 and 278) You can check your answers to the practice exercises, *Study planner* and *Additional exercises* in the keys. You will also find comments on some of the answers.
- *Indexes* (pages 281 and 287) Use the *Indexes* to help you find the grammar or vocabulary you need.

How to use the book

It is not necessary to work through the units in order. If you know which grammar points you have difficulty with, go straight to the units that deal with them, using the *Contents* or *Indexes* to help you find the relevant unit. When you have found a unit to study, read through any related material in the *Grammar reminder* before you begin.

You can use the units in a number of ways. You might study the explanations and examples first, do the exercises on the opposite page, check your answers in the *Key to Exercises*, and then look again at the explanations if you made any mistakes. If you just want to practise an area of grammar you think you already know, you could do the exercises first and then study the explanations for any you got wrong. You might of course simply use the book as a reference book without doing the exercises.

Corpus information

A corpus is a large collection of texts stored on a computer. In writing *Advanced Grammar in Use* we have worked with the Cambridge International Corpus (CIC), a multi-million word collection of real speech and writing, and the Cambridge Learner Corpus, a collection of exam answers written by students. From these corpora we can learn more about language in use, and about the common errors made by learners. Using this information, we can be sure that the grammar explanations and examples in the book reflect real language, and we can focus on problem areas for learners. We have also used the CIC to produce word boxes, listing the most common words found in particular grammar patterns.

To the teacher

Advanced Grammar in Use was written as a self-study grammar book but teachers might also find it useful for supplementing or supporting their classroom teaching. The book will probably be most useful for advanced level students for reference and practice.

No attempt has been made to order the units according to level of difficulty. Instead, you should select units as they are relevant to the syllabus that you are following with your students, or as particular difficulties arise, rather than working through from beginning to end. Alternatively, you could ask students to do the multiple-choice test in the *Study planner* (page 210) and focus on units that deal with areas of grammar where students are least successful.

Don't forget to point students to the *Grammar reminder* (page 222). This is a reference-only section which presents basic knowledge on a number of areas of grammar. It will be useful for students to read through a section before moving on to the more advanced material in the units. At the beginning of each section of the *Grammar reminder* you will find information about the unit(s) it relates to.

There are many ways in which you can use the book with a class. You might, for example, present the explanations on the left-hand page of a unit, and use the exercises for classroom practice. Alternatively, you might want to begin with the exercises and refer to the left-hand page only when students are having problems. You could also set particular units or groups of units (such as those on *Articles* or *Nouns*) for self-study if individual students are having difficulties. Another possibility might be to develop your own classroom-based activities around the explanations on the left-hand page of a unit, and then set the exercises as consolidation material for self-study. When students need further practice of grammar points from a number of different units, refer them to the *Additional exercises* (page 240). References at the bottom of the right-hand pages show where the relevant *Additional exercises* can be found.

An edition of *Advanced Grammar in Use* without the answers is also available, and some teachers might prefer to use it with their students.

The third edition of *Advanced Grammar in Use* has the same comprehensive grammar coverage as previous editions, but many of its exercises have been revised and its layout made more user-friendly.

Advanced Grammar in Use

Unit 1

Present continuous and present simple 1

A State verbs

Reminder ➜ A1–A5

We can use the present continuous with some state verbs (e.g. **attract**, **like**, **look**, **love**, **sound**) to emphasise that a situation is temporary or for a period of time around the present. Compare:

- Ella stays with us quite often. The children **love** having her here. *and*
- Ella's with us at the moment. The children **are loving** having her here.

State verbs which we rarely use with the present continuous include **believe**, **consist of**, **doubt**, **own**.

B

Some verbs have different meanings when they are used to talk about states and when they describe actions. With their 'state' meanings, they usually take simple rather than continuous forms. With their 'action' meanings, they may take simple or continuous forms, depending on context. Compare:

- The app **doesn't appear** to work on my phone. (appear: *state* = seem) *and*
- Carley Robb **is** currently **appearing** in a musical on Broadway. / She often **appears** in musicals. (appear: *action* = take part)

Also: **cost, expect, feel, fit, have, imagine, measure, think, weigh**

C Mental state verbs

With some verbs describing *mental* states (e.g. **find**, **realise**, **regret**, **think**, **understand**) we can use the present continuous to emphasise that we have recently started to think about something or that we are not sure about something. Compare:

- I **regret** that the company will have to be sold. (= I've made the decision and I'm sorry about it) *and*
- **I'm regretting** my decision to give her the job. (= I'm increasingly aware that it was the wrong decision)

When it means 'think carefully about', **consider** is only used with the present continuous:

- He**'s considering** taking early retirement. (*not* He considers taking early retirement.)

Some other verbs describing preferences and mental states (e.g. **agree**, **believe**, **conclude**, **know**, **prefer**) are rarely used with the present continuous:

- I **believe** you now. (*not* I'm believing you now.)

D Performatives

We use the present simple with verbs which perform the action they describe (= performatives):

- I **suggest** you park outside the city and get the bus to the centre.
- We **request** that you read the terms and conditions carefully before signing.

Also: **acknowledge, admit, advise, apologise, beg**, **confess**, **congratulate**, **declare**, **deny**, **forbid**, **guarantee**, **name**, **order**, **permit**, **predict**, **promise**, **refuse**, **remind**, **request**, **thank**, **warn**

Some verbs used as performatives with the present simple in affirmative (= positive) sentences (**apologise**, **deny**, **guarantee**, **promise**, **suggest**) have a similar meaning with either the present simple or the present continuous in negative sentences:

- I **don't deny** / **I'm not denying** taking the books, but Miguel said it would be okay.

Modals are often used with performatives to make what we say more tentative or polite:

- We **would advise** you to arrive two hours before the flight leaves.
- I **must beg** you to keep this a secret.

Exercises

1.1 **Complete each pair of sentences using the same verb (in a question form or negative if necessary) from the box. Use the present continuous; if this is not possible, use the present simple. Use ⁄\ to add any words outside the gap and use contracted forms where appropriate.** A & B

attract	consist of	doubt	feel	fit
have	like	look	measure	sound

1 a I hear you're having your house repainted. How it ....? (*or* How it ....?)
  b I bought this new dress today. How it ....?
2 a A: What are you doing with that ruler? B: I .... the area of the kitchen.
  b The garden .... 12 by 20 metres.
3 a I .... whether I'll get another chance to retake the exam.
  b I suppose she might be at home tonight, but I .... it.
4 a The new science museum currently .... 10,000 visitors a month.
  b Flowers .... bees with their brightly-coloured petals.
5 a Carlos won't work at the top of the 20-storey building because he .... heights.
  b A: How's the new job? B: Well, at the moment, I .... it at all.
6 a My car's in the garage today. They .... new brakes.
  b I bought this jumper for Anna, but it .... her so I'll have to take it back.
7 a What's your shirt made from? It .... like silk.
  b I won't be coming to work today. I .... very well.
8 a The roof of the house .... only plastic sheets nailed down in a few places.
  b Their school uniform .... black trousers and a dark green jumper.
9 a Simon's new song .... quite good, but he doesn't think he's ready yet to perform it in public.
  b A: What's that noise? B: It .... like a bird stuck in the chimney.
10 a Poulson .... treatment for a knee injury, but should be fit to play on Saturday.
  b My sister .... long blonde hair. You're bound to recognise her.

1.2 **Cross out any improbable answers.** C & D

Dear Aunt Mara,

Thanks for your message. I (1) *apologise / 'm apologising* for not getting back to you sooner, but I've been incredibly busy. When I went into nursing, you warned me that it would be really hard work, but I (2) *admit / 'm admitting* that I didn't really believe you. Don't get me wrong – I (3) *don't suggest / 'm not suggesting* that I'm not enjoying it. It's incredibly rewarding, but I (4) *now realise / 'm now realising* how hard the job is. When I get home I just eat (not very well, I (5) *confess / 'm confessing*) and go straight to bed. It doesn't help that the bus journey to the hospital is so slow. I (6) *consider / 'm considering* buying a car, which will make things easier, I hope.

And what about you? How (7) *do you find / are you finding* living in a village after so many years in the city? I (8) *know / 'm knowing* how difficult it is for you to travel such a long way, but it would be lovely if you could come and stay with me for a weekend. I've got plenty of room in my flat. I (9) *don't guarantee / 'm not guaranteeing* to cook as well as you do, but I (10) *promise / 'm promising* to find time to show you around this lovely old town.

Hope to see you soon. Keep in touch.

Love,

Martina

→ **Additional exercise 1** (page 240)

Unit 2

Present continuous and present simple 2

A

We often use the present simple and present continuous in stories and jokes in informal spoken English to create the impression that events are happening now. This can make them more direct and exciting and hold people's attention:

Reminder ➜ A1–A5

- She **goes** up to this man and **looks** straight into his eyes. He**'s** not **wearing** his glasses, and he **doesn't recognise** her ...
- This man**'s playing** golf when a kangaroo **bounds** up to him, **grabs** his club and **hits** his ball about half a mile ...

The main events are usually described in sequence using the present simple and longer background events are described using the present continuous.

In narratives and anecdotes the present simple can be used to highlight an event. Often it is used after past tenses and with a phrase such as **suddenly** or **all of a sudden**:

- So last night, I'm waiting for the bus when this man **walks** up to me and **says** ...
- I was in the park reading a newspaper, when *all of a sudden* this dog **jumps** at me.

B

We also use the present simple and present continuous in live commentaries (for example, on sports events) when the report takes place at the same time as the action:

- King **serves** to the left-hand court and Adams **makes** a wonderful return. She**'s playing** magnificent tennis in this match ...

C

We can use the present simple in phrases such as **It says here**, **I hear**, **I gather**, **I see**, **I understand** and **They say**, **(Someone) says**, **(Someone) tells me** to introduce news that we have heard, read, seen (e.g. on television), or been told. We can also use past tenses (e.g. **It said here**, **I heard**):

- **I gather** you're worried about Pedro.
- Sophia **tells me** you're thinking of emigrating.
- Professor Hendriks is at the conference and **I hear** she's an excellent speaker.

D

The present simple is often used in news headlines to talk about events that have recently happened:

SECOND QUAKE *HITS* JAPAN

FIRE *BREAKS OUT* IN HOTEL ROOM

SCIENTISTS *FIND* ICE ON THE MOON

FOREIGN MINISTER *RESIGNS*

We can use the present simple to refer to the contents of books, films, newspapers, etc:

- Thompson **gives** a list of the largest European companies in Chapter 6.
- At the beginning of the book, three men **find** $4 million in a crashed plane.
- In the film, Loni Baranski **takes** the role of a private detective.

E

We can use the present continuous with adverbs such as **always**, **constantly**, **continually** or **forever** to emphasise that something is done so often that it is characteristic of a person, group or thing:

- A: I think I'll stay here after all. B: You**'re** *constantly* **changing** your mind.
- Jacob is a really kind person. He**'s** *always* **offering** to help me with my work.

We often use this pattern to indicate disapproval. The past continuous is used in a similar way with these adverbs (e.g. **Was** Olivia *always* **asking** you for money, too?).

We can use the present continuous to describe something we regularly do at a certain time:

- At eight o'clock I**'m** usually **driving** to work, so phone me on my mobile.
- Seven o'clock is a bit early. We**'re** generally **eating** then.

Exercises

2.1 **Complete these sentences using the verbs in brackets. Use the present simple or present continuous.** A & B

1 Rodriguez ....passes.... to Messi who .... just over the bar. Barcelona .... much more in this half … (~~pass~~ – *shoot* – *attack*)

2 A man .... home late one night after the office Christmas party. His wife .... for him, and she .... to him … (*arrive* – *wait* – *say*)

3 I went to a concert yesterday in the Town Hall. In the middle of it, while the orchestra .... this man suddenly .... on his seat and .... to conduct them. (*play* – *stand* – *start*)

2.2 **Complete what each person says about the news they have read or heard using the present tense phrases in C.** C

1 **Government gives health service billions**

....I see.... the government's giving ....the health service a lot more money....

2 **Vegecorp to sack 1,000 workers.**

.... Vegecorp are going to ....

3 President Cartman announced a new public holiday on his birthday, August 6th. He made the announcement …

.... we're going to have ....

4 

Ed

.... Bruno's ....

5 

Julia

.... she's ....

6 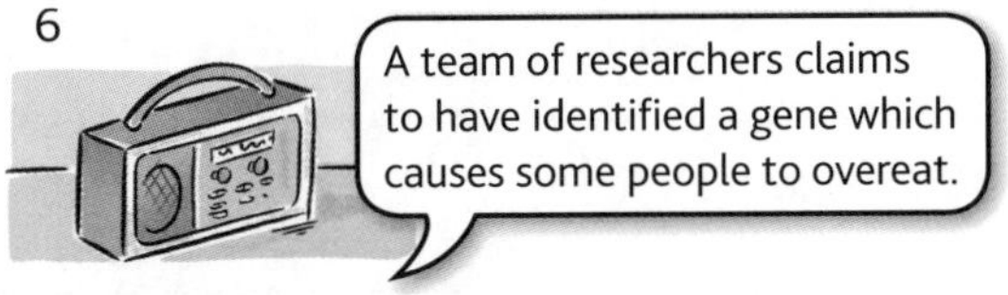

.... they've identified ....

2.3 **Expand one of the sets of notes below to complete each dialogue.** E

continually / change / mind	**forever / moan / work**	**forever / ask me / money**
constantly / criticise / driving	~~**always / complain / handwriting**~~	

1 A: I can't read this. B: You're ....always complaining about my handwriting....

2 A: Can I borrow €10? B: You're ....

3 A: That was a dangerous thing to do. B: You're ....

4 A: I think I'll stay here after all. B: You're ....

5 A: I had a bad day at the office again. B: You're ....

2.4 **Complete each pair of sentences using the same verb (in negative form if necessary). Use the present continuous or the present simple. Use ⋏ to add any words outside the gap.** D & E

1 a A: Shall I phone at six? B: No, we usually .... dinner at that time.
b I .... lamb, thanks. I'm a vegetarian.

2 a Gielman .... Henry V in the latest production at the Royal Theatre.
b They constantly .... loud music until the early hours of the morning.

3 a I normally .... the children to school at 8:30. Perhaps we could meet at 9:00.
b In his 2007 book, Wall .... a controversial view of Britain's role in the war.

→ Additional exercise 1 (page 240)

Unit 3

Past simple and present perfect

A

Time expressions that refer to the present, such as **this morning / week / month** and **today**, can be used with either past simple or present perfect verbs.

Reminder → A6–A12

If we think of **this morning** (etc.) as a past, completed time period, then we use the past simple; if we think of **this morning** (etc.) as a time period which includes the present moment, then we use the present perfect. Compare:

- I **didn't shave** *this morning*. (= the morning is over and I didn't shave) *and*
- I **haven't shaved** *this morning*. (= it is still the morning and I might shave later)

B

In a sentence which includes a time clause with **since**, we generally prefer a past simple verb in the time clause and a present perfect verb in the main clause. The time clause refers to a particular point in the past:

- *Since* Mr Dodson **became** president unemployment **has increased**. (*rather than* … has become …)
- She **hasn't been able** to play tennis *since* she **broke** her arm. (*rather than* … has broken …)

Note, however, that we use the present perfect in the time clause if the two situations described in the main clause and time clause extend until the present:

- **Have** you **met** any of your neighbours *since* you'**ve lived** here? (*not* … you lived …)

C

With time clauses introduced by **after**, **when**, **until**, **as soon as**, **once**, **by the time** and the time expressions **the minute / second / moment** the past simple refers to past, completed events and the present perfect refers to future events. Compare these examples:

- *After* she **left** hospital (past), she had a long holiday. *and*
- *After* Lucas **has left** school (future), he will be spending six months in India.
- *The minute* I **got** the news about Anna (past) I telephoned my parents. *and*
- I'll contact you *the minute* I'**ve got** my exam results. (future)

In the time clause in sentences like this it is possible to use the past perfect instead of the past simple (e.g. After she **had left** …) and the present simple instead of the present perfect (e.g. After Lucas **leaves** …) with the same meaning (see also Unit 5).

D

In news reports, you will often read about or hear recent events introduced with the present perfect, and then the past simple or other past tenses are used to give details:

- A Russian spacecraft **has returned** safely to Earth with its two passengers. US astronaut Scott Keane and Russian cosmonaut Olga Kaleri **landed** in the early hours of Wednesday.
- An American woman **has become** the first person to make 2 million contributions to Wikipedia. Esther Miller **began** editing the site eight years ago.

E

After the pattern **It / This / That** *is / will be* **the first time** … we generally use the present perfect in the next clause:

- *That's the first time* I'**ve seen** Jan look embarrassed. (reporting a past event)
- *It won't be the first time* she **has voted** against the government. (talking about a future event)

Note that after **It / This / That** *was* **the first time** … we generally use the *past* perfect (see Unit 5):

- *It was the first time* I'**d talked** to Dimitra outside the office.

Exercises

3.1 **Complete each sentence with a verb from the box. Use the present perfect or past simple, with a negative form where necessary.** A

have	go	oversleep	read	spend	wear

1 A: Shall I make us some dinner? It's already eight o'clock.
B: No, thanks. I .... to the dentist this afternoon and my mouth hurts too much to eat anything.
2 I .... three lectures today and I still have two more later this afternoon.
3 It was so hot today that I .... shorts and a T-shirt at work.
4 We .... £200 on food this month and there's another week to go before I get paid.
5 A: Do you want a lift home?
B: No, I .... this morning because my alarm clock didn't go off, so I need to work late.
6 I .... much of the report yet, but I have to finish it by the weekend.

3.2 **Complete the sentences with the pairs of verbs from the box. Choose the most appropriate tense — present perfect or past simple.** B

be able – feel	happen – speak	improve – be
not want – fall	rescue – be	work – not have

1 Maria .... to go swimming since she .... in the river.
2 Since she .... at the company she .... a day off through illness.
3 Since he .... the girl from a house fire, he .... on TV almost every day.
4 A lot .... since I last .... to you.
5 Since I .... to drive I .... much more independent
6 Stefan's reading .... enormously since he .... at school.

3.3 **One sentence in each pair is wrong. Correct it by replacing the past simple with the present perfect of the italicised verb.** C

1 a Remember that after you *signed* the contract you won't be able to change your mind.
b Carlo's injury only became apparent after he *signed* to play for Real Madrid.

2 a As soon as I *finished* college I want to travel around Australia.
b I didn't have time to check the essay. I handed it in as soon as I *finished* it.

3 a By the time Sarah *got* to work the meeting had finished.
b I'll probably have finished breakfast by the time the children *got* up.

4 a I recognised her the moment I *heard* her laugh.
b I'll tell you what time we're coming the moment I *heard* from Emil.

3.4 **Here are some extracts from a television news report. Choose the more appropriate tense – present perfect or past simple – for the verbs in brackets.** D & E

1 When President Nelson ...arrives... (*arrive*) in Paris this evening, it will be the first time she .... (*visit*) Europe since her election victory in May.
2 The Victoria Hospital in Milltown .... (*close*) to new patients after more cases of food poisoning. Three elderly patients .... (*die*) last week in the outbreak.
3 The rate of inflation .... (*drop*) to 4.8%. It's the first time in nearly two years that the rate .... (*fall*) below 5%.
4 Nearly 600 laptops .... (*steal*) from Ministry of Defence staff over the past five years. However, a spokesperson .... (*insist*) that there had been no security problems as none of the computers .... (*hold*) secret information.

→ **Additional exercise 2** (page 241)

Unit 4

Past continuous and past simple

A

When we talk about two events or activities that went on over the same period of past time, we can often use the past continuous or the past simple for both: Reminder ➜ A6–A8, A13

- Mia **was reading** to the children while Ben **was washing up**. (*or* … **read** … **washed up**.)

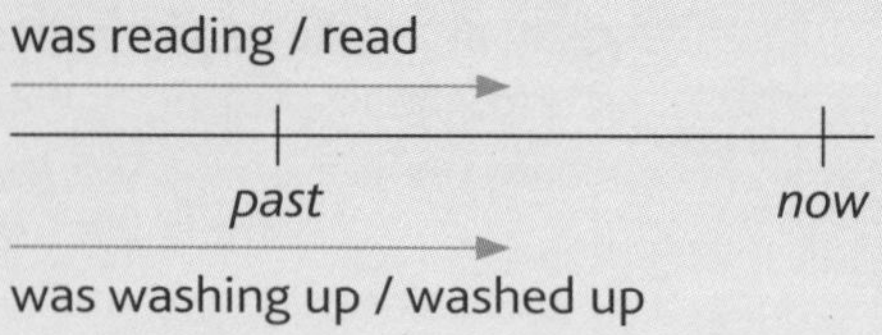

Using the past continuous emphasises that the event or activity ('was reading') was in progress during the past period of time ('while Ben was washing up'). Compare:

- When I **was learning / learned** to drive I was living with my parents.

Was learning emphasises that the activity was in progress ('I had lessons during this time') and **learned** emphasises completion ('I passed my test during this time').

When we talk about two or more past completed events that followed one another, we use the past simple, not the past continuous, for both (see also Unit 5C):

- She **got** up when the alarm clock **went** off.

B

We usually use the past simple rather than the past continuous to talk about repeated past actions:

- We **went** to Spain three times last year.
- **Did** you **drive** past her house every day?

However, we can use the past continuous, particularly in spoken English, when we want to emphasise that repeated actions went on for a limited and temporary period of past time:

- When Kata was in hospital, we **were visiting** her twice a day. (*or* … we **visited** …)
- To lose weight before the race, I **wasn't eating** any biscuits for weeks. (*or* … I **didn't eat** …)

or to talk about something that happened surprisingly often:

- Last week I **was having to** bring work home every night to get it all done. (*or* … **had** …)
- When the builders were here I **was making** them cups of tea all the time. (*or* … **made** …)

C

We often use the past simple in a narrative (e.g. a report or a story) to talk about a single complete past event and the past continuous to describe the situation that existed at the time. The event might have interrupted the situation, or happened while the situation was in progress:

- Erika **dropped** her bag while she **was getting** into her car.
- She **was shaking** with anger as she **left** the hotel.

D

We can use either the past continuous or past simple (or past perfect; see Unit 5E) with some verbs to talk about things we intended to do but didn't:

- We **were meaning** to call in and see you, but Marc wasn't feeling well. (*or* We **meant** …)

Also: **consider + -ing, expect to, hope to, intend to, plan to / on + -ing, think about / of + -ing, want to**

These verbs (with the exception of **mean** and **expect**) and **wonder about** can also be used with the present and past continuous to report what we might do in the future. The past continuous is less definite than the present continuous:

- I **was thinking of** going to China next year, but it depends how much money I've got. (*less definite than* I'**m thinking of** going …)
- We **were wondering about** inviting Eva over tomorrow. (*less definite than* We'**re wondering** about …)

Exercises

4.1 **Complete the sentences using these pairs of verbs. Use the past simple in one gap and the past continuous in the other.** A–D

come – show	**~~get – go~~**	**hope – give**	**live – spend**
look – see	**play – break**	**start – check in**	

1 Just as I ......was getting...... into the bath all the lights ......went...... off.
2 I .... to go away this weekend, but my boss .... me some work that I have to finish by Monday.
3 When I .... in Paris, I .... three hours a day travelling to and from work.
4 A friendly American couple .... chatting to him as he .... at the hotel reception.
5 I bumped into Lena last week. She .... a lot better than when I last .... her.
6 My boss .... into the office just as I .... everyone my holiday photos.
7 I .... badminton four times a week before I .... my ankle.

This time, use the *same* tense, either past simple or past continuous, in both spaces.

add – taste	**go off – light**	**not listen – explain**	**push – run**	**not watch – dream**

8 The smoke alarm .... when he .... a candle underneath it.
9 I can't remember how to answer this question. I must confess that I .... while the teacher .... it to us.
10 She .... more salt to the soup, and then it .... much better.
11 Although the television was on, I .... it. Instead I .... about my holidays.
12 She .... open the door and .... into the room.

4.2 **Look again at numbers 1, 4, 7 and 11 in 4.1. Which of these sentences could have both verbs in the past simple? What difference in meaning, if any, would there be?**

4.3 **Complete this email with either the past simple or the past continuous form of the verbs in brackets. Where alternatives are possible, think about any difference in meaning.** A–C

I (1) .... (*buy*) a new alarm clock the other day in Taylor's the jewellers, when I actually (2) .... (*see*) somebody shoplifting. I'd just finished paying for my clock and as I (3) .... (*turn*) round, an elderly woman (4) .... (*slowly put*) a silver plate into a bag that she (5) .... (*carry*). Then she (6) .... (*walk*) over to another part of the shop and (7) .... (*pick up*) an expensive-looking watch a number of times. When she (8) .... (*think*) that nobody (9) .... (*look*), she (10) .... (*drop*) it into the bag. Before I (11) .... (*have*) a chance to tell the staff in the shop, she (12) .... (*notice*) that I (13) .... (*watch*) her and (14) .... (*hurry*) out. Unfortunately for her, two police officers (15) .... (*walk*) past just at that moment and she (16) .... (*run*) straight into them.

→ Additional exercise 1 (page 240)

Unit 5

Past perfect and past simple

A

When we give an account of a sequence of past events we usually put these events in chronological order using the past simple. If we want to refer to an event out of order – that is, an event which happened *before* the last event in the sequence we have written or spoken about – we can use the past perfect. Study the use of the past perfect and past simple in the text on the right:

Reminder ➜ A6–A8, A14–A15

Order of events:	1 gave present 2 wrote email 3 made mistake 4 realised mistake
Order events are mentioned:	1 wrote email 2 **had given** present (*out of order*) 3 realised mistake 4 **had made** mistake (*out of order*)

I **wrote** Clara an email to thank her for the present she **had given** me for my birthday last week. But as soon as I pressed the 'send' button, I **realised** that I **had made** a mistake and sent it to her sister instead.

B

When we understand that we are talking about events before another past event, we don't have to continue using the past perfect:

- We **bought** a new car last month. We**'d driven** my parents' old car for ages, but it **started** (*or* **had started**) to fall apart. We **put** (*or* **had put**) a new engine in it, but that **didn't solve** (*or* **hadn't solved**) the problems we were having.

C

If the order of past events is clear from the context (for example, if time expressions make the order clear) we can often use either the past perfect or the past simple:

- *After* Ivan **had finished** reading, he put out the light. (*or* … Ivan **finished** …)
- The two leaders agreed to meet, even though *earlier* talks **had failed** to reach an agreement. (*or* … talks **failed** …)

D

The past perfect is often used in reporting what was originally said or thought in the present perfect or past simple (see also Unit 35):

Talking about a past event	Reporting this past event
'I **have met** him before.'	I was sure that I **had met** him before. (*not* … I met him …)
'The village **hasn't changed** much.'	I found that the village **hadn't changed** much. (*not* … the village didn't change …)
'225 people **drowned** in the recent floods.'	Police said that 225 people **had drowned** in the recent floods. (*or* … **drowned** …)
'I **stole** the watch.'	She admitted that she **had stolen** the watch. (*or* … **stole** …)

E

We can use either the past perfect or past simple (and often past continuous and past perfect continuous; see Units 4 and 7) when we talk about things that we intended to do, but didn't or won't now do in the future:

- I **had hoped** to visit the gallery before I left Florence, but it's closed on Mondays. (*or* I **hoped** …, I **was hoping** …, I **had been hoping** …)
- Aron **planned** to retire at 60, but we have persuaded him to stay for a few more years. (*or* Aron **had planned** …, Aron **was planning** …, Aron **had been planning** …)

Exercises

5.1 **The events mentioned in the magazine article are listed below. Write the order in which the events are mentioned and then the order in which they occurred (or were thought to occur). Compare the two lists and consider why the past perfect (in italics) was used.** A & B

How I bought my dream house

When I first saw the old house I *had* just *moved* to the area. It *had been* empty for about a year and was beginning to need some repairs, but the house was exactly what I wanted. But by the time I *had put together* enough money I learnt that a property developer *had bought* it and planned to turn it into a hotel. Six months later I *had* nearly *given up* hope of finding anywhere to live in the village when I heard that the house was for sale again. The property developer *had decided* to invest his money in a new housing development on the edge of the village. I bought the house immediately and I've lived there happily ever since.

Carla Bridges

events	order events are mentioned in text	order of events
I moved …	2	2
I learnt …		
The property developer decided …		
I heard …		
I first saw the old house	1	
A property developer bought it		
I nearly gave up…		
I put together enough money…		
It was empty		1

5.2 **Underline the correct options. In some cases only one is correct, and in others both are correct.** C & D

1 As Jonas was introduced to Mrs Lopez, he realised that he *had met / met* her before.
2 During the previous week, I *had been / went* to the gym every evening.
3 He denied that he *had taken / took* the money from the office.
4 I thought it was the best film I *had seen / saw* in my life.
5 The boy told me that he *had lost / lost* his train ticket and didn't know how he would get home.
6 At the conference, scientists reported that they *had found / found* a cure for malaria.
7 The teacher guessed that some of the children *had cheated / cheated* in the exam.
8 She said that she *had made up / made up* her mind who to vote for, and that I couldn't persuade her to change.
9 Thomas explained that he *had gone / went* home early because he felt ill.
10 When I asked Maria about Jakub, she admitted that she *hadn't heard / didn't hear* from him for ages.
11 The waiter took my plate away before I *had finished / finished* eating.
12 Julia said she didn't want any dinner. Apparently, she *had eaten / ate* already.

5.3 **Expand these sets of notes using the past perfect to begin each sentence.** E

I / expect / operation / painful	~~**I / hope / leave / by nine**~~
He / not mean / insult / her	**Lara / not intend / become / dentist**
I / not think of / cook rabbit	

1 I had hoped to leave by nine, but I overslept and missed the train.
2 ……………………; she always wanted to be a vet.
3 ……………………, but I didn't feel a thing.
4 ……………………, until Andrei told me how tasty it was.
5 ……………………, but Daria was very offended.

➔ **Additional exercise 3** (page 241)

Present perfect continuous and present perfect

A

We use the present perfect continuous to express the idea of an activity (a task, piece of work, etc.) in progress until recently or until the time of speaking:

Reminder ➔ A9–A12, A16–A17

- **Have** you **been working** in the garden *all day*? You look exhausted.
- She**'s been writing** the book *since she was in her twenties* and at last it's finished.

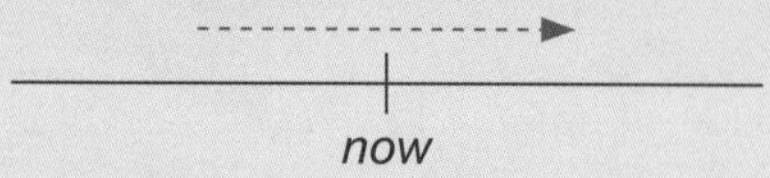

Note that we often use time expressions to say how long the activity has been in progress.

We don't use the present perfect continuous with verbs such as **belong**, **know**, (**dis**)**like**, and **understand** that describe unchanging states:

- **Have** you **known** each other long? (*not* Have you been knowing …)
- I **haven't liked** ice cream since I ate too much and was sick. (*not* I haven't been liking …)

When we talk about situations (general characteristics or circumstances) that exist until the present we can often use either the present perfect or present perfect continuous:

- We**'ve been looking forward to** this holiday for ages. (*or* We**'ve looked forward to** …)

B

We often use the present perfect or the present perfect continuous to talk about something that has recently finished if we can still see its results. However, we generally use the present perfect continuous with verbs that suggest extended or repeated activity. Compare:

- He**'s broken** his finger and is in a lot of pain. (*not* He's been breaking …) *and*
- **I've been playing** squash and need a shower! (*more likely than* I've played …)

We use the present perfect continuous rather than the present perfect when we draw a conclusion from what we can see, hear, etc. We often use this form to complain or criticise:

- Who**'s been messing** around with my papers? They're all over the place.
- You**'ve been eating** chocolate, haven't you? There's some on your shirt.

When we talk about the *result* of circumstances or an activity, we use the present perfect, rather than the present perfect continuous. When we focus on the *process* we often use either the present perfect or the present perfect continuous. Compare:

- Prices **have decreased** by 7%. (*not* Prices have been decreasing by 7%.) *and*
- Prices **have been decreasing** recently. (*or* Prices **have decreased** …)
- **I've used** three tins of paint on the kitchen walls. (*not* I've been using three tins of paint on the kitchen walls.) *and*
- **I've been using** a new kind of paint on the kitchen walls. (*or* I**'ve used** …)

C

The present perfect continuous emphasises that an activity is ongoing and repeated, while the present perfect suggests the activity happened only once or on a specified number of occasions:

- Miguel **has been kicking** a football against the wall all day. (*more likely than* … **has kicked** …)
- He **has played** for the national team in 65 matches so far. (*not* He has been playing for the national team in 65 matches so far.)

Compare:

- The workers **have been calling** for the chairman's resignation. (= emphasises a number of times, probably over an extended period) *and*
- Workers **have called** for management to begin negotiations on pay. (= maybe a number of times or only once.)

Exercises

6.1 **Complete each pair of sentences using the same verb. Use the present perfect in one sentence and the present perfect continuous in the other. Use negative forms where appropriate.** A–C

disappear	give	put	read	stay	stop	swim

1 a Martina Gonzalez .... in a rented flat since returning to Buenos Aires.
  b We .... at this hotel a couple of times before.
2 a All day, the police .... motorists to question them about the accident.
  b Good, the noise .... I can start concentrating on my work again.
3 a I .... any of Dickens' novels.
  b I .... this book on astrophysics for hours and I'm still only on page six.
4 a Dr Fletcher .... the same lecture to students for the last ten years.
  b Mr Sato .... nearly a million pounds to the charity this year.
5 a I did 20 lengths of the pool today. I .... that far since I was at school.
  b I .... and I feel exhausted.
6 a In recent years, companies .... increasing resources into internet marketing.
  b The South African coal company .... the Calverton Mine up for sale.
7 a An important file .... from my office.
  b Plants and vegetables .... from my garden since we had new neighbours.

6.2 **Here are two views on the government's announcement that it is to cut the money it gives to the Influenza Research Centre. If necessary, correct the present perfect continuous verbs using either the present perfect or past simple.** A–C and Unit 3

a *Dr Petra Adams, the Director of the Centre*

It's remarkable to think that since 1950 influenza (1) *has been claiming* more than 50,000 lives in this country, and in 1957 alone around 6,000 people (2) *have been dying*. But over the last 20 years we at the Centre (3) *have been making* considerable progress on understanding the illness. We (4) *have been producing* over a hundred books and articles reporting the results of our research and in 2012 they (5) *have been awarding* the Nobel Prize for medicine to one of my colleagues. In our more recent work we (6) *have been looking* into the effects of influenza on heart disease and we (7) *have also been exploring* a possible link between climate change and the recent increase in the number of cases of influenza. It is a tragedy that the government (8) *has been making* this decision now.

b *Sabir Khan, the Opposition spokesperson for science*

The previous government (1) *has been investing* huge amounts of money into the Centre and I think it's terrible that the present government (2) *has been announcing* this cut when the number of cases of influenza (3) *has been increasing*. The Centre (4) *has been running* successfully for many years. But this decision is just typical of this government. It (5) *has been neglecting* health research ever since it was elected, and (6) *has been cutting* back on spending on science generally. Although the government says that the cut is necessary because of the recent world economic problems, I (7) *have been finding* evidence that they (8) *have been planning* this for some time. I (9) *have been speaking* to the Minister about this yesterday and (10) *have also been writing* to the Prime Minister demanding that the decision should be reversed.

→ Additional exercise 2 (page 241)

Unit 7 Past perfect continuous, past perfect and past continuous

A We use the past perfect continuous to talk about something that was in progress recently before or up to a past point in time, and the past perfect when we talk about a finished activity before a past time:

Reminder ➜ A14–A15, A18

- I'**d been finishing** some work in the garden when Lea arrived, so I didn't hear her come in. (*not* I'd finished some work in the garden when Lea arrived, so I didn't hear her come in.) *and*
- I'**d finished** all the ironing so I started cleaning the windows. (*not* I'd been finishing all the ironing so I started cleaning the windows.)

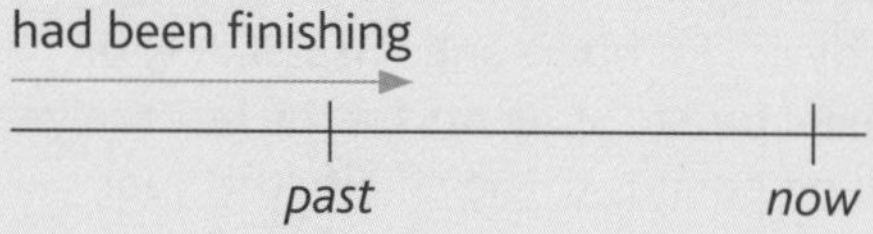

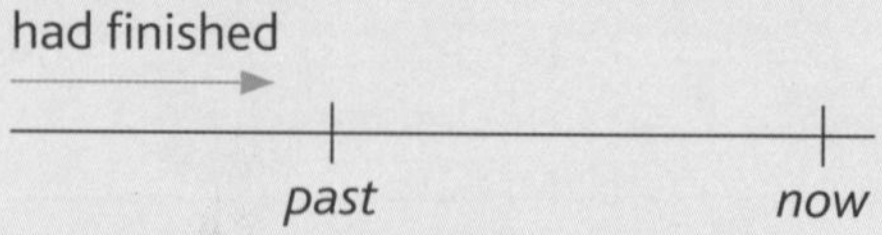

We can often use either the past perfect continuous or the past perfect with a similar meaning:

- I'**d been working / I'd worked** hard all year, so I felt that I deserved a holiday.

B If we talk about *how many* times something happened in a period up to a particular past time, we use the past perfect, not the past perfect continuous:

- How many times **had** you **met** him before yesterday? (*not* How many times had you been meeting ...)
- I **had stayed** in the hotel twice in the 1990s. (*not* I had been staying in the hotel twice ...)

C The past perfect continuous can be used to talk about a situation or activity that went on before a particular past time and (i) finished at that time, (ii) continued beyond it, or (iii) finished shortly before it:

- (i) We'**d been driving** for about an hour when the engine suddenly stopped.
- (ii) She felt terrible during the interview because she **had been suffering** from flu since the previous day.
- (iii) When I last saw Omar, he'**d been running** and was out of breath.

If we are not interested in how long the activity went on, we can use the past continuous instead of the past perfect continuous. Compare:

- When the merger was announced it became apparent that the two companies **had been discussing** the possibility *since last year*. *and*
- A friend told me about a conversation she'd recently overheard. Two women **were discussing** their holiday plans ...
- I first met Mateo and Lucia when they **had been going out** together *for five years*, and they didn't get married for another three years after that. *and*
- Karin met Lars when she **was going out** with his best friend.

D Remember that we don't describe states with continuous tenses (see Unit 1), and we use the past perfect, not the past perfect continuous, even when we focus on the length of a situation up to a particular past time:

- We **had** only **owned** the car for six weeks when the clutch broke. (*not* We had been owning the car for six weeks ...)

E The past perfect continuous is mainly used in written texts and is less common in speech. Here is an example in a newspaper article:

- The body of a climber who went missing in the Alps was finally found yesterday. Carl Sims **had been climbing** alone near the Harz Waterfall, which has claimed many lives in the past.

Exercises

7.1 **Complete each pair of sentences using one verb from the box. Use the past perfect continuous if possible; if not, use the past perfect.** A

apply	carry	fly	work

1 a She .... only .... for the company for a couple of months, so I was surprised to hear that she'd left.
  b She .... finally .... her way up from trainee to a management position, and she celebrated her promotion with a big party.
2 a The avalanche .... them 500 metres down the mountain but no one was hurt.
  b She took a bottle from the bag she .... all the way from home.
3 a We .... for visas early, but still hadn't got them by the week before the holiday.
  b She .... for jobs, without success, since leaving university.
4 a He .... all the way from New York to be at yesterday's meeting.
  b When the plane was diverted, shortly after take-off, it .... from London to Frankfurt.

7.2 **Use the past perfect continuous form of the verb in brackets if appropriate; if not, use the past perfect.** B–D

1 Mrs Bishop .... to have children for years, and only became pregnant at the age of 45. (*try*)
2 This was the first time we had been to the castle, even though we .... Prague a few times before. (*visit*)
3 She bought her first watch at the age of eight. It .... two pounds. (*cost*)
4 Emma Willems .... novels for ten years before she published her first book. (*write*)
5 For some time Daniel .... about passing the exams and eventually decided to change the course he was taking. (*worry*)
6 My teacher was really annoyed with me. It was the third time I .... late for school that week. (*arrive*)
7 I .... always .... it would be easy to get a job, and was disappointed to be rejected. (*believe*)
8 We .... about Sarah when, to our amazement, she walked through the door. (*talk*)

In which one of the sentences where you have used the past perfect continuous do you think the past continuous is more likely? C

7.3 **Study this conversation extract. If the italicised verbs are correct, write ✓. If they are wrong, correct them using either the past perfect (active or passive) or past perfect continuous.** A–E

A: How was your weekend?
B: Not great, actually. I (1)*'d really been looking* forward to a relaxing couple of days. But early on Saturday morning Mum phoned to say that Dad (2) *had been taking* ill.
A: Oh, no! What (3) *had happened*?
B: She (4) *had just been hearing* that he (5) *had been flown* by helicopter to hospital in Edinburgh from a village called Contin where he (6) *had fished* with my Uncle Mark.
A: And is he okay? What's wrong with him?
B: Well, Uncle Mark said that Dad (7) *had been complaining* of a bad headache most of yesterday, but he (8) *hadn't been wanting* to go back to the hotel and spoil the day. But then in the evening, just as they (9) *had stopped* fishing for the day, he (10) *had been collapsing*…

→ **Additional exercise 3** (page 241)

Unit 8

Present and past time: review

A Continuous and simple

Reminder → Section A

When we focus on an activity itself, starting before and continuing up to (and possibly beyond) a particular point of time, rather than focusing on actions as completed events, we use *continuous* forms:

- Ingrid can't come to the phone. She**'s washing** her hair.
- As you**'re not using** your car at the moment, can I borrow it?
- This time yesterday I **was flying** over the Pacific.
- **Was** she **wearing** that red dress when you saw her?

We use *simple* forms to talk about general situations, habits, and things that are or were always true:

- When I **worked** as a postman I **got up** at three o'clock every morning.
- Miguel **doesn't play** golf very well.
- These birds **build** their nests on the ground.
- The earthquake **struck** the area at midday yesterday. (past simple for completed events)

We use simple forms with verbs that describe unchanging states (that stay the same):

- She **intends** to work hard at school and go on to university.
- **Did** you **understand** the instructions we were given?

However, we can use continuous forms with these verbs when they describe something happening or changing:

- She **was intending** to talk to Tony about the idea, but she didn't get the opportunity.
- **I'm understanding** physics much better now that Mr Davies is teaching us.

B Perfect

We use *perfect* verb forms to describe one event or state from the point of view of a later time. The present perfect suggests a connection between something that happened in the past and the present time. Note, however, that the situation or event does not have to continue until the time of speaking, only to have some connection or relevance to the present time:

- **I've finished** that book you wanted, so you can borrow it now.
- **Have** you **turned** the heating off? I don't like it to be on when I'm not at home.
- Your nose is bleeding. **Has** somebody **hit** you?

The past perfect is used to locate a past event before another past event:

- I invited him out to dinner, but he said he **had** already **eaten**.
- By the time I picked up the phone, they **had rung off**.

C Combinations of perfect and continuous

We combine the perfect and continuous forms in the present perfect continuous to describe an activity in progress either at or recently before the time of speaking, and possibly beyond it:

- I **have been following** the discussions on the forum with great interest.

We can also use the present perfect continuous to talk about activities that have recently finished with some result that can be seen, heard, etc.:

- Look at the dirt on your clothes! **Have** you **been digging** in the garden again?

The past perfect continuous has a similar meaning. However, the point of reference is not 'now' (as it is with the present perfect continuous) but a point in the past:

- When we met Lena and Marko, they **had been riding**.
- It **had been snowing** heavily for hours and when I went to the door I couldn't open it.

Exercises

8.1 **Amy is writing a blog for her friends and family as she travels around Australia. Use the present simple, present continuous, past simple or past continuous of the verbs in the box to complete the extract.** A

In 1–10 use:

arrive	**feel** (×2)	**get**	**go**	**know**	**spend**	**text**	**wait**	~~**write**~~

In 11–20 use:

ask	**complain**	**enjoy**	**get**	**(not) get on**	**hear**	**look** (×2)	**seem**	**start**

I (1) ....am writing.... this blog in a hotel room in Perth. I (2) .... here a couple of hours ago after a long coach journey from Adelaide. I (3) .... pretty tired so this will only be a short post before I (4) .... to sleep. As you (5) .... , I (6) .... last week in Adelaide with Ruby. I (7) .... her a month or so ago to tell her when I would be arriving, and she (8) .... at the airport for me when I (9) .... there. For the first few days I (10) .... quite jet-lagged, but I soon (11) .... over that after a few days of lazing around on the beach. Ruby (12) .... living in Adelaide a lot, although she (13) .... for a new job just now. It (14) .... that she (15) .... very well with her colleagues. Apparently they constantly (16) .... about the working conditions and it (17) .... to annoy Ruby. She (18) .... me to pass on her best wishes to all her old friends. So now I (19) .... forward to exploring Perth. I (20) .... it's a wonderful place. I'll post again soon. Amy

8.2 **Complete this extract from a newspaper article using the past simple, present perfect or past perfect of the verbs in brackets.** B

RONSON SACKED IN UNITED CUTS

Aston United (1) ....have sacked.... (*sack*) their manager, Neil Ronson. The former England football international (2) .... (*say*) that he (3) .... (*hear*) the news when he (4) .... (*return*) from a three-week holiday in Spain and that it (5) .... (*come*) as a complete shock. 'There (6) .... (*be*) no hint of any problem when I (7) .... (*leave*) for the holiday.' Aston United (8) .... (*appoint*) Ronson as manager two years ago and last season they (9) .... (*finish*) second in the First Division. However, they (10) .... (*win*) only five matches so far this season. The chairman of the club, Peter White, last night (11) .... (*accuse*) Ronson of lack of commitment to the club. 'Neil's attitude (12) .... (*disappoint*) us recently. Over the last few months he (13) .... (*spend*) more time on Spanish beaches than working with the players in Aston.'

8.3 **Here is the rest of the conversation in Exercise 7.3. If the italicised verb is correct, write ✓. If it is wrong, correct it using the past simple, present perfect, past perfect, present perfect continuous or past perfect continuous.** A–C

A: (1) *Did he have* any health problems recently?

B: Well, he (2) *'s been suffering* from stress for some time, but we (3) *have thought* a holiday in Scotland would be relaxing for him. He (4) *worked* too hard for months, and we (5) *'ve been trying* to persuade him to have a break for ages before he agreed.

A: So (6) *have you gone* up to Scotland when you (7) *have heard*?

B: No, Mum (8) *has gone* up to be with him, but the doctors (9) *have checked* him over and (10) *had been saying* that it's not too serious. They (11) *gave* him some medicine to bring down his blood pressure and (12) *had told* him that he needs complete rest for a couple of months. So Mum's driving him back in the car tomorrow.

A: Well, send him my best wishes when you speak to him.

B: Thanks, I will do.

Unit 9 Will and be going to

A

We can use either **will** or **be going to** to talk about something that is planned, or something that we think is likely to happen in the future:

Reminder ➜ B1–B5

- We **will** study climate change in a later part of the course. (*or* We **are going to** study ...)
- Where **will** you stay in Berlin? (*or* Where **are you going to** stay ...?)
- The south of the city **won't** be affected by the power cuts. (*or* ... **isn't going to be** affected ...)

We often prefer **be going to** in informal contexts (see also **D**).

B

We use **will** rather than **be going to** to make a prediction based on our opinion or experience:

- Why not come over at the weekend? The children **will** enjoy seeing you again.
- 'Shall I ask Lamar?' 'No, she **won't** want to be disturbed.'

We use **be going to** rather than **will** when we make a prediction based on some present evidence:

- The sky's gone really dark. There**'s going to** be a storm.
- 'What's the matter with her?' 'It looks like she**'s going to** faint.'

C

To predict the future we often use **will** with **I bet** (informal), **I expect**, **I hope**, **I imagine**, **I reckon** (informal), **I think**, **I wonder** and **I'm sure**, and in questions with **think** and **reckon**:

- *I imagine* the stadium **will** be full for the match on Saturday.
- That cheese smells awful. *I bet* nobody **will** eat it.
- When *do* you *think* you**'ll** finish work?
- *Do* you *reckon* he**'ll** say yes?

Be going to can also be used with these phrases, particularly in informal contexts.

D

We use **will** when we make a decision at the moment of speaking and **be going to** for decisions about the future that have already been made. Compare:

- I**'ll** pick him up at eight. (an offer; making an arrangement now) *and*
- I**'m going to** collect the children at eight. (this was previously arranged)
- 'Pineapples are on special offer this week.' 'In that case, I**'ll** buy two.' *and*
- When I've saved up enough money, I**'m going to** buy a smartphone.

However, in a formal style, we use **will** rather than **be going to** to talk about future events that have been previously arranged in some detail. Compare:

- **Are** you **going to** talk at the meeting tonight? *and*
- The meeting **will** begin at 9 am. Refreshments **will** be available from 8:30 onwards.

E

We can use **will** or **be going to** with little difference in meaning in the main clause of an **if-sentence** when we say that something (often something negative) is conditional on something else:

- You**'ll** / You**'re going to** knock that glass over if you're not careful.

When the future event does not depend on the action described in the **if-clause**, we use **be going to**, not **will**. This kind of sentence is mainly found in spoken English. Compare:

- I**'m going to** open a bottle of lemonade, if you want some. (= I'm going to open a bottle of lemonade. Do you want some?) *and*
- I**'ll** open a bottle of lemonade if you want some. (= If you say you want some, I'll open it.)

However, we use **will**, not **be going to**, when the main clause refers to offers, requests, promises, etc. and ability:

- If Erik phones, I**'ll** let you know. (= an offer; '..., I'm going to let you know' suggests 'I intend to let you know when Erik phones')
- If you look to your left, you**'ll** see the lake. (= you'll be able to see; '... you're going to see ...' suggests 'I know this is what you can see when you look to your left')

and when one thing is the logical consequence of another:

- If you don't switch on the monitor first, the computer **won't** come on.

Exercises

9.1 **Correct or improve the sentences where necessary by changing the italicised will ('ll) forms to be going to forms.** A–D

1 Have you seen Nadia recently? She~~'ll have~~ another baby. 's going to have
2 The method is quite simple, and I'm sure it *will be* familiar to most of you already.
3 A: I can't come over during the day.
B: *I'll see* you tomorrow evening, then.
4 Are these new skis yours? *Will you take up* skiing?
5 Wherever you go in Brazil, you*'ll find* the people very friendly.
6 Jamie says he*'ll be* a politician when he grows up – and he's only five years old!
7 It's getting very humid – we*'ll have* a thunderstorm.
8 I hear you*'ll sell* your car. How much do you want for it?
9 You can't play football in the garden. I*'ll cut* the grass.
10 A: What's the matter with Paula?
B: She says she*'ll be sick*.
A: She*'ll feel* better with some fresh air.
11 A: I've been offered a new job in Munich, so I*'ll leave* Camco.
B: When *will you tell* your boss?
A: I'm not sure. Perhaps I*'ll try* to see him later today.
12 A: Did I tell you I*'ll have* dinner with Karl on Thursday?
B: But we*'ll see* a film with Hamid on Thursday. You've known about it for weeks.
A: Sorry. In that case, I*'ll sort out* a different day with Karl.
13 A: Did you get the theatre tickets?
B: No. I forgot all about them. I*'ll book* them tomorrow.
14 A: We've got small, medium and large. What size do you want?
B: I*'ll have* a large one, please.
15 A: Shall I give Ian another ring?
B: Yes, I expect he*'ll be* home by now.
16 A: What are those bricks for?
B: I*'ll build* a wall at the side of the garden.

9.2 **Complete the sentences with will ('ll) or be going to and an appropriate verb. If both will and be going to are possible, write them both.** E

1 If you want me to, I ..'ll explain.. how the equipment works.
2 If you want to help us, we .... these trees at the bottom of the garden.
3 You .... your back if you try to lift that box.
4 If I give you the money .... you .... me some oranges when you're out?
5 If you press the red button, the machine ....
6 I .... Laura this weekend, if you'd like to come too.
7 He's been told that if he's late once more he ....
8 If you listen carefully, you .... an owl in the trees over there.

→ Additional exercise 4 (page 242)

Unit 10

Present simple and present continuous for the future

A

Present simple

Reminder ➜ B6 & B7

We can often use either the present simple or **will** to talk about future events that are part of some timetabled or programmed arrangement or routine. However, we prefer the present simple for fixed, unchangeable events. Compare:

- **Does** the sale **finish** on Thursday or Friday? (*or* **Will** the sale **finish** ...?) *and*
- The sun **rises** at 5:16 tomorrow. (*more likely than* The sun will rise ...)

We avoid the present simple when we talk about less formal or less routine arrangements, or predictions. Instead we use **will**, **be going to**, or the present continuous:

- **Are** you **staying** in to watch TV tonight, or **are** you **coming** dancing? (*not* Do you stay to watch TV tonight, or do you come...)
- It's only a problem in Britain now, but it **will affect** the rest of Europe soon. (*not* ... but it affects the rest of Europe soon.)

B

We use the present simple, not **will**, to refer to the future –

☆ in time clauses with conjunctions such as **after**, **as soon as**, **before**, **by the time**, **when**, **while**, **until**:

- *When* you **see** Ben, tell him he still owes me some money. (*not* When you will see Ben ...)
- I should be finished *by the time* you **get** back. (*not* ... by the time you will get back.)

☆ in conditional clauses with **if**, **in case**, **provided**, and **unless**:

- *Provided* the right software **is** available, I should be able to solve the problem.
- I'll bring some sandwiches *in case* we **don't find** anywhere decent to eat.

☆ when we talk about possible future events with **suppose**, **supposing**, and **what if** at the beginning of a sentence. Note that the past simple can be used with a similar meaning:

- *Suppose* we **miss** the bus – how will we get home? (*or Suppose* we **missed** ...)
- *What if* the train**'s** late? Where shall I meet you then? (*or What if* the train **was** late?)

C

Present continuous

We can often use either the present continuous or **be going to** with a similar meaning to talk about planned future events. The present continuous indicates that we have a firm intention or have made a definite decision to do something, although this may not already be arranged:

- **Are** you **seeing** the doctor again next week? (*or* **Are** you **going to see** ...?)
- **I'm not asking** Tom to the party. (*or* **I'm not going to ask** ...)

However, we don't use the present continuous for the future –

☆ when we make or report predictions about activities or events over which we have no control (we can't arrange these):

- I think it**'s going to rain** soon.
- Scientists say that the satellite **won't cause** any damage when it falls to Earth.

☆ when we talk about permanent future situations:

- People **are going to live** / **will live** longer in the future.
- Her new house **is going to have** / **will have** three floors.

D

Many people avoid **be going to** + **go** / **come** and use the present continuous forms of **go** and **come** instead:

- **I'm going** to town on Saturday. (*rather than* I'm going to go to town ...)
- **Are** you **coming** home for lunch? (*rather than* Are you going to come ...?)

Exercises

10.1 **If possible, use the present simple of a verb from the box to complete each sentence. If not, use will + infinitive.** A–C

accept	change	get	give out	go	lend	look after
miss	play	rain	read	start	stop	want

1 We .... our exam results on the 20th August.
2 Alex .... our cats while we're away next week.
3 I think I'll take an umbrella in case it ....
4 There is a reading list to accompany my lecture, which I .... at the end.
5 The new drug .... on sale in the USA next year.
6 The concert .... at 7:30, not 7:15 as it says in the programme.
7 Provided it .... raining, we'll go for a walk this afternoon.
8 What if I .... my plans and decide to stay longer? Will I need to renew my visa?
9 We .... Mariam when she leaves, but she says she'll keep in touch.
10 Unless my parents .... me some money, I won't be able to go on holiday this year.
11 Tonight France .... Germany in a match important for both teams.
12 It is unlikely that the government .... the court's decision.
13 Supposing I .... to upload a video to YouTube? How do I do that?
14 By the time you .... this letter, I should be in New Zealand.

10.2 **Cross out any answers that are wrong or very unlikely. If two answers are possible, consider the difference in meaning, if any, between them.** C, D & Unit 9

1 It's not a deep cut, but it .... a scar.
a will leave b is going to leave c is leaving
2 Did you know I .... a new car next week?
a will buy b am going to buy c am buying
3 A: I'm not sure how I'll get to the concert. B: We can take you. We .... you up at eight.
a will pick b are going to pick c are picking
4 I'm sorry I can't come for dinner. I .... to York tonight.
a will drive b am going to drive c am driving
5 The high-speed rail link .... the journey time between the cities significantly.
a will cut b is going to cut c is cutting
6 I have to go now. I .... you back later today.
a will call b am going to call c am calling
7 Don't go out now. I .... lunch and it'll be cold by the time you get back.
a will serve b am going to serve c am serving
8 Unless help arrives within the next few days, thousands ....
a will starve b are going to starve c are starving

10.3 **Complete these dialogues with either present simple for the future or present continuous for the future using the verbs in brackets. If neither of these is correct, use will or be going to.** Units 9 & 10

1 A: Simon Bianchi (1) .... (*join*) us for dinner. You know, the novelist.
B: Yes, I've read some of his books.
A: I'm sure you (2) .... (*like*) him. His latest book (3) .... (*come*) out at the end of this week. If you want, I'm sure he (4) .... (*give*) you a signed copy.
2 A: Have you heard that BWM (1) .... (*sack*) 300 workers?
B: That's bad news. Supposing they (2) .... (*close*) completely – that would be awful.
A: But I've heard that they (3) .... (*build*) a new factory in Ireland. If you look on their website, you (4) .... (*see*) a lot of information about it.

➜ **Additional exercise 4** (page 242)

Unit 11

Future continuous and future perfect (continuous)

A

Future continuous: I will be doing

Reminder ➜ B8

We can use the future continuous to talk about:
(i) something that is predicted to start before a particular point of future time, and that may continue after this point (often the result of a previous decision or arrangement):

- When it goes into orbit, the spacecraft **will be carrying** 30 kilos of plutonium.
- Anna **will be helping** us to organise the party.

(ii) a future activity that is part of the normal course of events or that is one of a repeated or regular series of events:

- Dr Lin **will be giving** the same talk in room 103 at ten next Thursday.
- **Will you be driving** to work, as usual?

We can often use either the future continuous or the present continuous when we talk about arranged activities or events in the future (see also Unit 10). Compare:

- We **will be leaving** for Istanbul at 7:00 in the evening. (timetabled; *or* … **are leaving** …) *and*
- When the race starts later this afternoon the drivers **will be hoping** for drier weather than last year. (*not* … are hoping …; not reporting the details of a programme or timetable)

B

When we don't want to indicate willingness, intention, invitation, etc., we prefer to use the future continuous instead of **will**. For example, if guests have stayed longer than you wanted, and you don't know when they are leaving, you might ask:

- **Will** you **be staying** with us again tonight? (asking about their plans) *rather than*
- **Will** you **stay** with us again tonight? (they might think this is an invitation)

C

Future perfect and future perfect continuous: I will have done and I will have been doing

We use the future perfect to say that something will be ended, completed, or achieved by a particular point in the future:

- *By the time you get home* I **will have cleaned** the house from top to bottom.
- I'm sure his awful behaviour **will** *soon* **have been forgotten**. (= passive form)

We use the future perfect continuous to emphasise the duration of an activity in progress at a particular point in the future:

- *Next year* I **will have been working** in the company for 30 years.

With both the future perfect and future perfect continuous we usually mention the future time (e.g. *By the time you get home* …, *Next year* …).

D

The future continuous, future perfect and future perfect continuous can also be used to say what we believe or imagine is happening around now:

- We could ask to borrow Joe's car. He **won't be using** it today – he went to work by bike.
- Most people **will have forgotten** the fire by now.
- Tennis fans **will have been queuing** at Wimbledon all day to buy tickets.

We can use the future perfect continuous to say what we think was happening at a point in the past:

- Motorist Vicky Hesketh **will have been asking** herself whether speed cameras are a good idea after she was fined £100 last week for driving at 33 mph in a 30 mph zone.

Exercises

11.1 **Complete both sentences in each pair with one verb from the box. Use the future continuous (will / won't be + -ing) in one sentence and will / won't + infinitive in the other.** A & B

give leave move use work

1 a We .... in an hour or so, so make sure your suitcase is packed.
  b Without more cheap housing, families .... the village and find homes in town.
2 a .... you .... late at the office again? I want to know when to cook.
  b A: We need to get this order sent out before Monday.
    B: Well, I .... over the weekend if that will help.
3 a I .... my car until next week, so you can borrow it if you like.
  b My grandad .... a computer. He says he's very happy with his old typewriter.
4 a Is your suitcase very heavy? I .... you a hand with it if you like.
  b Dr Sankey .... evidence at the trial of James Morgan next week.
5 a He's parked his car across our drive and says he .... it. Shall I call the police?
  b The two schools .... to a single campus at the beginning of September.

11.2 **Make sentences with a beginning from (i), a verb from (ii) (either in the future perfect or future perfect continuous), and an ending from (iii).** C & D

(i)	(ii)	(iii)
1 The weather forecast says that the rain ...	act	... the objective we set ourselves when we took over.
2 If the company is making a profit by the end of the year then we ...	achieve	~~... by the morning and tomorrow will be dry.~~
3 In two years' time Morneau ...	~~clear~~	... for 50 years, and shows no sign of retiring from the theatre.
4 I am confident that I ...	finish	... the report before the end of the week.
5 This book on Proust is really difficult. On Saturday I ...	discover	... it for a month, and I'm still only half way.
6 As delegates who arrived early ...	read	... there have been some late changes to the conference programme.

1 *The weather forecast says that the rain will have cleared by the morning and tomorrow will be dry.*

11.3 **Here is part of an email from Emily, an English teacher in Japan, to her friend Rosa. Underline the correct option.** A & D

Delete Junk Reply Reply All Forward Print To Do

Hi Rosa

Greetings from Osaka! Hope this finds you all well. I suppose by now school (1) *will close / will have closed* for Christmas and you (2) *will be enjoying / will have been enjoying* a rest. It's hard to believe that Tim's already 18 and that it's only a few months until he (3) *will be leaving / will have been leaving* school for college.

My main news is that my brother, Joe, and his family (4) *will have been arriving / will be arriving* next Friday as part of their big trip around the world. By the time they get here they (5) *will be going / will have been* to California and New Zealand. No doubt Joe's children (6) *will have been planning / will plan* it all out for months! They (7) *won't be spending / won't have spent* all their time with me. Joe has to go to Tokyo on business, so I (8) *will have kept / will be keeping* the rest of the family entertained while he's away. Then they (9) *will all be going / will all have been going* to Kyoto ...

Unit 12

Be to + infinitive; **be about to** + infinitive

A

Be to + infinitive is commonly used in news reports to talk about events that are likely to happen in the near future:

- Police officers **are to visit** every home in the area.
- The main Rome-to-Naples railway line **is to be reopened** today. (passive form)

It is also used to talk about formal or official arrangements, formal instructions, and to give orders:

- You **are not to leave** the school without my permission.
- The European Parliament **is to introduce** a new law on safety at work.
- Children **are not to be left** unsupervised in the museum. (passive form)

Passive forms are often used to make orders and instructions more impersonal.

Note that we only use **be to + infinitive** to talk about future events that can be controlled by people. Compare:

- In the next few years, thousands of speed cameras **are to appear** on major roads. (*or* … **will appear** …) *and*
- Scientists say they can't predict when or where the disease **will appear** again. (*not* … the disease is to appear again; the appearance of the disease can't be controlled)
- The President **is to return** to Brazil later today. (*or* … **will return** …) *and*
- The comet **will return** to our solar system in around 500 years. (*not* The comet is to return …; the movement of the comet can't be controlled)

However, when **be to + infinitive** refers to the future from the past (see Unit 14B), we often use it to describe what happened to someone, whether they were able to influence events or not:

- Matthew Flinders sailed past Tasmania in 1770, but it **was to be** a further 30 years before he landed there.
- Clare Atkins **was to write** two more books about her experiences in Africa before her death in 1997.

B

We often use **be to + infinitive** in **if-clauses** to say that something must happen first (in the main clause) before something else can happen (in the **if-clause**):

- *If* the human race **is to survive**, we must look at environmental problems now.
- The law needs to be revised *if* justice **is to be done**. (passive form)

Compare the use of **be to + infinitive** and the present simple for the future in **if-clauses**:

- If Lopez **is to win** gold at the next Olympics, he needs to work on his fitness. *and*
- If Lopez **wins** gold at the next Olympics, he has said that he will retire from athletics.

Note how the order of cause and effects in **if-sentences** is reversed with these two tenses:

- If Lopez **is to win** gold … (= effect), he needs to work … (= cause) *and*
- If Lopez **wins** gold … (= cause), he has said that he will retire … (= effect)

C

We use **be about to + infinitive** mainly in conversation to say that something will (not) happen in the very near future:

- We**'re about to eat**. Do you want to join us?
- Appearing on TV might make her famous, but it**'s not about to make** her rich.
- A: Why don't you switch it off and turn it back on again?
  B: Yes, I **was about to try** that when you came in.
  (*not* Yes, I was to try …) (referring to the future from the past)

Exercises

12.1 **Complete these news extracts using the verbs in brackets. Use be to + infinitive if possible and will + infinitive if not. Use active or passive forms as necessary.** A

1 Jon Stobbard has written his first new play for 15 years. Its first performance .... (*stage*) at the New Victoria Theatre.
2 The new safety system .... (*stop*) trains automatically if they pass a danger signal.
3 Stafford Boys' School .... (*merge*) with the nearby Bicton Girls' School to form a new co-educational establishment.
4 There are fears that sea levels .... (*rise*) catastrophically in the next 50 years.
5 The old design and technology programme .... (*replace*) with a new computer science course.

Now use the verbs in the box to do the same in 6 to 10.

become	**create**	**increase**	**receive**	**retire**	**succeed**

6 Managing Director Lars Lindberg, 59, ... this summer a year early. He .... by Christina Fontana, who joined the company last year.
7 As the temperatures fall with the onset of winter, the refugee crisis .... more severe.
8 Production line staff at the Heathcote garden furniture factory in Northam .... a pay rise following a big new order from Italy.
9 Seventy new posts .... at the factory following a major investment by the parent company in the United States.
10 The recent rapid rise in house prices in the south-east .... the demand for higher salaries among lower-paid workers.

12.2 **Underline the correct answers. In some cases both alternatives are possible.** B & C

1 You need to work much harder if you *have* / *are to have* any chance of passing the exam.
2 My sister *is to start* / *is about to start* a PhD in Physics.
3 Mrs Patel is likely to become the Foreign Minister if the party *wins* / *is to win* power at the next election.
4 If you *enjoy* / *are to enjoy* romantic comedies, then this is a film you must see.
5 A: Can you type this letter for me?
B: Sorry, I*'m just to go* / *'m just about to go* home. It'll have to wait until tomorrow.
6 If Beckman *recovers* / *is to recover* from a foot injury, it seems certain that he will play in Saturday's match against Spain.
7 If the university *keeps* / *is to keep* its international reputation, it must first invest in better facilities for students.
8 Jonas Fischer has denied that he *is to resign* / *is about to resign* as marketing manager.
9 It started snowing an hour ago, and from the look of those clouds things *are to get* / *are about to get* a lot worse.
10 If the railway system *is improved* / *is to be improved*, the government should invest substantial amounts of money now.

Unit 13

Other ways of talking about the future

A

Some phrases are commonly used to refer to actions or events in the future with a meaning similar to **be about to + infinitive** (see Unit 12C). We can use **be on the verge of** … / **brink of** … / **point of** … (+ **-ing** or **noun**) to say that something will happen soon:

- People **are on the verge of** starvation as the drought continues.
- Scientists **are on the brink of** making major advances in the fight against AIDS.
- Exhausted, mentally and physically, she **was on the point of** collapse.

Be on the brink of usually refers to something important, exciting, or very bad.

We use **be due to** (+ **infinitive**) to say that something is expected to happen at a particular time, **be sure / bound to** (+ **infinitive**) to say that something is likely or certain to happen, and **be set to** (+ **infinitive**) to say that something is ready to happen:

- The company's chief executive **is due to** retire next year, but following today's announcement of further losses she **is sure to** be asked to leave sooner.
- 'Will there be somewhere to get a coffee at the station?' 'Oh, yes, there**'s bound to** be.'
- Her new film **is set to** be a great success.

Note that we use **due to** + **noun** to give the reason for something, not to talk about the future (e.g. **Due to fog**, all flights from the airport have been cancelled).

B

We use some verbs with a **to-infinitive** to talk about intentions:

- We **guarantee** *to refund* your money if you are dissatisfied with the computer.

The **present simple + to-infinitive** or **present continuous** + **to-infinitive** can be used with the verbs marked * to talk about intentions:

- I **aim** *to get* to Bangkok by the end of June. (*or* I**'m aiming** *to get* …; I **was aiming** *to get* … is also possible, but more tentative)

Also: **aim*, agree, expect*, hope*, intend*, mean, plan*, promise, propose*, resolve, undertake, want***

Some people, particularly in speech and in journalism, use **be looking** + **to-infinitive** to mean planning a course of action:

- We**'re looking** *to create* 3,000 jobs in the city over the next year.

C

When the phrases and verbs in **A** and **B** are used with past tense forms, they are usually concerned with future events seen from the past (see also Unit 14):

- It was his 64th birthday in 2006 and he **was due** *to retire* the following year.
- Nathan **had resolved** *to become* fluent in Spanish before he left university.
- The new management **had been looking** *to create* 20 new jobs.

D

Some people use **shall** (and **shan't**) instead of **will** (and **won't**) in statements about the future with **I** and **we**. However, it is more common to use **will** (particularly its contracted form **'ll**) and **won't**:

- He was a good friend and we **shall** miss him greatly. (*more commonly* … we**'ll** miss …)
- I'm just going to buy a newspaper. I **shan't** be long. (*more commonly* I **won't** …)

In current English we don't usually use **shall / shan't** with other subjects to talk about the future, although this is found in formal rules and in older literary styles:

- The match referee **shall** be the sole judge of fair play.
- All people of the world **shall** live together as brothers.

Exercises

13.1 **Expand the notes to complete the news extracts, using the phrases in A.**

verge – become	sure – face	brink – go	set – launch
set – make	sure – provide	~~bound – raise~~	due – return
point – sign	~~point – move~~	verge – quit	due – undergo

1/2 The decision of Cornico to relocate its international headquarters to Switzerland is *bound to raise* questions about the government's new profits tax. It seems that other major financial firms are also *on the point of moving* their headquarters out of London.

3/4 NASA's latest Mars probe is .... to Earth later today. A spokesperson for NASA said that the probe would be bringing back rock samples that are .... exciting new information about the planet.

5/6 The Countryside Conservation Society is .... a new million-Euro scheme for the protection of endangered plant species. It is estimated that over 200 species are .... extinct in the country.

7/8 Sources at the United Nations have said that the governments of North and South Alicia are .... an agreement to end their long-running border dispute. However, any agreement is .... resistance from rebel forces in South Alicia, who have said they will fight on.

9/10 Tennis star Sancho Gomez is .... a second operation on his injured shoulder. He was .... tennis earlier this year after a first operation was unsuccessful.

11/12 EU agriculture ministers are .... an important announcement on increasing support to farmers when they meet in Brussels on Monday. 'Many farmers are .... out of business,' said the Italian representative, 'and the matter must be decided very soon.'

13.2 **Complete the sentences with the verb pairs from the box. Use either the present simple or present continuous for the first verb. If both tenses are possible, write them both.** B & C

aim – to study	expect – to finish	~~look – to replace~~	intend – to move
propose – to deal	resolve – to give up	guarantee – to find	

1 My computer is now five years old, and I *'m looking to replace* it with a faster one.
2 In the first half of the course we'll study microbiology, and in the second half I .... with genetic engineering.
3 We haven't completed the work yet, but we .... it later this week.
4 I haven't done much work at college so far, but I .... harder from now on.
5 Every New Year he .... eating biscuits, but by February he has started again.
6 We can't provide the spare parts ourselves, but we .... a supplier who can.
7 At the moment I commute for over three hours a day, but I .... closer to my work in the next few months.

13.3 **Underline the possible options.** D

1 I have passed your letter on to the manager who *shall / will* reply shortly.
2 Sorry, but I *shan't / won't* be able to give you a lift after all.
3 I think your parents *shall / will* be very happy with your decision.
4 Only people over the age of 18 *shall / will* be eligible to vote in the referendum.
5 You *shan't / won't* want to eat your dinner tonight after all that chocolate.

Unit 14

The future seen from the past

A

There are a number of ways of talking about an activity or event that was in the future at a particular point in the past. In order to express this idea, we can use the past tenses of the verb forms we would normally use to talk about the future. These forms are often used in reporting (see Units 32–36). Compare the following sentences:

The future from now …	*The future from the past …*
I haven't got much money, so I think **I'll stay** at home this summer.	Eleni decided that she **would stay** at home for the summer.
I'm not going to say anything about the exams today, because I don't have time.	I **wasn't going to say** anything about the exams, but the students asked me to.
I'm having a meeting with my tutor tomorrow to discuss my work.	I couldn't go to the match because I **was having** a meeting with my tutor.
Will you **be going** alone, or is Louise going with you?	At the time, I thought I **would be going** alone, but then Jan said he wanted to come.
The exam **will have finished** by three o'clock, so I'll see you then.	The exam was so easy that most people **would have finished** after 30 minutes.
There **is to be** a meeting of ministers this evening.	It was announced that there **was to be** a meeting of ministers that evening.
When the school closes, all the children **are to be moved** to one nearby.	Mrs Novak heard that she **was to be moved** to a post in a nearby school.
As the bell **is about to go** for the end of the lesson, pack your books away.	The bell **was about to go** when all the children started to pack their books away.

If the future seen from the past is still in the future for the speaker, then either form is possible:

- It was announced this morning that there **is / was to be** a statement this evening.

In some cases we don't know whether the activity or event happened or not. Compare:

- I didn't phone to give him the news because we **were seeing** each other later. He was very upset when I told him. (= we saw each other) *and*
- We **were seeing** each other later that day, but I had to phone and cancel. (= we didn't see each other)

B

To talk about an activity or event that was in the future at a particular point in the past, we can use **was / were to + infinitive** (for things that actually happened) and **was / were to have + past participle** (for things that were expected, but didn't happen):

- At the time she was probably the best actor in the theatre company, but in fact some of her colleagues **were to become** much better known.
- The boat, which **was to have taken** them to the island, failed to arrive.
- He **was to find out** years later that the car he had bought was stolen.

Note, however, that in less formal contexts it is more natural to use **be supposed to**:

- I **was supposed to help**, but I was ill. (*more natural than* I was to have helped …)

Exercises

14.1 Write ✓ if the italicised parts are correct. If they are wrong, correct them. A

1 I'*m going to do* the washing, but we'd run out of washing powder.
2 The concert tonight *would be* over by about 9:30. We could eat after that.
3 When we *were passing* Ivan's house, we thought we'd drop in and see him.
4 A: Where shall I hang my coat? B: Sorry, I thought Ella *will have shown* you. Over there.
5 The manager of Newtown United said that the team *is to be announced* at nine tomorrow.
6 The second half *was about to start*, so shall we go back to our seats now?
7 I knew that by the morning I *would be feeling* exhausted, but I just wanted to go dancing.
8 A: Where's Oliver? He *is supposed* to be here yesterday, and there's still no sign of him.
B: I'*m about to ask* the same question.
9 I didn't phone Ben this morning because I *was going to see* him when I've finished work.
10 DNA testing *was to be used* by police in the search for the missing Dublin schoolboy. His parents have welcomed the news.
11 We *are meeting* at seven in the Globe coffee bar. Can you be there, too?
12 We didn't expect that having a rabbit as a pet *will cause* so many problems.

In which *three* cases can we use either a past or present tense form in the italicised parts?

14.2 Choose the more appropriate option, (a) or (b), to complete these sentences. B

1 The meeting was to have taken place in the hall, …
a but had to be cancelled at the last minute.
b and was well attended.
2 She was to have appeared with Heath Ledger in his last film…
a and was a tremendous success.
b but the part went to her sister.
3 Later, in Rome, I was to meet Professor Pearce …
a and was very impressed by his knowledge of Italian culture.
b but he left before I got there.
4 The twenty police officers who were to have gone off duty at eight …
a went to the Christmas party.
b had to remain in the police station.
5 It was to take 48 hours to get to Japan …
a and we were exhausted when we arrived.
b but we managed to do it in only a day.
6 After the war he was to teach at London University …
a but no money was available to employ him.
b for ten years.
7 The bridge was to have been completed this year …
a but a number of accidents have led to delays.
b and is to be opened by the president next month.
8 The new road was to have a major impact on traffic in the busy town centre, …
a making life much easier for commuters.
b but the crowded roads continued.
9 The construction of the cathedral was to have begun in 1650 …
a and go on for over 80 years.
b but a shortage of labour delayed the start for a further 20 years.
10 We were to stay with Rodrigo in Lisbon …
a many times before he moved to Madrid.
b but he moved to Madrid.

Unit 15

Can, could, be able to and be allowed to

A

Can, could and be able to: ability

Reminder ➜ C1 – C7

We sometimes use **be able to** instead of **can** and **could** to talk about ability. We avoid **be able to** –

☆ when we talk about something that is happening as we speak:

- Watch me, Mum; I **can** stand on one leg. (*not* … I'm able to stand on one leg.)

☆ before passives:

- Films **can** now easily *be streamed* online. (*rather than* Films are now easily able to be streamed …)

☆ when the meaning is 'know how to':

- **Can** you cook? (*rather than* Are you able to cook?)

B

If we talk about a single achievement, rather than a general ability in the past, we usually use **be able to** rather than **could**. Compare:

- Sophie **could** play the flute quite well. (*or* … **was able to** …; a general ability) *and*
- She swam strongly and **was able to** cross the river easily, even though it was swollen by the heavy rain. (*not* She swam strongly and could cross …; a specific achievement)

However, **could** is usually more natural than **be able to** –

☆ in negative sentences:

- I tried to get up but I **couldn't** move.

☆ with verbs of the senses, e.g. **feel**, **hear**, **see**, **smell**, **taste**, and with verbs of 'thinking', e.g. **believe**, **decide**, **remember**, **understand**:

- I **could** *remember* the crash, but nothing after that.

☆ after the phrases **the only thing / place / time,** and after **all** when it means 'the only thing':

- *All* we **could** see were his feet.

☆ to suggest that something almost didn't happen, particularly with **almost**, **hardly**, **just, nearly**:

- I **could** *nearly* touch the ceiling.

C

Can and could: possibility

To talk about the theoretical possibility of something happening we use **could**, not **can**. However, we use **can**, not **could**, to say that something is possible and actually happens. Compare:

- It **could** be expensive to keep a cat. (= if we had one, it could or it may not be expensive) *and*
- It **can** be expensive to keep a cat. (= it can be, and it sometimes is)

We use **can't**, not **couldn't**, to say that something is theoretically or actually impossible:

- There **can't** be many people in the world who haven't watched television.
- The doctor **can't** see you this morning; he's busy at the hospital.

D

We use **can** to indicate that there is a very real possibility of a future event happening. Using **could** suggests that something is less likely or that there is some doubt about it. Compare:

- We **can** stay with Jake in Oslo. (= we will be able to stay) *and*
- We **could** stay with Jake in Oslo. (= it's possible; if he's there)

E

Could and be allowed to: permission

To say that in the past someone had *general* permission to do something – that is, to do it at any time – we can use either **could** or **was / were allowed to**. However, to talk about permission for one *particular* past action, we use **was / were allowed to**, but not **could**. Compare:

- Anyone **was allowed to** fish in the lake when the council owned it. (*or* … **could** fish …) *and*
- Although he didn't have a ticket, Ned **was allowed to** come in. (*not* … could come in.)

In negative sentences, we can use either **couldn't** or **wasn't / weren't allowed to** to say that permission was not given in general *or* particular situations:

- I **couldn't / wasn't allowed to** open the present until my birthday.

Exercises

15.1 **Underline the correct or more natural option (or both if possible).** A & B

1 Valuables *can / are able to* be left in the hotel safe. Please ask at the reception desk.
2 We *could / were able to* finish the hockey match before it started snowing too heavily.
3 The rebels *could / were able to* draw on the support of over 20,000 soldiers.
4 *Could you / Were you able to* understand Professor Larsen's lecture? I found it really difficult.
5 A: Do you want a game? B: Sorry, I *can't / 'm not able to* play chess.
6 Look at me, I *can / 'm able to* ride my bike without any help.
7 When the firefighters arrived they *could / were able to* put out the flames in a couple of minutes.
8 The air was so polluted in the city centre, I *could hardly / was hardly able to* breathe.
9 I knew Petra had been decorating. I *could / was able to* smell the paint when I came in.
10 *Can you / Are you able to* drive without your glasses?
11 No changes *can / are able to* be made to this rail ticket after purchase.
12 He *could / was able to* untie the ropes without the guards noticing.
13 She looked all over the house, but *couldn't / wasn't able to* find her keys anywhere.
14 I was very busy at work, but I *could / was able to* have a couple of days off last week.

15.2 **Complete these blog posts with can, could and be allowed to (or two forms if possible). Use negative forms where necessary.** A–E

a

We went camping in the north of Spain last July. As you probably know, it (1) .... rain a lot on the coast, even in midsummer, and the day we arrived we (2) .... believe how heavy the rain was. Eventually we found a place to camp, in a field next to a beach. We had a new tent – the advertisement for it said, 'This tent (3) .... be assembled in two minutes with no previous experience.' What a joke! Now, there (4) .... be many people who haven't had difficulty putting up a tent at some time, but it took us more than two hours. And then, just as it was done, a man came along and said that we (5) .... camp there – it was private property. So we had to take the tent down again. Then Eva just said, 'Well, we (6) .... stay here all night. Let's go to that hotel in the last village we drove through.' Unfortunately, when we got there they were full. But they were very kind and we (7) .... camp at the end of their garden!

b

It is often said that sports coaches (1) .... be strict, but athlete Lance Jordan's was incredibly hard on him in the year before the Olympic Games. For instance, Lance (2) .... stay up later than nine, although on his birthday he (3) .... watch television until ten as it was a special occasion! Of course, all Lance (4) .... think of was going out with his friends in the evening, and he (5) .... hardly wait for the Games to finish to get back to a normal life. When he complained, his coach just said, 'Trust me and you'll win gold – you (6) .... lose!' And his coach was right. He won a gold medal in the 400 metres in a world record time. And on the night of his victory Lance (7) .... celebrate – by staying up until 11 o'clock! 'But no later,' said his coach. 'The World Championships are only two years away.'

→ Additional exercise 5 (page 242)

Unit 16

Will, would and used to

A Will and would

Reminder → C8 – C14

We can use **will** (for the present) and **would** (for the past) to talk about –

☆ characteristic behaviour or habits:

- Every day Dan **will** come home from work and turn on the TV.
- At school she **would** always sit quietly and pay attention.

☆ things that are or were always true:

- Cold weather **will** kill certain plants.
- During the war, people **would** eat all kinds of things that we don't eat now.

(For the use of **will** to talk about the future, see Unit 9.)

We don't use **will** or **would** in this way to talk about a *particular* occasion. Compare:

- Each time I gave him a problem he **would solve** it for me. *and*
- Last night I gave him a problem and he **solved** it for me. (*not* … he would solve it …)

However, we can use **will not** (**won't**) and **would not** (**wouldn't**) in either case. Compare:

- He **would / wouldn't** walk the five miles to his place of work. (characteristic behaviour) *and*
- She **wouldn't** say what was wrong when I asked her.

B

In speech, we can stress **will** or **would** to criticise people's characteristic behaviour or habits:

- She just **won't** do the washing up when I ask her.
- I was happy when Ryan left. He **would** talk about people behind their backs.

We can also express disapproval of something they have done using **will**:

- 'I feel sick.' 'Well, if you **will** eat so much, I'm not surprised.'

C

We can use use **will** to draw conclusions or state assumptions about things that are the case now (see also Unit 9B):

- Martina **will** be at home by now. Let's go and see her.
- You **will** know that Ewan and Lucy are engaged. (= I assume you already know)

D Would and used to

When we talk about repeated events in the past that don't happen now we can use either **would** or **used to + infinitive**. However, we can use **would** only if the time reference is clear. Compare:

- We **used to play** in the garden. (*not* We would play …; time reference not given) *and*
- Whenever we went to my uncle's house, we **would / used to play** in the garden.

We can use **used to** but not **would** when we talk about past states that have changed:

- The factory **used to** be over there.
- Didn't you **use to** have red hair?

We don't use either **used to** or **would** when we say exactly how many times in total something happened, how long something took, or that a single event happened at a given past time:

- We **visited** Switzerland four times during the 1990s. (*not* We would / used to visit …)
- She **went** to Jamaica last month. (*not* She would / used to go to Jamaica last month.)

E Would / will have + past participle

To talk about an *unreal past* situation – that is, an imaginary situation or a situation that might have happened in the past, but didn't – we use **would have + past participle**:

- I **would have been** happy to see him, but I didn't have time.

However, to say that we think a past situation actually happened, we use **will have + past participle**:

- As it was cloudy, few people **will have seen** last night's lunar eclipse. (*rather than* … would have seen …)

Exercises

16.1 Complete the doctor and patient speech bubbles using **will** or **would** followed by one of these verbs. If **will** or **would** are not possible, use a verb in the past simple. A & C

be	cause	exercise	find	have	know	sit	spend

1 Most days I .... eight hours or more in front of my computer.

2 Yesterday I .... a sharp pain in my lower back.

3 No, I'm not that fit now. When I was at college, I .... in the gym most days.

4 When I tried to stand I .... that I couldn't straighten up.

5 5 Over time poor posture .... back pain.

6 Before computers came along, people .... rarely .... still for so long.

7 I'm sure you .... about the need to take regular breaks.

8 That .... probably .... the result of sitting badly.

16.2 If necessary, correct these sentences using **would** or **used to**. If neither **would** nor **used to** is correct, use a past simple verb form. D

1 I would enjoy studying Latin when I was at school.
2 Orwell would spend winters in Spain and summers in England.
3 We would live in a bungalow on the south coast, and then we moved to a flat in town.
4 You used to teach at Halston University, didn't you?
5 On Saturdays and Sundays the ferry used to take tourists across to the island.
6 The committee would meet four times last week, but still no decision has been reached.

16.3 Complete these sentences with **will have** or **would have** and the past participle of one of these verbs. E

approve	buy	hear	hurt	notice	prefer	watch

1 According to official figures, over half the population .... the final of the song contest on TV last night.
2 I enjoyed the exhibition – but I don't think my grandmother .... of it.
3 I don't think the dog .... anyone, but I was still glad when the owner took it away.
4 I'm sure by now you .... about yesterday's robbery at the supermarket.
5 The train journey was quite comfortable, although I .... to fly.
6 Regular readers .... the return of a popular feature to our website.
7 A: Did you like the present Justin gave you for your birthday? B: Well, an umbrella stand isn't something I .... myself, but I suppose it might be useful.

16.4 Complete B's responses below to show criticism or disapproval. B

1 A: I think I'm putting on weight. B: Well, if you ....
2 A: I've got a headache. B: Well, if you ....
3 A: I'm really hot. B: Well, if you ....

→ **Additional exercise 5** (page 242)

Unit 17

May and **might**

A

May and **might** often have a similar meaning when we talk about possibility. Reminder ➔ C15 – C19
However, we prefer **may** in academic or formal language to talk about characteristics or behaviour:

- The seeds from the plant **may** grow up to 20 centimetres in length.

and in speech we prefer **might** to say what we will possibly do in the future:

- I **might** paint the kitchen purple.

B

We don't use **may** to ask questions about the possibility of something happening. Instead we use, for example, **could(n't)** or the phrase **be likely**:

- **Could** it be that you don't want to leave? (*not* May it be that you ...?)
- **Are** you **likely** to be in Spain again this summer? (*not* May you be in Spain ...?)

It is possible to use **might** in this type of question, but it is rather formal:

- **Might** they be persuaded to change their minds?

Note that we can use **may** in formally asking for permission and offering help:

- **May** I leave now?
- **May** I help you?

C

Might (not 'may') + **bare infinitive** is sometimes used to talk about what was *typically* the case in the past. This is a formal or literary use:

- During the war, the police **might** *arrest* you for criticising the government.
- Years ago children **might** *be sent* down mines at the age of six. (passive form)

We can also use **could** + **bare infinitive** in examples like this to talk about past ability (see Unit 15). For example, 'During the war, the police could arrest you ...' means that the police were legally able to arrest you.

D

When we say that a person or thing compensates to some extent for a limitation or weakness by having another characteristic, we can use a pattern with **may / might not** + **bare infinitive** ... **but** ... or **may / might not have** + **past participle** ... **but** ...:

- The painting **may not** *be* a masterpiece, **but** the colours are remarkable.
- She **might not** *have danced* very gracefully, **but** she had a lot of energy and enthusiasm.

E

We use **may / might** (not 'can') + **have** + **past participle** and **may / might** (not 'can') + **be** + **-ing** to talk about possible events in the past, present and future:

- Do you think Laura **may / might have completed** the report by now? (past)
- His maths **may / might have improved** by the time the exam comes round. (future)
- Marco isn't in his office. He **may / might be working** at home today. (present)
- When I go to Vienna I **may / might be staying** with Max, but I'm not sure yet. (future)

Note that **could** can be used in these sentences instead of **may** or **might**:

- Do you think Laura **could have completed** the report by now?

We can use **may / might have been** + **-ing** to talk about possible situations or activities that went on over a period of past time:

- Callum didn't know where the ball was, but he thought his sister **might have been playing** with it before she left for school.

Exercises

17.1 **Complete the sentences with either may or might, whichever is more likely. If neither is possible, use an alternative.** A & B

1 We .... go to Majorca for our holiday this summer.
2 The planet Venus .... be seen clearly in the night sky this month.
3 .... you see Yasemin this weekend?
4 I feel really sore after playing tennis. I think I .... have a bath.
5 A: Someone's left their coat. B: .... it be Nadia's?
6 Exceeding the stated dose .... cause drowsiness.

17.2 **Underline the correct answer.** C & E

1 You should have come dancing. You *might have enjoyed / might enjoy* it.
2 She *might have tried / might have been trying* to get a book off the top shelf when she fell.
3 Dr Carter *might have come / might be coming* over this evening, so can you tidy the house up a bit?
4 As recently as the 1950s, employers *might be requiring / might require* a woman to leave her job when she got married.
5 I've been offered a new job, so I *may be moving / may have moved* to Dubai.
6 Why not come and see us in March? The weather *may have been improving / may have improved* by then.
7 During the riots of the 1960s, people *might be imprisoned / may be imprisoned* simply for being on the streets.
8 He said he was in a lot of pain, but he *may have been exaggerating / may exaggerate*.
9 In the past, left-handed children *might be punishing / might be punished* for not holding a pen in their right hand.
10 I *may have told / may tell* you this before. I can't remember.

17.3 **Complete these sentences in any appropriate way.** D

1 He may not be the best singer in the world, but ....
....
2 Hugh's old car might not be terribly comfortable, but ....
....
3 Her English grammar may not be very accurate, but ....
....

Now expand these notes to complete the sentences below.

sound / exciting	agree / him	express / feelings openly	~~work / quickly~~

4 *He may / might not work very quickly* but at least he's very reliable.
5 ...., but his opinions on music make you think.
6 ...., but she is really very fond of you.
7 ...., but the new museum of fishing is actually very good.

→ Additional exercise 5 (page 242)

Unit 18

Must and have (got) to

A

We use **must** and **must not** in formal rules and regulations and in warnings: Reminder ➔ C20– C24

- Bookings **must** be made at least seven days before departure.
- The government **must not** be allowed to appoint judges.

In spoken English we often use **must** and **mustn't** (= must not) to propose a future arrangement, such as a meeting or social event, without making detailed plans:

- We **must** get together more often.
- We **mustn't** leave it so long next time.

We can also use **I must** … to remind ourselves to do something:

- **I must** charge my phone. I meant to do it yesterday, but I forgot.

B

To draw a conclusion about –

☆ something that happened in the past we use **must** + **have** + **past participle**:

- That's not Clara's car. She **must have borrowed** it from her parents.

☆ something happening at or around the time of speaking we use **must be** + **-ing**:

- I can't hear a noise. You **must be imagining** things.

☆ something that is likely to happen in the future we use **must be going to** or **must be** + **-ing**:

- 'What are all those workmen doing?' 'I think they **must be going to** dig up the road.'
- I was wrong about the meeting being today. It **must be happening** <u>next</u> Friday.

☆ a present situation we use **must be**, or **have (got) to be** in informal speech:

- Their goalkeeper **has got to be** at least two metres tall! (*or* … **must be** …)

We can use **must have to** to say that we conclude something based on what we know about a present situation and **must have had to** to conclude something about a past situation:

- I can't access the database. You **must have to put in** a password. (= a password is necessary)
- Matt wasn't at home when I went round. He **must have had to go** out unexpectedly.

Note that we can't say 'must've (got) to' but we can say **must've had to**.

C

In questions that hope for or expect a negative answer we prefer **have (got) to**, although in formal contexts **must** is sometimes used:

- **Do** we **have to** answer <u>all</u> the questions? (*or* **Have** we **got to** …?; *formally* <u>**Must**</u> **we** …?)

We use **have to** in questions that imply a criticism. **Must** can also be used, although some people think this is rather old-fashioned. We usually stress **have** and **must** in sentences like this:

- **Do** you <u>**have**</u> **to** play your trumpet here? It's deafening! (*formally* <u>**Must**</u> you play …?)

D

Sometimes we can use either **have to** or **have got to**. However –

☆ we use **have to** with frequency adverbs:

- I *often* **have to** work at the weekend to get everything done.

Also: **always**, **never**, **normally**, **rarely**, **sometimes**, etc.

☆ with the past simple we use **had to** especially in questions and negative sentences:

- When **did** you **have to** give it back? (*not* When had you got to give it back?)
- We **didn't have to** wait too long for an answer. (*not* We hadn't got to wait too long …)

☆ if **have** is contracted (e.g. I've, He's, It'd) then we must include **got**:

- I need a new pair of shoes, and they**'ve got to** be blue. (*not* … they've to be …)

☆ we don't use **have got to** with other modal verbs:

- Motorists *will* **have to** wait until next year to use the bridge. (*not* Motorists will have got to wait …)

Note also that **have got to** is often preferred in informal speech.

Exercises

18.1 Complete the sentences with one of these forms: **must have + past participle; must + bare infinitive; must be + -ing;** or **must have (had) to**. Use the verbs given. B

1 When I left my laptop on the train I thought I'd never see it again. But someone .... it and handed it in to the lost property office. (*find*)
2 Luisa owns a big car and a yacht. She .... incredibly rich. (*be*)
3 A: Everyone's going into the hall. B: The meeting .... soon. Let's go. (*start*)
4 Without things like washing machines and dishwashers our grandparents .... much harder in the kitchen than we do today. (*work*)
5 I didn't think Rob was coming to the meeting. He .... his mind. (*change*)
6 A: I wonder how you get past security.
B: I suppose you .... some form of ID. (*show*)
7 A: I thought Paul would be home.
B: He .... Lotta to work. He said he would. (*take*)
8 Look at all those birds. There .... at least a thousand of them. (*be*)

18.2 Write new sentences with a similar meaning. Use **have / has got to** where possible or preferable; if not, use **have / has to.** D

1 It is necessary to do all of this photocopying before lunchtime.
All of this photocopying has got to be done / has to be done before lunchtime
2 It is rarely necessary to ask Hannah to tidy her room. *Hannah* ...
3 Is it necessary for us to hand in the homework tomorrow? *Have* ...
4 It wasn't necessary for me to go to the hospital after all. *I* ...
5 Was it necessary for Ben to go alone? *Did* ...
6 It is sometimes necessary for Adam to start work at 6:30. *Adam* ...
7 It is necessary to extend the college to accommodate the new students. *The college* ...
8 It may be necessary to cancel our holiday because my mother is ill. *We* ...

18.3 If necessary, correct the italicised parts of this email message. A–D

Delete Junk Reply Reply All Forward Print To Do

Hello Maria,

Sorry I haven't been in touch for a while. You (1) *must have been wondering* what's been happening. Well, I must admit I've had a pretty awful week. When I got home from work last Monday, the front door was wide open. The door's very stiff, and I (2) *always have got to pull* it very hard to shut it. My neighbour's always saying, '(3) *Have you to bang* the door so hard?' When I went in I found that the house had been burgled. They (4) *must have climbed* over the fence in the back garden. None of the windows and doors were damaged, so someone very small (5) *must have to squeeze* through the tiny window in the kitchen. I suppose I (6) *must leave* it open, but I didn't expect anyone to be able to get in. Then they (7) *must have come* through the house and opened the front door for the others. Of course, the first thing I did was to call the police and I (8) *mustn't wait* very long for them to get here. Fortunately, the only thing that was taken was my TV. I think the burglars (9) *must be disturbed*, perhaps when the postman came. So now (10) *I've to get* a new lock for the front door and replace the TV, and I (11) *must put* some locks on the windows. I suppose I (12) *may must* get a burglar alarm, too. I must say I've never really wanted one, but needs must!

Anyway, (13) *I've to go*. Hope the family is well. Jessica (14) *must get* ready to go back to university. And you (15) *must be busy* with the new school year just about to start. When you have time, we (16) *have to get* together for a weekend.

All the best for now,

Amy

Can you find three other common expressions with must?

→ **Additional exercise 5** (page 242)

Unit 19

Need(n't), don't need to and don't have to

A

We can use **need** as an ordinary or a modal verb (followed by a bare infinitive). As a modal verb it doesn't change its tense and doesn't add '-s' for the third person singular. Compare:

Reminder ➔ C25–C28

- I **needed** to leave early. *or* She's thirsty. She **needs** a drink. (= ordinary verb) *and*
- You **needn't** *speak* so loudly. (= modal verb)

When it is a modal verb **need** is most commonly used in negative sentences:

- I've already cleaned the car so you **needn't** *bother* to do it.
- I was very nervous before the interview, but I **needn't** *have worried* – I got the job!

Other verbs often used with **need not (needn't): apply, concern, fear, involve, mean, panic**

It is sometimes used in questions, but we prefer to use **need** as an ordinary verb or **have to**:

- **Need** you **go** so soon? (= modal verb; less common and rather formal)
- **Do** you **need to go** so soon? (= ordinary verb) *or* **Do** you **have to go** so soon?

It is rarely used in affirmative sentences (that is, not questions or negatives), but is sometimes found in written English, particularly in fiction:

- We **need** *have* no fear for Nicole, she can take care of herself.

In other styles of formal written English it is used in this way with negative words such as **hardly**, **never**, **nobody / no one**, and **only**:

- The changes **need** *only* be small to make the proposals acceptable. (*less formally* The changes only need to be ...)
- *Nobody* ever **need** know about the money. (*less formally* Nobody ever needs to know ...)
- 'I don't want my parents to know.' 'They **need** *never* find out.' (*less formally* They never need to find out.)

B

To give permission not to do something we can use either **needn't** or **don't need to**:

- You **needn't cut** the grass, I'll do it later. (*or* You **don't need to cut** the grass ...)

To talk about a general necessity, we prefer **don't need to**:

- You **don't need to be** over 18 to get into a nightclub. (*rather than* You needn't be ...)

C

We can often use either **needn't** or **don't have to** with little difference in meaning to say that it is unnecessary to do something:

- You **needn't** whisper. Nobody can hear us. (*or* You **don't have to** ...)

However, some people prefer **needn't** when it is the speaker who decides the lack of necessity, and **don't have to** when somebody else or external rules make something unnecessary. Compare:

- As you worked late yesterday you **needn't** come in until ten tomorrow morning. (the speaker's decision) *and*
- We've been told that we **don't have to** be at work until ten tomorrow. (reporting someone else's decision.)

D

We can use **needn't** (or **don't have to**) to say that something is not necessarily true. We don't use **mustn't** in this way (see also Unit 18C):

- Volcanoes **needn't** erupt constantly to be classified as 'active'. (*or* Volcanoes **don't have to** erupt ...; *not* Volcanoes mustn't erupt ...)
- Nowadays it **needn't** cost a fortune to own an eBook reader. (*or* Nowadays it **doesn't have to** cost ...; *not* Nowadays it mustn't cost ...)

Exercises

19.1 **Match the sentence beginnings and ends. Join them with needn't and the bare infinitive of one of the verbs from the box.** A

bother	change	concern	panic	worry

1 I'll give you a lift to the station so you ...
2 The questions are in the book so you ...
3 All the windows have screens so you ...
4 Our software provides full computer security so you ...
5 The new tax laws don't come into force until next year so you ...

... the details on the form.
... yourself with viruses.
... to copy them down.
... about booking a taxi.
... about being bitten by mosquitoes.

19.2 **Rewrite the following in a formal style using need.** A

1 It is hardly necessary for us to remind you that the money is now due.
We need hardly remind you that the money is now due.
2 It is only necessary for us to look at the rainfall figures to see the seriousness of the problem.
3 With such a lead in the opinion polls it is hardly necessary for the Democrats to bother campaigning before the election.
4 It is not necessary for anyone to know who paid the ransom to the kidnappers.
5 After such a huge lottery win, it is not necessary for him to work again.

19.3 **Underline the more likely option. If the options are equally likely, underline them both.** B

1 In most developed countries, people *needn't / don't need to* boil water before they drink it.
2 You *needn't / don't need to* walk. I'll give you a lift.
3 I'll email a summary of the lecture so you *needn't / don't need to* take notes.
4 You *needn't / don't need to* have a university degree to become a police officer.
5 You *needn't / don't need to* buy me a birthday present.
6 In most cities you *needn't / don't need to* pay to get into the galleries and museums.

19.4 **Correct any mistakes in the extracts from a speech made by the managing director of a company to her employees.** A–D

1 You needn't to worry about losing your jobs.
2 Need we make any changes in company policy?
3 Changes in technology mustn't be a problem, but in fact provide opportunities.
4 I don't have to remind you that we are competing with two other companies.
5 I need hardly to tell you how important it is that we get this order.
6 You don't have to cancel your holiday plans.
7 We mustn't allow our rate of production to drop.
8 The present financial difficulties mustn't mean that people will lose their jobs.

→ Additional exercise 5 (page 242)

Should, ought to and had better

A

Reminder ➜ C29– C32

We can often use either **should** or **ought to** to talk about obligations and recommendations (e.g. You **should** / **ought to** finish your homework before you go out) and probability (e.g. It **should** / **ought to** be ready by now) although in general **should** is used more frequently. **Ought to** is used particularly in speech and most often to talk about obligation rather than probability.

When we conclude, on the basis of some evidence we have, that something is certain or very likely we can use **must** (see Unit 18) but not **should** / **ought to**:

- It's the third time she's been skating this week. She **must** really enjoy it.

Note also the following details –

☆ we prefer **should** when we say what an outside authority recommends:

- The manual says that the computer **should** be disconnected from the power supply before the cover is removed. (*rather than* … ought to be disconnected …)

☆ we use **should** (or **would**), not **ought to**, when we give advice with **I** …:

- I **should** leave early tomorrow, if I were you. (*or* **I would** leave …; *or* **I'd** leave …)

☆ we prefer **should** in questions, particularly **wh-questions**:

- What **should** I do if I have any problems?
- **Should** I ring you at home?

B

We use **should / ought to** + **have** + **past participle** to talk about something that didn't happen in the past and we are sorry that it didn't:

- We **should** / **ought to have waited** for the rain to stop. (I'm sorry we didn't)

We often use this pattern to indicate some regret or criticism and the negative forms **shouldn't / oughtn't to have** are almost always used in this way.

We also use **should / ought to** + **have** + **past participle** to talk about an expectation that something happened, has happened, or will happen:

- If the flight was on time, he **should** / **ought to have arrived** in Jakarta early this morning.

C

We can use **should** in questions that are offers or that request confirmation or advice:

- **Should** I phone for a taxi for you?
- Who **should** I pass the message to?

Note that in sentences like these we can also use **shall** with a very similar meaning.

Compare the use of **shall** and **should** in sentences such as the following, where 'I shall' means 'I intend to' and 'I should' means 'I ought to':

- I **shall** read the script on the train tomorrow. (*or* **I'll** read …) *and*
- I **should** read the script on the train tomorrow but I know that I'll be too tired.

D

We can use **had better** instead of **should** / **ought to**, especially in spoken English, to say that we think it is a good idea to do something:

- If you're not well, you**'d better** ask Clare to go instead. (*or* … you **should** / **ought to** …)

although we don't use it to talk about the past or to make general comments:

- You **should** / **ought to** have caught a later train. (*not* You had better have caught …)
- I don't think parents **should** / **ought to** give children sweets. (*not* … parents had better give …)

We prefer **had better** if we want to express particular urgency or in demands and threats:

- There's someone moving about downstairs. We**'d better** call the police, quickly.

Note that the negative form is **had better not**, and in questions the subject comes after **had**:

- He**'d better not** be late again or he'll be in trouble.
- **Had** we **better** get a taxi? (*or* **Should** we get …?)

Exercises

20.1 Complete these sentences with **should / ought to + infinitive** (active), **should / ought to be + past participle** (passive), or **should / ought to have + past participle** using each of the verbs from the box once only. A & B

answer	arrive	be	go	put	remove	resign	send	wear	win

1 Thomas is running so well at the moment that he .... the 800 metres easily.
2 Where .... the cheese? In the fridge?
3 The tickets .... a couple of weeks before we go on holiday.
4 Payment for the full amount .... with this application form.
5 All packaging .... before switching on the printer for the first time.
6 It's important to look smart at the interview. You .... a suit.
7 There are many people who think the President .... years ago.
8 .... we .... the questions in English or in French?
9 If you want my advice, I .... by train rather than car.
10 I can't imagine what's happened to Nadia. She .... here by now.

20.2 **In which sentences can you use should or must and in which can you only use must? Where both are possible, consider the difference between should and must.** A

1 A timetable .... be set for withdrawing the army.
2 Lev isn't home yet. He .... have been held up at work.
3 A: I wonder how old Louis is?
B: Well, he went to school with my mother, so he .... be well over 50.
4 If you smell gas, you .... phone the emergency number.
5 You .... try to visit Nepal – it's a beautiful country.
6 A: I know I'm always complaining that my house is small, but it's very convenient for work.
B: Yes, it .... be handy living so close to your office.

20.3 If necessary correct these conversations using **should / ought to**, **must**, **shall**, or **had better**, or write ✓. A, C & D

1 A: There's something wrong with David's computer yet again.
B: He should wish he'd never bought it.
2 A: The next meeting's on 3rd April.
B: I'd better make a note of that, or I'll forget.
3 A: Have you put on weight recently?
B: Yes. I shall do more exercise, but I never seem to have time.
4 A: The children from next door have been throwing stones at our windows.
B: Well, they shouldn't do it again, otherwise I'll call the police.
5 A: I'm freezing.
B: You'd better have worn a thicker coat.
6 A: Businesses had better not be allowed to give money to political parties.
B: I totally agree.
7 A: When have we got to be in Bristol?
B: By four. I think we'd better get started.
8 A: Do you want to go out for lunch?
B: Well, I should be revising for my maths exam ... but okay.
9 A: I've looked all over the house and can't find the keys.
B: Well, if they're not here, they must still be in the car.
10 A: It's so expensive to park here.
B: Yes, I don't think people had better pay to park at work at all.

→ Additional exercise 5 (page 242)

Linking verbs: **be, appear, seem; become, get**, etc.

A

When an adjective or noun phrase is used after a verb to describe the subject or say what or who the subject is, the adjective or noun phrase is a *complement* and the verb is a *linking verb*:

- ▢ Clara **is** *a doctor*.
- ▢ She **seemed** *unable to concentrate*.

Other linking verbs:
'being' linking verbs: e.g. **be, keep, prove, remain, stay**
'becoming' linking verbs: e.g. **become, come, end up, grow, turn out**
'seeming' linking verbs: e.g. **appear, look, seem, sound**

Most of these verbs can be followed by either an adjective or noun phrase (e.g. It **sounds nice / a nice place**).

When they are used as linking verbs, **come** and **grow** (e.g. **come to know**, **grow thoughtful**) can't be followed by a noun phrase.

Keep is only followed by a noun if an adjective follows it (e.g. It **kept him awake**).

B

After the verbs **appear** (= seems true), **look** (= seem), **prove**, **seem**, and **turn out** we can often either include or omit **to be**:

- ▢ The room **appears (to be)** *brighter* than when I last saw it.

However, following these verbs **to be** is usually included before the adjectives **alive**, **alone**, **asleep**, and **awake**, and before the **-ing** forms of verbs:

- ▢ I didn't go in because **she appeared to be** *asleep*. (*not* … she appeared asleep.)

Before a noun we include **to be** when the noun tells us what the subject is, but often leave it out when we give our opinion of the person or thing in the subject. We leave out **to be** in formal English. Compare:

- ▢ He walked into what **seemed to be** *a cave*. (*not* … what seemed a cave.) *and*
- ▢ She **seems (to be)** *a very efficient salesperson*.

C

We use the linking verb **become** to describe a process of change. A number of other linking verbs can be used instead of **become**, including **come**, **get**, **go**, **grow**, **turn (into)**.

We use **get** rather than **become**: in informal speech and writing before **difficult**, **ill**, **interested**, **pregnant**, **suspicious**, **unhappy**, and **worried**; in imperatives; and in phrases such as **get changed** (clothes), **get dressed**, **get married / divorced**:

- ▢ I first **got** *suspicious* when he looked into all the cars. (*more formally* … **became** *suspicious* …)
- ▢ *Don't* **get** *upset* about it!
- ▢ Where did you live before you **got** *married*?

We prefer **become** to talk about a more abstract or technical process of change:

- ▢ He **became** *recognised* as an expert.
- ▢ Their bodies **have become** *adapted* to high altitudes.

Also with: **apparent, aware, convinced, infected, irrelevant, obvious**

We use **become**, not **get**, if there is a noun phrase after the linking verb:

- ▢ Dr Morales **became** *an adviser* to the government.

D

We use **go** or **turn**, not usually **get** or **become**, when we talk about colours changing:

- ▢ The traffic lights **turned / went** *green* and I pulled away.

We often use **go** to talk about changes, particularly for unwanted situations. For example:

go deaf / blind / bald; **go mad / crazy / wild**; **go bad / off / mouldy / rotten**; **go bust**; **go dead**; **go missing**; **go wrong**. But note: **get ill**, **get old**, **get tired**.

- ▢ The company **went bust** and had to close.
- ▢ My computer's **gone wrong** again.
- ▢ Some people **get ill** very easily.

After the verbs **come**, **get**, and **grow** (but not after **become**) we can use a **to-infinitive**. **Come** and **grow** are often used to talk about gradual change:

- ▢ I eventually **came / grew** *to appreciate* his work. (*not* … became to appreciate his work.)

Exercises

21.1 Put brackets around to be in these sentences if it can be left out. B

1 The job turned out to be far easier than I'd expected.
2 When I looked through the window, Ella appeared to be alone.
3 What he called his 'little cottage in the country' proved to be a castle.
4 Hassan proved to be an excellent source of information about the town.
5 She appeared to be satisfied with the work I'd done.
6 I've adjusted the aerial and the television seems to be working okay now.
7 When I picked the crab up I thought it was dead, but it turned out to be alive and pinched me.
8 With only five minutes of the match left, Spain look to be heading to victory.
9 A: We've decided to buy a Ford. B: That seems to be a very good choice.
10 He only looked to be about ten years old, but I knew he must be a lot older.

21.2 Complete the sentences with an appropriate form of become or get. C

1 Give me a few minutes to .... changed, and then I'll be ready to go.
2 The state of the railways .... a major political issue during the last election campaign.
3 Research has shown that women who .... pregnant while dieting increase their child's risk of obesity.
4 The reasons for my decision will .... clear at the next meeting.
5 Don't .... annoyed with me, but I've lost the car keys.
6 I didn't finish the book. I just couldn't .... interested in it.
7 After the strange events in the house she .... convinced that it was haunted.
8 I had just .... divorced when I met Marianne.

21.3 Complete each sentence with an appropriate form of one of the verbs in brackets and a word or phrase from the box. D

~~berserk~~	blind	bust	dead	to know	to like	red	tired

1 I was at a zoo once when an elephant *went berserk* and attacked its keeper. (*go / turn*)
2 A few seconds later the line .... and Marc put down the handset. (*go / turn*)
3 After the spider bit Rachel her ankle .... and started to swell up. (*go / get*)
4 He's actually quite friendly when you .... him. (*become / get*)
5 I'll take over driving when you .... (*get / go*)
6 We soon .... each other and have been great friends ever since. (*become / come*)
7 The doctor told me that without immediate treatment I might .... (*go / turn*)
8 The company .... when the bank wouldn't lend it any more money. (*go / get*)

21.4 If necessary, correct the italicised parts of this blog. A–D

The morning we were going on holiday everything seemed to (1) *turn wrong*. The taxi was due at 8:00 to take us to the airport. When I looked in on Adam at 7:00 he (2) *seemed awake*, so I went downstairs to make breakfast. When I opened the fridge I found that the milk (3) *had gone off*, so we couldn't have breakfast. Then Adam (4) *seemed taking* a long time to come down, so at 7:30 I went back upstairs and he still (5) *hadn't become dressed*. He said he wasn't feeling well, but I just shouted, 'You can't (6) *get ill* when we're going on holiday!' After that the keys to the luggage (7) *got missing*, but Adam eventually found them in his jacket pocket. By 8:30 the taxi hadn't arrived and I was starting (8) *to become worried*. It was (9) *getting obvious* that we were going to miss our plane if we didn't leave soon. But just then the taxi arrived and we made it to the airport with minutes to spare. Surprisingly, after such a bad start, it (10) *turned out to be* an excellent holiday.

Unit 22 Forming passive sentences 1

A

Verbs such as **give** take both a direct object (DO) and an indirect object (IO) in two patterns: **V + IO + DO** or **V + DO + preposition + IO**. These verbs have two corresponding passives:

Reminder ➔ Section D & Appendix 2

active **V + IO + DO** **V + DO + prep + IO**	passive
Alice gave us that vase. ✓	We were given that vase (by Alice). ✓
Alice gave that vase to us. ✓	That vase was given (to) us (by Alice). ✓

Also: **award, hand, lend, offer, send, throw** (= 'giving' verbs)**; ask, read, teach** (= 'telling' verbs)

The passive form you choose depends on which is more appropriate in a particular context. If we specify an agent (see Appendix 2), this follows **by** at the end of the clause. Note that in informal contexts 'to' can be left out in the second passive pattern.

Verbs that can't be followed by **IO + DO** in the active have only one of these passive forms:

active **V + DO + prep + IO**	passive
~~He explained me the problem.~~ ✗ He explained the problem to me. ✓	~~I was explained the problem.~~ ✗ The problem was explained to me. ✓

Also: **announce, demonstrate, describe, introduce, mention, propose, report, suggest** (= 'reporting' verbs)

B

Verbs followed by **object + complement** in the active have one passive form:

active **V + object + complement**	passive
They elected her president.	She was elected president.

Also: **appoint, declare, make, nominate, vote** (to do with giving a particular position)**; call, name, title** (= 'naming' verbs)

C

Some verbs that are followed by **object + bare infinitive** (= an infinitive without 'to') in the active are followed by a **to-infinitive** in the passive:

active **V + object + bare infinitive**	passive
They have made him return the money.	He has been made to return the money.

Also: **feel, hear, help** (*also* + object + **to-infinitive**), **observe, see** (see also Unit 23A)

D

Transitive two- and three-word verbs (see also Unit 94)

Some have passive forms:

active	passive
Ella **looked after** him.	He was looked after (by Ella).

Also: **carry out** (= put into practice), **disapprove of, hold over** (= delay), **talk down to** (= patronise)

Some are not used in the passive:

active	no passive
We **came up against** a problem.	~~A problem was come up against.~~ ✗

Also: **brush up on** (= revise), **cast (your mind) back** (= try to remember), **get (something) down** (= write), **take after** (= resemble)

Some can be only used in the passive with certain senses:

active	passive
They **put out** the fire. I **put out** a hand to steady myself.	The fire was put out. ~~A hand was put out to steady myself.~~ ✗

Also: (passive possible meaning / no passive meaning): **call (someone) up** (order to join the army / telephone); **call (someone) back** (ask to return / telephone); **let in** (allow into a place / allow rain, etc. in); **let out** (allow to leave / let out a sound)

Exercises

22.1 Rewrite the sentences using one or, if possible, two passive forms. Look carefully at the tense. A

1 Someone handed me a note. I was handed a note. / A note was handed to me.
2 Someone offered her a second-hand bicycle.
3 Someone has proposed improvements to the developers.
4 Someone suggested some interesting changes to me.
5 Someone awarded him a prize.
6 Someone will announce the President's arrival to the waiting journalists.
7 Someone had mentioned the password to the thieves.
8 Someone has lent me some skis.
9 Someone is sending me a lot of spam emails.
10 Someone is going to explain the changes to the students.

22.2 Complete each first sentence with a suitable form of a verb from the box. Then complete the second sentence using the same verb and the passive. A, B & C

appoint	declare	demonstrate	~~help~~	introduce	see

1 People helped Rob to his feet after the accident.
Rob was helped to his feet after the accident.
2 Tony .... me to Mrs Rossi at his birthday party. I ....
....
3 Has anyone .... Chris this morning? Has Chris ....
.... ?
4 They .... Sven Larsen Regional Sales Director for Scandinavia.
Sven Larsen ....
5 I am certain that Sarah .... her suitability as company director to those who still have any doubt. I am certain that Sarah's suitability as company director ....
....
6 They .... Alan Watson winner of the election after a recount.
Alan Watson ....

22.3 If possible, rewrite each sentence using a passive form of the italicised two- or three-word verb. If not, write 'No passive'. D

1 Children often *look up to* strict teachers.
Strict teachers are often looked up to by children.
2 The company *phased out* the product over a period of three years.
....
3 The students *got* the information *down* as fast as they could.
....
4 The decision has *deprived* many people *of* the right to vote.
....
5 People often *brush up on* a foreign language just before a holiday.
....
6 Ben *called* Mrs Patel *back* as soon as he got home.
....
7 The chairperson *held over* the last two items until the next committee meeting.
....
8 The farmer *prevented* walkers *from* crossing the field after he *fenced* it *off*.
....

→ **Additional exercise 6** (page 243)

Unit 23

Forming passive sentences 2: verb + **-ing** or **to-infinitive**

A

Active patterns with verb + -ing

Verbs followed by **object** + **-ing** in the active are made passive with **'be'** + **past participle** + **-ing**:

- They **saw** *the monkey* **climbing** over the fence. (= active)
- *The monkey* **was seen climbing** over the fence. (= passive)

Also: **bring**, **catch**, **hear**, **find**, **keep**, **notice**, **observe**, **send**, **show**

B

Some verbs that can be followed by an **-ing** form can be used with a passive form **being** + **past participle**:

- I really **love being given** presents.
- The children **enjoyed being taken** to the zoo.

Also: **avoid, deny, describe, dislike, face, hate, (not) imagine, like, remember**, **report**, **resent**

C

Verbs which in the active are followed by an object consisting of a noun phrase and **-ing clause** usually have no passive:

- I dread **him** (*or* **his**) **finding out**. (*but not* He is dreaded finding out)

Also: **anticipate, appreciate, dislike, forget, hate, imagine, like, (not) mind**, **recall**, **remember**

D

Active patterns with verb + to-infinitive

The active pattern **verb** + **object** + **to-infinitive** is made passive with **'be'** + **past participle** + **to-infinitive**. Compare:

- Mr Wang **has taught** *Peter* **to sing** for years. *and*
- Peter **has been taught to sing** (by Mr Wang) for years.

Also: **advise**, **allow**, **ask**, **believe**, **consider**, **expect**, **feel**, **instruct**, **mean**, **order**, **require**, **tell**, **understand**

Note that in some contexts it is possible to make both verbs passive:

- Changes to the taxation system **are expected to be proposed**. (*compare the active* We **expect** the government **to propose** changes to the taxation system.)

Some verbs followed by an **object + to-infinitive** in the active have no passive:

- Susan **liked Karl to be** there. (*but not* Karl was liked to be there.)

Also: **(can't) bear**, **hate**, **love**, **need**, **prefer**, **want**, **wish** (= 'liking' and 'wanting' verbs)

E

The active pattern **verb** + **to-infinitive** + **object** is made passive with **verb** + **to be** + **past participle**. Compare:

- Supermarkets **started to sell** *fresh pasta* only in the 1990s. *and*
- *Fresh pasta* **started to be sold** by supermarkets only in the 1990s.

Also: (i) **appear**, **begin**, **come**, **continue**, **seem**, **tend**; (ii) **agree**, **aim**, **arrange**, **attempt**, **hope**, **refuse**, **want**

The verbs in group (i) (and **start**) have corresponding meanings in active and passive sentences, but the verbs in group (ii) do not. Compare:

- People have come to see organic food as something only the wealthy eat. (active) *corresponds to*
- Organic food has come to be seen as something only the wealthy eat. (passive)
- Petra wanted to help me. (active) *does not correspond to*
- I wanted to be helped by Petra. (passive)

Exercises

23.1 Complete each sentence using one pair of verbs from the box. Use either **was / were + past participle + -ing** or **past simple + being + past participle.** A & B

avoid – take	deny – involve	face – expel	find – wander	~~keep – wait~~
leave – hold	observe – hide	remember – bite	resent – give	send – tumble

1 Inger ......was kept waiting...... for over three hours when she went for her dental appointment.
2 When the police first questioned him, Wayne .... in the robbery.
3 I .... the baby while Karen went to answer the door.
4 When I woke up in hospital, I .... by the snake but nothing after that.
5 They .... prisoner by pretending to be dead.
6 The man .... a suspicious package under a seat in the train.
7 When the bike hit her, Ana .... to the ground.
8 Two teenagers yesterday .... from school after they were found with over a hundred stolen mobile phones.
9 The man was taken to hospital when he .... lost and alone in the forest.
10 Tarik had worked in the company for 30 years and he rather .... orders by people who had been there only weeks.

23.2 Rewrite the sentences using one pair of words from the box. Use passive forms with **past participle + -ing, past participle + to-infinitive,** or **past simple + being + past participle.** A–D

~~ask – show~~	catch – shoplift	expect – attract	hear – argue
hate – tease	mind – criticise	observe – enter	require – complete

1 They wanted us to show our passports at the border.
We were asked to show our passports at the border.
2 They could hear Emil and Laura shouting at each other next door.
Emil and Laura ....
3 The other children made Ollie unhappy when they teased him.
Ollie ....
4 They saw the burglar getting into the museum through a window.
The burglar ....
5 They think that over 20,000 people will go to the pop concert.
The pop concert ....
6 They criticised her but she wasn't unhappy about it.
She ....
7 They said I had to fill in two copies of the customs declaration.
I ....
8 They caught Mrs Dee taking things from the shop.
Mrs Dee ....

23.3 Make passive sentences beginning with the italicised word(s). E

1 Kay's questions began to irritate *Marco*.
Marco began to be irritated by Kay's questions. (corresponding meaning)
2 The team captain hopes to select *Omar*.
3 Alastair arranged to take *Kathy* to the station.
4 Critics have come to recognise *Galdos* as one of Spain's greatest novelists.
5 The south coast continues to attract *holidaymakers*.
6 Harris has agreed to interview *the Finance Minister*.

Do the sentences you have written have a corresponding meaning to the original, or a different meaning? Look carefully at the tense in the sentences given.

→ **Additional exercise 6** (page 243)

Unit 24

Using passives

A

We typically use a passive rather than an active in the following situations.

Reminder → Section D & Appendix 2

☆ Using a passive allows us to omit the agent (= the subject of the corresponding active sentence) by leaving out the prepositional phrase with **by**. We prefer passives when the agent:

– is not known: ◯ My office **was broken into** when I was on holiday.
– is 'people in general': ◯ An order form **can be found** on page 2.
– is unimportant: ◯ He **is thought** to be somewhere in Russia.
– is obvious: ◯ She **is being treated** in hospital. (the agent is clearly 'medical staff')

☆ In factual writing (e.g. describing procedures or processes) we often omit the agent, and use passives:

◯ Nuclear waste will still be radioactive even after 20,000 years, so it **must be disposed of** very carefully. It **can be stored** as a liquid in stainless-steel containers which **are encased** in concrete. The most dangerous nuclear waste **can be turned** into glass which **will be stored** in deep underground mines.

☆ In informal contexts, particularly in conversation, we often use active sentences with a subject such as **people**, **somebody / someone**, **something**, **they**, **we**, or **you** even when we do not know who the agent is. In more formal contexts, we often prefer to use a passive so that we can avoid any mention of an agent. Compare:

◯ **They're installing** the new computer system next month. *and*
◯ The new computer system **is being installed** next month. (*more formal*)

B

Note also that some verbs have related nouns which express the same meaning. These nouns can be used as the subject of passive sentences, with a new passive verb introduced. Compare the example above and:

◯ The **installation** of the new computer system **will be completed** by next month.

C

In English we usually prefer to put the topic (what is already being talked about) at the beginning of a sentence (or clause) and a comment on that topic at the end. Choosing the passive often allows us to do this. Compare these two texts and note where the topic (in *italics*) is placed in the second sentence of each. The second text uses a passive where the emphasis is on the (safety) valves:

◯ The three machines tested for the report contained different types of safety valve. The Boron Group in Germany manufactured *all the valves*.
◯ The three machines tested for the report contained different types of safety valve. *All the valves* were manufactured by the Boron Group in Germany.

Using the passive allows us to put long subjects at the end of a sentence. So, for example:

◯ **I was surprised** by Dev's decision to give up his job and move to Sydney.

is more natural than '*Dev's decision to give up his job and move to Sydney* surprised me', although the choice can depend on considerations of style and context.

D

Instead of making a **that-clause** the subject of a passive sentence, it is normal to use an **it-clause** (see also Unit 25):

◯ Everybody **believed** (that) the plan would fail. (*active*)
◯ **It was believed** that the plan would fail. (*passive*) *is more natural than*
◯ *That the plan would fail* **was believed** by everybody.

Exercises

24.1 **Write passive sentences about the development of an Olympic Games site starting with the italicised words.** A & Appendix 2

1 They built *the main stadium* in under three years.
The main stadium was built in under three years.

2 They have designed *the main stadium* to accommodate many different sports.

3 They will take down *the temporary stands* after the Games.

4 They will have completed *the basketball arena* by the end of May.

5 They are holding *the rowing competition* on the River Nene.

6 They had completed *the athletics track* only a year after the city got the Olympics.

7 They were using *the handball venue* as a warehouse until a year ago.

8 They should have finished *the badminton arena* by now.

24.2 **Rewrite these sentences beginning with a noun formed from the italicised verb (with the if necessary). Use a passive form of the verb in brackets, and make any other necessary changes.** B

1 They will *consider* the issue at next week's meeting. (*give*)
Consideration will be given to the issue at next week's meeting.
2 They will *appoint* a new managing director next week. (*make*)
3 People have *accused* the local council of corruption. (*make*)
4 They *demolished* the building in only two days. (*complete*)
5 They will *present* the trophy after the speeches. (*make*)
6 Local residents will certainly *resist* the proposed new industrial area. (*expect*)

24.3 **Complete the text with appropriate forms (active or passive) of the verbs in brackets.** A–D

Slowly but surely the coastline of Britain (1) is being worn away (*wear away*) by an advancing sea. The country which once 'ruled the waves' now (2) .... (*rule*) by them, with huge forces threatening to destroy vast areas of human and wildlife habitat. Already some of Britain's last wild, natural areas (3) .... (*disappear*), and experts (4) .... (*fear*) that this is just the beginning. It (5) .... (*estimate*) that there will be a 38–55 cm rise in average sea levels by the year 2100. According to the Department of the Environment, during the next 50 years at least 10,000 hectares of farmland (6) .... (*turn into*) mud flats and salt marshes by the increases in sea levels. Rather than trying to prevent the erosion, the present government (7) .... (*use*) a method of 'managed retreat' by creating new defences further inland and allowing low-lying coastal farmland (8) .... (*abandon*) to the sea. However, many of the country's major cities could also (9) .... (*affect*). London, Bristol and Cardiff all (10) .... (*expect*) severe flooding as our sea defences (11) .... (*destroy*) by the rising tides.

→ Additional exercise 6 (page 243)

Unit 25 Reporting with passives; **It is said that …**

A

We often use a passive to report what people say, think, etc., particularly if it is not important to mention who is being reported:

- People in the area **have been told** that they should stay indoors.
- Everyone **was asked** to bring some food to the party.

B

Another common way of reporting what is said by an unspecified group of people is to use **it** + **passive verb** + **that-clause** (see Unit 33 for more on **that-clauses**). Using this pattern allows us to put important information at the end of the sentence (see Unit 24C):

- **It is reported** *that* the damage is extensive. (*compare* The damage is extensive, according to government sources.)
- **It was decided** *that* the meeting should be cancelled. (*or* It was decided to cancel the meeting.)

> *Also*: **allege, announce, assume, believe, calculate, claim, consider, demonstrate, discover, establish, estimate, expect, feel, find, know, mention, recommend, reveal, say, show, suggest, suppose, think, understand; agree, decide, hope, intend, plan**, **propose** (can also be followed by a **to-infinitive clause**)

Note that many other verbs connected with reporting are *not* used with **it + passive verb + that-clause**, but can be used as in **A:**

- We **have been informed** that we have to leave. (*but not* It has informed us …)

> *Also*: **encourage, persuade, reassure, remind, tell, warn**

These verbs need a personal object before the **that-clause** in an active form (e.g. They have informed **us** that …)

C

An alternative to **it** + **passive verb** + **that-clause** is to use **subject** + **passive verb** + **to-infinitive** if we want the subject to be the topic of the sentence (see Unit 24C). Compare:

- **It is reported** *that* the damage is extensive. *and*
- **The damage is reported** *to be* extensive.

Most of the verbs listed in the first white box in **B** can also be used in this pattern except for **announce**, **decide**, **mention**, **propose**, **recommend**, **suggest**.

We can only use **tell** in this pattern when it means 'order'. So we can say:

- **I was told** (= ordered) **to go** with them to the railway station.

but not 'The accident was told (= said) to have happened just after midnight'.

D

With some verbs we can also use **it** + **passive verb** + **wh-clause** to report information given or found out:

- **It has now been revealed** *who* was responsible for the accident.
- The decision to build the bridge was taken before **it was established** *whether* it was actually needed.

> *Also*: **discover**, **explain**, **find**, **know**, **reveal**, **show**, **understand**

E

When a **that-clause** begins **that** + **there** …, we can make a corresponding passive form **there** + **passive verb** + **to be** / **to have been**. Compare:

- **It is thought** (**that**) **there are** too many obstacles to peace. *and*
- **There are thought to be** too many obstacles to peace.

We can use the same verbs in this pattern as with **subject** + **passive verb** + **to-infinitive** (see **C**).

Exercises

25.1 Which of the verbs in brackets can complete the sentence? Underline one or both. B & D

1 It was .... to hold new negotiations next month. (*agreed / announced*)
2 It has been .... that the crash was the result of pilot error. (*proposed / shown*)
3 It was .... that Mrs Ho would chair the meeting. (*hoped / explained*)
4 It has been .... to appoint Dr Ahmadi as head teacher. (*decided / suggested*)
5 It has not yet been .... who was responsible for the error. (*claimed / explained*)
6 It has now been .... that half of cancer cases are lifestyle-related. (*established / revealed*)
7 It is .... to employ 500 people in the factory. (*expected / intended*)
8 It is .... to close the library permanently from next April. (*planned / recommended*)
9 It is .... that another moon landing will take place next year. (*assumed / thought*)
10 It has been .... how spiders are able to travel across the sea. (*discovered / said*)

25.2 If possible, rewrite these newspaper headlines as passive sentences with it. If not, write ✗. A & B

1 AGREEMENT THAT UN WILL SEND IN TROOPS
It has been agreed that the UN will send in troops.

2 PATIENTS REASSURED ABOUT HOSPITAL SAFETY

3 WATER DISCOVERED ON MARS

4 *TERRORISTS BELIEVED TO BE OPERATING IN BERLIN*

5 MOON ASTRONAUTS EXPECTED TO RETURN TODAY

6 EX-PRESIDENT JULIUS REVEALED AS SPY

7 WARNING GIVEN ABOUT COMPUTER VIRUS

8 KING SAID TO BE MAKING GOOD RECOVERY

9 RESTAURANT ESTABLISHED AS SOURCE OF FOOD POISONING OUTBREAK

10 POLICE TOLD TO WORK LONGER HOURS

25.3 Write two new sentences for each numbered sentence below, using it + passive verb + that-clause in one sentence and subject + passive verb + to-infinitive in the other. (The second pattern may not always be possible.) C

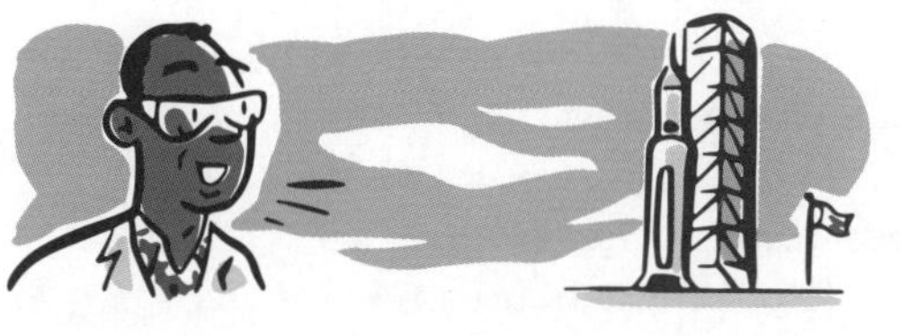

(1) We have discovered that a mechanical fault caused the problem. (2) We don't think that the fault is serious. (3) We expect that it will take several weeks to correct the fault. (4) We have decided to postpone the next rocket launch, and (5) we suggest that the next launch should take place in May.

1 *It has been discovered that a mechanical fault caused the problem. / A mechanical fault was discovered to have caused the problem.*

→ **Additional exercise 6** (page 243)

Unit 26 Wh-questions with who, whom, which, how and whose

A

Who refers to people, and can be used as subject, object or complement: Reminder ➜ Section E

- **Who** owns that car?
- **Who** did you meet?
- **Who** was her father?

Whom is used as a formal alternative to **who** as object, and also directly after prepositions:

- **Whom** did you meet?
- **To whom** were you talking?

Which is used to refer to people when we want to identify somebody in a group:

- '**Which** is your brother?' 'The one next to Luka.' (talking about a photograph)

and we can use **which** instead of **who** to talk about particular classes of people:

- **Which** do you think earns more, a teacher or a police officer? (*or* **Who** do you think ...?)

B

We usually use **which**, rather than **who** or **what**, in questions before **one**(**s**) and **of**, as **which** is commonly used to ask or talk about a choice between one or more things:

- I've decided to buy one of these jumpers. **Which** *one* do you think I should choose?
- **Which** *of* you would like to go first? (*rather than* Who of ...?)

C

When we use **who** or **what** as *subjects*, the verb that follows is usually singular, even if a plural answer is expected:

- **What** *is* there to see in the town? (expects an answer giving a number of things to see; *not* What are there to see in the town?)

However, the verb can be plural in echo questions (see Unit 27E) after a plural subject or a subject consisting of two or more noun phrases joined by **and**:

- 'Mr Almeida and his family are here to see you.' '**Who** *are* here?' (*or* **Who***'s* here?)

and when **who** and **what** function as *complements*:

- **Who** *are* those people over there?
- **What** *are* the consequences of the decision?

D

How or what?

How	What
How was the journey? (asking a general opinion)	**What** was the journey **like**? (asking a general opinion)
How is your brother? (asking about general health)	**What** do you **like about** the job? (asking for details)
How do you like your coffee? (asking about food and drink preferences)	**What if** your plan doesn't work? (asking about consequences)
	What's it **called**? (asking about a name)

How / What (about)

- **How / What about** a swim? (making a suggestion)
- 'He's a bit scary sometimes.' '**How / What** do you mean?' (asking for more information)

E

We can use **whose** to ask about the person that owns or is responsible for something. **Whose** can be used either before a verb (as a pronoun):

- **Whose** *are* these boots?

or before a noun or noun phrase (as a determiner) introducing direct or indirect questions:

- **Whose** *boots* are these?
- She asked me **whose** *coat* I was wearing.

In formal contexts we can use a preposition before **whose** (see also Unit 55B):

- *In* **whose** desk was it found? (*less formally* **Whose** desk was it found *in*?)

However, in questions without a verb a preposition comes before **whose**:

- 'We're meeting at nine.' '*In* **whose** house?' (*not* Whose house in?)

Exercises

26.1 Underline the correct option (or both if possible). A & B

1 To *whom / who* should the documents be sent?
2 *Which / Who* of you is Dr Hansen? I have a message for you.
3 A: Here's a photo of our children at the fancy dress party. B: *Who / Which* is Isabella?
4 A: Is your sister at home? B: *What / Which* one do you want to speak to?
5 *Whom / Who* do you hold responsible for the damage?
6 *Who / Which* will captain the team if Zeinab isn't available?
7 *Which / Who* would you rather be – a doctor or a vet?
8 *Who / Whom* translated the book?

26.2 Complete the sentences with an appropriate present simple form of the verbs in brackets. C

1 What .... those cakes made from? (*be*)
2 Who .... you for Maths and English? (*teach*)
3 What .... there to see on the island? (*be*)
4 Who .... the major decisions in the company? (*make*)
5 A: The Turners are in France. B: Who .... in France? (*be*)
6 Who .... their textbook with them? Put your hands up. (*have*)

26.3 First, complete the sentences with how, what, or how / what if both are possible. Then choose an appropriate answer for each question. D

1 '...What... do you like about your new job?' [g]
2 '............ if Omar calls while you're out?' [ ]
3 '............ about a coffee?' [ ]
4 '............ are your parents these days?' [ ]
5 '............'s your boss like?' [ ]
6 '............ do you like your new job?' [ ]
7 '............ was the camping trip?' [ ]
8 '............'s your boss called?' [ ]
9 '............ do you mean, "Smart clothes"?' [ ]
10 '............ was the camping trip like?' [ ]

a 'It's really boring.'
b 'I'd love one.'
c 'I mean you've got to wear a suit.'
d 'Tell him I'll call back.'
e 'It was great.'
f 'Lucia Garcia.'
g 'It's never boring.'
h 'Quite well, thanks.'
i 'We had an excellent time.'
j 'She works us really hard.'

26.4 Correct any mistakes in the italicised words or, if necessary, suggest ways of making the sentence more natural. If the sentence is already correct, write ✓. B, C & E

1 *Who's* caravan were you staying in? ....
2 *Whose are* all these books? ....
3 He asked us *who's* car was parked in front of his house. ....
4 A: *Who live* in the flat upstairs? B: The Thompson family. ....
5 *Whose* going with you to Canada? ....
6 *About whose* travels in Nepal did Liam Wilson write a book? ....
7 *What* one of the following statements is true? ....
8 *Who* of us has not told a lie at some time in our lives? ....
9 A: Can you post the books to us? B: *Whose address to?* ....
10 A: Ants have got into the fridge! B: *What has* got into the fridge? ....

Unit 27

Negative questions; echo questions; questions with **that-clauses**

A

Negative questions

Reminder ➜ E5– E7

We usually make a negative **yes / no** or **wh-question** with an auxiliary verb (*have*, *did*, *would*, etc.) + **-n't** to suggest, persuade, criticise, etc.

- **Wouldn't** it be better to go tomorrow?
- Why **don't** we go out for a meal?

In formal contexts, or when we want to give some special emphasis to the negative (perhaps to show that we are angry, very surprised, or to strongly persuade someone), we can use **not** after the subject in negative questions. This happens particularly in **yes / no** rather than **wh-questions**:

- **Did** *she* **not** realise that she'd broken it? (*less emphatically* **Didn't** *she* realise that ...?)
- **Can** *you* **not** get there a bit earlier? (*less emphatically* **Can't** *you* ...?)

B

We sometimes use negative words other than **-n't** such as **never**, **no**, **nobody**, **nothing**, **nowhere**:

- Why do you **never** help?
- Have you **nowhere** to go? (*or* Do you have **nowhere** to go?)

or less emphatically or more informally:

- Why do**n't** you ever help?
- Have**n't** you got anywhere to go? (*or* Do**n't** you have anywhere ...?)

C

We can make a suggestion with **Why not + verb** or **Why don't / doesn't ...** (*but not* Why do not / does not ...):

- **Why not** *decorate* the house yourself? (*or* **Why don't** you decorate ...?)

Why didn't ... isn't used to make a suggestion, but can show that we think an action was wrong. For example, depending on intonation and context, it can be used to criticise someone:

- **Why didn't** you tell me that in the first place? (I'm annoyed that you didn't)

D

Negative question forms, usually with a falling intonation, are used in exclamations giving opinions:

- Have**n't** you grown!
- Does**n't** she look lovely!
- Did**n't** it snow a lot!

E

Echo questions

Echo questions are used when we haven't understood what has been said or to check that we heard correctly, perhaps because we found it very surprising. We might repeat, usually with a rising intonation, the whole of what was said:

- 'Tala's lost her job.' 'Tala's lost her job?'

or focus on part of what was said using a stressed **wh-word** or a phrase with **how**:

- 'Leon's arriving at 6:30.' '**When's** Leon arriving? / Leon's arriving **when**?'
- 'We paid £3,000 for the painting.' '**How much** did you pay? / You paid **how much**?'

We can use **what** or '**do**' **what** to focus on the verb or part of the sentence beginning with the verb:

- 'We paid £3,000 for the painting.' 'You **what**?' (*or* 'You **did what**?')
- 'I think she's having a sleep.' 'She's **what**?' (*or* 'She's **doing what**?')

F

Questions with that-clauses

A **wh-question** can refer to a following **that-clause**, particularly after verbs such as **expect**, **hope**, **reckon**, **say**, **suggest**, **suppose**, and **think**. We can leave out **that** in these questions:

- **When** do you *reckon* (that) you'll finish the job?

However, when the **wh-word** is the subject, object or complement of the verb in the subordinate clause, we do not use **that**:

- **What** did you *think* was in the box? (*not* What did you think that was in the box?)

Exercises

27.1 **Write negative questions for B in these dialogues, using -n't with the words in brackets.** A

1 A: Can you lend me €10?
B: Again? Haven't you got any money left? (... *money left?*)

2 A: I'm annoyed that you didn't come to the meeting.
B: Why? .... (... *my email / on holiday?*)

3 A: I've had to bring the children with me.
B: Why? .... (... *babysitter?*)

4 A: I'll just finish my homework before I go to school.
B: But .... (... *be supposed to / last night?*)

5 A: I've put my bike in the sitting room.
B: The sitting room! .... (... *outside?*)

6 A: I'm taking the coach to Vienna.
B: But that will take ages. .... (... *rather / plane?*)

27.2 **Use the notes to complete these dialogues with two negative questions. In the first use -n't; in the second use never, no, nobody, nothing or nowhere.** B

1 (*ever / considered you might / wrong*)
A: Haven't you ever considered you might be wrong? / Have you never considered you might be wrong?
B: No, I'm sure I'm right.

2 (*you / any interest / maths at all*) A: ....?
B: No, I've always hated it.

3 A: I spent the night in the railway station. (*could / find anywhere else / sleep*)
B: ....?

4 (*can / remember anything about / accident*) A: ....
............?
B: Not after getting into the car, no.

5 (*why / ever do well / exams*) A: ....?
B: Perhaps you don't revise enough.

6 (*there anybody / you can ask / help*) A: ....?
B: I can't think of anyone.'

27.3 **Complete the echo questions using appropriate question words or phrases.** E

1 A: Jake's going to Chile. B: He's going where? / He's doing what? / He's what?

2 A: He's leaving at the end of next week.
B: He's leaving ....?/ He's doing ....?/ He's ....?

3 A: He'll be away for three months. B: He'll be away for ....?/ He'll ....?

4 A: It will cost about £15,000. B: It'll cost ....? / It'll ....?

5 A: He's sold his house to pay for the trip.
B: He's sold ....?/ He's done ....?/ He's ....?

6 A: He's going climbing in the Andes.
B: He's going climbing ....?/ He's doing ....?/ He's ....?

27.4 **If necessary, correct any mistakes in these sentences. Put a tick if they are already correct.** C, D & F

1 A: Mariam isn't answering her phone. B: Why do you not email her?
2 Who do you expect that will read your blog?
3 Why did they suggest that we should avoid using the motorway?
4 Was not it a brilliant film!
5 If she really wants to go rock climbing, why not let her?
6 What did you say that is in these biscuits?
7 How do you think that Twitter will have changed our lives in ten years' time?
8 Why did not you tell me you'd changed your number?

Unit 28

Verbs, objects and complements

A

Some verbs can be either transitive or intransitive, allowing us to focus on either the person or thing performing the action, or the person or thing affected by the action. Compare:

Reminder ➜ F1– F3

- She **closed** *the door*. (transitive) *and* The door **closed**. (intransitive)
- I've **ripped** *my shirt*. (transitive) *and* My shirt **has ripped**. (intransitive)

Also: **begin**, **bend**, **break**, **burn**, **change**, **decrease**, **drop**, **finish**, **increase**, **move**, **open**, **shut**, **start**, **vary**, **wake** (most are 'change' verbs)

B

Some transitive verbs don't need an object when the meaning is clear from the context:

- I often **sing** (*songs*) in the shower.
- She **plays** (*the saxophone*) beautifully.

Also: **answer**, **ask**, **change**, **cook**, **dance**, **drink**, **drive**, **eat**, **fail**, **park**, **phone**, **read**, **smoke**, **study**, **wash**, **wash up**, **wave**, **win**, **write**

C

After some verbs we usually add a *complement* – a phrase which completes the meaning of a verb, noun or adjective – which is an adverb or prepositional phrase:

- The disease **originated** *in Britain*. (*not* The disease originated. We need to add something about where or how it originated.)

Other verbs usually have a complement but may not. Compare:

- He **paused** *for a few moments*. *and* He **paused**. (no complement needed)

D

Some verbs are commonly followed by a particular preposition or prepositions and then an object (see also Unit 94):

- We had to **deal with** *hundreds of complaints*. (*not* We had to deal.)
- I'm sure that blue car **belongs to** *Murad*. (*not* I'm sure that blue car belongs.)

Also: **adhere to**, **aspire to**, **culminate in / with**, **detract from**, **differentiate between**, **incline to / towards**, **specialise in**

E

Some verbs are usually followed by an **object** + **prepositional phrase** complement:

- I always **associate** *pizza with Italy*. (*not* I always associate pizza.)
- She **put** *the report on the floor*. (*not* She put the report.)

Also: **attribute … to**, **base … on / upon**, **equate … with**, **inflict … on**, **mistake … for**, **regard … as / with**, **remind … of**

F

Some verbs are often followed by an **object** + **adjective** (or **adjective phrase**) complement:

- The people of this country will **hold** *the government responsible*.
- Conti **pronounced** *herself fit for the match*.

Also: **assume**, **believe**, **consider**, **declare**, **find**, **judge**, **prove**, **report**, **think**.
(The object after **declare**, **find**, **pronounce** and **prove** is usually a reflexive pronoun.)

Sentences with an **object** + **adjective** complement after these verbs are usually rather formal. Adding **to be** after the object or using a **that-clause** can make sentences less formal:

- Dr Adams argues that house prices will fall, but other economists **believe** *the opposite true*. (*or less formally* … believe the opposite to be true. *or* … believe that the opposite is true.)

Exercises

28.1 **If it is possible to omit the object (*in italics*) after the underlined verbs, put brackets around it.** B

Aya was (1) reading (*a book*) when the telephone rang. It was Val. She said, 'I called you earlier, but nobody (2) answered *the phone*. Would you like to come over to (3) eat *dinner* tonight with me and Tom? Is eight/seven okay?' Aya (4) thanked *Val* and said that she'd love to come. At about seven Aya started to get ready. She (5) washed *herself* and (6) brushed *her hair*. Then she (7) changed *her clothes* and (8) put on *some makeup*. After that, she (9) drove *her car* to Malstowe, the village where Val and Tom lived. Val was gardening when Aya (10) reached *their house* and she (11) waved *her hand* when she saw Aya. Aya (12) parked *her car* on the drive and walked over to Val. Val said, 'Tom's still (13) cooking *dinner*, so I thought I had time (14) to pick *some flowers*. By the way, my sister Kate is staying with us. She's (15) studying *French* at university, but is on holiday at the moment. I forgot to (16) mention *her* when I spoke to you earlier. I'll (17) introduce *you* when we go inside.' Aya (18) enjoyed *the evening* very much. The food was excellent and they talked a lot about their holiday plans. Aya hoped to go to Canada, but wasn't sure yet that she could (19) afford *it*. Before she left, Aya helped (20) wash up *the dishes*. As she drove home, she decided that she must (21) invite *Val and Tom* for a meal at her house very soon.

28.2 **Complete sentences 1–4 with a correct verb + preposition + noun phrase. Complete 5–8 with a correct verb + noun phrase + preposition.** D & E

Verbs (*Use an appropriate form.*)	Prepositions	Noun phrases
~~aspire~~ attribute base culminate differentiate inflict mistake specialise	between for in in on on ~~to~~ to	the black car ~~national leadership~~ his success the discovery of penicillin a surprise defeat fantasy and reality her new novel seafood

1 Electors deserve more from a political party that aspires to national leadership.
2 Years of research by Fleming ....
3 Her mental condition makes it difficult for her to ....
4 There's a great restaurant by the harbour which ....
5 The team of amateur footballers .... the first division leaders.
6 After Lewis's victory, he .... the advice of his new trainer.
7 It was dark and raining and she .... a taxi.
8 Emma Janse has .... events that took place in 16th-century Denmark.

28.3 **Complete these sentences with any appropriate adjective.** F

1 The scientific evidence proved him guilty.
2 She declared herself .... with the result.
3 They considered the food ....
4 I'm surprised the plumber hasn't turned up. I've always found him ....
5 We believed her .... at school.

Now write less formal versions using either to be after the object or a that-clause.

1 The scientific evidence proved him *to be guilty*. / The scientific evidence *proved that he was guilty*.

Unit 29

Verb + two objects

A

Some verbs can be followed by two objects. Usually the first object (= the *indirect object* (IO)) is a person or group of people and the second object (= the *direct object* (DO)) is a thing:

- Can you **bring** *me* (= IO) *some milk* (= DO) from the shops?
- He **made** *himself* (= IO) *a cup of coffee*. (= DO).

Many verbs that can have two objects may also be used with a DO only (e.g. I read a story). With many verbs that can have two objects, it is possible to reverse the order of the objects if we put **for** or **to** before the IO (this is then called a *prepositional object*). Compare:

- I **built** my daughter a doll's house. *and* I **built** a doll's house **for** my daughter.
- Can you **pass** me that bandage? *and* Can you **pass** that bandage **to** me?

*Other verbs with **for + object***: **book, buy, catch, choose, cook, fetch, find, get, make, order, pour, save**

*Other verbs with **to + object***: **award, give, hand, lend, offer, owe, show, teach, tell, throw**

We often use this pattern if we want to focus particular attention on the object after **for / to**. We also use it if the IO is a lot longer than the DO:

- Jasmin taught music **to** a large number of children at the school. (*not* Jasmin taught a large number of children at the school music.)

If the DO is a pronoun, a pattern with **DO + preposition + IO** is usual. Patterns without a preposition are avoided because they are considered to be bad style:

- I gave them **to** Isa. (*rather than* I gave Isa them. / I gave them Isa.)
- We bought it **for** them. (*rather than* We bought them it. / We bought it them.)

B

Some verbs can be used with either **for** or **to**. Often there is a difference in meaning: **to** suggests that there is a transfer of something to someone, and **for** suggests that someone benefits from something. Compare:

- I hadn't got time to visit Mira, so I **wrote** a letter **to** her. *and*
- Mira had broken her wrist, so I **wrote** a letter **for** her.

Also: **bring**, **leave**, **pay**, **play**, **post**, **read**, **sell**, **send**, **sing**, **take**

Sometimes, however, the meaning is very similar:

- He **played** the piece **to** (*or* **for**) me.
- Can you **sing** that song again **to** (*or* **for**) us?

Note that when **object + object** is used after these verbs it usually has a similar meaning to the verb with **object + to + object**. For example:

- I sold him the car. (*means* I sold the car **to** him, *not* I sold the car **for** him.)

C

Some verbs that are followed by two objects cannot have their objects reversed with **for / to**:

- We all **envied** him his lifestyle. (*but not* We all envied his lifestyle for / to him.)

Also: **allow**, **ask**, **cost**, **deny**, **forgive**, **guarantee**, **permit**, **refuse**

D

Some verbs, such as **describe** and **fix**, can *only* have a second object if this is a prepositional object –

☆ with **to** (see also Unit 22A). Compare:

- She **described** the situation (**to** me). (*but not* She described me the situation.) *and*
- She **told** this joke (**to** me). *or* She **told** me this joke.

Also: **admit, announce, demonstrate, explain, introduce, mention, point out, prove, report, say, suggest**

☆ with **for.** Compare:

- He **fixed** the tap (**for** me). (*but not* He fixed me the tap.) *and*
- I **booked** a room (**for** her). *or* I **booked** her a room.

Also: **collect, mend, repair**

Exercises

29.1 **Complete each sentence with a suitable form of a verb from the box and insert to or for in an appropriate place. Write to / for if either can be used.** A & B

choose	offer	pass	~~pay~~	post	read	save	sell	take	teach

1 Elias hasn't got any money so I'll have to ...pay... the bill for him.
2 Kaspar hates going shopping. I have to .... his clothes him.
3 You're staying with Dimitra at the weekend, aren't you? Can you .... this present her?
4 I can't reach the salt. Could you .... it me, please?
5 When Mr Durand bought the house, we .... all the carpets him as well.
6 He's got a very rewarding job. He .... sports disabled children.
7 I haven't got my glasses. Can you .... these instructions me, please?
8 Jane .... the letter me on her way to work because I had flu and couldn't go out.
9 I .... my old bike him, but he said he wanted something more modern.
10 I'll be in late tonight. Can you .... some dinner me, please?

29.2 **If necessary, correct these sentences. If the sentence is already correct, write ✓.** C & D

1 He kindly collected me some library books.
2 He admitted his error for his colleagues.
3 I have to prepare a report for the meeting.
4 Can I ask a favour to you?
5 A special ticket allows entry for people to all the museums in the city.
6 I'd like to introduce you to my sister.

29.3 **Complete these texts with objects chosen from the box. Give all possible word orders and add prepositions where necessary.** A–D

the problem / our teacher	**her photograph / me**	**the glass / him**
another half an hour / us	**his sister / me**	**three bedtime stories / him**
~~**an email / him**~~	**his broken car / him**	**the money / me**
a drink / Ben	**a paper aeroplane / him**	~~**the problem / him**~~
a fortune / you		

1 A: Samuel phoned. He wants to come and stay with us at the beginning of September.
B: But that's when my parents will be with us. I'll have to send
...him an email / an email to him... to explain ...the problem to him....

2 When he described .... I didn't think I knew her, but when he showed .... I realised that I had seen her at work.

3 The clock on the wall was wrong. When we pointed out .... , she allowed .... to finish the exam.

4 My three-year-old nephew, Luis, always keeps me busy when I babysit. Last night I first had to make .... , then I had to mend .... and after that he insisted that I read ....

5 A: Your new motorbike must have cost ....
B: Well, actually, my parents lent ....

6 I poured ....
and gave ....

Unit 30

Verb + -ing forms and infinitives 1

A

Reminder → F4– F13

Some verbs can be followed either by an **object** + **-ing** or a **possessive** + **-ing** with a similar meaning, although the **possessive** + **-ing** form is usually considered to be rather formal:

- ☐ I resented **Tom** winning the prize. (*more formally* I resented **Tom's** winning the prize.)
- ☐ Mia recalled **him** buying the book. (*more formally* Mia recalled **his** buying the book.)

Also: **detest, (dis)approve of, (dis)like, hate, love, object to** (= '(dis)liking' verbs); **forget, imagine, remember, think of** (= 'thinking' verbs)

Note that we only use a possessive form (Tom's, his) here to talk about a person or group of people:

- ☐ I remember **the horse** winning the race. (*but not* … the horse's winning …)

B

Some verbs can be followed by **to** + **-ing** where **to** is a preposition:

- ☐ She **confessed to** *stealing* the money.
- ☐ You **don't object to** *working* late tonight, do you?

Also: **adapt, adjust, admit, look forward, own up, resort**

Note that these verbs can also be followed by **to** + **noun phrase**:

- ☐ She **confessed to** *the crime*.
- ☐ You **don't object to** *the work*, do you?

C

Other verbs can be followed by different prepositions + **-ing**. For example:

☆ **by** + **-ing** (**begin**, **close**, **end**, **finish** (**off** / **up**), **open**, **start** (**off** / **out**))

- ☐ Can you **begin by** *cleaning* the floors, and then do the windows?

☆ **on** + **-ing** or **on** + **object** + **-ing** (**concentrate**, **count**, **depend**, **focus**, **insist**, **rely**)

- ☐ Clare **insisted on** (*Jack*) *wearing* a suit to the party.

☆ **of** + **-ing** or **of** + **object** + **-ing** (**approve**, **hear**, **know**, **speak**, **talk**, **tell**)

- ☐ Have you ever **heard of** *(anyone) getting* arrested for gossiping before?

☆ **object** + **from** + **-ing** (**deter**, **discourage**, **keep**, **prevent**, **prohibit**, **stop**)

- ☐ The noise from next door **prevented me from** *sleeping*.

D

Some verbs (**feel**, **hear**, **notice**, **observe**, **overhear**, **see**, **watch**) can be followed by an object and then either by an **-ing** form or **bare infinitive**, but the meanings may be slightly different. Compare:

- ☐ I **saw** *them playing* football from my window. (**-ing** indicates an action in progress) *and*
- ☐ I **saw** *him smash* the bottle. (**bare infinitive** indicates a completed action)
- ☐ I was able to **watch** *them building* the new car park from my office window. (**-ing** suggests that I watched, but not from start to finish) *and*
- ☐ I **watched** *him climb* through the window, and then I called the police. (**bare infinitive** suggests I watched the whole action from start to finish)

E

After the verbs **dare** and **help** we can use either a **bare infinitive** or **to-infinitive**:

- ☐ I was angry with him, but I **didn't dare** (*to*) *say* anything.
- ☐ We hope the Twitter campaign will **help** (*to*) *raise* awareness of the problem.

When **dare** has an object, we can only use a **to-infinitive**. Compare:

- ☐ I **dared** *him to cross* the river. (*not* I dared him cross …) *and*
- ☐ I **helped** *them* (*to*) *pack*.

After **have**, **let** and **make** we can use an **object** + **bare infinitive** but not **to-infinitive**:

- ☐ His exam results might **make** *him work* harder. (*not* … might make him to work …)
- ☐ I **had** *Irena clean* up her bedroom before I **let** *her go* out to play.

Exercises

30.1 **If possible, rewrite these sentences using the possessive form of the object. If not, write ✗.** A

1 I really hate you having to be away from home so much.
I really hate your having to be away from home so much.
2 We don't approve of the developer locating the factory so close to houses.
3 I have always detested the dog jumping up at me when I visit them.
4 No one heard the man shouting for help.
5 It is difficult to imagine him accepting the decision without any objection.
6 No one in the crowd that day will forget Ashe fighting so hard to win the match.
7 I remember them arguing a great deal when they were children.
8 The police investigated him stealing cars from the city centre.

30.2 **Rewrite the italicised part of each sentence so that it has a similar meaning. Use one of the verbs from the box and an -ing form.** B & C

adapt	approve	discourage	end	~~own up~~	rely

1 In a survey, 65% of dentists *said that they had made* mistakes in treating patients.
owned up to making
2 I don't *think children should wear* jewellery in school. ....
3 I would like to *finish with a summary of* the main points of my talk. ....
4 My parents *said they thought I shouldn't go* to university. ....
5 You can't *trust Sophie to turn up* on time. ....
6 I grew up in the countryside, and I found it difficult to *get used to life* in a big city.
....

30.3 **Underline the most likely verb form. Consider why it is the most likely.** A

1 I heard the tyre *burst / bursting* and then the lorry skidded across the road.
2 Carl noticed someone *watch / watching* him from an upstairs window.
3 She felt the wasp *sting / stinging* her just before she brushed it off her arm.
4 With a good telescope you can see the eagles *feed / feeding* their chicks in the nest.

30.4 **Match the sentence beginnings and endings, adding an appropriate object where necessary and write (to) where this might be included.** E

1 When Lana thought of going on the roller-coaster it made ...
2 The new course is intended to help ...
3 Scientists hope the new drug will help ...
4 We didn't agree with the decision, but we didn't dare ...
5 When Ethan arrives, have ...
6 The dial on the left lets ...

a prevent hay fever.
b ~~feel quite ill.~~
c control the speed of the fan.
d wait outside my office.
e understand modern art.
f protest against it.

1 + b *When Lana thought of going on the roller-coaster it made her feel quite ill.*

→ Additional exercise 7 (page 244)

Unit 31

Verb + -ing forms and infinitives 2

A

After some verbs we need to include an object before a **to-infinitive** in active sentences:

Reminder ➔ F4– F13

- The police **warned** *everyone* **to stay** inside with their windows closed. (*not* The police warned to stay ...)

Also: **advise, allow, believe, cause, command, enable, encourage, entitle, force, invite, order, persuade, remind, show, teach, tell**

After other verbs, however, we can't include an object before a **to-infinitive**:

- We**'ve decided to leave** early. (*not* We've decided us to leave early.)

Also: **agree, consent, fail, hope, manage, offer, pretend, refuse, start, threaten, volunteer**

B

After some verbs we have to put a preposition, usually **for**, immediately after the verb before an **object + to-infinitive** (see also Unit 29):

- They *arranged* **for** *Rania to stay* in London. (*not* They arranged Rania to stay ...)
- They *applied* **for** *the court appearance to be postponed.*

Also: **advertise**, **campaign**, **long**, **plan**, **wait** (After **apply** and **campaign**, the **to-infinitive** is usually passive.)

Other verbs can be followed by different prepositions + **object** + **to-infinitive**. For example:

☆ **at** + **object** + **to-infinitive** (**go on** [= to criticise continually], **keep on** [= to talk about something many times], **scream**, **shout**, **yell**)

- I *shouted* **at** *the man to open* the door.

☆ **on** + **object** + **to-infinitive** (**call** [= to officially ask someone to do something], **count**, **depend**, **prevail**, **rely**)

- We*'re depending* **on** *you to find* a solution soon.

☆ **to** + **object** + **to-infinitive** (**appeal**, **gesture**, **motion, signal**)

- He closed the door and *signalled* **to** *the pilot to take off*.

C

A number of other **to-infinitive** and **-ing** forms can also follow verbs –

☆ **verb** + negative **to-infinitive** and negative **-ing** forms

- We **decided not to go** to Paris after all. (*compare* The people **didn't decide to go** to war, it was their political leaders.)
- Some of my friends **have considered not going** to college because of the cost. (*compare* I **haven't considered going** to college – I don't want to go on studying after school.)

☆ **verb** + **to have** + **past participle**

- The accident **seems to have happened** at around 1 pm yesterday.
- Simmons **is alleged to have assaulted** a police officer.

This form is often used to give an opinion (after verbs like **seem** and **appear**) about a past event, or to report what is or was said (after passive verbs like **is / was alleged**, **believed**, **said**, **thought**) about past events.

☆ **verb** + **having** + **past participle**

The **verb** + **-ing** and **verb** + **having** + **past participle** forms have a similar meaning with these verbs:

- I now **regret buying** the car. *and* ▢ I now **regret having bought** the car.

This form is most often used with **admit**, **deny**, **forget**, **recall**, **regret** and **remember**.

Exercises

31.1 Complete each sentence with one of the verbs in brackets. A

1 a My mother .... me to throw away my old toys. (*threatened / told*)
  b My mother .... to throw away my old toys.
2 a They .... to visit Riko in hospital. (*allowed / offered*)
  b They .... us to visit Riko in hospital.
3 a I .... to carry the heavy boxes up the stairs. (*managed / persuaded*)
  b I .... Hamza to carry the heavy boxes up the stairs.
4 a She .... Lars to help in the garden. (*agreed / encouraged*)
  b She .... to help in the garden.
5 a I .... her to tidy up the house. (*pretended / reminded*)
  b I .... to tidy up the house.
6 a Jonas .... to study economics at university. (*advised / hoped*)
  b Jonas .... me to study economics at university.

31.2 Write one word that is missing from each line in these texts. Put a ‸ where the word should be. B

a 1 2 3 4	When I advertised ‸ a website designer for the business, Greta got the job. But I've now learnt that you can't rely Greta to do anything. I waited ages her to come up with some initial ideas for the site, and then I had to keep on her to do any more work on it. Finally, she said she couldn't do it after all.	....for.... ....
b 1 2 3 4	Managers of the National Electricity Company have appealed workers to end their strike, and have called the government to intervene in the dispute. The Energy Minister said that he has arranged employers and employees to meet next week, and he prevailed strikers to return to work in the meantime.	....

31.3 Complete the sentences with the verbs in brackets using one of the patterns in section C opposite. Give alternatives where possible. C

1 I .... anyone Marta's new address. (*agree – not tell*)
2 The prisoners .... through a broken window last night. (*think – escape*)
3 I .... him at the conference. (*not recall – see*)
4 He .... any stolen property. (*deny – receive*)
5 He .... as the person who donated the money. (*ask – not name*)
6 She .... all the way back home. (*not feel like – walk*)
7 I am sure my purse was on the table a few minutes ago, but now it .... (*seem – disappear*)
8 The Etruscans .... in Italy in the 8th or 9th century BC. (*believe – arrive*)

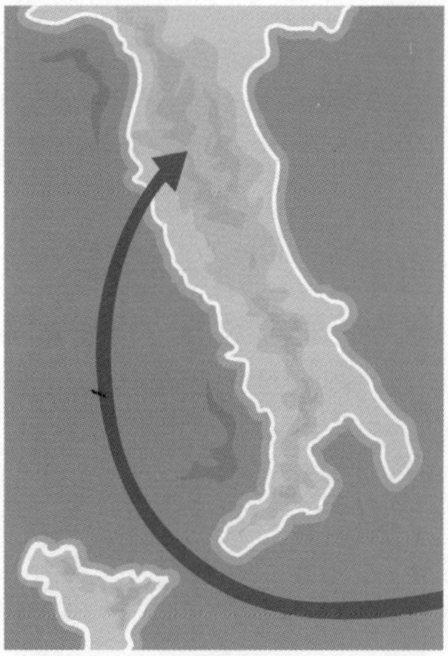

→ Additional exercise 7 (page 244)

Unit 32

Reporting people's words and thoughts

A Quoting and reporting in our own words

Reminder → G1– G11

When we report what people think or what they have said, we often give the information using our own words. We do this with sentences that have a *reporting clause* and a *reported clause* (see also Units 33–39):

reporting clause	reported clause
She explained He didn't tell me	(that) she couldn't take the job until January. where to put the boxes.

B

If the exact words are important, we might report the actual words someone said. In writing this is done in a *quotation*:

- 'I suppose you've heard the latest news,' she said to me.
- 'Of course,' Carter replied, 'you'll have to pay him to do the job.'

The *reporting clause* can come before, within, or at the end of the quotation.

In the English used in stories and novels, the *reporting verb* (e.g. **ask, continue**) is often placed before the subject when the *reporting clause* comes after the quotation except when the subject is a pronoun:

- 'When will you be back?' asked Jimin. (*or* … Jimin asked.)
- 'And after that I moved to Italy,' she continued. (*not* … continued she.)

C Negatives in reporting

To report what somebody **didn't** say or think, we make the reporting verb negative:

- He **didn't tell me** how he would get to London.

If we want to report a negative sentence, then we usually report this in the *reported clause*:

- 'You're right, it isn't a good idea.' → He **agreed** that it **wasn't** a good idea.

although it may be reported in the *reporting clause*, depending on meaning:

- 'I disagree. It's not a good idea at all.' → He **didn't agree** that it was a good idea.

However, with some verbs, to report a negative sentence we usually make the verb in the *reporting clause* negative:

- 'I expect he won't come.'/ 'I don't expect he will come.' → She **didn't expect** him to come.

Also: **believe**, **feel**, **intend**, **plan**, **propose**, **suppose**, **think**, **want**

D Reporting questions

To report a **wh-question** we use a *reporting clause* and a clause with a **wh-word**:

- She asked me **what** the problem was.
- I asked him **where** to go next.

When we report a **yes / no question** we use a *reporting clause* followed by a clause beginning with either **if** or **whether** (but note that we can't use **if** + **to-infinitive**; see Unit 34):

- Liz wanted to know **if / whether** we had any photos of our holiday.

The usual word order in a **wh-**, **if-**, or **whether-clause** is the one we would use in a statement:

- 'Have you seen Paul recently?' → She wanted to know if *I had seen* Paul recently.

However, if the original question begins **what**, **which**, or **who** followed by **be** + **complement**, we can put the complement before or after **be** in the report:

- 'Who was the winner?' → I asked who *the winner was*. (*or* … who *was the winner*.)

Note that we don't use a form of **do** in the **wh-**, **if-**, or **whether-clause**:

- She asked me where I found it. (*not* … where did I find it. /… where I did find it.)

However, if we are reporting a negative question, we can use a negative form of **do**:

- He asked (me) why I **didn't** want anything to eat.

Exercises

32.1 **Report what was said, quoting the speaker's exact words using one of the reporting verbs from the box. Put the reporting clause after the quotation and give alternative word orders where possible.** B & G8–G11

boast	chorus	~~command~~	confess	explain	grumble	suggest	wonder

1 Come in out of the rain now. (*her mother*)
'Come in out of the rain now,' commanded her mother / her mother commanded.
2 Why don't we stop for a coffee? (*she*)
3 All right, Georgia, it was me. (*he*)
4 My novel is more exciting than a Dan Brown thriller. (*she*)
5 I always carry two umbrellas with me because I'm always losing them. (*Lena*)
6 Oh, no, it's raining again. (*Matt*)
7 Good morning, Miss Novak. (*the children*)
8 Have I done the right thing? (*I*)

32.2 **Complete each sentence using a pair of verbs from the box. Make one of the verbs negative.** C

announce – go	expect – be	feel – could	~~intend – hurt~~
insist – be	promise – would	think – would	threaten – repay

1 'I didn't mean to upset Astrid.' → He didn't intend to hurt her feelings.
2 'I won't give you the money back if you keep on at me.' → He .... the money if she kept on at him.
3 'I can't ask my parents to help me again.' → He .... that he .... ask his parents to help him again.
4 'I wasn't anywhere near the school at the time of the break-in.' → He .... that he .... anywhere near the school at the time of the break-in.
5 'I'm not going back to college.' → She .... that she .... back to college.
6 'I was surprised that Mum was angry.' → He .... his mother .... angry.
7 'Adam won't mind waiting.' → She .... Adam .... mind waiting.
8 'I won't be late again.' → She .... that she ....be late again.

32.3 **Complete the email by reporting these questions using a wh-, if- or whether-clause.** D

1 ~~'How did you hear about the job?'~~
2 'What are your long-term career plans?'
3 'How many languages do you speak?'
4 'Where did you learn Chinese?'
5 'Can you use a spreadsheet?'
6 'Have you organised international conferences before?'
7 'Would you be willing to live overseas for periods of time?'
8 'When can you start work?'

Hi Karim,

The interview went well, although it was long and they asked lots of questions. First, they wondered (1) how I'd heard about the job, and then they asked me (2) .... They were very interested in the travelling I'd done. They asked me (3) .... , and they wondered (4) .... There were questions about my previous experience. They wanted to know (5) .... , and they asked me (6) .... At the end they asked (7) .... When I said 'Yes', they asked me (8) .... !

I'll phone later and tell you more about it.

Emily

Unit 33

Reporting statements: **that-clauses**

A

When we report statements, we often use a **that-clause** in the *reported clause* (see Unit 32): Reminder → G1–G7

- He **said** (**that**) he was enjoying his work.
- The members of the Security Council **warned that** further action may be taken.

After the more common reporting verbs such as **agree**, **mention**, **notice**, **promise**, **say**, and **think**, we often leave out **that**, particularly in informal speech. However, it is not usually left out –

- ☆ after less common reporting verbs such as **complain**, **confide**, **deny**, **grumble**, **speculate**, **warn** (and after the common reporting verbs **answer**, **argue**, and **reply**)
- ☆ in formal writing
- ☆ if the **that-clause** doesn't immediately follow the verb:
  - She **agreed** *with her parents and brothers* **that** it would be safer to buy a car than a motorbike. (*rather than* … and brothers it would be safer …)

B

Some reporting verbs which are followed by a **that-clause** have an alternative with an **object** + **to-infinitive** (often **to be**), although the alternatives are often rather formal. Compare:

- I **felt that the results** were satisfactory. *and* I **felt the results to be** satisfactory.

Also: **acknowledge, assume, believe, consider, declare, expect, find, presume, report, think, understand**

C

If we use a **that-clause** after an active form of some verbs, we must include an object between the verb and the **that-clause**. This object can't be a prepositional object (see **D** below):

- I **notified the bank that** I had changed my address. (*but not* I notified that I … / I notified to the bank that I …)

Also: **assure, convince, inform, persuade, reassure, remind, tell**

However, after some other verbs an object before a **that-clause** is not always necessary:

- They **promised (me) that** they would come to the party.

Also: **advise, show, teach, warn**

D

After some verbs we can use a **that-clause** with or without a personal object before the **that-clause**. However, if we *do* include an object, we put a preposition before it.

- ☆ After some verbs we use **to**:
  - She **admitted** (**to me**) **that** she was seriously ill.
  - I **pointed out** (**to the driver**) that he had parked across the entrance.

Also: **announce**, **complain**, **confess**, **explain**, **indicate**, **mention**, **propose**, **recommend**, **report**, **say**, **suggest**

- ☆ After some verbs we use **with**:
  - We **agreed** (**with Ella**) **that** the information should go no further.

Also: **argue**, **check**, **disagree**, **joke**

- ☆ After the verbs **ask**, **demand** and **require** we use **of**:
  - The club **asks** (**of its members**) **that** they pay their fees by 31st December.
  - The company **demands** (**of its staff**) **that** they should be at work by 8:30.

This pattern is usually used in formal contexts. Less formally we can use a **to-infinitive clause** after **ask** and **require** (e.g. The club asks its members to pay their fees by 31st December). However, we can't use a **to-infinitive clause** after **demand** (*not* The company demands its staff to …).

Exercises

33.1 Underline the correct verb. If both are possible, underline them both. C

1 The doctors *advised / persuaded* that I should rest for three months.
2 The police *assured / promised* residents that everything possible was being done to catch the thieves.
3 A spokesperson for the company *reminded / warned* that there may be delays on the railways this summer due to major engineering work.
4 We should *inform / teach* children that diet is of vital importance to health.
5 Russian scientists *have shown / have convinced* that honey can prevent the growth of bacteria.
6 The company *has reassured / has advised* customers that cars ordered before 1st August would be delivered by the end of the month.
7 Katarina *told / promised* that she would be home before midnight.

33.2 If possible, rewrite these sentences in a more formal way with a to-infinitive clause. If not, write ✗. B

1 Two days after the launch Houston reported that the satellite was missing.
Two days after the launch Houston reported the satellite to be missing.
2 The employees argued that the reduction in wages was unlawful.
3 The judge thought that his explanation was unconvincing.
4 I expected that her plans would fail.
5 She stressed that her stories were aimed primarily at children.
6 Lucas acknowledged that his chances of winning the race were slim.
7 We found that the rugby supporters were very well behaved.
8 The president's spokesman commented that the election result was a victory for democracy.

33.3 Complete each sentence with an appropriate form of a verb from the box + to, with, or of. More than one verb may be possible, but use each verb at least once. D

announce	**complain**	**disagree**	**joke**	**mention**	**require**

1 Martina .... the shop assistant that the laptop she'd bought there was faulty.
2 She .... her neighbours that their dog was keeping her awake at night.
3 He .... his friends that he'd won the lottery and was going to Barbados.
4 The minister .... shocked journalists that she was to resign immediately.
5 The college .... its students that they attend all classes.
6 I .... Mr Jacobs that the students were lazy. I thought they were very enthusiastic.
7 I forgot to .... Chris that I'd be home late.

33.4 Suggest corrections to the italicised words in this news article. A, C & D

PIK TO CUT WORKFORCE

PIK, the toy manufacturer, (1) *has warned they* are to make over 100 employees redundant over the next month. Managing Director Beth Edwards yesterday (2) *explained employees* that a national fall in demand for traditional toys is to blame. She (3) *confessed her audience* that management had been surprised by the downturn, but she (4) *denied management* had been incompetent. When asked whether staff would receive redundancy pay, Ms Edwards (5) *replied an announcement* would be made within a few days, but (6) *reassured that* they would receive financial compensation. She (7) *went on to complain government help* for small businesses was insufficient and (8) *demanded ministers* that they provide more support. She (9) *asked staff that* they continue to work as normal until details of the redundancies were given. She (10) *reassured that* the company would not close completely.

→ Additional exercise 8 (page 245)

Verb + wh-clause

A

Some verbs can be followed by a clause beginning with a **wh-word** (**how**, **what**, **when**, **where**, **which**, **who**, or **why**):

- That might **explain** *why* he's unhappy.
- I couldn't **decide** *which* train to catch.
- Let's **consider** *how* we can solve the problem.

Also: **arrange**, **calculate**, **check**, **choose**, **debate**, **determine**, **discover**, **discuss**, **establish**, **find out**, **forget**, **guess**, **imagine**, **know**, **learn**, **notice**, **plan**, **realise**, **remember**, **say**, **see**, **talk about**, **think** (**about**), **understand**, **wonder**

Many of these verbs can also be followed by –

☆ a **that-clause** (see Unit 33):

- I **decided** *that* I ought to leave.

☆ a **wh-clause** (except 'why') + **to-infinitive**:

- **Did** you **find out** *where to go*?

Note that if we add a subject in the **wh-clause** we don't use a **to-infinitive**:

- I can't imagine what **he** likes about jazz.

B

Some verbs must have an object before the **wh-clause**:

- She *reminded* **me** *what* (I had) to do.
- I *told* **Linda** *how* to get to my house.

Also: **advise**, **inform**, **instruct**, **teach**, **warn**

The verbs **ask** and **show** often have an object before a **wh-clause**, but not always:

- I *asked* (**him**) *how* I could get to the station, and he told me.

These verbs can also be followed by **object** + **wh-word** + **to-infinitive**:

- She **taught me** *how to play* chess.
- I **showed her** *where to put* her coat.

C

We can often use **the way** instead of **how** referring to either the route or the means:

- Go back **the way** (that / by which) you came. (*or informally* Go back **how** you came.)
- Have you noticed **the way** (that / in which) he spins the ball? (*or* … noticed **how** he spins …?)

Note that we don't use 'the way how'. (e.g. *not* Go back the way how you came.)

D

Whether

We can use **whether** as the **wh-word** in a **wh-clause** when we want to show possible choices. **Whether** has a similar meaning to 'if' (see Unit 86):

- He couldn't remember **whether** / **if** he had turned the computer off.

Some verbs can be followed by **whether + to-infinitive** to talk about the choice between two or more possibilities. Note that 'if' is never used before a **to-infinitive**:

- You have 14 days to **decide whether to keep** it or not. (*not* … to decide if to keep it or not.)

Also: **choose, consider, debate, determine, discuss, know** (in questions and negatives), **think about, wonder** (= 'talking' or 'thinking about choices' verbs)

Some other 'talking' and 'thinking about choices' verbs are *not* used with **whether + to-infinitive**, including **ask, conclude, explain, imagine, realise, speculate, think**.

E

Note the difference between these sentences. The first has a **wh-clause** with **whether** and the second has a **that-clause** (see Unit 33):

- I didn't know **whether** the shop was shut. (= if the shop was shut or not)
- I didn't know **that** the shop was shut. (suggests that the shop was shut)

F

In rather formal contexts, particularly in writing, we can use **as to** with a meaning similar to 'about' or 'concerning' before a **wh-clause**. This is most common before **whether**:

- Opinion was divided **as to whether** the findings from the study were representative of the population as a whole. (*or less formally* … divided whether …)

Exercises

34.1 Match sentence beginnings 1–10 to endings a–j and choose an appropriate wh-word to connect them. If necessary, add an appropriate object. A & B

1 Before the meeting finished they arranged …
2 He took my hands and showed …
3 I explained carefully so that the students understood …
4 Anna was new in the office and I had to keep reminding …
5 I saw Sarah leave the building, but I didn't notice …
6 When I saw Hugo alone at the party I wondered …
7 As we walked over the hills the guide warned …
8 After I'd dismantled the motor I couldn't remember …
9 To win a prize you had to guess …
10 As the guests came in Diego told …

a … to fit the parts back together.
b … she went after that.
c … to put their coats.
d ~~… to meet next.~~
e … Helen wasn't with him.
f … many sweets were in the jar.
g … they had to do in the test.
h … the path was dangerous.
i … everyone was.
j … to hold the golf club properly.

1 + d *Before the meeting finished they arranged when / where to meet next.*

34.2 Underline the correct or more appropriate verb. D

1 She was *thinking / debating* whether to invite Jeremy over for dinner.
2 The council is meeting this morning to *discuss / ask* whether to increase local taxes.
3 Apparently Louis and Eva are *considering / speculating* whether to emigrate to Australia.
4 I have to *imagine / choose* whether to get a job or apply to go to college.
5 Scientists will have to *decide / conclude* soon whether to start testing the new drugs on people.

34.3 Zak Miles has written a book about mountain climbing in the Andes. Correct any mistakes in these extracts. A–F

The villagers warned *me* what the conditions were like at higher altitudes, and advised to take enough food for a week. There was some discussion through the day as whether the snow would arrive before my descent from the mountain, but I never imagined how hard the conditions would be. In the morning they showed me the way how to get to the track up the mountain.

When the snow started falling it was very light, and I couldn't decide if to carry on or go back down. Soon, however, I couldn't see where to go.

I wondered if to retrace my steps and try to find the track again, but by the time I decided whether I should go back, the track had disappeared.

As the snow got heavier I began to realise whether my life was in danger. Fortunately, my years in the Andes had taught what to do in extreme conditions. I knew that there was a shepherd's hut somewhere on this side of the mountain that I could shelter in, but I didn't know that it was nearby or miles away.

Unit 35

Tense choice in reporting

A

Verb tense in the *reported* clause

Reminder ➜ G1– G7

When the situation described in the *reported* clause (see Unit 32) is in the *past* when we are reporting it, we use a past tense (past simple, past continuous, etc.):

- ▢ 'I don't want anything to eat.' → Yusuf **said** that he **didn't want** anything to eat.
- ▢ 'I'm leaving!' → Lamar **announced** that she **was leaving**.

When the situation described in the *reported* clause was *already* in the past when it was spoken about originally, we often use the past perfect to report it:

- ▢ 'We have found the missing girl.' → Police **said** that they **had found** the missing girl.

However, if it is clear that one event took place before another, then it may not be necessary to indicate this by using the past perfect and we use the past simple instead:

- ▢ 'I've sent out the invitations. I did it well before the wedding.' → She **reassured** me that she **sent** out the invitations well before the wedding. (*or*… **had sent** …)

B

When the situation described in the *reported* clause is a *permanent / habitual situation*, or still exists or is relevant at the time we are reporting it, then we use a present tense (or present perfect) if we also use a present tense for the verb in the *reporting* clause:

- ▢ Dr Weir **thinks** that he **spends** about five minutes on a typical appointment with a patient.
- ▢ US scientists **claim** that they **have developed** a new vaccine against malaria.

Note that the present perfect focuses attention on the *result* of the action, not the action itself.

However, when we use a past tense in the *reporting* clause we can use either a present or past tense (or present perfect or past perfect) in the *reported* clause:

- ▢ She **argued** that Carl **is / was** the best person for the job.
- ▢ They **noted** that the rate of inflation **has / had slowed** down.

Choosing a present tense (or present perfect) in the *reported* clause emphasises that the situation being reported still exists or is still relevant when we report it.

If we are not sure that what we are reporting is necessarily true, or a situation may not still exist now, we prefer a *past* rather than a present tense. Compare:

- ▢ Yasemin told me that she **has** two houses. (= might suggest that this is true) *and*
- ▢ Yasemin told me that she **had** two houses. (= might suggest either that this is perhaps not true, or that she once had two houses but doesn't have two houses now)

C

Verb tense in the *reporting* clause

To report something said or thought in the past, the verb in the *reporting* clause is often in a *past* tense:

- ▢ Just before her wedding, she **revealed** that she had been married before.

When we report current news, opinions, etc. we can use a present tense for the verb in the *reporting* clause. In some cases, either a present or past tense is possible, although we prefer a present tense to emphasise that what was said is true or still relevant when we report it:

- ▢ She **says** that she'll have to close the shop unless business improves. (*or* … **said** …)

We often prefer a present rather than a past tense –

☆ to report information that we have been told or heard, but don't know whether it is true:

- ▢ I **hear** you're unhappy with your job.

☆ to report what is said by some authority:

- ▢ The law **says** that no one under the age of 16 can buy a lottery ticket.

☆ to report what many people say:

- ▢ Every teacher I've spoken to **tells** me that standards of spelling are in decline.

Exercises

35.1 **Report these sentences using the verbs from the box in the reporting clauses and either the past simple or past perfect (or both if possible) in the that-clause.** A

alleged	conceded	~~denied~~	estimated	recalled	repeated

1 'I have never been in love with Oliver.' →
She denied that she had ever been / was ever in love with Oliver.
2 'Markus has stolen jewellery from my house.' → She ....
3 'I think the vase is around 250 years old.' → She ....
4 'I've told you once. I've already seen the film.' → She ....
5 'Well, perhaps you're right. Maybe I did treat Lara unkindly.' → She ....
6 'I seem to remember that Wilma's great-grandmother was from Spain.' → She ....

35.2 **Complete the sentences with a verb chosen from a suitable pair. If both verbs in the pair are possible, write both.** B

has / had	is / was	looks / looked	solved / have solved
states / stated	understand / understood		

1 Engineers hope that they .... the problems with the bridge now that new supports have been built, and they plan to reopen it next week.
2 The current law .... that an employee has the right to appeal against dismissal.
3 Simon is already a good tennis player, but he accepts that he still .... a lot to learn.
4 I .... that you want to buy a second-hand car. Your brother just told me.
5 Health officials warn that anyone who .... directly at the sun during an eclipse may put their sight at risk.
6 They reassured us that the path .... perfectly safe.

35.3 **Jamie Barnes and Daniel Nokes have been interviewed by the police in connection with a robbery last week. If necessary, correct the tenses in the that-clauses in these extracts from the interview reports. If not, write ✓. Suggest possible alternatives.** A–C

1

When I mentioned to Nokes that he had been seen in a local shop last Monday, he protested that he is at home all day. He swears that he didn't own a blue Ford Focus. He claimed that he had been to the paint factory two weeks ago to look for work. Nokes alleges that he is a good friend of Jamie Barnes. He insisted that he didn't telephone Barnes last Monday morning. When I pointed out to Nokes that a large quantity of paint had been found in his house, he replied that he is storing it for a friend.

2

At the beginning of the interview I reminded Barnes that he is entitled to have a lawyer present. He denied that he knew anyone by the name of Daniel Nokes. Barnes confirmed that he is in the area of the paint factory last Monday, but said that he is visiting his mother. He admitted that he is walking along New Street at around ten. He maintains that he was a very honest person and would never be involved in anything illegal.

→ Additional exercise 8 (page 245)

Unit 36

Reporting offers, suggestions, orders, intentions, etc.

A

Verb + (object) + to-infinitive clause

When we report offers, suggestions, orders, intentions, promises, requests, etc. we can follow some verbs in the *reporting clause* (see Unit 33) with –

☆ a **to-infinitive clause**

- 'The theatre will be built next to the town hall.'→ They **propose to build** the theatre next to the town hall. (*not* They propose them to build ...)

Also: **agree, demand, guarantee, offer, promise, swear, threaten, volunteer**

☆ an **object + to-infinitive clause**

- 'You should take the job, Fran.' → She **encouraged Fran to take** the job.

Also: **advise, ask, call on, command, instruct, invite, order, persuade, recommend, remind, request, urge, warn, tell**

The object usually refers to the person who the offer, suggestion, etc. is made to; that is, the person who performs the action in the reported clause.

Compare the use of **ask** with and without an object before a **to-infinitive clause**:

- We **asked** *to leave* our bags outside the exam room. (= this is something we wanted) *and*
- They **asked** *us to leave* our bags outside the exam room. (= this is something they wanted)

B

Verb + that-clause *or* verb + to-infinitive clause

After some verbs we can use a **that-clause** instead of a **to-infinitive clause**:

- He **promised** *to arrive* on time. *or*
- He **promised** *that* he would arrive on time.

Also: **agree, demand, expect**, **guarantee**, **hope**, **propose**, **request**, **vow**

With a **that-clause** the person promising, etc. and the person referred to in the *reported* clause may be different:

- He **promised** *that* he wouldn't be late. ('He ...' and '... he ...' may refer to different people)

C

After the verbs **insist, order, say** and **suggest** we use a **that-clause** but not a **to-infinitive clause**:

- There were cheers when he **suggested** *that* we went home early. (*not* ... suggested to go ...)

Advise and **order** can be used with an **object + to-infinitive clause** (see **A**) or a **that-clause**:

- I **advised** *that* she should accept. (*or* I **advised** *her to accept*.; *but not* I advised to accept ...)

D

Verb + to-infinitive clause (*not* verb + that-clause)

After some verbs we use a **to-infinitive clause** but not a **that-clause**:

- Carolyn **intends** *to return* to Dublin after a year in Canada. (*not* Carolyn intends that she should return ...)

Also: **long**, **offer**, **refuse**, **volunteer, want**

E

When we report a suggestion, either what the person reported might do themselves, or what someone else might do, we can use a *reporting clause* with **advise**, **propose**, **recommend** or **suggest** followed by an **-ing clause** rather than a **that-clause**:

- The lecturer **recommended** *reading* a number of books before the exam. (*or* ... **recommended** *that* the students should read a number of books before the exam.)

Exercises

36.1 **Report each sentence using a verb from the box and a to-infinitive clause. Use each verb once only. If necessary, add an appropriate object after the verb.** A

~~advise~~	agree	ask	call on	expect	hope	order	urge	vow

1 'If I were you, I'd read the exam questions very carefully.' →
He advised us to read the exam questions very carefully.
2 'Okay, I'll collect Declan from school.' → He …
3 'Be quiet!' → He …
4 'Please stay for a few more days.' → He …
5 'I will fight the ban on smoking in public places.' → He …
6 'I imagine I'll see Olivia at the party.' → He …
7 'Can you lend me ten pounds?' → He …
8 'The government should do more to help the homeless.' → He …
9 'If I leave early, I'll avoid the heavy traffic.' → He …

36.2 **Replace any incorrect verbs with ones from the boxes. (It may not be necessary to use all the boxed verbs.)** B, C & D

expected	promised	refused	said

In a major speech today, the Health Minister (1) *suggested* to improve the country's health care. She (2) *guaranteed* to reduce waiting times for operations, and (3) *intended* that this could be done without raising taxes. She said that she (4) *insisted* to see significant improvements within a year.

hoped	ordered	proposed	volunteered

The President of Guwandi has (5) *demanded* Narian troops to withdraw from the border area between the two countries, and said that he (6) *wanted* that the Narian president would act now to prevent war. In a separate development, the UN Secretary General has (7) *agreed* to meet the leaders of both countries and has (8) *offered* that a peace conference should be held in New York early next week.

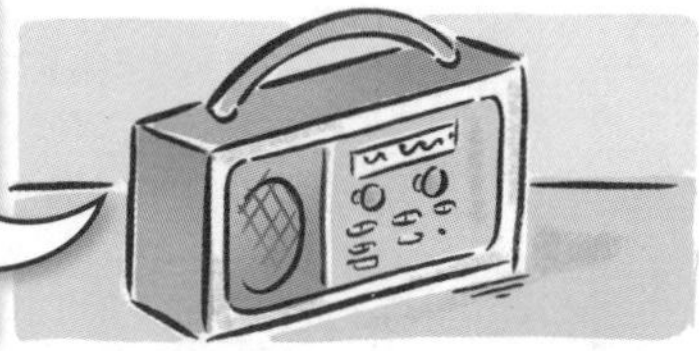

36.3 **Complete the sentences in any appropriate way using a clause beginning with the -ing form of a verb.** E

1 To avoid the road works, police have advised leaving the motorway at Junction 3 .
2 To encourage people to use public transport the council proposed ……………… .
3 Ricardo said the play was very entertaining and he recommended ……………… .
4 To find my way around London, Reza suggested ……………… .
5 I'd been feeling unwell for a few days and my mother advised ……………… .
6 The capital urgently needs a new airport, and the government proposes ……………… .
7 I've been putting on weight and my doctor has recommended ……………… .
8 It was a lovely morning and Nina suggested ……………… .

Can any of these sentences be rewritten with a to-infinitive clause without an object?

→ **Additional exercise 8** (page 245)

Unit 37

Modal verbs in reporting

A

When there is a modal verb in the original statement, suggestion, etc., it sometimes changes when we report what was said or thought. The changes are summarised here:

	modal verb in original	*modal verb in report*
B	**could, would, should, might, needn't, ought to, used to, could have, should have, etc.**	**could, would, should, might, needn't, ought to, used to,** (*i.e. no change*) 1–3 **could have, should have, etc.**
C	**will, can, may**	☐ **would, could, might** 4 & 5 ☐ **will, can, may** (existing or future situations and *present* tense verb in reporting clause) 6 ☐ **will** or **would**, **can** or **could**, **may** or **might** (existing or future situations and *past* tense verb in reporting clause) 7
D	**shall**	☐ **would** (talking about the future) 8 ☐ **should** (offers, requests for advice, etc.) 9
E	**must** (= necessity) **must** (= conclude; see Unit 18B) **mustn't**	**must** or **had to** 10 **must** 11 **mustn't** 12

B

- ☐ 'I **could** meet you at the airport.' → He said that he **could** meet us at the airport. 1
- ☐ 'We **might** drop in if we have time.' → They said they **might** drop in if they have time. 2
- ☐ 'You **should have** contacted me earlier.' → She said I **should have** contacted her earlier. 3

C

- ☐ 'She **may** have already left.' → He thought she **might** have already left. 4

If the situation we are reporting still exists or is still in the future and the verb in the *reporting clause* has a *present tense*, we use **will**, **can**, and **may** in the *reported clause* (see Unit 32). Compare:

- ☐ 'Careful! You**'ll** fall through the ice!' → I **warned** him he **would** fall through the ice. 5 *and*
- ☐ 'I**'ll** be in Paris at Christmas.' → She **tells** me she**'ll** be in Paris at Christmas. 6

If the situation we are reporting still exists or is still in the future and the verb in the *reporting clause* has a *past* tense, we can use either **would** or **will**, **can** or **could**, or **may** or **might** in the *reported clause*:

- ☐ 'The problem can be solved.' → They **said** the problem **can / could** be solved. 7

D

- ☐ 'I **shall** (I**'ll**) call you on Monday.' → She told me she **would** call me on Monday. 8
- ☐ 'Where **shall** I put this box?' → He asked where he **should** put the box. 9

E

- ☐ 'You **must** be home by 9 o'clock.' → She said I **must / had to** be home by 9 o'clock. 10 (*had to* is more natural in speech)
- ☐ 'I didn't hear the phone. I **must** be going deaf.' → Alex thought he **must** be going deaf. 11
- ☐ 'You **mustn't** tell my brother.' → He warned me that I **mustn't** tell his brother. 12

F

Note that we sometimes use a modal verb in a reported sentence when there is no modal verb in the original:

- ☐ 'You're not allowed to smoke here.' → She told me that I **mustn't** smoke there.
- ☐ 'My advice is to look for a new job now.' → She said that I **should** look for a new job now.

Exercises

37.1 Underline the more appropriate verb. If both are possible, underline them both. C

1 The doctor says that he *will / would* see you in 20 minutes.
2 In her letter, Elizabeth revealed that she *may / might* be getting married soon.
3 Maxim tells me that he *can / could* come for dinner with us tonight after all.
4 Inge promised that she *will / would* be at home by nine, so I phoned her shortly after that.
5 The mechanic admitted that he *can't / couldn't* repair the radiator and had to replace it instead.
6 Olivia reckons that she *can / could* save enough money to go on holiday to Canada.
7 Mario explained that he *will / would* be living in Austria for the next six months.

37.2 Complete the reported sentences using a that-clause with a modal verb. A & C

1 'If all goes to plan, I'll study medicine.' → He hoped that he would study medicine but instead he became a vet.
2 'I won't be late.' → She promised .... and she kept her word.
3 'Perhaps we can go to Paris for the weekend.' → He suggested .... but I was busy.
4 'I can get you there in good time.' → She guaranteed .... but I didn't believe her.
5 'I'll pay for the meal.' → He insisted .... and I accepted, of course.

37.3 Complete this message left on an answering machine by reporting what Chloe said, using modal verbs in the reports. D & E

'You mustn't forget to bring your student discount card.'

'Where shall we meet?'

~~'I must be getting old.'~~

'I must be in the city centre by one.'

'I shall be there this time.'

'I can't come to the phone at the moment. Please leave a message after the tone.'

'Hi, Mia. I've just spoken to Chloe and she's keen to come to the pool with us tomorrow. She apologised for not turning up last week – she said she was always forgetting things and that she (1) must be getting old! But she promised (2) .... She's meeting Jack for lunch, and she said she (3) ...., so I suggested meeting at 10:30. She (4) .... and I said just by the pool entrance. Hope that's okay for you. Oh, and she said I (5) .... Remember yours, too. See you there. Bye.'

37.4 Complete the reported sentences using appropriate modal verbs. Give alternative modal verbs where possible. F

1 'It's vital that you attend the meeting.' →
She said that I had to / must attend the meeting.
2 'If you want to travel with us, that's fine.' → She said that ....
3 'I'm not prepared to answer his questions.' → She said that ....
4 'Karl's likely to be back soon.' → She said that ....
5 'There's a possibility that I'll have to move to Milan.' → She said that ....
6 'I refuse to accept that Jason is dishonest.' → She said that ....
7 'Maria is sure to be disappointed if you leave without seeing her.' → She said that ... .

Unit 38 Reporting what people say using nouns and adjectives

A Reporting using nouns

We sometimes report people's words and thoughts using a **noun** in the reporting clause followed by a reported clause beginning with **that**, a **to-infinitive**-, or **wh-word**. Most of these nouns are related to reporting verbs (acknowledgement – acknowledge, statement – state, etc.). Note that when we report using **nouns** and **adjectives** (see **C**) the exact original words are not necessarily reported. Instead we might use our own words, or report that something was said without reporting *what* was said.

☆ Noun + **that-clause**

- The **claim** is often made *that* smoking causes heart disease.
- The jury came to the **conclusion** *that* the woman was guilty.

> *Also*: **acknowledgement, advice, allegation, announcement, answer, argument, comment, decision, explanation, forecast, guarantee, indication, observation, promise, recommendation, reply, speculation, statement, suggestion, threat, warning**

Note that we don't usually leave out **that** in sentences like this (see Unit 33).

☆ Noun + **to-infinitive clause**

- I accepted Luisa's **invitation** *to visit* her in Rome.
- He gave me every **encouragement** *to take up* painting again.

> *Also*: **decision, instruction, order, promise, recommendation, refusal, threat, warning**

Note that some of these nouns can be followed by a **that-clause**:

- They carried out their **threat** *to dismiss* workers on strike. (*or* ... their **threat** *that* they would dismiss workers on strike.)

☆ Noun + **wh-clause**

- Juan raised the **question** *of when* the money would be collected.
- Our previous meeting looked at the **issue** *of how* to increase income.

> *Also*: **explanation, discussion, problem**

We usually use **of** after these nouns in reporting.

B

After many of the nouns listed in **A** we can use **as to** + **wh-clause** or **as to** + **wh-word** + **to-infinitive** to introduce the subject of a question or topic discussed or thought about (see also Unit 34F). Note that an alternative preposition can usually be used instead of **as to**:

- She asked my *advice* **as to** *what* subject she should study at university. (*or* ... advice **on** ...)
- There was some *discussion* **as to** *whether* the price included tax or not. (*or* ... discussion **of** ...)
- Before we left we gave them strict *instructions* **as to** *how to cook* it. (*or* ... **about** how to ...)

C Reporting using adjectives

Some adjectives used to report a speaker's feelings or opinion are followed by a **that-clause**:

- The builders are **certain** *that* they'll be finished by the end of next week.

> *Also*: **adamant, agreed, angry, annoyed, grateful, insistent, sure**

Adjectives expressing uncertainty are usually followed by a **wh-clause**:

- Scientists are**n't sure** *where* the remains of the satellite will land.

> *Also*: **doubtful** (*usually* + whether), **uncertain, not certain, unsure**

Some adjectives are usually followed by a preposition + noun phrase:

- Today's newspapers are very **critical** *of* the President's decision to appoint Mr Walters.

> *Also*: **apologetic, complimentary, insulting, tactful** (+ about); **dismissive, scornful** (+ of); **abusive, sympathetic** (+ to / towards)

Exercises

38.1 **Complete the sentences with the nouns from the box and the notes in brackets. Use a that-, to-infinitive or wh-clause. Suggest alternatives where possible.** A

announcement	~~**decision**~~	**encouragement**	**explanation**		
invitation	**issue**	**observation**	**promise**	**question**	**warning**

1 The turning point in his life came when he took the decision to become an actor. / ... that he would become an actor (*become – actor*)
2 He failed to address the ... (*who – pay – repairs – building*)
3 I was delighted to get an ... (*spend the holidays – them – Scotland*)
4 I think it was Aristotle who made the ... (*no such thing – bad publicity*)
5 Amazingly the police accepted Rudi's ... (*taken – wallet – mistake*)
6 On the webinar they debated the ... (*assisted suicide – criminal offence*)
7 The letter from the company gave a final ... (*pay – bill by – end of – week*)
8 The government has broken its ... (*reduce – rate – income tax*)
9 The positive reaction to my work gave me considerable ... (*take up photography – career*)
10 Waiting passengers were angry when they heard the ... (*flight – cancelled*)

38.2 **Complete the rewritten sentences using a noun formed from the italicised verb + as to and then a wh-word.** B

1 At the end the writers *suggest* when it is appropriate to correct students' grammar mistakes.
The writers end with suggestions as to when it is appropriate to correct students' grammar mistakes.
2 People have *argued* a great deal about how to define poverty.
There has been ...
3 For months people have *speculated* about whether President Malik would stand again.
There have been months ...
4 Scientists might *conclude* something about what their results imply.
Scientists might ...
5 We have still not *explained* definitely why the dinosaurs disappeared.
There is still ...

38.3 **Complete each sentence using an adjective from the box with that, a wh-word, or a preposition.** C

abusive	**adamant**	**agreed**	**angry**	**apologetic**	
not certain	**complimentary**	**dismissive**	~~**doubtful**~~	**unsure**	

1 The climbers were doubtful whether the clothes would be warm enough at high altitudes.
2 My boss is very unsympathetic and was .... my complaints about the new software.
3 The company is .... the child car seats are safe.
4 Mona tried to pick up the rabbit, but was .... to hold it.
5 She was very .... the window had been broken.
6 Rachel is normally very reliable and was extremely .... turning up late.
7 Karim left for New York in September but he was .... he would return.
8 The court heard that Hughes became .... a police officer and was arrested.
9 Judi doesn't normally like spicy food, but was quite .... my fish curry.
10 All the players are .... the game should go on despite the weather.

→ **Additional exercise 8** (page 245)

Unit 39

Should in **that-clauses**; the present subjunctive

A

We can sometimes report advice, orders, requests, suggestions, etc. about things that need to be done or are desirable using a **that-clause** with **should** + **bare infinitive**:

- They have proposed that Felix **should** *move* to their Munich office.
- We advised **that** the company **should not** *raise* its prices.

After **should** we often use **be** + **past participle** (passive) or **be** + **adjective**:

- They directed **that** the building **should** *be pulled down*.
- We insist **that** the money **should** *be available* to all students in financial difficulties.

B

In formal contexts, particularly in written English, we can often leave out **should** and use only the base form of the verb (that is, the form you would look up in a dictionary). This form is the *present subjunctive* (see Unit 85A for the *past subjunctive*) and is used to describe bringing about the situation expressed in the **that-clause**:

- They have proposed that Felix **move** to their Munich office.
- They directed that the building **be pulled down**.

> *Other verbs used with the present subjunctive*: **advise, ask, beg, command, demand, insist, instruct, intend, order, prefer, recommend, request, require, stipulate, suggest, urge, warn**

To make a negative form, we use **not** (*not* 'do not') before the verb:

- We advised that the company **not raise** its prices.

In less formal contexts we can use ordinary forms of the verb instead of the *subjunctive*. Compare:

- I suggested that he **should give up** golf. (*negative*: ... that he **shouldn't** give up ...)
- I suggested that he **give** up golf. (more formal) (*negative*: ... that he **not** give up ...)
- I suggested that he **gives** up golf. (less formal) (*negative*: ... that he **doesn't** give up ...)

C

We can also use **that-clauses** with **should** or the subjunctive after *reporting clauses* with nouns related to the verbs in **B** (e.g. **advice, order, proposal, warning**):

- The police issued an **order** that all weapons (should) be handed in immediately.
- The weather forecast gave a **warning** that people (should) prepare for heavy snow.

D

We can also use **should** or sometimes the subjunctive in a **that-clause** after **it + be + adjective**:

- **It is inappropriate** that he *(should) receive* the award again. (*or* ... that he *receives* ...)

> *Also*: **advisable, appalling, appropriate, (in)conceivable, crucial, essential, imperative, important, obligatory, (un)necessary, urgent, vital**

E

We can use **should** in a **that-clause** when we talk about our own reaction to something we are reporting, particularly after **be** + **adjective**. Compare:

- *I am concerned* that she **should think** I stole the money (*or* … that she **thinks** …)

> *Also:* **amazed**, **amused**, **anxious**, **astounded**, **disappointed**, **shocked**, **surprised**, **upset**

Note that when we leave out **should** in sentences like this (= less formal) we use an ordinary tense, not a subjunctive.

F

We can use **should** in a **that-clause** to talk about a situation that exists now:

- It's not surprising that they **should** *be seen* together – they're brothers.

or one that may exist in the future:

- We believe it is important that she **should** *take* the exam next year.

If we are talking about an intention or plan, we can often use a *subjunctive* rather than **should**:

- I've arranged that she **come** to the first part of the meeting. (*or* … that she **should come** … / … that she **comes** … / … for her **to come** …)

Exercises

39.1 **Report these statements from a Spanit Engineering Company board meeting. Use a that-clause with should (should + bare infinitive or should + be + past participle).** A–C

1 Lee said: 'I think it's important to expand business in South America.'
Lee felt that business in South America should be expanded.

2 Lee said: 'Mara Bianchi would make an excellent export manager. Let's promote her.'
Lee urged ....

3 Alice said: 'It would be valuable for us to send a sales representative to South Africa.'
Alice recommended ....

4 Alice said: 'The Delaware Bridge project ought to be completed by August next year.'
Alice reported ....

5 Simon said: 'It is vital to keep to our work schedules.'
Simon insisted ....

6 Simon said: 'I'd like all monthly reports sent to me directly.'
Simon instructed ....

7 Alina said: 'Perhaps we could use web conferencing for meetings to save money on air fares.'
Alina suggested ....

8 Alina said: 'Our head office must remain in London.'
Alina declared ....

9 Nathan said: 'It's okay for us to sponsor the European chess league for the next three years.'
Nathan agreed ....

10 Nathan said: 'In future, all claims for travel expenses are to be made in US dollars.'
Nathan announced ....

39.2 **Look again at your answers for 39.1. Can any of the sentences be written without should and still be correct? Write 'yes' if it is possible and 'no' if not.** A–C

1 ~~Lee felt that business in South America be expanded~~. *No*

39.3 **Expand the notes using a that-clause with should and an adjective from the box to make reporting sentences. More than one adjective may be possible, but use each once only.** D & E

amused	**appalling**	**astounded**	**imperative**
~~**inconceivable**~~	**shocked**	**upset**	**urgent**

1 It is … / she / marry Ben.
It is inconceivable that she should marry Ben.

2 I am … / Kristina / behave so badly.
....

3 I am … / anyone / vote for him.
....

4 It is … / he / return home immediately.
....

5 I am … / he / take his appearance so seriously.
....

6 I am … / they / think I had cheated them.
....

7 It is … / they / allowed to go free.
....

8 It is … / we / act now to avoid war.
....

Unit 40

Agreement between subject and verb 1

A

If a sentence has a singular subject, it is followed by a singular verb, and if it has a plural subject, it is followed by a plural verb; that is, the verb *agrees with* the subject. Compare:

Reminder → H1–H3

- **She** *lives* in China. *and* **More people** *live* in Asia than in any other continent.

When the subject of the sentence is complex the following verb must agree with the main noun in the subject. In the examples below the subject is underlined and the main noun is circled. Note how the verb, in italics, agrees with the main noun:

- <u>Many leading members of the opposition party</u> *have* criticised the delay.
- <u>The only excuse that he gave for his actions</u> *was* that he was tired.

The verb must agree with the subject when the subject follows the verb (see Units 99 & 100):

- Displayed on the board *were* **the exam results**. (*compare* The exam results *were* displayed …)

B

If the subject is a clause, we usually use a singular verb:

- <u>To keep these young people in prison</u> *is* inhuman.
- <u>Having overall responsibility for the course</u> *means* that I have a lot of meetings.
- <u>Whoever took them</u> *remains* a mystery.

However, if we use a **what-clause** as subject (see Unit 98B), we use a singular verb if the following main noun is singular, and either a singular or a plural verb if the following main noun is plural (although a plural verb is preferred in more formal contexts):

- <u>What worries us</u> *is* the poor selection **process**.
- <u>What is needed</u> *are* additional **resources**. (*or more colloquially* … needed *is* …)

C

Some nouns with a singular form, referring to groups of some kind, can be used with either a singular or plural form of the verb. These nouns are sometimes called *collective nouns*:

- **The council** *has* (or *have*) postponed a decision on the new road.

We use a singular verb if the focus is on the institution or organisation as a whole unit, and a plural verb if the focus is on a collection of individuals. Often you can use either with very little difference in meaning, although in formal contexts (such as academic writing) it is common to use a singular verb.

Also: **army, association, audience, class, club, college, commission, committee, community, company, crew, crowd, department, electorate, enemy, family, federation, generation, government, group, institute, jury, opposition, orchestra, population, press, public, school, team, university; the Bank of England, the BBC, IBM, Sony, the United Nations** (specific organisations)

In some contexts we have to use a singular or a plural form of the verb.

The committee usually **raise** their hands to vote 'Yes'. (*not* The committee usually raises its hands …)	This is something the individuals do, not the committee as a whole.
The school **is** to close next year. (*not* The school are to close …)	This is something that will happen to the school as a building or institution, not to the individuals in the school.

D

When names and titles ending in **-s** refer to a single unit we use a singular verb. Examples include countries; newspapers; titles of books, films, etc.; and quoted plural words or phrases:

- At this time of the year *the Netherlands* **is** one hour ahead of the UK.
- *The Machine Gunners* **was** one of Robert Westall's most successful books.
- '*Daps*' **is** the word used in the south-west of the country for sports shoes.

Exercises

40.1 Correct ten mistakes in the italicised verbs in this museum review. A & B

Museums and historic sites
The Rivers Museum
Open: 9 am – 5 pm, Mon – Sat
Entrance: Free

The Rivers Museum on the corner of Corn Street and New Road 1 ~~*house*~~ houses a fascinating collection of art and other objects which begins as soon as you step through the door. Among the most eye-catching pieces in the whole collection 2 *is* the marble animal sculptures under two arches on the left of the entrance hall. Whoever created these figures apparently 3 *remain* a mystery, but the skill of the craftspeople who worked on them 4 *is* obvious. Hanging on the wall directly opposite the carvings 5 *is* over a hundred swords from the 17th century. The narrow doorway between the arches 6 *let* you into a series of smaller rooms where paintings from the 18th and 19th centuries 7 *are* on display. If paintings aren't your thing, the museum's incredible collection of seashells and fossils in the final room 8 *are* sure to be of interest. Perhaps what is most surprising about the building itself 9 *are* the bell tower in the small courtyard. Only since the restoration work was completed in 2011 10 *have* the tower been open, and climbing the 150 steps to the top to take in the view over the city 11 *is* well worth the effort. Over 50 full-time staff and volunteers 12 *is* employed and having so many of them available to answer questions about the collection 13 *add* to the pleasure of this must-see museum.

40.2 Complete each sentence with a noun from the box and an appropriate form of the verb in brackets (singular, plural or both). C

audience	class	jury	orchestra	press
~~team~~	the United Nations		university	

1 The volleyball ..... team ..... play / plays ..... twice a week in the summer. (*play*)
2 If the .... to host the conference, I just don't know where we will be able to hold it. (*refuse*)
3 The worldwide television .... for tomorrow's cup final .... expected to be 200 million. (*be*)
4 The .... classical concerts throughout the year. (*perform*)
5 The Waterman's Junior Book Prize .... three adults and three children. (*include*)
6 The .... all passed the end-of-year exam. (*have*)
7 The .... a picture of chaos in our schools, but it's just not like that at all. (*present*)
8 .... ordered an investigation into the capture of members of its peace-keeping force in eastern Africa. (*have*)

40.3 If necessary, correct the mistakes in these sentences or write ✓ if they are already correct. A–D

1 The United States come top of the list of countries ranked by economic performance.
2 The people I know who have seen the film say that it's really good.
3 The *New Straits Times* report that tourism is booming in Malaysia.
4 *Northern Lights* are one of Suzanne's favourite books.
5 The stairs leading to the first floor were steep and poorly lit.
6 Chequers is the country house of the British Prime Minister.
7 Whoever made all the mess in the kitchen have to clear it up.
8 The phrase 'men in white coats' are used to talk about psychiatrists.
9 The public needs to be kept informed about progress in the peace talks.
10 Musical chairs are a party game where everyone dashes for a seat when the music stops.

→ Additional exercise 9 (page 245)

Agreement between subject and verb 2

A

With **any of**, **each of**, **either of**, **neither of**, or **none of** and a **plural noun / pronoun** we can use a *singular* or *plural* verb. (We use a singular verb for careful written English.)	▢ I don't think **any of** them *knows* (or *know*) where the money is hidden. ▢ **Neither of** the French athletes *has* (or *have*) won this year.
With **a / the majority of, a number of**, **a lot of**, **plenty of**, **all** (**of**), or **some** (**of**) and a **plural noun / pronoun** we use a *plural* verb. (We use a singular verb with **the number of**.)	▢ **A number of** refugees *have* been turned back at the border. ▢ **The number of** books in the library *has* risen to over five million.
After **one of** and a **plural noun / pronoun** we use a *singular* verb. However, after **one of** + **plural noun / pronoun** + **who** we can often use either a singular or plural verb. (A plural verb is more grammatical.)	▢ **One of** the reasons I took the job *was* that I could work from home. ▢ He's **one of** those teachers who *insist / insists* on pupils sitting silently in class.
With **any of**, **none of**, **the majority of**, **a lot of**, **plenty of**, **all** (**of**), **some** (**of**) and an **uncountable noun** we use a *singular* verb.	▢ **All** the furniture *was* destroyed in the fire. ▢ **None of** the equipment *appears* to be damaged.
With **every** or **each** and a **singular noun** or **coordinated noun** (x *and* y) we use a *singular* verb. (For **each of**, see above.)	▢ **Every** room *looks* over the harbour. ▢ **Every** boy and girl *takes* part in the activity. ▢ **Each** child *has* drawn a picture. *but* ▢ The children *have* **each** drawn a picture.
With **everyone**, **everybody**, **everything** (and similar words beginning **any-**, **some-** and **no-**) we use a *singular* verb.	▢ Practically **everyone** *thinks* that Phil should be given the job.

B

When a subject has two or more items joined by **and**, we usually use a plural verb:

▢ **Ingrid and Tobias** *are* moving back to Australia.

However, phrases connected by **and** can also be followed by singular verbs if we think of them as making up a single item:

▢ **The lorry, its cargo and passengers** *weighs* around 35 tonnes. (*or* … *weigh* …)

C

When a subject is made up of two or more items joined by (**either**) **…** **or** **…** or (**neither**) **…** **nor** **…** we use a singular verb if the last item is singular (although a plural verb is sometimes used in informal English), and a plural verb if the last item is plural:

▢ **Either the station or the cinema** *is* a good place to meet. (*or* … *are* … in informal English)

▢ **The President or his representatives** *are* to attend the meeting.

If the last item is singular and previous item plural, we can use a singular or plural verb:

▢ **Either the teachers or the principal** *is* to blame for the accident. (*or* … *are* to blame …)

D

In **there** + **be** / **have** (see Unit 95) we use a singular verb form with singular and uncountable nouns and a plural form with plural nouns. However, in informal speech we often use a shortened singular form of **be** or **have** (= **There's**) with plural nouns:

▢ Over the last few years **there** *have* been many **improvements** in car safety.

▢ **There**'*s* been lots of good films on lately. (*or* **There**'*ve* been …)

Exercises

41.1 **Complete each set of sentences using nouns or phrases from (i) and appropriate present simple verb forms (active or passive) from (ii). If singular and plural verb forms are possible, write both.** A

(i) his early paintings ~~my children~~ Dr Jones's acquaintances the food

(ii) remain ~~remember~~ taste know

1 a I'd be surprised if any of my children remember / remembers my birthday.
  b It's unlikely that any of .... It seems that he destroyed most of the work he produced during the 1930s.
  c I don't think any of .... particularly good. In fact, the restaurant is rather disappointing.
  d An investigation is underway to discover whether any of .... where he is.

(i) vegetarians victims other museums medicines

(ii) exceed charge expect relieve

2 a Mainly because of recent health scares involving beef and chicken, the number of .... to rise dramatically in the next five years.
  b A number of .... the symptoms of influenza, but none can cure it.
  c It is estimated that the number of .... of the flooding .... 100,000.
  d You can still go into the National Museum for free, although a number of .... in the capital .... people for entry.

(i) player these factors the cars the pieces

(ii) last test influence try

3 a The whole concert includes twenty short items from young musicians. Each of .... about five minutes.
  b The aim of the game is quite simple. Each .... to buy as many properties on the board as possible.
  c Each of .... for safety, fuel economy and reliability.
  d There are four major influences on exchange rates: price levels, tariffs, preference for imported goods, and productivity. Here we investigate how each of .... the exchange rate.

41.2 **Complete the sentences with present simple forms of the verb in brackets. If both singular and plural verb forms are possible, write both.** A–D

1 Plenty of jobs .... available, but no one .... them because they're so poorly paid. (*be / want*)
2 The majority of those questioned .... that the government's economic policies have failed, although neither the Prime Minister nor the Education Minister .... indicated that these policies will change. (*think / have*)
3 It's the first time that either of us .... been to China, but everyone we've met here .... been very welcoming and helpful. (*have / have*)
4 Professor Smith and Dr Peters .... that the wreck of the ship and its cargo .... a danger to local people fishing near the island. (*claim / constitute*)
5 A: Oh, good, sausages and chips .... my favourite.
B: Sorry, all the sausages .... gone, but there .... plenty of chips left if you want some. (*be / have / be*)

→ Additional exercise 9 (page 245)

Unit 42

Agreement between subject and verb 3

A Plural nouns

Some nouns are usually plural and take a plural verb:

- The company's **earnings** *have increased* for the last five years.

> *Also:* **belongings, clothes, congratulations, goods, outskirts, overheads, particulars** (= information), **premises** (= building), **riches, savings, stairs, surroundings, thanks**

Note that **whereabouts** can be used with either a singular or plural verb, **police** and **people** always take a plural verb, and **staff** usually does:

- **Police** *believe* that Thomas is in Brazil, although his exact **whereabouts** *are / is* unknown.
- **Staff** *say* that the new computer system has led to greater levels of stress in their work.

B Plural nouns used with singular verbs

Although the words **data** and **media** (= newspaper, television, etc.) are plural (singular **datum** and **medium**), they are commonly used with a singular verb. However, in formal contexts such as academic writing a plural verb is preferred. Note that other similar plurals such as **criteria** and **phenomena** (singular **criterion** and **phenomenon**) are always used with plural verbs. Compare:

- All the **data** *is* available for public inspection. (*or* … *are* available …) *and*
- I agree that the **criteria** *are* not of equal importance. (*not* … the criteria is not …)

C Uncountable nouns ending in -s

Some uncountable nouns always end in **-s** and look as if they are plural, but when we use them as the subject they have a singular verb:

- The **news** from the Middle East *seems* very encouraging.

> *Also:* **means** (= 'method' or 'money'); **economics, linguistics, mathematics, phonetics, physics; politics, statistics; athletics, gymnastics; diabetes, measles, rabies**

However, compare:

academic subject	*general use*
Politics *is* popular at this university.	Her **politics** *are* bordering on the fascist. (= political belief)
Statistics *was* always my worst subject.	**Statistics** *are* able to prove anything you want them to. (= numerical information)
Economics *has* only recently been recognised as a scientific study.	The **economics** behind their policies *are* unreasonable. (= the financial system)

D Agrement with measurements, percentages, etc.

With a phrase referring to a measurement, amount or quantity we usually prefer a singular verb:

- Only **three metres** *separates* the runners in first and second places. (*rather than* … separate …)

and a singular verb must be used when the complement is a singular noun phrase (e.g. a long time):

- **Three hours** *seems* a long time to take on the homework. (*not* Three hours seem …)

When the first noun in a complex subject is a percentage or a fraction the verb agrees with the noun closest to the verb. Compare:

- **An inflation rate** of only 2% *makes* a difference to exports. (verb agrees with main noun) *and*
- About 50% / half of **the houses** *need* major repairs. (verb agrees with closest noun)

Where we use a singular noun that can be thought of as either a whole unit or a collection of individuals, we can use either a singular or plural verb:

- Some 80% of **the electorate** *is* expected to vote. (*or* … *are* expected …)

Exercises

42.1 If necessary, correct the italicised verbs. A & B

1 Dr Darsee's present whereabouts *is* unknown.
2 Phenomena such as sun spots *have* puzzled scientists for centuries.
3 Over the last decade the company's overheads *has* increased dramatically.
4 The research data *was* collected during the period 12th–29th July 2012.
5 Congratulations *goes* to Ricky Branch for his excellent exam results.
6 The coastal surroundings of the village *is* particularly attractive.
7 He feels that the media *have* criticised him unfairly.
8 Further particulars about the house *is* available from the owner.
9 People *says* the house is haunted.

42.2 Complete the sentences using suitable present simple verbs. C

1 Modern linguistics .... often said to have begun at the start of the 20th century.
2 I think the Senator's politics .... extremely right-wing.
3 If athletics .... neglected in schools, this will have a big impact on future national teams.
4 Measles .... killed a large number of children in the Nagola region.
5 Contact us by whatever means .... most convenient for you: phone, email or fax.
6 Recent statistics .... evidence of a rapid increase in living standards in Asia.

42.3 Complete these extracts from news articles with a singular or plural form of the verbs in brackets. If both singular and plural forms are possible, write both. A–D; also Unit 40

1 The outskirts of our cities .... (*have*) benefited from the new out-of-town shopping centres that .... (*have*) recently been built. Around a third of the population regularly .... (*shop*) out of town.

2 On average, 25 litres of water .... (*be*) used each day per household and as the population .... (*expect*) higher living standards, this figure will rise.

3 Some 30% of the office space in London .... (*be*) presently empty and the Department for Employment .... (*blame*) high property prices.

4 Three centimetres .... (*be*) all that separated the first two runners in last night's 10,000 metres and the sports club .... (*have*) declared the race a dead-heat.

5 The research group now .... (*admit*) that the criteria they used .... (*be*) not totally reliable, and that the figure of 85% .... (*be*) exaggerated.

6 Following last week's major art theft from the Arcon Art Gallery, the premises .... (*be*) searched by police last night and the owner's belongings .... (*have*) been taken away for further inspection.

7 A survey of the opinions of students .... (*show*) that economics .... (*be*) the least popular university subject. However, 90% of the economics students surveyed .... (*believe*) that their courses are well taught.

8 Sufferers from diabetes .... (*have*) welcomed the launch by Federex of a new drug to combat the disease. The company .... (*say*) that earnings from the drug .... (*be*) to be put back into further research.

→ Additional exercise 9 (page 245)

Unit 43

Compound nouns and noun phrases

A

Reminder ➔ H4– H12

In a compound consisting of **noun** + **noun**, often the second noun gives the general class of things to which the compound belongs and the first noun indicates the type within this class. The first noun usually has a singular form:

- **an address book** (= a book for addresses; *not* an addresses book)

However, there are a number of exceptions. These include –

☆ when the first noun only has a plural form:

- **a savings account** **a customs officer** **a clothes shop** (compare **a shoe shop**) **the arms trade** (arms = weapons) **a glasses case** (glasses = spectacles. Compare 'a glass case' = a case made of glass) **an arts festival** (arts = music, drama, film, dance, painting, etc. Compare 'an art festival'; art = painting, drawing and sculpture)

☆ when we refer to an institution (an industry, department, etc.), such as

- **the building materials industry** **the publications department**

which deals with more than one kind of item or activity (different types of building material, different forms of publication).

Note that to make a compound noun plural we usually make the second noun plural:

- **coal mine(s)** **office-worker(s)** **tea leaf / leaves**

B

Sometimes a **noun** + **noun** is not appropriate and instead we use **noun** + **-'s** + **noun** (possessive form) or **noun** + **preposition** + **noun**. In general, we prefer **noun** + **-'s** + **noun** –

☆ when the first noun is the user (a person or animal) of the item in the second noun:

- **a baby's bedroom** **a lion's den** **a women's clinic** **a girls' school** **birds' nests**

☆ when the item in the second noun is produced by the thing (often an animal) in the first: **goat's cheese** **duck's eggs** **cow's milk** (but note **lamb chops** and **chicken drumsticks**)

☆ when we talk about parts of people or animals; but we usually use **noun** + **noun** to talk about parts of things. Compare:

- **a woman's face** **a boy's arm** *but* **a pen top** **a computer keyboard**

We prefer **noun** + **preposition** + **noun** –

☆ when we talk about some kind of container together with its contents. Compare:

- **a cup of tea** (= a cup with tea in it) *and* **a tea cup** (= a cup for drinking tea from)

☆ when the combination of nouns does not refer to a well-known class of items. Compare:

- **income tax** (a recognised class of tax) *and* **a tax on children's clothes** (*rather than* 'a children's clothes tax')

C

Some compound nouns are made up of verbs and prepositions or adverbs, and may be related to a two- or three-word verb (see Unit 94). Compare:

- Mansen **broke out** of the prison by dressing as a woman. (= escaped) *and*
- There was a major **break-out** from the prison last night. (= prisoners escaped)

Countable compound nouns like this have a plural form ending in **-s**:

- **read-out(s)** **push-up(s)** **intake(s)** **outcome(s)**

However, there are exceptions. For example:

- **looker(s)-on** (*or* **onlooker[s]**) **runner(s)-up** **passer(s)-by** **hanger(s)-on**

D

We can form other kinds of hyphenated phrases that are placed before nouns to say more precisely what the noun refers to:

- a **state-of-the-art** (= very modern) tablet PC **up-to-date** information

Exercises

43.1 If necessary, correct the italicised words. A & B

1 Ali worked for a long time in (a) *the parks department*, but a few years ago he retrained, and now he's (b) *a computers programmer*. Of course, what he really wants to be is (c) *a films star!*
2 I was waiting at (a) *the bus stop* this morning when a cyclist on her way to the (b) *girl school* up the road got knocked off her bike. Someone got out of a car without looking and (c) *the car's door* hit her. She was very lucky not to be badly hurt, although she did have (d) *a head cut*.
3 I shouldn't be long at (a) *the corner shop*. I've just got three things on my (b) *shopping list* – (c) *a milk bottle*, (d) *a biscuit packet*, and (e) *some teethpaste*. I'll also look for (f) *some goat's cheese*, but I don't think they'll have any.
4 The tracks on his latest CD range from (a) *love songs* to (b) *pollution songs*.
5 Marta hated going into her grandfather's old (a) *tools shed*. It was full of (b) *spider webs*.
6 When Jake was cleaning his (a) *armschair*, he found a lot of things that had slipped down the back. There was an old (b) *pen top*, a piece from (c) *the 500-pieces jigsaw puzzle* that his daughter had been doing, and his (d) *glass case* with his sunglasses inside.

43.2 Underline the two-word verbs in sentences 1–4, then complete sentences 5–8 with the corresponding compound nouns. C

1 Nathan tried to cover up the fact that he had gambled and lost most of his money.
2 It is reported that cholera has broken out in the refugee camp.
3 I'm flying to Sydney, but I'm stopping over in Singapore for a few days on the way.
4 On the first Friday of each month, a few of us get together and go ten-pin bowling.
5 The minister was taken ill in Iceland during a short .... on his way back to Canada.
6 We didn't have a big party for Jo's 50th birthday, just a family ....
7 Allegations of a .... of a major leak of radioactive waste from the nuclear power plant have been strongly denied by the Energy Ministry.
8 Only two years ago there was a serious .... of malaria in the town.

43.3 Match the halves of these phrases, then use them to complete the sentences below. The meaning of the correct phrase is given in brackets. D

~~day-to-~~	down-to-	larger-than-	man / woman-in-the-
once-in-a-	step-by-	middle-of-the-	round-the

clock	~~day~~	earth	life	lifetime	road	step	street

1 Although the Managing Director of Transcom was involved in major decisions, she left the ...day-to-day... running of the company to her staff. (*routine*)
2 The party will never regain power unless it can persuade .... voters that it has rid itself of corruption. (*not politically extreme*)
3 Since the attempt to assassinate him last year, the Defence Minister has been given .... protection by the police. (*all day and all night*)
4 The bookcase came with simple, ... instructions on how to assemble it. (*progressing from one stage to the next*)
5 When the comet passes close to Earth next week, scientists will have a .... opportunity to study its effects on our atmosphere. (*very rare*)
6 Eleni has a refreshing, ... approach to management. She's much less concerned with theory than with getting things done in the most efficient way possible. (*practical*)
7 The .... isn't interested in the finer points of the government's tax policy. They just want to know if they are going to take home more or less pay. (*ordinary person*)
8 Her father was a .... character who was well known throughout the village for his eccentric way of dressing and outspoken views. (*more exaggerated than usual*)

→ Additional exercise 9 (page 245)

A / an and one

A

We use **a** before nouns and noun phrases that begin with a consonant sound. Reminder ➜ I6–7
If the noun or noun phrase starts with a vowel *letter* but begins with a consonant *sound*, we also use **a**:

a university (/ə juːn …/) a European (/ə jʊər …/) a one-parent family (/ə wʌn …/)

We use **an** before words that begin with a vowel sound, including a silent letter 'h':

- **an o**range **an I**talian **an u**mbrella **an h**our **an h**onour

and abbreviations said as individual letters that begin with A, E, F, H, I, L, M, N, O, R, S or X:

- an MP (/ən em piː/) an FBI agent (/ən ef biː aɪ …/) an IOU (/ən aɪ əʊ juː /)

But compare abbreviations said as words:

- **a NATO** general (/ə neɪtəʊ … /) **a FIFA** official (/ə fiːfə … /) *but* **an OPEC** meeting (/ən əʊpek … /)

Note that we say:

- **a history** (book) *but* **an** (*or* **a**) **historical** (novel)

B

We use **a / an** (not **one**) to talk about a particular but unspecified person, thing or event:

- I really need **a** cup of coffee.
- You never see **a** police officer in this part of town, do you?

We also use **a / an**, not **one**, in number and quantity expressions such as:

- three times **a** year half **an** hour **a** quarter of **an** hour **a** day or so (= 'about a day')
  50 cents **a** (= each) litre (note we can also say '50 cents for one litre')
  a week or two (= between one and two weeks; note we can also say 'one or two weeks')
  a few **a** little **a** huge number of …

We use **a** rather than **one** in the pattern **a** … **of** … with possessives, as in:

- She's **a** colleague **of** mine.
- That'**s a** friend **of** Gabriel's.

C

Before a singular countable noun **one** and **a / an** both refer to one thing:

- We'll be in Australia for **one** year. (*or* … **a** year.)
- Wait here for **one** minute, and I'll be with you. (*or* … **a** minute …)

Using **one** gives a little more emphasis to the length of time, quantity, amount, etc.:

- He weighs **one** hundred and twenty kilos! Would you believe it! (using **one** emphasises the weight more than using **a**)

However, we use **one** rather than **a / an** if we want to emphasise that we are talking about *only* one thing or person rather than two or more:

- Do you want **one** sandwich or two?
- Are you staying only **one** night?
- I just took **one** look at her and she started crying.

We use **one**, not **a / an**, in the pattern **one** … **other / another**:

- Close **one** eye, and then the **other**.
- Bees carry pollen from **one** plant to **another**.

We also use **one** in phrases such as **one day**, **one evening**, **one spring**, etc. to mean a particular, but unspecified, day, evening, spring, etc.:

- Hope to see you again **one day**.
- **One evening**, while he was working late at the office …

Exercises

44.1 **Write a or an in the spaces.** A

1 .... unpaid bill
2 .... DIY shop
3 .... MP3 player
4 .... Euro
5 .... MiG fighter plane
6 .... Olympic medal
7 .... AGM
8 .... U-turn
9 .... heirloom
10 .... NASA space launch
11 .... UN decision
12 .... SOS message
13 .... F grade
14 .... hero

44.2 **If necessary, correct a / an or one in these sentences, or write ✓. In which sentences are a / an and one both possible?** B & C

1 I usually go to the gym four times one week.
2 There's more than one way to solve the problem.
3 I phoned the council to complain, but just got passed on from a person to another.
4 The rate of pay is really good here. You can earn over £20 one hour.
5 Maybe we could go skiing one winter.
6 The apples are 90 cents one kilo.
7 Are you hungry? Would you like one piece of cake?
8 The rules say that there is only one vote per member.
9 You can get seven hours of recording on one disc.
10 A: What would Moritz like for his birthday?
B: Why don't you ask Leah? She's one good friend of his and will have some ideas.
11 There's one pen on the floor. Is it yours?
12 The library books are due back in one month.
13 Do you want some of my chips? There are too many here for a person.
14 I'm going to London for one day or two.
15 Either I'll work late tonight or I'll come in early tomorrow, but the report's got to be finished by lunchtime a way or another.
16 It will take more than one morning to finish the decorating.

44.3 **Which is more appropriate, a / an or one? If both a / an and one are possible, write them both.** B & C

1 If you wait .... second I'll get my coat and come too.
2 I want to see the river .... last time before I leave.
3 The President is visiting the city .... day in November.
4 It was announced that the plane would be approximately .... hour late.
5 I could hear the sound of .... helicopter in the distance.
6 I'd just like to say .... thing before I go.
7 Misaki's baby is .... year old already.
8 Dinner should be ready in .... hour or so.
9 Hugo came over .... evening last week.
10 I've painted .... wall already and I'll do the other tomorrow.
11 I'd like to make .... point here, Carlos, if I may.
12 .... large number of people had gathered in the square.

→ **Additional exercise 10** (page 246)

Unit 45

A / an, the and zero article 1

A

We usually use **the** when we talk about –

Reminder ➔ I1– I9

☆ things which are unique; that is, there is only one of them (or one set of them):

- **the world** **the sky** **the atmosphere** **the sun** **the ground** **the climate** **the horizon** **the human race** **the environment** **the travel industry** **the Internet**

☆ general geographical areas with **the** as in:

- **the beach** **the town** **the sea(side)** **the land** **the country(side)** (where 'the country' or 'the countryside' means 'the area where there are no towns')

☆
- **the past** **the present** **the future**

Note, however, that some nouns like this can be used with **zero article** (i.e. no article) to refer to a concept in general:

- **Climate** is one of the many factors involved in changing farming methods. (*or* **The climate** …)
- These flowers grow best in sandy soil and **sun**. (= sunshine)
- In autumn the temperature difference between **land** and **sea** decreases. (*or* … **the land** and **the sea** …)

If we want to describe a particular instance of these we can use **a / an**. Compare:

- I could see the plane high up in **the sky**. *and*
- When I woke up there was **a bright blue sky**.
- What are your plans for **the future**? *and*
- She dreamt of **a future where she could spend more time painting**.

B

We can use **the** when we make generalisations about classes of things using singular countable nouns. (See also Unit 47A.) Compare the use of **the** and **a / an** in these sentences:

- **The computer** has revolutionised publishing. (this refers to computers in general) *but not* A computer has revolutionised publishing. (computers *in general* have done this, not an individual computer)
- **The computer** is an important research tool. *and*
- **A computer** is an important research tool. (this statement is true of both the general class and the individual item)

As an alternative to **the** + **singular countable noun** we can use a plural countable noun to talk about a class of things:

- **Computers** are an important research tool.

Note that if **the** is used with plural and uncountable nouns we refer to a specific thing or group:

- **The computers** have arrived. Where shall I put them?
- **The music** was wonderful. I could have listened to the orchestra all night.

When we define something or say what is typical of a particular class of people or things, we generally use **a / an** rather than **the**:

- **A corkscrew** is a gadget for getting corks out of bottles.
- **A garden** is there to give you pleasure, not to be a constant worry.

C

Some nouns can be used uncountably when we talk about the whole substance or idea, but countably when we talk about an instance or more than one instance of it. When these nouns are used countably we can use **a / an** (and plurals). Compare:

- I don't drink **coffee**. *and* Would you like **a coffee**? (= a cup of coffee)
- He shook with **fear**. *and* He has **a fear** of heights.

There are many other nouns like this, including **conversation**, **grammar**, **importance**, **iron**, **pleasure**, **shampoo**, **sound**. Some of these nouns (e.g. **grammar**, **iron**) have different meanings when they are used countably and uncountably.

Exercises

45.1 **Complete both sentences in each pair using one word from the box. Add the or a / an in an appropriate place.** A

beach	future	past	world

1 a I think the best Australian wine is as good as any in ....
b As a child, Dariya would often daydream about travelling forward in time to .... very different from the one she lived in.

2 a If we are elected, we will build our policies on the simple belief that our purpose is to create bright .... for our children rather than achieving short-term goals for ourselves.
b Although our current financial position is worrying, we have many new orders for our products and .... is looking very positive.

3 a As I get older, I remember .... better than things that happened recently.
b Many tourists come to the village looking for .... that never really existed.

4 a If you want to get away from it all, you can take a small boat to deserted .... on one of the islands.
b Dear Mum and Dad, We're having a great holiday. The weather's wonderful and we're spending most of our time on ....

45.2 **Underline the correct or more likely answer. If both answers are possible, underline them both.** B

1 We get some strange requests in our shop. We had *the customer / a customer* in the other day who wanted to buy chocolate-covered ants.
2 It often seems that *the individual / an individual* can have little impact on government policy.
3 The invention of *a car / the car* is normally attributed to the German engineer Gottlieb Daimler.
4 *The television / A television* has changed the way we think more than any other modern invention.
5 The campaign against smoking in public places argues that its harmful effects are not confined to *the smoker / a smoker*.

45.3 **Complete the sentences using the nouns from the box. Use each noun twice. If necessary, insert a / an in the correct place.** C

conversation	grammar	iron	pleasure	sound

1 My sisters were clearly having ^a serious conversation so I didn't like to disturb them.
2 It now gives me great .... to introduce that marvellous ventriloquist, Marco Lutman.
3 As we walked through the rainforest we heard .... we weren't expecting – the ring of a mobile phone.
4 The failure to teach .... in schools has affected people's ability to write well.
5 Most red meat is relatively high in ....
6 .... travels at different speeds, depending on the temperature of the air.
7 It's real .... to travel by rail in Sweden. The trains are clean and punctual.
8 I have .... of English printed in 1890 on very thin paper.
9 Although he's got .... he never seems to use it. His shirts are always creased.
10 As she walked into the party, ... ceased and everyone in the crowded room stared at her.

→ Additional exercise 10 (page 246)

Unit 46

A / an, the and zero article 2

A

Reminder → I1– I9

We use **a / an** to say what a person's job is, was, or will be:

- She was **a company director** when she retired.
- Against her parents' wishes, she wants to be **a journalist**.

However, when we give a person's job title, or their unique position, we use **the** or **zero article** (i.e. no article), not **a / an**. Compare:

- She's been appointed **(the) head of the company.** *and*
- I'm **a production manager** at Fino. (= there may be more than one production manager)

After **the position of**, **the post of**, or **the role of** we use **zero article** before a job title:

- Dr Simons has taken on **the position of** Head of Department.

B

We usually use **zero article** (i.e. no article) before the name of an individual person or place. However, we use **the** –

☆ when there are two people with the same name to specify which one we mean:

- That's not **the Stephen Fraser** I went to school with.

but compare 'There was **a** Stephen Fraser in my class.' (= a person named Stephen Fraser)

☆ when we want to emphasise that the person we are referring to is the most famous person with that name. Used this way, **the** is stressed and pronounced /ðiː/:

- Do they mean ***the*** **Neil Armstrong**, or someone else?

☆ with an adjective to describe a person, or another noun which tells us their job:

- **the late Michael Jackson**
- **(the) artist Joseph Turner** ('the' is sometimes left out, particularly in journalism)

☆ when we talk about a family as a whole:

- **The Robinsons** are away this weekend.

C

Note that **a / an**, or sometimes **zero article**, is used with a name when referring to the particular excellent qualities of the person named:

- Majid plays tennis well, but he'll never be **(a) Roger Federer**.

We also use **a / an** when we refer to an individual example of a product made by a particular manufacturer (e.g I've just bought **a** Mercedes) or a work by a particular artist (e.g. Do you think it could be **a** Van Gogh / **a** Rembrandt?).

You can use **a / an** before a person's name if you don't know the person yourself. Compare:

- Dr Lee is here for you. (= I know Dr Lee) *and*
- There's **a** Dr Amy Lee on the phone. (= I haven't heard of her before) Do you want to talk to her?

D

In stories and jokes in conversation, **this** is commonly used instead of **a / an** to introduce a new person or thing. Using **this** highlights the person or thing as the topic of what is to come next:

- As I was walking along, **this** spider (= a spider) landed on my head, and …
- **This** man (= a man) goes into a chemist and he says …

E

We use **the** before a *superlative adjective* (**the biggest**, **the most expensive**, etc.) when the superlative adjective is followed by a noun or defining phrase:

- He is **the finest** *young player* around at the moment.

However, we can often leave out **the**, particularly in an informal style, when there is no noun or defining phrase after the superlative adjective. Compare:

- A: Why did you decide to stay in this hotel?
  B: It was **(the) cheapest**. *and* It was **the cheapest** I could find.

Exercises

46.1 **If necessary, correct any mistakes in these sentences. If they are already correct, write ✓.** A–C

1 She was determined to be author one day.
2 She recently became the minister in the new government.
3 A: What make is your computer? B: It's Mac.
4 I found myself talking to George Clooney! Not George Clooney, of course, but someone with the same name.
5 I didn't even know Clara was interested in art until I heard that she owns Van Gogh.
6 I've been offered the position of Director of Personnel.
7 We're going on holiday with Nielsens.
8 He's really keen on athletics. He likes to think of himself as the Usain Bolt.

46.2 **Put a / an, the or zero article (–) in the spaces. Give all possible answers.** A–C

1 I'm .... marketing adviser at Unifleet.
2 Leon's .... manager of his local football team.
3 She has been appointed .... Minister for Industry.
4 A special award was given to .... novelist Ian McMurphy.
5 Let me introduce you to .... Georgia Rossi.
6 We met our good friend .... Eliza Borg when we were in .... Malta.
7 When Lucia was young she knew .... Picasso.
8 .... Linda Green is outside. Do you want to see her?

46.3 **If the italicised the can be left out of these sentences, put brackets around it.** E

1. It's *the* best ice-cream I've ever tasted.
2 Rodrigo's boat wasn't the most elegant in the harbour, but it was certainly *the* biggest.
3 I thought the second competitor was *the* best, even though he didn't win a prize.
4 This is by far *the* most valuable painting in the collection.
5 A: Why did you ask Martina to go first? B: Because she's *the* oldest.
6 Sapphires occur in a variety of colours, but blue ones are *the* most valuable.
7 The Pacific is *the* biggest ocean in the world.
8 It's supposed to be *the* oldest post office in the country.

46.4 **Complete the email with a / an, the, zero article or this. Give alternatives where possible.** Units 45 & 46

Something very strange happened to me the other night. As I was going home (1) .... man came up to me. He had (2) .... untidy hair and (3) .... paint all over his clothes. He told me that he was (4) .... head of the local council and that he was offering me a job as (5) .... road sweeper. He said that (6) .... road sweeper earns a great deal of money and that I would become very rich in (7) .... future. Well, I just said 'No, thanks' and walked on. When I looked back he had stopped (8) .... woman. He was telling her that he was (9) .... President of the United States and that he wanted her to be (10) .... Defence Secretary ...

→ Additional exercise 10 (page 246)

Unit 47

A / an, the and zero article 3

A

Reminder ➔ I1– I9

With plural and uncountable nouns, **zero article** (i.e. no article) is used to talk generally, without definite people or things in mind. **The** is used when we assume the listener or reader will understand who or what we are referring to, or when other words in the noun phrase make the reference specific. Compare:

- The government has promised not to tax **books**. (= books generally) *and*
- **The books** have arrived. (= the books you ordered)
- **Music** played an important part in his life. (= music generally) *and*
- I thought **the music** used in the film was the best part. (= that particular music)

B

We often use **zero article** with the names of holidays, special times of the year, months, and days of the week including **Easter**, **Ramadan**, **New Year's Day**. But compare:

- I'll see you on **Saturday**. (= next Saturday)
- We met on **Saturday**. (= last Saturday)
- They came on **a Saturday** as far as I can remember. (we are only interested in the day of the week, not which particular Saturday)
- They came on **the Saturday** after our party. (a particular Saturday, specifying which one)

With **winter**, **summer**, **spring**, **autumn**, and **New Year** (meaning the holiday period), we can use either **zero article** or **the**:

- In (**the**) **summer** I try to spend as much time as I can in the garden.

We use **the** when it is understood or we go on to specify which summer, spring, etc. we mean:

- I'd like to go skiing in **the autumn**. (= this year)
- I first went skiing in **the spring** of 2002.

We say 'in the New Year' to mean near the beginning of next year:

- I'll see you again in **the New Year**.

When we want to describe the features of a particular holiday, season, or other period of time and say that it was somehow special when compared with others, we can use **It / That was ... + a / an + noun + modifying phrase**. Compare:

- That was **a** winter I'll never forget. (= compared to other winters it was unforgettable) *and*
- That was **the** winter we went to Norway. (= a statement about a particular winter)

C

We use **zero article** with times of the day and night such as **midnight**, **midday**, and **noon**:

- If possible, I'd like it finished by **midday**.
- **Midnight** couldn't come quickly enough.

But note that we can say either **the dawn** or **dawn**:

- He got back into bed and waited for (**the**) **dawn**.

We use **the** + **morning / afternoon / evening** for a day which is understood or already specified:

- I enjoyed **the morning**, but in **the afternoon** the course was boring.

But compare:

- **Morning** is the time I work best. (= mornings in general; **The morning** ... is also possible)
- I'll be there **by** (**the**) **morning / evening**. (*but* ... **by the afternoon**, *not* ... by afternoon)
- I waited **all morning**. (*more usual than* all the morning / afternoon, etc.)
- 'You look upset.' 'Yes, I've had **a** terrible **morning**.' (= compared to other mornings)

D

We often use **by** + **zero article** to talk about means of transport and communication. Compare:

- I generally go **by bus** to work. *and*
- I generally take **the bus** to work.

> *Also*: **go / travel *by* car / taxi / bus / plane / train / air / sea**; **contact / communicate *by* post / email / phone**

Exercises

47.1 **Complete both sentences in each pair using one word from the box. Add the where necessary.** A

agriculture	**children**	**fire**	**holidays**	**islands**	**money**	**parents**	**rain**

1 a .... as young as ten are working in the clothing industry.
  b While you're painting the sitting room, I'll take .... over to the park.
2 a As the soil quality deteriorated, so too did .... on which the region depended.
  b Around 60% of the labour force in the county is supported by ....
3 a Around the world .... are being threatened by rising sea levels.
  b .... off the east coast of Malaysia are beautiful.
4 a I've been really busy at work, so I'm really looking forward to ....
  b .... in the Brazilian rainforests are now becoming popular with travellers.
5 a Farmers will be hoping for .... in the next few weeks.
  b Last night .... was torrential.
6 a I've left .... I owe you on your desk.
  b It is said that .... is the root of all evil.
7 a .... will be able to use this software to check their child's use of the Internet.
  b .... of Paul Thomas claimed that he was at home at the time of the robbery.
8 a It isn't known how .... started.
  b Animals fear .... more than anything else.

47.2 **Complete the dialogues with a / an, the or zero article (–), whichever is more likely. Where more than one answer is possible, consider any difference in meaning.** B & C

1 A: What's the matter?
  B: I've been working in the garden all .... afternoon and my back aches.
2 A: Can you remember when we last saw Alex?
  B: It was .... Sunday in June, I think.
3 A: When did you get your laptop?
  B: July 15th last year. I remember because it was also .... day I passed my driving test.
4 A: I haven't seen Subin for months. B: He's been away in South Africa for .... winter.
5 A: I've spent .... afternoon on the phone to my mother. B: Why? Is there a problem?
6 A: Shall we go out walking on .... Sunday? B: No, I'm busy this weekend.
7 A: Do you remember when Mateo did all the cooking?
  B: Of course. It was .... Christmas the rest of us had flu.
8 A: I'll see you again after .... Christmas. B: Okay. Have a good holiday.
9 A: That old coat of yours won't be warm enough for .... winter.
  B: You're right. I need a new one.
10 A: Remember when Lars and Ella had that terrible row?
  B: How could I forget? That was .... day I wouldn't want to go through again.

47.3 **Complete the sentences using the words from the box (more than once). Add any other necessary words.** D

air	**car**	**email**	**post**

1 A: I got .... from Carla yesterday. B: How is she now?
2 The train was cancelled so I had to come ....
3 Research has found that living plants are efficient at absorbing pollutants in ....
4 The application forms came in .... this morning.
5 The exam results will be sent .... on 24th August.
6 It's raining so I think I'll take ....
7 A: Shall I send Goran a letter? B: No, the quickest way to get in touch with him is ....
8 Thailand – Getting there ....: The main international airport in Thailand is Suvarnabhumi Airport ...

→ **Additional exercise 10** (page 246)

Some and any

A

Some

Reminder ➜ I10–I21

Before plural and uncountable nouns we sometimes use **some** or **zero article** (i.e. no article) with very little difference in meaning:

- 'Where were you last week?' 'I was visiting (**some**) friends.'
- Before serving, pour (**some**) yoghurt over the top.

With both **some** and **zero article** we are referring to particular people or things but in an indefinite way. When it is used in this way, **some** is usually pronounced /səm/.

We don't use **some** to make general statements about whole classes of things or people:

- **Machinery** can be dangerous unless used properly.
- **Babies** need a lot of attention.

B

Some is used before a number to mean 'approximately':

- **Some** eighty per cent of all residents took part in the vote. (= approximately eighty per cent; beginning 'Eighty per cent ...' suggests a more precise figure)

When it is used in this way, **some** is usually pronounced /sʌm/.

C

When we can't say exactly which person or thing we are talking about because we don't know, can't remember, or want to emphasise that it is not important, we can use **some** instead of **a** / **an** with a singular noun. When it is used in this way, **some** is usually pronounced /sʌm/.

- He was interrupted twice by **some** troublemaker in the audience.

We use the phrase **some** (**thing**) **or other** in a similar way:

- I bought them from **some** shop **or other** in New Street. (*not* ... from a shop or other ...)

D

Any

We usually use **any** not **some** (and **anyone**, **anything**, etc. not **someone**, **something**, etc.) –

☆ in non-affirmative contexts; that is, lacking positive, affirmative meaning.

☆ to refer to non-specific, unspecified things.

For example, we generally use **any** in sentences with a negative meaning:

- There's *hardly* **any** sugar left.
- I closed the windows to *prevent* **any** flies getting in.
- It was *impossible* to see **anything** in the dark.
- We got to the airport *without* **any** difficulty.

Also when sentences include: **barely, never, rarely, scarcely, seldom** (= negative adverbs); **deny, fail, forbid, prohibit, refuse** (= negative verbs); **reluctant, unable, unlikely** (= negative adjectives)

However, we use **some** with these negative words–

☆ when **some** (pronounced /sʌm/) has the implication 'not all':

- I talk to colleagues *before* I make **some** decisions, but I had to make this one on my own.

☆ when the basic meaning is positive:

- **Somebody** isn't telling the truth. (= There is some person [who isn't telling the truth])

☆ when we are talking about a particular but unspecified person or thing:

- I was *reluctant* to repeat **something** so critical of Paul. (= a specific criticism)

E

We often use **any** in clauses that begin with **before**, and with comparisons:

- I cleared up the mess *before* **anyone** saw it. ('... before someone saw it' suggests that I have a particular person in mind who might see it)
- The material felt *softer than* **anything** she had ever touched before.

Exercises

48.1 If necessary, correct these sentences by writing **some** in an appropriate place or crossing it out. If the sentence is already correct, write ✓. A & Reminder I10–I14

1 If you're going to the library, could you take back books that I've finished reading?
2 The price of some coffee is at an all-time low.
3 Tony knows more about some jazz than anyone I've ever met.
4 The door kept flying open in the wind so I tied it up with string.
5 Sports are dangerous.
6 I need to get some bread from the supermarket.
7 Money can't buy you some happiness.
8 Children are taller than expected at a given age.

48.2 Rewrite these news headlines as full sentences using **some** to mean 'approximately'. B

1 **250 people charged with assault following Molton riots**
Some 250 people have been charged with assault following the Molton riots.

2 **30% OF ALL CITY BUSES FOUND TO BE UNSAFE**

3 Unexploded bomb found 5 miles from Newham centre

4 25% OF ELECTRICITY FROM WIND BY 2025
....

5 **200 jobs to be lost at Encon steelworks**

48.3 Complete the sentences in any appropriate way using **some + singular noun** or **some + singular noun + or other**. C

1 I don't know where I got the information from. I must have heard it *on some radio programme (or other).*
2 I don't know where Jakub is. He's probably ....
3 I don't know where the book is. Maybe I lent it ....
4 I don't know where Zuzanna works. I think it's in ....
5 I don't know why Nika is still at work. Perhaps she's got to ....

48.4 Complete these sentences with **some, someone, something, any, anyone** or **anything**. Where both **some(one / thing)** or **any(one / thing)** are possible, write both and consider any difference in meaning. D & E

1 Elias worked hard at learning Japanese but failed to make .... real progress.
2 I was unable to eat .... of the food.
3 I always offer to help organise school concerts, but there is seldom .... for me to do.
4 Fiona Jones is .... I rarely see these days.
5 He denied that he had done .... wrong.
6 I always get to work before .... else.
7 The theatre is unlikely to have .... tickets left for tonight's performance.
8 Despite rowing as hard as we could, we had gone barely .... distance from the shore.
9 .... parents never seem to have time to sit down and talk to their children.
10 When I last lent my laptop out it got damaged, so I'm reluctant to lend it to .... else.

→ Additional exercise 10 (page 246)

No, none (of) and not any

A

We can use **no** and **none (of)** instead of **not a** or **not any** for particular emphasis. Compare:

Reminder → 129–134

- There is**n't a** train until tomorrow. *and* There's **no** train until tomorrow. (more emphatic)
- Sorry, there is**n't any** left. *and* Sorry, there's **none** left.
- He did**n't** have **any** of the usual symptoms. *and* He had **none of** the usual symptoms.

We use other pairs of negative words and phrases in a similar way:

- There is**n't anyone / anybody** here. *and* There's **no one / nobody** here. (more emphatic)
- She was**n't anywhere** to be seen. *and* She was **nowhere** to be seen.
- Why do**n't** you **ever** call me? *and* Why do you **never** call me?

B

We don't usually use **not a / any**, **not anyone**, etc. in initial position in a sentence or clause, or straight after **and**, **but** or **that** at the beginning of a clause. Instead we use **no**, **none of**, **no one**, etc.:

- **No** force was needed to make them move. (*not* Not any force was needed ...)
- Most players are under 16 *and* **none of** them is over 20. (*not* ... and not any of them ...)
- I'm sure *that* **nothing** can go wrong. (*not* ... that not anything can ...)

C

In a formal or literary style we can use **not a** in initial position or after **and**, **but** or **that** (see also Unit 100):

- **Not a** sound came from the room. (*less formally* There wasn't a sound from the room.)
- She kept so quiet *that* **not a** soul in the house knew she was there.

D

After **no**, we can often use either a singular or a plural noun with little difference in meaning, although a singular noun is usually more formal:

- **No answers** could be found. (*or more formally* **No answer** ...)
- We want to go to the island but there are **no boats** to take us. (*or more formally* ... there is **no boat**.)

However, we use a *singular* noun in situations where we would expect one of something, and a *plural* noun where we would expect more than one. Compare:

- I phoned Sarah at home, but there *was* **no answer**. (*not* ... but there were no answers.) *and*
- He seems very lonely at school, and *has* **no friends**. (*not* ... no friend.)

E

We can give special emphasis to **no** or **none of** using phrases like **no amount of** with uncountable nouns, **not one ... / not a single ...** with singular countable nouns, and **not one of ...** with plural nouns:

- The company is so badly managed that **no amount of** *investment* will make it successful.
- **Not one** *person* remembered my birthday. (*or* **Not a single** *person* ...)
- **Not one of** *the families* affected by the noise wants to move.

F

Some phrases with **no** are commonly used in informal spoken English: **No wonder** (= it's not surprising); **No idea** (= I don't know); **No comment** (= I have nothing to say); **No way**, **No chance** (= emphatic ways of saying 'no', particularly to express refusal to do or believe something); **No problem**, **No bother** (= it isn't / wasn't difficult to do something):

- 'The computer's not working again.' '**No wonder**. It's not plugged in!'
- 'Thanks for the lift.' '**No problem**. I had to go past the station anyway.'

Exercises

49.1 **Complete the sentences with a word or phrase from (i) followed by a word or phrase from (ii). Use each word or phrase once only.** A–C

(i)

no ~~none~~ none of no one nothing nowhere never not

(ii)

a drop else going to get heard the hotels ~~in the cupboard~~ point wrong

1 Where are the biscuits? There are *none in the cupboard.*
2 We left the house as quietly as possible and .... us.
3 .... was spilt as she poured the liquid into the flask.
4 She was determined to leave and I knew there was .... in protesting.
5 The door was locked and he had .... to go.
6 I found that .... in the city centre had any rooms left.
7 Liam's so lazy. Is he .... a job?
8 The doctors reassured Emily that they could find .... with her.

49.2 **Look again at the sentences in 49.1. Which of them can you rewrite to make less emphatic using not (n't) any / anyone, etc.?** A & B

49.3 **If necessary, correct the italicised parts of this email.** D

Hi. Just back from a week on the island of Lumos – but I certainly wouldn't recommend it! Their economy is in a really bad way. A lot of people just sit around all day – there (1) *is no job* to be found outside the main town. I had to hire a car because there (2) *is no train or bus* on the island. But it was incredibly old – it's ages since I've seen a car with (3) *no seatbelt*. And then when I had a puncture I discovered there (4) *were no spare tyres* either. It was in the hills in the north, and as there (5) *were no people* around to help, I phoned the car hire company and had to wait hours for someone to turn up. It was hot and there (6) *was no shade* as there (7) *is no tree* in that part of the island. The hotel wasn't much better. There (8) *were no swimming pools* – even though it showed one on its website! There (9) *were no televisions* in my room, and on the first night there (10) *was no hot water*. But when I phoned down to reception to complain, there (11) *were no replies*. The food was awful at the hotel, but as there (12) *were no restaurants* for miles around there (13) *were no choices* – I had to eat there. But I don't think I'll be going back!
Speak soon,
Karl

49.4 **Complete these sentences in any appropriate way beginning not one (of) or no amount of.** E

1 I made lots of cakes for the party but *not one of the children liked them.*
2 Mr Carlson didn't want to sell the painting, and …
3 I sent job applications to over a hundred companies, but …
4 Smallpox used to be common all over the world but since 1978 …
5 The floor had dirty black marks all over it, and …

49.5 **Choose one of the No … phrases from section F opposite to complete these dialogues.** F

1 A: Can you give me a lift to the station? B: .... I'll pick you up at eight.
2 A: I've got a headache.
B: .... You've been in front of that computer screen for hours.
3 A: Do you think Kim will pass her maths?
B: .... She just doesn't work hard enough.
4 A: Where's Stefan?
B: .... Last time I saw him he was in the kitchen.
5 A: I'm from News World, Dr James. Do you have anything to say about the accusation that you stole from your patients? B: .... Goodbye.

Unit 50 Much (of), many (of), a lot of, lots (of), etc.

A

Reminder ➜ 138–142

In affirmative sentences we generally use **a lot of** and **lots (of)** rather than **much (of)** and **many (of)**, particularly in informal contexts. However, there are a number of exceptions –

☆ In formal contexts, such as academic writing, **much (of)** and **many (of)** are often preferred. We can also use phrases such as **a large / considerable / substantial amount of** (with uncountable nouns), or **a large / considerable / great / substantial number of** (with plural nouns):

- **Much** debate has been heard about Thornton's new book.
- There could be **many** explanations for this.
- **Much of** her fiction describes women in unhappy marriages.
- **A large amount of** the food was inedible. (*or* **Much of** …)
- The book contains **a large number of** pictures, many in colour. (*or* … **many** …)

☆ In formal contexts we can use **much** and **many** as pronouns:

- There is no guarantee she will recover. **Much** depends on how well she responds to treatment.
- **Many** (= many people) have argued that she is the finest poet of our generation.
- Not once did I see a tiger in the jungle, although I heard **many**. (referring back to 'tiger(s)')

☆ We usually use **many** rather than **a lot of** or **lots of** with time expressions (**days**, **minutes**, **months**, **weeks**, **years**) and **number + of** (e.g. **thousands of voters**, **millions of pounds**):

- We used to spend **many** *hours* driving to Melbourne and back.
- He was the founder of a company now worth **many** *millions of pounds*.

B

We can use **many** following **the**, **my**, **its**, **his**, **her**, etc. and plural countable nouns:

- Among *the* **many** *unknowns* after the earthquake is the extent of damage to the foundations of buildings.
- The gallery is exhibiting some of *his* **many** *famous paintings of ships*.

We can use the phrase **many a** with a singular noun to talk about a repeated event or a large number of people or things:

- **Many a** *pupil* at the school will be pleased that Latin is no longer compulsory.

C

To emphasise that we are talking about a large number we can use **a good / great many** with a plural noun:

- She has **a good / great many** *friends* in New Zealand.

To emphasise that we are talking about a large amount we can use **a good / great deal of** with a singular or uncountable noun:

- **A good / great deal of** *the exhibition* was devoted to her recent work.

D

We use **far** (not 'much' or 'many') before **too many + a plural countable noun** or **too much + an uncountable noun**:

- **Far too many** *students* failed the end-of-year maths exam. (*not* Much / Many too many …)
- **Far too much** *time* is wasted filling in forms. (*not* Much / Many too much time …)

E

We often use **plenty of** instead of **a lot of** or **lots of** with uncountable and plural countable nouns. However, **plenty of** means 'enough, or more than enough' and is therefore not likely in certain contexts. Compare:

- We took **lots of / plenty of** food and drink on our walk through the hills. *and*
- Nina doesn't look well. She's lost **a lot of** weight. ('plenty of' is unlikely here)

Exercises

50.1 **Make corrections or improvements to these extracts from conversations (1–3) and from academic writing (4–6).** A, C, D & E

1 Lola's had many problems with her back for a lot of years. She's having an operation next week and she won't be back at work for a good deal of weeks afterwards.

2 A: There's bound to be much traffic on the way to the station. Perhaps we should leave now.

B: No, there's plenty time left, and at this time of day many people will already be at work.

3 Many think that hedgehogs are very rare nowadays, but when I was in Wales I saw many.

4 A lot have claimed that Professor Dowman's study on current attitudes to politics is flawed. One criticism is that much too many people questioned in the survey were under 18.

5 A lot of research has been conducted on the effects of diet on health, with a lot of studies focusing on the link between fat intake and heart disease. However, a lot remains to be done.

6 While it is true that a lot of thousands of jobs were lost with the decline of the northern coal and steel industries, a lot of advantages have also followed. Much too many cases of lung disease were recorded in the region, but with lower levels of pollution the number has declined. In addition, a great deal of hi-tech companies have moved in to take advantage of the newly available workforce.

50.2 **Complete the sentences with either the / my / its / his / her many or many a / an and one item from the box.** B

coffee shops	**expeditions**	**~~German relatives~~**	**golf courses**
emails	**ship**	**sunny afternoon**	**teacher**

1 She went to stay in Munich with one of *her many German relatives.*
2 I spent .... sitting on the terrace looking out over the hills.
3 .... has been lost in the dangerous waters off the south coast of the island.
4 The area is most famous for .... that attract players from all over the world.
5 Since the end of last year he has refused to speak to me on the phone or answer ....
6 Oliver Svensson accompanied Colonel Colombo on .... to the Himalayas and the Andes.
7 .... will be looking forward to the start of the school holidays.
8 I went into the first of .... along New Street and ordered an espresso.

50.3 **If possible, complete these sentences using plenty of. If not, use a lot of.** E

1 It will be very hot on the journey, so make sure you bring .... drinking water.
2 .... staff at the hospital have come down with a mysterious illness.
3 He didn't have .... money, so he decided to catch the bus rather than take a taxi.
4 We were surprised when .... students failed to attend the lecture.
5 I'm looking forward to a relaxing holiday, and I'm taking .... books to read.

Unit 51

All (of), whole, every, each

A All (of)

Reminder ➜ 143–146

We sometimes use **all** after the noun it refers to:

- *His songs* **all** sound much the same to me. (*or* **All** [**of**] *his songs* sound ...)
- *We* **all** think Kushi's working too hard. (*or* **All of** *us* think ...)

Note that we usually put **all** after the verb **be** and after the first auxiliary verb if there is one:

- They *are* **all** going to Athens during the vacation. (*not* They all are going ...)
- You *should* **all** have three question papers. (*not* You all should have ...; however, note that we can say 'You all should have ...' for particular emphasis in spoken English)

B

To make negative sentences with **all (of)** we usually use **not all (of)** rather than **all** ... **not** (although **all** ... **not** is sometimes used in informal spoken English):

- **Not all (of)** the seats were taken. *or* The seats were **not all** taken.

Note that **not all (of)** and **none of** have a different meaning. Compare:

- **Not all (of)** my cousins were at the wedding. (= some of them were there) *and*
- **None of** my cousins were at the wedding. (= not one of them was there)

C All and whole

Before singular countable nouns we usually use **the whole** rather than **all the**:

- They weren't able to stay for **the whole** concert. (*rather than* ... for all the concert.)

However, we can say **all** + **day / week / night / month / winter**, etc. (*but not usually* all October / 2001 / 21st May, etc.; **all Monday / Tuesday**, etc. are only usually used in informal contexts); **all the time**, **all the way**; and in informal speech we can use **all the** with things that we see as being made up of parts (**all the world / house / city / country / department**, etc.):

- After the fire **the whole** *city* was covered in dust. (*or* ... **all** *the city* ... in informal speech)

Note that we can use **entire** instead of **whole** immediately before a noun:

- The **whole / entire** building has recently been renovated.

Before plural nouns we can use **all (of)** or **whole**, but they have different meanings. Compare:

- **All (of) the towns** had their electricity cut off. (= every town in an area) *and*
- After the storm, **whole towns** were left without electricity. (= some towns were completely affected; note that we don't say '... whole the towns ...')

D Every and each

Often we can use **every** or **each** with little difference in meaning. However, we use **every** –

☆ with **almost**, **virtually**, etc. + noun to emphasise we are talking about a group as a whole:
- *Almost* **every** visitor stopped and stared. (*not* Almost each visitor ...)

☆ with a plural noun when **every** is followed by a number:
- I go to the dentist **every** six months. (*rather than* ... each six months.)

☆ with abstract uncountable nouns such as **chance**, **confidence**, **hope**, **reason**, and **sympathy** to show a positive attitude to what we are saying. Here **every** means 'complete' or 'total':
- She has **every** *chance* of success in her application for the job.

☆ in phrases referring to regular or repeated events such as: **every other (kilometre)**, **every single (day)**, **every so often**, **every few (months)**, and **every now and again** (= occasionally).

We use **each** –

☆ before a noun or **one** to talk about both people or things in a pair:
- I only had two suitcases, but **each** one weighed over 20 kilos.

☆ as a pronoun:
- I asked many people and **each** gave the same answer. (*or* ... **each / every** one gave ...)

Exercises

51.1 **Put all in the more appropriate space in each sentence.** A

1 They .... were .... sitting around the table waiting for me.
2 You .... can .... stay for dinner if you want.
3 It .... had .... happened so quickly, I couldn't remember much about it.
4 We .... are .... going to be late if we don't hurry.
5 .... the children .... started to speak at once.
6 We have .... been .... involved in the decision.

51.2 **Underline the more appropriate answer. If both are possible, underline them both.** C

1 *All the process / The whole process* takes only a few minutes.
2 *All areas of the country / Whole areas of the country* have been devastated by the floods, although others haven't had rain for months.
3 *All the trip / The whole trip* cost me less than $1,000.
4 The new rail network links *all of the towns / whole towns* in the region.
5 When I picked up the book I found that *all of the pages / whole pages* had been ripped out. There wasn't a single one left.
6 The new heating system makes *all the building / the whole building* warmer.
7 *All the room / The whole room* was full of books.

51.3 **Complete these sentences with every or each, whichever is more appropriate. If you can use either every or each, write them both.** D

1 I had .... reason to believe that she would keep my secret.
2 The ten lucky winners will .... receive £1,000.
3 We've discussed the problem in virtually .... meeting for the last year.
4 Hugh sends us a postcard from .... place he visits.
5 In a rugby league game .... side has 13 players.
6 They had to take out .... single part of the engine and clean it.
7 Antibiotics were given to .... child in the school as a precaution.
8 The two girls walked in, ... one carrying a bouquet of flowers.
9 .... household in the country is to be sent a booklet giving advice on first aid.
10 You should take two tablets .... four hours.

51.4 **Find any mistakes in the italicised parts of this blog post and suggest corrections.** A–D

(1) *Each so often* I like to invite (2) *my entire family* – my parents, six brothers and their families – over for dinner on Saturday evening. My parents are quite old now, so I like to see them (3) *each few weeks*. It's quite a lot of work and I usually spend (4) *all Friday* shopping and cooking. Some of my family are fussy about what they eat, so I generally have to cook different things for (5) *every of them*. Fortunately, (6) *all the food doesn't usually get eaten*, so I have plenty left for the rest of the week. (7) *None of my brothers always come*, but the ones who live locally usually do. Last Saturday (8) *Neil and his family all were on holiday* so they couldn't make it. Anyway, (9) *the rest of us had all a great time* and we spent (10) *the whole evening* talking about when we were children.

Unit 52

Few, little, less, fewer

A

We often use **(a) few** and **(a) little** with nouns. However, we can also use them as pronouns:

Reminder ➜ 147–152

- It is a part of the world visited by **few**. (= few people)
- Do you want a chocolate? There's still **a few** left. (= a few chocolates)
- **Little** is known about the painter's early life.
- 'Do you know anything about car engines?' '**A little**.' (= I know a little about car engines)

Note that **quite a few** means 'quite a large number':

- She's been away from work for **quite a few** weeks.

B

We can use **the few** and **the little** followed by a noun to suggest 'not enough' when we talk about a group of things or people (with **few**) or part of a group or amount (with **little**):

- It's one of **the few** shops in the city centre where you can buy food.
- We should use **the little** time we have available to discuss Jon's proposal.

Instead of **the few / little** we can use **what few / little** to mean 'the small (number / amount)':

- She gave **what little** money she had in her purse to the man. (*or* ... **the little** money ...)
- **What few** visitors we have are always made welcome. (*or* **The few** visitors ...)

Note that we can also say 'She gave **what / the little** she had ...' and '**What / The few** we have ...' when it is clear from the context what is being referred to.

We can use **few** (but rarely **little**) after personal pronouns (**my**, **her**, etc.) and **these** and **those**:

- I learned to play golf during **my few** days off during the summer.
- **These few** miles of motorway have taken over ten years to build.

C

In speech and informal writing, we use **not many / much** or **only / just** ... **a few / little** to talk about a small amount or number, and we often use **a bit (of)** instead of **a little**:

- Sorry I haven't finished, I **haven't** had **much** time today. (*rather than* ... I had little time ...)
- I won't be long. I've **only** got **a few** things to get. (*rather than* ... I've got few things ...)
- Want **a bit** of chocolate? (*rather than* ... a little chocolate?)

In more formal contexts, such as academic writing, we generally prefer **few** and **little**:

- The results take **little** account of personal preference. (*rather than* ... don't take much ...)

D

Less (than) and fewer (than)

We use **less** with uncountable nouns and **fewer** with plural countable nouns:

- You should eat **less pasta**.
- There are **fewer cars** on the road today.

Less is sometimes used with a plural countable noun (e.g. ... **less cars** ...), particularly in conversation. However, this is grammatically incorrect.

We use **less than** with a noun phrase indicating an amount and **fewer than** with a noun phrase referring to a group of things or people:

- I used to earn **less than** *a pound a week* when I first started work.
- There were **fewer than** *20 students* at the lecture. (*or informally* ... **less than** ...; but note that some people think this use of 'less than' is incorrect)

When we talk about a distance or a sum of money we use **less than**, not **fewer than**:

- The beach is **less than** a mile away.

To emphasise that a number is surprisingly large we can use **no less than** or **no fewer than**:

- The team has had **no fewer than** ten managers in just five years. (*or* ... **no less than** ...)

Note that we prefer **no less than** with percentages, periods of time and quantities:

- Profits have increased by **no less than** 95% in the last year. (*rather than* ... no fewer than ...)

Exercises

52.1 **Complete the sentences with (a) few, (a) little, the few, the little, what few or what little, giving alternatives where possible.** A & B

1 Thomas was named sportsperson of the year, and .... would disagree.
2 .... remains of the old castle walls except the Black Gate.
3 She called her .... remaining relatives together and told them she was leaving.
4 Simpson is among .... foreign journalists allowed into the country.
5 A: Has my explanation helped? B: .... , yes.
6 .... belongings she had were packed into a small suitcase.
7 Maya hasn't been looking well recently, and I'm .... worried about her.
8 A: Have there been many applications for the job? B: Yes, quite ....
9 The children weren't well so I had to take .... days off.
10 I don't have much money, but I'm happy to lend you .... I have.

52.2 **Suggest changes to the italicised text in these examples from conversations (1–4) and from academic writing (5–8).** C

1 A: Did you do anything last night? B: I just watched *a little TV* and then went to bed.
2 Take some sweets if you want, although *there are few left*.
3 I've tried to help her, but *there's little more* I can do.
4 See that old car over there? There's *few like that* left now.
5 The country *hasn't had many* female politicians since independence.
6 It is thought that the two leaders *didn't exchange many words* on their first meeting.
7 Teachers were found to be *a bit more confident* after the extra training.
8 *There doesn't seem to be much prospect* of ever recovering the missing manuscript.

52.3 **A survey of British university students was conducted in 2000 and recently repeated. Some of the results are given below. Comment on them in sentences using fewer (than) or less (than).** D

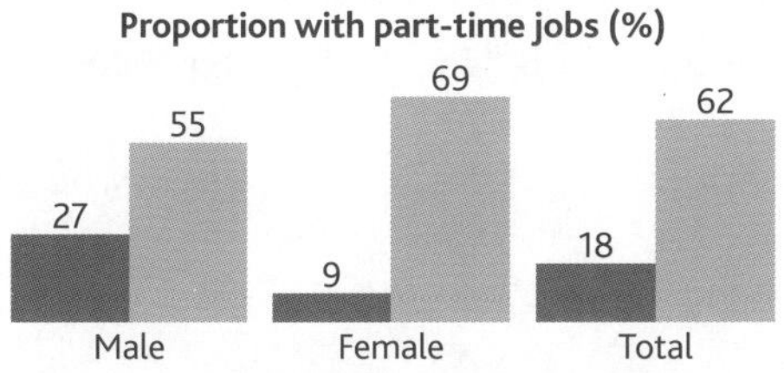

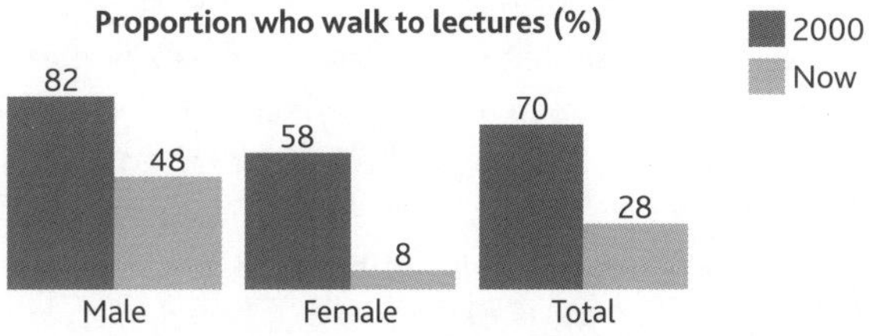

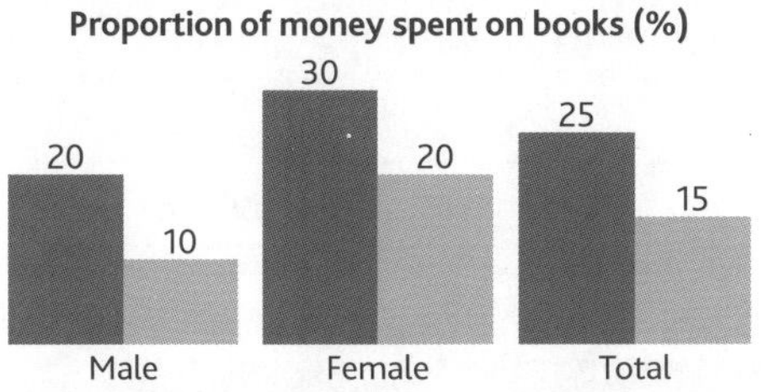

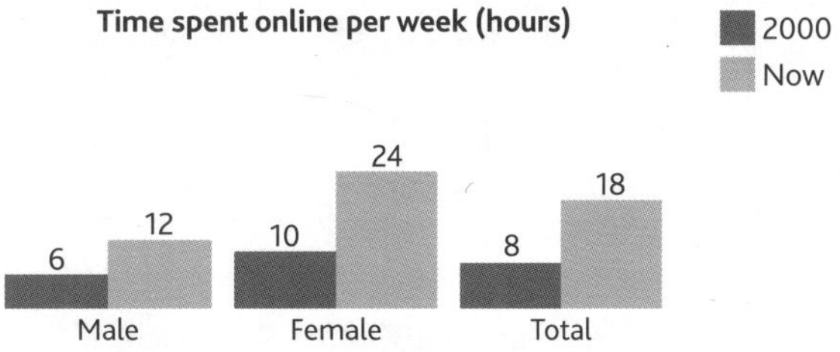

1 Proportion with part-time jobs (%)
Fewer students had a part-time job in 2000 than now.
2 Proportion of money spent on books (%)
3 Proportion who walk to lectures (%)
4 Time spent online per week (hours)

Are there any results that surprise you? Comment on them using no less than or no fewer than.

Unit 53 Relative pronouns

A

Defining and *non-defining relative clauses* begin with a *relative pronoun*, which can sometimes be omitted:

Reminder ➜ J1–J5

- We went to a beach (**which / that**) Ali had recommended to us.

Here the relative pronoun refers to 'a beach', and the subject of the relative clause is 'Ali'. Compare:

- I know a man **who / that** ran in the New York Marathon last year.

where the relative pronoun refers to 'a man', and the subject of the relative clause is also 'a man'. In this case, the relative pronoun can't be omitted.

B

Relative pronouns are used to add information in *defining relative clauses* as follows:

adding information about things

subject	**which**	**that**	
object	**which**	**that**	no relative pronoun

adding information about people

subject	**who**	**that**		
object	**who**	**that**	no relative pronoun	**whom**

☆ When we add information about things, we can use **that** (or **no relative pronoun**) as object in conversation and **which** in more formal contexts:

- Decorating's a job (**that**) I hate. (*rather than* '... which ...' in this informal context)

☆ When we add information about people, we generally prefer **that** (or **no relative pronoun**) as object in informal contexts rather than **who** or **whom**:

- He's the man (**that**) I met at Aisha's party (*rather than* ... who / whom I met ...)

☆ **whom** is very formal and rarely used in spoken English:

- The boy **whom** Elena had shouted at smiled. (*less formally* **that**, **no relative pronoun** *or* **who**)

☆ We use **that** as subject after: **something** and **anything**; words such as **all**, **little**, **much**, and **none** used as pronouns; and noun phrases that include superlatives. **Which** is also used as subject after **something** and **anything**, but less commonly:

- These walls are *all* **that** *remain* of the city. (*not* ... which remain of the city.)

☆ Note that we can use **that** (or **no relative pronoun**) as object after **something / anything**; **all**, etc.; and noun phrases with superlatives. For example:

- She's one of *the kindest* people (**that**) I know. (*not* ... one of the kindest people who I know.)

C

Relative pronouns are used to add information in *non-defining relative clauses* as follows:

adding information about things

subject	**which**	**that**
object	**which**	**that**

adding information about people

subject	**who**	
object	**who**	**whom**

☆ Note that we must include a relative pronoun in a non-defining relative clause.

☆ We can use **who** or **whom** as object, although **whom** is very formal:

- Professor Johnson, **who(m)** I have long admired, is to visit the university next week.

☆ When we add information about things, we can use **which** as subject or object. **That** is sometimes used instead of **which**, but some people think this is incorrect:

- The Master's course, **which** I took in 2001, is no longer taught. (*or* ... **that** I took ...)

Exercises

53.1 Put brackets around the italicised relative pronoun if it can be omitted. A

1 We talked about the party *which* Natalia wants to organise for my birthday.
2 To get to Maxim's house, take the main road *that* bypasses the village.
3 The paintings *which* Mr Flowers has in his house are worth around £100,000.
4 Let's go through the main points *that* he made in his lecture.
5 He received a low mark for his essay, *which* was only one page long.
6 Mrs Yang, *who* is 42, has three children.
7 Dev is a friend *who* we stayed with in Australia.
8 In the shop window there's a sign *that* says '10% off'.
9 The couple *who* live next to us have 16 grandchildren.
10 There was little *that* we could do to help her.

53.2 Rewrite these sentences including the information in brackets as relative clauses (defining or non-defining). Give alternative relative pronouns if possible. (Use (–) to indicate 'no relative pronoun'.) B & C

1 Oliver said something. (I couldn't hear it clearly) Oliver said something that / which / – I couldn't hear clearly.
2 Eva's father has just come back from a skiing holiday. (he is over 80)
....
3 The problems faced by the company are being resolved. (I'll look at these in detail in a moment)
....
4 She was greatly influenced by her father. (she adored him)
....
5 He pointed to the stairs. (they led down to the cellar)
....
6 These drugs have been withdrawn from sale. (they are used to treat stomach ulcers)
....
7 The singer had to cancel her concert. (she was recovering from flu)
....
8 The minister talked about the plans for tax reform. (he will reveal them next month)
....
9 I have two older sisters. (I love them very much)
....

53.3 If necessary, correct or make improvements to these sentences. If they are already correct, write ✓. A–C

1 There's something which I should tell you.
2 The doctor whom Ingrid went to see was very thorough.
3 Yesterday was the hottest day I can remember.
4 There isn't much can go wrong with the machine.
5 Thieves whom stole paintings from Notford art gallery have been arrested in Paris.
6 It may be the most important decision which you will ever take.
7 The boy took the photograph was paid £100.
8 I heard many different accents in the room, but none which I could identify as Polish.
9 He just said anything which came into his head.
10 There's this dream which I have every night about falling downstairs.

➔ **Additional exercise 11** (page 247)

Unit 54

Other relative words: **whose, when, whereby**, etc.

A Clauses with whose

Reminder ➜ J1–J5

We use a relative clause beginning with the relative pronoun **whose** + **noun**, particularly in written English, when we talk about something belonging to or associated with a person, animal or plant:

- Stevenson is an architect **whose designs** have won international praise.
- Suzy was taking care of a dog **whose ears** were badly damaged in a fight with a cat.

We can use **whose** in both *defining* and *non-defining relative clauses*.

We generally avoid using **whose** to talk about something belonging to or associated with a *thing*:

- I received a letter, and its poor spelling made me think it was written by a child. (*more natural than* I received a letter, **whose** poor spelling made me think ...)

However, we sometimes use **whose** when we talk about towns, countries, or organisations:

- The film was made in *Botswana*, **whose wildlife parks** are larger than those in Kenya.
- We need to learn from *companies* **whose trading** is healthier than our own.

In academic writing **whose** is used to talk about a wide variety of 'belonging to' relationships:

- Students have to solve *problems* **whose** solutions require a knowledge of calculus.

B Clauses with when, whereby, where and why

We can begin relative and other clauses with **when** (referring to time), **whereby** (method or means; used mainly in formal contexts), and **where** (location). In formal English in particular, a phrase with **preposition** + **which** can often be used instead of these:

- The camera records the time **when** the photo is taken. (*or* ... the time **at which** ...)
- Do you know the date **when** we have to hand in the essay? (*or* ... the date **on / by which** ...)
- We need to develop a system **whereby** workers and management can communicate more effectively. (*or* ... the system **in / by which** workers ...)
- This was the place **where** we first met. (*or* ... the place **at / in which** we ...)

In academic English, we can also use **where** to refer to features other than location, particularly after words such as **case**, **condition**, **example**, **situation**, **system**:

- Later in this chapter we will introduce *cases* **where** consumer complaints have resulted in changes in the law. (*or more formally* ... cases **in which** ...)

We can also use **a / the reason why** or **a / the reason that** or just **a / the reason**:

- I didn't get a pay rise, but this wasn't **the reason why** I left. (*or* ... **the reason** (**that**) I left.)

C Clauses with who and what; whatever, whoever and whichever

Some clauses beginning with a **wh-word** are used like a noun phrase in a sentence. These are sometimes called *nominal relative clauses*:

- Can you give me a list of **who's** been invited? (= the people who have been invited)
- I didn't know **what** I should do next. (= the thing that I should do next)

Note that we can't use **what** in this way after a noun:

- I managed to get all the *books* **that** you asked for. (*not* ... all the books what you asked for.)

We use clauses beginning with **whatever** (= anything *or* it doesn't matter what), **whoever** (= the person / group who *or* any person / group who), or **whichever** (= one thing or person from a limited number), to talk about things or people that are indefinite or unknown:

- I'm sure I'll enjoy eating **whatever** you cook.
- **Whoever** wins will go on to play Barcelona in the final.
- **Whichever** one of you broke the window will have to pay for it.

Exercises

54.1 **Combine a sentence from (i) with a sentence from (ii) to make new sentences with whose.** A

(i)	(ii)
1 Dr Rowan has had to do all her own typing.	a Its chairperson is Miss Jiu Kim.
2 The newspaper is owned by the Mears group.	b Their diets contain high levels of protein.
3 Parents are being asked to take part in the survey.	c Their flowers are attractive to bees.
4 Children do better in examinations.	d ~~Her secretary resigned two weeks ago.~~
5 My aunt is now CEO of a department store.	e Her first job was filling shelves in a supermarket.
6 I enjoy growing plants.	f Their children are between four and six.

1 + d Dr Rowan, whose secretary resigned two weeks ago, has had to do all her own typing.

54.2 **Define the words using whose (1–3) and in which (4–6). You may need to use a dictionary.** A & B

1 A lexicographer is a person whose job is to write dictionaries.
2 A widow is a woman ....
3 An actuary is a person ....
4 A furnace is a container ....
5 A gazebo is a small garden building ....
6 Polo is ....

54.3 **Complete these sentences using phrases from the box and when, whereby, where or why.** B

the area **an agreement** **a condition** **a method** **the moment** **the reason**

1 Sunset is defined in astronomy as .... the whole of the sun's disc disappears below the horizon.
2 In 1951, China and the Soviet Union signed .... China provided uranium ore in exchange for technical assistance.
3 The coastline is .... the land meets the sea or ocean.
4 The river is prone to sudden flooding which is .... there are no major towns along its banks.
5 Freeze-drying is .... water is rapidly evaporated from frozen food in order to preserve it.
6 Hypoglycaemia is .... the level of sugar in the blood drops suddenly.

54.4 **If the italicised word is correct, write ✓. If not, suggest another word.** C

1 I think *whatever* was responsible for damaging the trees should be fined or sent to prison.
2 Do they really understand *that* they are doing?
3 I don't envy *whoever* buys that house. It's in a terrible condition.
4 Now that I no longer have to wear a school uniform, I'll be able to wear *which* I want.
5 I think the government should improve the health service, *whichever* the cost.
6 It's a question *that* I've been asking for many years.
7 The clock makes a noise *what* keeps me awake at night.
8 I'm sure that Rashid will do well at university, *which* one he goes to.

→ **Additional exercise 11** (page 247)

Unit 55

Prepositions in relative clauses

A

In formal styles **noun + of which** is often preferred to –

Reminder ➜ J1–J5

☆ **whose + noun**:

- A huge amount of oil was spilled, *the effects* **of which** are still being felt. (*or* … **whose** *effects* are still being felt.)

☆ **that / which … of** in relative clauses:

- The school **of which** she is head is closing. (*less formally* The school **(that / which)** she is head **of** is closing.)

After **both** we can use **of which** and **of whose**, but not usually **which** or **whose**:

- Lotta was able to switch between German and Russian, **both of which** she spoke fluently. (*not* … both which she spoke fluently.)

Also after: **all**, **each**, **many**, **most**, **neither**, **none**, **part**, **some**, **a number** (one, two, etc.; the first, the second, etc.; half, a third, etc.), and **superlatives** (the best, the biggest, etc.)

B

In formal, mainly written, English **whose** can come after a preposition in a relative clause. Putting the preposition at the end of the clause is more natural in informal and spoken English:

- I now turn to Freud, **from whose** work the following quotation is taken. (*less formally* … Freud, **whose** work the following quotation is taken **from**.)

C

When a preposition is needed with the relative pronouns **which** and **whom** we usually put it before the relative pronoun in formal styles:

- The rate **at which** a material heats up depends on its chemical composition.
- There are 80 teachers in the Physics Department, **among whom** 24 are professors.

After a preposition we usually use **whom** rather than **who** in formal styles:

- Is it right that politicians should make important decisions without consulting the public **to whom** they are accountable? (*rather than* … the public to who they are accountable.)

and we don't use **that** or **no relative pronoun**:

- The valley **in which** the town lies is heavily polluted. (*not* The valley in that the town lies is heavily polluted.; *not* The valley in the town lies is heavily polluted.)

In less formal English we usually put the preposition later in the relative clause:

- The office **that** Juan took us **to** was filled with books. (*rather than* The office **to which** Juan took us …)

and we prefer **who** (or **that**) rather than **whom** (see also Unit 26A):

- The playground wasn't used by the children **who** it was built **for**.

D

If the verb in the relative clause is a two-word verb (e.g. **come across**, **fill in**, **look after**, **take on**) we don't usually put the preposition before the relative pronoun:

- The Roman coins, **which** a local farmer **came across** in a field, are now on display in the National Museum. (*not* … coins, across which the local farmer came, are …)

With three-word verbs, we only put the preposition before the relative pronoun in a very formal or literary style, and many people avoid this pattern:

- She is one of the few people **to whom** I **look up**. (*or less formally* … **who** I **look up to**.)

Exercises

55.1 **Rewrite these sentences so that they are more appropriate for formal written English. Use preposition + which or preposition + whose, as appropriate.** A & B

1 Fleming's discovery of penicillin, which he was awarded the Nobel Prize for, had a major influence on the lives of people in the 20th century. *Fleming's discovery of penicillin, for which he was awarded the Nobel Prize, had a major influence on the lives of people in the 20th century.*
2 He was the uncle of Anne Boleyn, whose execution in 1536 he lost power after.
3 It is her unmarried name which she is better known by.
4 Mr Wang, whose land the road will be built across, is unhappy about the plans.
5 The election result, which there can be no doubt about, is a great disappointment.
6 The building which Marcus emerged from was little more than a ruin.
7 It is a medieval palace, whose tower the king hid in during the civil war.
8 I am grateful to Aarav Basu, whose book on the history of the bicycle this information comes from.

55.2 **Complete the sentences using the endings from the box and which or whom after an appropriate preposition.** C

the furniture is to be delivered.	**she was divorced in 2005.**	**he had shown his novel.**
~~I had great respect.~~	**it was named.**	**the printer was supplied.**
most world trade was conducted.	**you should be aware.**	

1 My Maths teacher, Mr Kato, was someone *for whom I had great respect.*
2 Until 1914 the pound sterling was the currency ....
3 They have changed the date ....
4 Pasteurisation was discovered by the French chemist Louis Pasteur, ...
5 He was persuaded to stay in England by Charles Dickens, ...
6 There are a number of safety procedures ....
7 Details are in the instruction manual ....
8 Ms Park was left the money by her former husband, ...

55.3 **Rewrite the sentences from 55.2 in a less formal way, putting the preposition at the end of the relative clause.** A

1 *My Maths teacher, Mr Kato, was someone who / that / – I had great respect for.*

55.4 **If necessary, suggest corrections or improvements to these sentences or write ✓ if they are already correct.** A, C & D

1 The house into which the thieves broke is owned by Caleb Cruz.
2 The school has been given 20 laptops, half of which are brand new.
3 JKL Motorbikes sells six different models, the first which they started making in 1985.
4 The party, to which I've been looking forward all week, is at Maxine's house.
5 The water that she fell into was freezing cold.
6 I have heard her on the violin and clarinet, both which she plays extremely well.
7 The film was made at Tulloch Castle, part which dates back to 1466.
8 The college is home to 30 students from Nepal, almost all of who are studying economics.

→ Additional exercise 11 (page 247)

Unit 56 Other ways of adding information to noun phrases 1: additional noun phrases, etc.

A

We sometimes add information about a person or thing referred to in one noun phrase by talking about the same person or thing in a different way in a following noun phrase:

- *A hooded cobra*, *one of the world's most dangerous snakes*, has escaped from Dudley Zoo.
- *Dr Alex Parr*, *director of the State Museum*, is to become the government's arts adviser.

In writing, the items are usually separated by a comma, and in speech they are often separated by a pause or other intonation break. However, when the second item acts like a defining relative clause, when it is usually a name, there is usually no punctuation in writing or intonation break in speech:

- *My friend Mia* has moved to Sweden. (*rather than* My friend, Mia, …)
- The current champion is expected to survive her first-round match with *the Italian Silvia Farina*. (*rather than* … the Italian, Silvia Farina.)

B

We can add information to a noun phrase with a conjunction such as **and** or **or**:

- Kurt Svensson, her teacher **and** *well-known concert pianist*, thinks that she has great talent. (= her teacher is also a well-known concert pianist)
- Phonetics **or** *the study of speech sounds* is a common component on courses in teaching English as a foreign language.

C

The adverb **namely** and the phrase **that is** are used to add details about a noun phrase:

- This side effect of the treatment, **namely** *weight gain*, is counteracted with other drugs.
- The main cause of global warming, **that is** *the burning of fossil fuels*, is to be the focus of negotiations at the international conference.

D

We can also add information to a noun phrase using a participle clause beginning with an **-ing**, **-ed** or **being** + **-ed** verb form. These are often similar to *defining relative clauses*:

- The people ***living*** *next door* come from Italy. (*or* The people who are living next door …)
- The weapon ***used*** *in the murder* has now been found. (*or* The weapon that was used ...)
- The prisoners ***being released*** are all women. (*or* The prisoners who are being released …)

Note that **-ing** participle clauses correspond to defining relative clauses with an active verb, while **-ed** and **being** + **-ed** clauses correspond to defining relative clauses with a passive verb.

We can also use a **to-infinitive clause**, as in:

- Have you brought a book **to read**?
- My decision **to resign** *from the company* was made after a great deal of thought.
- I thought that the management's offer, **to increase** *staff holidays*, was a good one.

E

In written English, particularly in newspapers, **-ing** and **-ed clauses** are also used instead of *non-defining relative clauses*. These are usually written between commas or dashes (–):

- The men, *wearing anoraks and hats*, made off in a stolen Volvo estate.

- The proposals – *expected to be agreed by ministers* – are less radical than many employers had feared.

Exercises

56.1 **Add the information in brackets to the sentences and rewrite them in an appropriate way, using the examples in A and B as models.** A & B

1. Gofast Technology has launched its new generation of high-speed trains. *(Gofast Technology is part of the Maddison Enterprises Group)*
   Gofast Technology, part of the Maddison Enterprises Group, has launched its new generation of high-speed trains.
2. I went on an IT training course with my colleague. *(My colleague is Mateo)*
3. Rubella is still a common childhood disease in many countries. *(Another name for rubella is German measles)*
4. Four kilos of Beluga caviar has been ordered for the reception. *(Beluga caviar is among the most expensive foods in the world)*
5. One of the most popular modern writers for children is John Marsden. *(John Marsden is Australian)*
6. Tonya's father was in the crowd to watch her victory. *(Tonya's father has also been her trainer for the last ten years)*
7. Dr Sofia Lopez has criticised government plans to cut health funding. *(Sofia Lopez is head of Downlands Hospital)*
8. Klaus Schmidt is running in the Stockholm Marathon. *(Klaus Schmidt is the current European champion) (The German 10,000 metres record holder is also the current European champion)*

56.2 **Make sentences by matching the beginnings (in i) to the endings (in ii) and adding appropriate information (from iii) after namely or that is.** C

(i)

1. Leo Tolstoy's most celebrated novel,
2. The two countries having land borders with the USA,
3. The three most popular pets in Britain,
4. The capital of Estonia,
5. The largest island in the world,
6. The 'consumers' of education,

(ii)

a. are found in 25% of households.
b. covers over 2 million square kilometres.
c. should have ways of complaining about poor teaching.
d. have complained to the President about the new customs regulations.
e. ~~was published in 1869.~~
f. is situated on the Gulf of Finland.

(iii)

Tallinn **students**
cats, dogs and rabbits
~~**War and Peace**~~
Mexico and Canada
Greenland

1 + e Leo Tolstoy's most celebrated novel, namely War and Peace, was published in 1869.

56.3 **Complete the sentences with an -ing, -ed or being + -ed form of the verbs from the box. Then rewrite each sentence using a relative clause instead of the participle clause.** D

~~drive~~ educate flow introduce need print say tell off

1. The man driving the bus is my brother. The man who is driving the bus is my brother.
2. I went to a reunion for students .... in the physics department during the 1990s.
3. As my aunt told me what she thought, I felt like a schoolboy .... by his headteacher.
4. There is a sign on the gate .... 'Entry forbidden'.
5. Across the river were some of the deer .... into the park in the 19th century.
6. Rivers .... into the Baltic Sea are much cleaner now than ten years ago.
7. The booklets .... as we speak will be on sale later this afternoon.
8. Anyone .... further information can see me in my office.

Unit 57 Other ways of adding information to noun phrases 2: prepositional phrases, etc.

A

We commonly add information about a thing or person using a prepositional phrase. Often these have a meaning similar to a relative clause:

- What's the name of the *man* **by** the window? (*or* … the man **who's** by the window?)
- It's in the *cupboard* **under** the stairs. (*or* … the cupboard **that's** under the stairs.)
- She lives in the *house* **with** the red door. (*or* … the house **which has** the red door.)

In some cases, however, these prepositional phrases do not have a corresponding relative clause:

- You need to keep a careful *record* **of** what you spend.
- There is likely to be an *increase* **in** temperature tomorrow.

We often prefer a relative clause rather than a prepositional phrase in non-defining relative clauses with **be + preposition** or with **have** as a main verb:

- *Mr Chen*, **who was in** the store at the time of the robbery, was able to identify two of the men. (*rather than* … Mr Chen, in the store …)
- *Davide Gallo*, **who has** a farm near Pisa, has decided to grow only organic vegetables. (*rather than* Davide Gallo, with a farm near Pisa, has …)

B

In written English, particularly in academic writing, a series of prepositional phrases and relative clauses is often used to add information about a previous noun phrase. Note that prepositional phrases can also be used with an adverbial function (e.g. '… taken the drug *in the last six months*' in the sentence below):

- Doctors are contacting patients with diabetes who have taken the drug in the last six months.
- Scientists in Spain who have developed the technique are optimistic that it will be widely used in laboratories within the next decade.

We can also use participle clauses and noun phrases (see Unit 56) in a series of clauses / phrases which add information to the preceding noun phrase:

- The waxwing is the only bird found in Britain with yellow and red tail feathers.
- Mr Bob Timms, leader of the Democratic Party, MP for Threeoaks, has announced his resignation.

C

Note that adding a series of prepositional phrases can often lead to ambiguity. For example:

- The protesters were demonstrating against the mistreatment of animals on farms.

could mean either that the place the protesters were demonstrating was 'on farms' or that the animals were 'on farms'. We could make the sentence unambiguous with, for example:

- The protesters were demonstrating on farms against the mistreatment of animals. *or*
- The protesters were demonstrating against the mistreatment of animals kept on farms.

Exercises

57.1 Match the sentence halves (there may be more than one possible answer), adding an appropriate preposition. A

1 Maja's the girl ...
2 She's in the photograph ...
3 I plan to cut down the tree ...
4 There's a team of people ...
5 We took the footpath ...
6 The children can't get over the fence ...
7 Go along the lane ...
8 Nico's a boy...
9 Follow the main road...
10 She's a teacher...

a ... green shirts.
b ... the back garden.
c ~~... blonde hair.~~
d ... the canal.
e ... the piano.
f ... Paris to Lyons.
g ... the houses.
h ... New Zealand.
i ... the pool.
j ... a quick temper.

1 + c *Maja's the girl with blonde hair.*

57.2 Rewrite the sentences in 57.1 using defining relative clauses. A

1 *Maja's the girl who has blonde hair.*

57.3 Complete the sentences by adding the information in brackets. Use relative clauses (Unit 53), additional noun phrases and participle clauses (Unit 56) and prepositional phrases (Unit 57).

1 Police are questioning men ... *between 25 and 30 living in the village, who are known to have a criminal record.*
(The men are between 25 and 30. They live in the village. They are known to have a criminal record.)

2 Teachers ....
....
(The teachers work at Queen's College. Queen's College is in the city centre. The teachers went on strike last week. They have appointed Kristina Borg as their spokesperson. She is the head of English.)

3 Marge Scott ....
....
(Marge Scott has died. She was aged 95. She was educated at Marston College. She was the first woman to be educated there. Marston College is in south Wales.)

4 The conference ....
....
(The conference was held in Singapore. It approved the world trade agreement. The agreement was drawn up by European and Asian states. The conference has now ended.)

5 A book ....
....
(The book is on gardening. It is called All about Plants. *Anna wanted to borrow it. It wasn't available in the library.)*

6 A painting ....
....
(The painting was found in a second-hand shop. It was found by Lara Gruber. She is an antique dealer. She is from Austria. The painting is thought to be by J.M.W. Turner. Turner was a British landscape artist.)

57.4 Why are these sentences ambiguous? Can you rewrite them to remove the ambiguity? C

1 A man was talking with a grey suit. ....
2 A lorry was stopped by a police officer carrying thousands of stolen cigarettes. ....
....
3 I discussed my plan to decorate the room with my parents. ....
....

Unit 58

Participle clauses with adverbial meaning 1

A

We can use **present participle (-ing)** and **past participle (-ed) clauses** with an adverbial meaning. (See also Unit 59.) They often give information about the timing, causes, and results of the events described:

Reminder → J6–J10

- *Opening her eyes*, the baby began to cry. (= When she opened her eyes ...)
- *Faced with a bill for £10,000*, Ivan has taken an extra job. (= Because he is faced ...)
- *Looked after carefully*, the plant can live through the winter. (= If it is looked after ...)
- *Having finished the book*, I had a holiday. (perfect; = When / Because I had finished ...)
- The fruit was expensive, *being imported*. (simple passive; = ... because it was imported)
- *Having been hunted close to extinction*, the rhino is once again common in this area. (perfect passive; = Although it had been hunted close to extinction ...)

B

The implied subject of a participle clause (that is, a subject known but not directly mentioned) is usually the same as the subject of the main clause:

- *Arriving* at the party, we saw Ruth standing alone. (= When **we** arrived ... **we** saw ...)

However, sometimes the implied subject is not referred to in the main clause:

- *Having wanted* to drive a train all his life, this was an opportunity not to be missed.

In careful speech and writing we avoid different subjects for the participle and main clause:

- Turning round quickly, the door hit me in the face. (first implied subject = 'I'; second subject = 'the door')

would be better as:

- When I turned round quickly, the door hit me in the face.

C

In formal English, the participle clause sometimes has its own subject, which is often a pronoun or includes one:

- The collection of vases is priceless, **some** *being over 2000 years old.*
- **Her voice** *breaking with emotion*, Vasiliki spoke about her father's illness.

We use the present participle (-**ing**) clause to talk about something happening at the same time as an event in the main clause, or to give information about the facts given in the main clause.

D

When we use **not** in a participle clause it usually comes before the participle. However, it can follow the participle, depending on meaning:

- **Not** *understanding* the rules, I found the cricket match boring. (= because I didn't understand the rules)
- *Hoping* **not** to be recognised, I chose a seat in a dark corner. (= I hoped that I wouldn't be recognised)

E

We use a clause beginning with **having + past participle** rather than a present participle if the action in the main clause is the consequence of the event in the participle clause:

- **Having broken** her leg the last time she went, Giorgia decided not to go on the school skiing trip this year. (*or* **After breaking** her leg ...; *not* Breaking her leg ...)

We can use either a **present participle (-ing)** clause or a **having** + **past participle** clause with a similar meaning when the action in the participle clause is complete before the action in the main clause begins. Compare:

- **Taking off** his shoes, Ram walked into the house. (*Having taken off* ... has a similar meaning) *and*
- **Running** across the field, I fell and hurt my ankle. (= While I was running ...; 'Having run ...' would suggest that I fell *after* I had run across the field)

Exercises

58.1 **Rewrite the sentences beginning with one of the clause forms from sections A and D opposite.** A & D

1 When she saw the dog coming towards her, she quickly crossed the road. *Seeing the dog coming towards her, she quickly crossed the road.*
2 As she was dressed all in black, she was almost invisible in the starless night.
3 As I don't have a credit card, I found it difficult to book an airline ticket online.
4 Antonio spent a lot of time filling in job application forms because he was unemployed.
5 Because I was walking quickly, I soon caught up with her.
6 The house was built of wood, so it was clearly a fire risk.
7 I was eager to catch the bus in good time because I had been told off the day before for arriving late.
8 She didn't know where the theatre was, so she asked for directions at the hotel reception.
9 As she was a nurse, she knew what to do after the accident.
10 He had spent his childhood in Oslo, so he knew the city well.

58.2 **If the implied subject of the two clauses is the same write S and if it is different write D. Rewrite the D sentences to make them more acceptable.** B

1 Waiting for the bus, a car went through a puddle and splashed water all over me.
2 Known mainly as a writer of novels, Rashid has now written a successful biography.
3 Keeping a careful eye on the spider, Suzanne hurried out of the bathroom.
4 Looking down from the hill, the town spread out before us towards the coast.
5 Feeling rather sick, the boat ploughed through the huge waves.
6 Found only in the Andes, the plant is used by local people to treat skin diseases.

58.3 **Write not in the more appropriate place in each sentence.** D

1 .... wishing .... to boast, she said nothing about her success.
2 .... pretending .... to notice that people were staring at me, I carried on looking on the floor for my lost contact lens.
3 .... determined .... to be beaten, she put all her energy into the serve.
4 .... feeling .... well, she went home early.
5 .... bothering .... to put on his coat, he left the house.
6 .... trying .... to cry, she waved to Harun as the train pulled out.

58.4 **Join these sentences using having + past participle or the -ing form of the first verb. Which sentences can have either form?** E

1 I moved house recently.
2 I looked over my shoulder.
3 I walked through the tunnel.
4 I waited six weeks for the washing machine to be delivered.
5 I suffered from depression myself as a teenager.
6 I parked the car about a kilometre from the stadium.
7 I reached my mid-thirties.
8 I learned some Swahili as a child.

a I decided to cancel the order.
b I felt I needed to change my life.
c I could see Ida running after me.
d ~~I don't yet have internet access.~~
e I was able to understand most of what she said.
f I banged my head on the low roof.
g I could understand how Nathan was feeling.
h I walked the rest of the way.

1 + d *Having moved house recently, I don't yet have internet access.*

Unit 59

Participle clauses with adverbial meaning 2

Reminder ➜ J6–J10

A

We can use prepositions such as **after**, **before**, **besides**, **by**, **in**, **on**, **since**, **through**, **while**, **with**, and **without** in a present participle (**-ing**) clause with an adverbial meaning (see also Unit 58):

- **While understanding** her problem, I don't know how I can help. (= Although I understand ...)
- **After spending** so much money on the car, I can't afford a holiday.
- **Before being changed** last year, the speed limit was 70 kph. (passive form)

An alternative is a clause with a verb that can change according to tense and subject. Compare:

- **Since moving** to London, we haven't had time to go to the theatre. *and*
- **Since we moved** to London, we haven't had time to go to the theatre. (less formal)

B

by, in, on + -ing

By working hard, she passed her maths exam. They only survived **by eating** roots and berries in the forest.	= the **-ing clause** indicates 'the method or means used'
On returning from Beijing, he wrote to the Chinese embassy. Josh was the first person I saw **on leaving** hospital.	= the **-ing clause** indicates 'when'
In criticising the painting, I knew I would offend her. **In choosing** Marco, the People's Party has moved to the left.	= the **-ing clause** indicates 'cause'

We can often use **by** + **-ing** or **in** + **-ing** with a similar meaning, although **by** + **-ing** is preferred in informal contexts:

- **In / By writing** about Spanish culture, I came to understand the country better. ('In writing ...' = the consequence of writing was to understand ...; 'By writing ...' = the method I used to understand the country better was to write...)

But compare:

- **By telephoning** every hour, she managed to speak to the doctor. (*not* In telephoning ...; the method is the focus here, not the consequence)

C

with -ing; without -ing

With + **-ing** often introduces a reason for something in the main clause. This use is fairly informal. Note that a subject has to come between **with** and **-ing**:

- **With** Louise **living** in Spain, we don't see her often. (= Because Louise lives in Spain ...)

With and **what with** can also be used with a noun phrase to introduce a reason:

- **With** *my bad back* I won't be able to lift a heavy suitcase.
- **What with** *the traffic* and *the heavy rain*, it's no wonder you were late.

We can use **without** + **-ing** to say that a second action doesn't happen:

- I went to work **without eating** breakfast.
- They left **without paying**.

Often, however, it has a similar meaning to 'although ... not' or 'unless':

- **Without meaning** to, I seem to have offended her. (= Although I didn't mean to ...)
- **Without using** the app, I can't judge how good it is. (= Unless I use the app ...)

D

Adverbial meanings can also be added by a clause beginning with a conjunction or adjective but with no verb. This kind of clause has the same meaning as a clause beginning with a **conjunction** + **subject** + **be** and is used in fairly formal English (more informal alternatives are given in brackets):

- **While in Poland**, they will play two concerts in Warsaw. (*or* **While** they are in Poland ...)
- **Although just two feet apart**, they didn't speak. (*or* **Although** they were just ...)
- I try to use public transport **whenever possible**. (*or* ... **whenever** it is possible.)
- **Unhappy with the decision**, Johnson swore at the referee. (*or* **Because** he was unhappy ...)

Exercises

59.1 **Complete these sentences using a preposition from (i) and the -ing form or being + past participle form of a verb from (ii). You may use the words from (i) more than once.** A

(i)

after	**before**	**since**
through	**while**	

(ii)

~~**come**~~	**interview**	**leave**	**overthrow**
sell	**take**	**welcome**	**work**

1 ...Since coming... out of hospital, I have been to the gym every day.
2 .... on TV last night, the minister mentioned that she would be retiring soon.
3 .... the back off the computer, make sure it is unplugged.
4 .... the government's new policy, I think it should have been introduced months ago.
5 .... in a military takeover, the king has been under house arrest.
6 .... with young children for the last 40 years, she has come to understand their behaviour better than most.
7 .... to the public, most milk is pasteurised.
8 .... Oxford University in 1983, Painter spent three years teaching at a local school.

59.2 **Join the sentences, beginning them with by + -ing, on + -ing, or in + -ing.** B

1 She returned home.
2 She gave up sugar.
3 She turned down the job.
4 She moved to a smaller flat.
5 She entered the classroom.
6 She criticised her father.

a She soon began to lose weight.
b She saved over a hundred pounds a month.
c She knew that she might offend him.
d ~~She found Dave waiting outside her front door.~~
e She gave up the possibility of a huge salary.
f She was surprised when all the children stood up.

1 + d ...On returning home, she found Dave waiting outside her front door....

59.3 **Rewrite these sentences beginning With ... -ing or Without ... -ing.** C

1 We couldn't go on holiday because Maryam had flu.

....

2 I won't be able to advise you unless I have more information.

....

3 He had solved the problem, although he didn't realise it.

....

4 I couldn't wait for Andrei any longer as time was running out before the train left. .

....

59.4 **Revise this biography by replacing six more full clauses with reduced clauses (as in the examples in section D opposite), and making any other necessary changes.** D

Although from a poor background

~~Although she was from a poor background~~, Paula Regis gained a place at Southam University. She was always fascinated by the stars and she took a first degree in astrophysics. Once she was at university she also became interested in student politics and, because she was popular with her fellow students, was elected University President in her second year. This didn't distract her from her studies, however, and while she was in the final year of her degree, she won the International Young Scientist of the Year award for her work on star classification. When she was asked what was the secret of her success she said, 'Just hard work and a little luck.' She is determined to continue her research and she has recently begun work on her PhD.

Unit 60 Reflexive pronouns: **herself**, **himself**, **themselves**, etc.

A

Reminder ➜ K1–K4

In addition to the usual reflexive pronouns (**myself**, **yourself**, etc.) some people use **themselves** to refer to the person who is the subject of the sentence, to avoid saying whether the subject is male or female:

- *The author of the letter* describes **themselves** as 'a senior government official'.
- *Who* wants to go through life by **themselves**, without friends?

Oneself (or less formally **yourself**) is used to refer to people in general:

- I think *one* has to have the courage to be **oneself** and say whatever comes naturally. (*less formally* I think *you* have to have the courage to be **yourself** …)

B

We can use reflexive pronouns for emphasis in various ways. We also use reflexive pronouns to emphasise that the subject caused a certain action. Compare

- Salma worked hard and *got promoted*.
- Salma worked hard and *got* **herself** *promoted*. (emphasises that it was through her own efforts)
- Salma encouraged me to apply for the senior manager position, but she *got promoted* **herself**. (emphasises that Salma got promoted, not me)

C

If the object of a transitive verb refers to the same person or thing as the subject, then that object must be a reflexive pronoun. Compare:

- **He** walked around the golf course to **familiarise** *himself* **with** it. *and*
- **We** walked around to **familiarise** *the children* **with** their new surroundings.

Also: **absent … from, avail … of, busy … with, concern … with, occupy … by / with, pride … on, tear … away from, trouble … about / with**

With some verbs we can use a reflexive pronoun or leave it out with little difference in meaning:

- We are confident that both sets of fans will **behave (themselves)** at the match.

Also: **acclimatise, adapt, (un)dress, hide, move, prepare, shave, wash**

We include the reflexive pronoun if we want to emphasise that the person or thing referred to in the subject is affected by the action:

- Although she helped other athletes in their preparations for competing at high altitudes, she found it difficult to **acclimatise herself**.

D

When the subject and object after a preposition refer to the same person or thing we use a reflexive pronoun after the preposition:

- **He** was pleased *with* **himself**. (*not* … pleased with him.)

If the verb has a direct object we use a personal pronoun, not a reflexive pronoun:

- **I** remember closing *the door behind* **me**. (*not* … closing the door behind myself.)

However, if we need to make it clear that the subject and prepositional phrase refer to the same person or thing, we use a reflexive pronoun after the preposition:

- **She** bought *the bracelet for* **herself**. ('… for her' suggests it was bought for someone else)

E

Myself is sometimes used after **and** and **or** rather than 'I' or 'me', although some people consider this use incorrect and avoid it:

- I believe that Lizi **and myself** have done a pretty good job.
- When you've finished the job can you send the bill either to Mrs Petrov **or myself**?

Using **myself** reduces focus on the speaker or writer and so sounds less forceful or more polite.

Exercises

60.1 **Complete each sentence with a suitable form of a verb from the box followed by a reflexive pronoun and, if necessary, a preposition. If the reflexive pronoun can be omitted, put brackets around it.** C

absent	**adapt**	~~**concern**~~	**dress**	**occupy**	**prepare**	**pride**	**trouble**

1 She works for a charity which ...concerns itself with... the welfare of children.
2 She .... for the interview by reading the job description again.
3 It is a town that .... being welcoming to visitors.
4 While I was working, the children .... playing computer games.
5 It will take you some time to .... to the pace of life in Tokyo.
6 Jack just expects to be given a job without making any effort. He won't even .... filling in any application forms.
7 When Jade broke her arm she couldn't .... properly, so I had to go round each morning to help.
8 Peter arranged to .... the company for the first time in his life so that he could spend time with his father in hospital.

60.2 **Underline the correct option. If both options are possible, note the difference in meaning.** D

1 Can you post this letter for *myself / me*, please?
2 All my friends were away, I was bored, and I just didn't know what to do with *myself / me*.
3 We put the voice recorder on the table between *ourselves / us*.
4 They dragged the tree behind *themselves / them* all the way to the trailer.
5 Now that you're a famous actor, you must hear a lot about *yourself / you* in the media.
6 He ought to be ashamed of *himself / him*, being rude to his parents like that.
7 She should take care of *herself / her* better. She's looking really ill.
8 I opened the window in front of *myself / me* and took a deep breath of fresh air.

60.3 **If necessary, correct the italicised parts of this email or write ✓. Give alternatives where possible.** A–E

Delete Junk Reply Reply All Forward Print To Do

Hi Dana,

Yes, Jan's a lot better, thanks. We (1) *got vaccinated ourselves* against hepatitis before we went to West Africa, so Jan was just unlucky to get it. He went into work after we got back although he was feeling bad, and some of his colleagues were worried about (2) *getting it themselves*. I know that some of them (3) *had checked themselves* by their doctors. By coincidence, his boss said that (4) *he'd caught himself hepatitis* when he was in Africa a few years ago. When he's completely recovered, (5) *Jan and myself* are off to Paris for a few days – if I can get Jan (6) *to tear him away* from his office! – and (7) we're *going to occupy us* with looking at the galleries and having a rest.

Must go now. The children have just shouted that they want some juice and (8) *they can't reach it themself*.

Will be in touch, Nika

Unit 61

One and ones

A

We can use **one** instead of repeating a singular countable noun and **ones** instead of repeating a plural noun when it is clear from the context what we are talking about:

- 'Can I get you a drink?' 'It's okay, I've already got **one**.' (= a drink)
- I think his best poems are his early **ones**. (= poems)

We don't use **one / ones** instead of an uncountable noun:

- If you need any more paper, I'll bring you some. (*not* … I'll bring you one / ones.)
- I asked him to get apple juice, but he got orange. (*not* … but he got orange one / ones.)

We can't use **ones** without defining precisely which group of things we are talking about. Instead, we use **some**. Compare:

- 'We need new curtains.' 'Okay, let's buy *green* **ones** this time. / … **ones** *with flowers on* / … *those* **ones**.' *and*
- 'We need new curtains.' 'Okay, let's buy **some**.' (*not* Okay, let's buy ones.)

B

We don't use **one / ones** after nouns used as adjectives:

- I thought my memory stick was in my trouser pocket, but it was in my **coat** pocket. (*not* … my coat one.)

Instead of using **one / ones** after possessive determiners (**my**, **your**, **her**, etc.) we prefer **mine**, **yours**, **hers**, etc. However, a possessive determiner + **one / ones** is often heard in informal speech:

- I'd really like a smartphone like **yours**. (*or* '… like your one' in informal speech)

We usually use **ones** to refer to things rather than people:

- We need two people to help. We could ask those men over there. (*not* … ask those ones …)

However, **ones** is more likely to be used in comparative sentences to refer to groups of people:

- Older students seem to work harder than younger **ones**. (*or* … than younger students.)

Note also that we use **ones** to refer to people in **the little ones** (= small children), **(your) loved ones** (= usually close family), **(one of) the lucky ones**.

C

We can leave out **one / ones** –

☆ after **which**:

- When we buy medicines, we have no way of knowing *which* (**ones**) contain sugar.

☆ after superlatives:

- Look at that pumpkin! It's the *biggest* (**one**) I've seen this year.

☆ after **this**, **that**, **these**, and **those**:

- The last test I did was quite easy, but some parts of *this* (**one**) are really difficult.
- Help yourself to grapes. *These* (**ones**) are the sweetest, but *those* (**ones**) taste best.

(Note that some people think 'those / these ones' is incorrect, particularly in formal English.)

☆ after **either**, **neither**, **another**, **each**, **the first / second / last**, (etc.):

- Karl pointed to the paintings and said I could take *either* (**one**). (*or* … either of them.)
- She cleared away the cups, washed *each* (**one**) thoroughly, and put them on the shelf.

D

We don't leave out **one / ones** –

☆ after **the**, **the only**, **the main**, and **every**:

- When you cook clams you shouldn't eat *the* **ones** that have broken shells.
- After I got the glasses home, I found that *every* **one** was broken.

☆ after adjectives:

- My shoes were so uncomfortable that I had to go out today and buy some *new* **ones**.

However, after colour adjectives we can often leave out **one / ones** in answers:

- 'Have you decided which jumper to buy?' 'Yes, I think I'll take the *blue* (**one**).'

Exercises

61.1 **If necessary, correct these sentences. If they are already correct, write ✓.** A

1. Bilal brought in the wood and put ones on the fire.
2 Normally I don't like wearing a scarf, but it was so cold I put one on.
3 A: We've run out of potatoes. B: I'll get ones when I go to the shops.
4 We haven't got lemon tea, but you could have mint one instead.
5 Those aren't your gloves. You must have picked up the wrong ones.
6 A: What kind of cakes do you like best? B: Ones with cream inside.
7 I couldn't fit all the boxes in the car, so I had to leave ones behind and pick it up later.
8 Most of the trees in our garden are less than ten years old but ones are much older than that.

61.2 **If appropriate, replace the italicised words or phrases with one or ones. If it is not possible or unlikely, write 'No' after the sentence.** A & B

1 I answered most of the questions, but had to miss out some very difficult *questions*.
2 The female violinists in the orchestra outnumber the male *violinists* by about three to one.
3 He used to work for a finance company, but he's moved to an insurance *company*.
4 The issue discussed at the meeting was an extremely complicated *issue*.
5 Many people are happy about the new road being built, but there are some angry *people*, too.
6 A: Was it these earrings you wanted? B: No, the *earrings* on the left of those, please.
7 Diana is really good at taking photos of old buildings. There's an excellent *photo* of a local church in her office.
8 A: Are you picking Jo up at the train station? B: No, she's arriving at the bus *station*.
9 On one channel was a war film and on the other was a horror *film*, so I turned the TV off.
10 There are lots of gloves here. Are these your *gloves*?

61.3 **If the italicised one or ones can be omitted in these sentences, put brackets around it. If not, write ✓.** C & D

1 The children had eaten all the pizza and were still hungry so I had to make them another (*one*).
2 I drove around the houses, looking for the *ones* with 'For Sale' notices outside. ✓
3 I'm not keen on those *ones* with the cherry on top. I think I'll have a chocolate biscuit instead.
4 I like both of these jackets. I don't know which *one* to choose.
5 The vases are all handmade and every *one* looks different.
6 Each winter seemed to be colder than the last *one*.
7 There are many excellent food markets in town but the main *one* is near the port.
8 She tried on lots of pairs of shoes and finally chose the purple *ones*.
9 The books were so disorganised that I soon lost track of which *ones* I had already counted.
10 Can you remember where you bought this *one*? I'd like to get one myself.

61.4 **Complete these sentences with one or ones followed by an ending of your own.** C & D

1 Carmen drove to the restaurant because she was the only ...
....
2 To help keep fit, go to shops you can walk or cycle to rather than ...
....
3 A number of causes of climate change have been suggested, but the main ...
....
4 Camera tripods come in a variety of sizes and materials, but the most convenient ...
....

Unit 62

So and **not** as substitutes for clauses, etc.

A

We can use **so** instead of repeating an adjective, adverb, or a whole clause:

Reminder ➜ K10–K12

- The workers were angry and they had every right to be **so**. (= angry)
- Joe took the work seriously and Petra perhaps even more **so**. (= took the work seriously)
- Usman's giving us a lift. At least I presume **so**. (= that he's giving us a lift)

B

We often use **so** instead of a clause after verbs concerned with thinking and speaking:

- 'Is Lewis going back to Scotland to see his parents this summer?' 'I've no idea, but I'd **imagine so**. He goes most years.'
- I found it ridiculous, and **said so**. / ... and **told them so**. (= that I found it ridiculous)

Also: **be afraid** (expressing regret), **appear / seem** (after 'it'), **assume, believe, expect, guess, hope, presume, suppose, suspect, think**

Note that after 'tell' we include an indirect object.

We don't use **so** after certain other verbs:

- 'Will Stefan know how to mend it?' 'I **doubt** it. / I **doubt** (that) he will.' (*not* I doubt so.)

Also: **accept, admit, agree, be certain, hear, know, promise, suggest, be sure**

Note that in informal English, particularly in an argument, we can use 'I **know so**'.

C

In negative sentences, we use **not** or **not ... so**:

- Is the Socialist Party offering anything new in its statement? It would *appear* **not**.
- They want to buy the house, although they did**n't** *say* **so** directly.

We can use *either* **not** or **not ... so** with **appear**, **seem**, **suppose**:

- 'I don't suppose there'll be any seats left.' 'No, I do**n't** *suppose* **so**.' (*or* ... I *suppose* **not**.)

We prefer **not ... so** with **believe**, **expect**, **imagine**, **think**. With these verbs, **not** is rather formal:

- 'Will we need to show our passports?' 'I do**n't** *think* **so**.' (*rather than* I think not.)

We use **not** with **be afraid** (expressing regret), **assume**, **guess** (in the phrase 'I guess ...', = 'I think ...'), **hope**, **presume**, **suspect**:

- 'You'd better do it yourself. Eva won't help.' 'No, I **guess not**.' (*not* No, I don't guess so.)

Compare the use of **not** (**to**) and **not ... so** with **say**:

- 'Do we have to do all ten questions?' 'The teacher *said* **not**.' (= the teacher said that we didn't have to) *or* 'The teacher *said* **not to**.' (= the teacher said that we shouldn't)
- 'Do we have to do all ten questions?' 'The teacher did**n't** *say* **so**.' (= the teacher didn't say that we should do all ten, but perhaps we should)

D

We can use **so** in a short answer, instead of a short answer with 'Yes, ...', when we want to say that we can see that something is true now that we have been told, particularly if we are surprised. In answers like this we use **so** + **pronoun** + **auxiliary verb** (*be*, *can*, etc.):

- 'Lisa and Sara are here.' '**So they are.**' (*or* **Yes, they are.**) (= I can now see that, too)

However, if we already know something we use 'Yes, ...', not 'So ...'. Compare:

- 'Your bike's been moved.' '**So it has. / Yes, it has.** I wonder who did it.' (= I didn't know before you told me) *and*
- 'Your bike's been moved.' '**Yes, it has.** Philip borrowed it this morning.' (= I knew before you told me; *not* So it has.)

E

We can use **so** in a similar way in short answers with verbs such as **appear** (after 'it'), **believe**, **gather**, **hear**, **say**, **seem**, **tell** (e.g. So she tells me.), **understand**. However, with these verbs, the pattern implies 'I knew before you told me':

- 'I found that lecture really boring.' '**So I gather** (= I knew that). I saw you sleeping.'

Exercises

62.1 **If possible, complete the dialogues with so. If not, use an appropriate that-clause.** B

1 A: Is Zak ill again? B: Well, he hasn't come to work, so I assume ...so...
2 A: Will we need to pay to get in? B: I doubt ...that we will...
3 A: Will you be able to come over this weekend? B: I hope ....
4 A: Can you give me a lift to work? B: I suppose ....
5 A: Is this one by Van Gogh, too? B: I think ....
6 A: Apparently Carol's getting married again. B: Yes, I hear ....
7 A: The weather's awful, so we'll need to take a taxi. B: I guess ....
8 A: Will the decorator be finished this week? B: He says ....
9 A: You will remember to pick me up at one, won't you? B: I promise ....
10 A: I hope I'll be able to get a ticket. B: I'm sure ....

62.2 **Underline all the correct B responses.** B & C

1 A: With the children being ill I haven't had time to do much housework.
B: No, I *suppose not / don't suppose / don't suppose so*.
2 A: Did I leave my handbag in your car yesterday?
B: I *don't think / don't think so / think not*.
3 A: I'm sure the bank has charged me too much. Will they refund the money?
B: I *don't suspect / suspect not / don't suspect so*.
4 A: Didn't Alice hear you? B: It *doesn't appear so / appears not / doesn't appear*.
5 A: What did you think of Sadia's work?
B: Well, I thought it was pretty awful, although I *didn't say so / said not / said so*.

62.3 **Complete B's responses with short answers beginning Yes, ... If possible, give an alternative response with So ....** D

1 A: That horse is walking with a limp.
B: ...Yes, it is. / So it is.... Perhaps we should tell the owner.
2 A: The children from next door are taking the apples from our trees.
B: .... I said they could come round and get them.
3 A: The DVD player's gone again. B: .... Dr Adams has probably borrowed it.
4 A: I told you I'd be late for work today.
B: .... I agree. But you didn't say *how* late – it's nearly two.

62.4 **Choose any appropriate short answer beginning So ... to respond to A's comments below, to say that B already knew what is being said. Use the verbs in E opposite.** E

1 A: My car won't start again. B: ...So I hear....
2 A: Maria's not very well. B: ....
3 A: The class has been cancelled again. B: ....
4 A: I see income tax is going up. B: ....
5 A: Fred's moving to Berlin. B: ....

→ Additional exercise 12 (page 248)

Unit 63

Do so; such

A

Do so

We use **do so** (or **does so**, **did so**, **doing so**, etc.) instead of repeating a verb phrase (a verb and what follows it to complete its meaning) when the context makes clear what we are talking about:

- She won in 2012 and seems likely to **do so** (= win) again this year.
- Dr Lawson said, 'Sit down.' Katia **did so** (= sat down), and explained her problem.
- The climbers will try again today to reach the summit of the mountain. Their chances of **doing so** (= reaching the summit of the mountain) are better than they were last week. (In very formal English we can also use **so doing**.)
- When he was asked to check the figures, he claimed that he **had** already **done so**. (= checked the figures)

Do so is most often used in formal spoken and written English. In informal English we can use **do it** or **do that** instead:

- Mrs Chen waved as she walked past. She **does so / it / that** every morning.
- Ricardo told me to put in a new battery. I **did so / it / that**, but the radio still doesn't work.

We can also use **do** alone rather than **do so** in less formal English, especially after modals or perfect tenses (see also **B**):

- 'Will this program work on your computer?' 'It *should* **do**.'
- I told you that I'd finish the work by today, and I *have* **done**. ('have' is stressed here)

B

We can use **do so** instead of verbs that describe *actions*, but we avoid **do so** with verbs that describe *states* and *habitual actions*. Compare:

- 65% of the members voted for Katie Brown this time, whereas 84% **did so** last year.
- Kenyon confessed to the murder, although he only **did so** after a number of witnesses had identified him as the killer.
- I gave her the medicine, and I take full responsibility for **doing so**. *and*
- Lars doesn't like Facebook but Emma **does**.
- He earned a lot more than I **did**.
- I don't have time to go swimming every day, but I *usually* **do**.

C

Such

We can use **such** + (**a / an**) + **noun** to refer back to something mentioned before, with the meaning 'of this / that kind'. We use **such** + **noun** when the noun is uncountable or plural, and **such** + **a / an** + **noun** when the noun is countable and singular. **Such** is used in this way mainly in formal speech and writing:

- The students refer to teachers by their first names and will often criticise them for badly prepared lessons. **Such behaviour** is unacceptable in most schools. (*more informally* Behaviour like this ...)
- When asked about rumours that the company is preparing to lose more than 200 jobs, a spokeswoman said: 'I know of no **such plans**.' (*more informally* ... no plans of this kind.)
- They needed someone who was both an excellent administrator and manager. **Such a person** was not easy to find. (*more informally* A person like this ...)
- We allow both men and women to have time off work to look after children. We were the first department to introduce **such a scheme**. (*more informally* ... a scheme like this.)

Exercises

63.1 **Join each pair of sentences with either and or but, replacing the repeated verb + object / complement with a form of do followed by so.** A

1 Johnson never won an Olympic medal. He twice came close to winning an Olympic medal.
Johnson never won an Olympic medal, but twice came close to doing so.

2 She was asked to teach more classes. She was happy to teach more classes.
....

3 My French hosts gave me snails to eat. I ate them very reluctantly.
....

4 The company wanted to build a new dam on the site. They were prevented from building the dam by local opposition.
....

5 All EU countries agreed to implement the new regulations on recycling plastic. So far only Finland and Austria have implemented the new regulations.
....

6 The water freezes in the cracks in rocks. As it freezes, it expands.
....

63.2 **Complete these sentences with a form of do (+ so if possible).** B

1 If you have not already handed in the form, then please .... without delay.
2 Olav drives much faster than you ....
3 He jumped down from the window, but in .... twisted his ankle.
4 I know that many people don't enjoy Felipe's blog, but I ....
5 Anyone crossing the railway .... at their own risk.
6 I thought Julie was joking when she said these apples smell like oranges. But they .... !
7 When we play tennis Leyla usually wins, and she gets upset if I ....
8 She pointed to the old box, her hand shaking as she ....

63.3 **Complete the sentences with such or such a / an followed by a word from the box in the singular or plural.** C

claim	destruction	~~device~~	project	research	tactic

1 Manufacturers often claim that their washing machines have built-in computers, but is there really a computer in *such a device ?*
2 After Professor Sharma spoke about her work on climate change, she called on the government to put more money into ....
3 Television is sometimes said to harm children's social development, yet the evidence for .... is often lacking.
4 Building a new power station would undoubtedly create new jobs, but has the environmental impact of .... been considered fully?
5 The earthquake demolished thousands of buildings. The country has rarely seen .... before.
6 United played very defensively in the second half, but .... were criticised by the team's supporters.

63.4 **Rewrite the sentences in 63.3 to make them less formal.** C

1 *...but is there really a computer in a device like this? / ... like that?*

➜ Additional exercise 12 (page 248)

Unit 64

More on leaving out words after auxiliary verbs

A

To avoid repeating words from a previous clause or sentence we use an auxiliary verb (**be**, **have**, **can**, **will**, **would**, etc.) instead of a whole verb group or instead of a verb and what follows it:

- She says she's finished, but I don't think she **has**. (*instead of* … has finished.)
- 'Would any of you like to go to Paris?' 'I **would**.' (*instead of* I would like to go to Paris.)

If there is more than one auxiliary verb in the previous clause or sentence, we leave out all the auxiliary verbs except the first instead of repeating the main verb. Alternatively, we can use two (or more) auxiliary verbs:

- 'They **could have been** delayed by the snow.' 'Yes, they **could**.' (*or* … **could have** (**been**).)

B

If there is no auxiliary verb in the previous clause or sentence, or if the auxiliary is a form of **do**, we can use a form of **do** instead of repeating the main verb. We use **do** when the main verb is a present simple form and **did** when it is a past simple form:

- Mona **plays** golf on Saturdays, and I **do** too. (*instead of* … and I play golf on Saturdays too.; '… and so do I' is also possible)
- 'I **didn't steal** the money.' 'No one thinks that you **did**.' (*instead of* … thinks that you stole it.; 'No one thinks so' is also possible.)

If **be** is the main verb in the previous clause or sentence, we repeat a form of the verb **be**:

- 'The children **are** noisy again.' 'They always **are**.'

If **have** or **have got** is the main verb in the previous clause or sentence, we can usually use a form of either **do** or **have**:

- 'Do you think I **have** a chance of winning?' 'Yes, I think you **have**.' (*or* … you **do**.; 'Yes, I think so' is also possible.)
- Even if he **hasn't got** a map himself, he may know someone who **has**. (*or* … who **does**.)

However, if we use **have** + **noun** in the previous clause or sentence to talk about actions (**have a shower**, **have a shave**, **have a good time**, etc.) we prefer **do**:

- I wasn't expecting to *have a good time* at the party, but I **did**.

Note that sometimes we can use either **do**, **be** or **have** with a similar meaning (see also **C**):

- I asked Clara to tidy her room, and she **has / did**. ('has' replaces 'has tidied her room'; 'did' replaces 'tidied her room'.)

C

If we use **have** as an auxiliary verb, we can often follow it with **done** instead of repeating the main verb. This happens particularly in spoken English:

- 'She's never made a mistake before.' 'Well, she **has** (**done**) this time.'

However, this is usually not possible when the verb being substituted is intransitive:

- 'They've already gone.' 'I don't think Daniel **has**.' (*not* … Daniel has done.)

Similarly, after a *modal* auxiliary verb (**can**, **could**, **may**, **might**, **must**, **ought to**, **shall**, **should**, **will**, **would**) we can use **do**, particularly in spoken English:

- 'Will you be seeing David today?' 'I **might** (**do**).'

Sometimes we can use **be** instead of **do** with a similar meaning (see also **D**):

- 'Will you be seeing Felix today?' 'I **might** (**do / be**).' ('do' replaces 'see Felix today'; 'be' replaces 'be seeing Felix today'.)

D

If we use **be** as an *auxiliary* verb in the previous clause or sentence, we can use **be** after a modal:

- 'Is Ella staying for lunch?' 'Yes, I think she **will** (**be**).' (*or* … she will **do**.)

However, if **be** is used as a *main* verb in the previous clause or sentence, or as an auxiliary verb within a passive, we can usually leave out **be** after a modal in informal contexts only. Compare:

- 'Lina'**s** late again.' 'I thought she **might** (**be**).' *and*
- It has been found that the comet is made entirely of gas, as it was predicted it **would be**.

Exercises

64.1 **Make B's replies shorter by crossing out some of the words in italics. Give alternatives if possible.** A

1 A: Have you ever played squash before? B: Yes, I *have* ~~*played squash before.*~~
2 A: I suppose we should have booked tickets. B: Yes, we *should have booked tickets.*
3 A: Will you be staying in Brazil permanently? B: Yes, *we will be staying in Brazil permanently.*
4 A: All the parking places will probably have been taken by now.
B: Yes, I'm sure they *will have been taken by now.*
5 A: Have you had dinner yet? B: No, I *haven't had dinner yet.*
6 A: Are you going to Katalin's party? B: Yes, I *am going to Katalin's party.*
7 A: If Diane hadn't given you a lift, you would have missed the train.
B: Yes, I *would have missed the train.*
8 A: Can you see Joe anywhere? B: No, I *can't see him anywhere.*
9 A: Did you see that cyclist go through the red light? He couldn't have been looking.
B: No, he *couldn't have been looking.*

64.2 **Complete the sentences with an appropriate form of do, be or have (plus any alternatives). Put brackets around the word if it can be omitted, and write (done) after forms of have where this might be added.** B & C

1 I haven't finished doing the translation yet, but I will ......have (done)...... by tomorrow morning.
2 As a child I always enjoyed watching cartoons on TV, and I still ....
3 A: Has the post arrived yet? B: No, I don't think it ....
4 Have a shower if you want, but take a towel from the cupboard when you ....
5 A: It costs a fortune to rent a flat in the city centre. B: I'm sure it must ....
6 I was hoping Ryan had an electric drill that I could borrow, but he ....
7 I'm not a member of the tennis club myself, but I know someone who ....
8 I told the class that they had to hand in their books by nine and they all ....
9 A: Have you got a copy of *Great Expectations*? B: Yes, I think I ....
10 A: I've got £100 with me. Will that be enough? B: It should ....

64.3 **Complete the sentences with might, should, will or would, (plus any alternatives). If necessary, write be after the modal, or (be) if it is possible to omit it.** D

1 It's not snowing at the moment, but they say it ......will / might (be)...... .
2 Chris was cleaning the house when I got home, as I hoped he ....
3 A: Are they staying for lunch? B: They .... I'll ask them.
4 A: Are you revising a lot for the exams? B: Not as much as I ....
5 The company has not been as successful as it was claimed it ....
6 Natalie says she's very sorry – as she ....
7 The book is a bestseller, as we hoped it ....
8 A: My photograph was awarded first prize. B: I thought it ....

→ Additional exercise 12 (page 248)

Unit 65

Leaving out **to-infinitives**

A

We can sometimes use **to** instead of a clause beginning with a **to-infinitive** when it is clear from the context what we are talking about:

- I wanted to come with you, but I won't be able **to**. (*instead of* … to come with you.)
- It might have been better if Rosa had asked for my help, but she chose **not to**. (*instead of* … chose not to ask for my help.)

However, when we use the verb **be** in the previous sentence or clause the **to-infinitive** form of **be** is repeated in the next clause or sentence:

- Leon **was** frightened – or maybe he just pretended **to be**. (*not* … just pretended to.)

B

After most nouns and adjectives that can be followed by a **to-infinitive clause**, we can leave out the **to-infinitive clause** or use **to**:

- I'm not going to write another book – at least I don't have any **plans (to)**. (*or* … plans to write another book.)
- 'Could you and Tom help me move house?' 'Well, I'm **willing (to)**, and I'll ask Tom.'

Also: **chance, idea, opportunity, promise, suggestion; afraid, delighted, determined**

We can also leave out a **to-infinitive** or use **to** with some verbs:

- Alex will collect us by 10 o'clock. He **promised (to)**.
- 'You were supposed to buy some sugar.' 'Sorry, I **forgot (to)**.'

Also: **agree, ask, begin, refuse, start, try**

After verbs which must have a complement (i.e. a phrase which completes the meaning of the verb) we can't leave out **to**:

- I admit that I took her watch, but I didn't **mean to**.
- Have you thought about getting vaccinated against cholera before going there? I'd certainly **advise** you **to**.

Also: **afford, be able, choose, deserve, expect, fail, hate, hope, intend, love, need, prefer**

C

After **want** and **would like** in **if-clauses** and **wh-clauses** we can often leave out a **to-infinitive** or use **to**:

- You're welcome to dance *if* you'**d like** (**to**).
- You can do *whatever* you **would like** (**to**).
- Call me Ben *if* you **want** (**to**).
- Come and see us *when* you **want** (**to**).

In other clauses (not **if-** and **wh-clauses)** we include **to**:

- I was planning to see you tomorrow, and I **would** still **like to**.
- I offered to clean your car because I really **want to**, not because I hope to be paid.

In **if-clauses** and **wh-clauses** we usually leave out **to** after **like**. Compare:

- You can have one if you **like**. *and* You can have one if you**'d like** (**to**).
- Leave whenever you **like**. *and* Leave whenever you**'d like** (**to**).

However, we include **to** with negative forms of **want**, **would like**, and **like**, including in **if-clauses** and **wh-clauses**:

- 'Shall we go and visit Laura?' 'I **don't** really **want to**.'
- I should have phoned Jo last night, but it was so late when I got home I **didn't like to**.
- 'He won't mind you asking him for a loan.' 'Oh, no, I **wouldn't like to**.'

Exercises

65.1 **Rewrite the italicised part of each sentence so that it has a similar meaning. Use a verb from the box (use each verb twice) followed by to or to be.** A

claimed	expected	pretended	used

1 Was she really as good at tennis as she *said she was?* ......claimed to be......
2 She occupies a much less important role in the company than she *did before*.
....
3 Lucia was frightened – or maybe she just *acted as if she was*.
....
4 Dan has lost a lot of weight. He's much thinner than he *was before*.
....
5 The last government didn't represent the majority of people, although it *said that it did*.
....
6 My family enjoyed my singing, or at least they *made believe that they did*.
....
7 The Pantheon in Rome wasn't anything like I *imagined it*.
....
8 I didn't get an interview for the job although I *thought that I would*.
....

65.2 **Complete the sentences. Write to if it is necessary; write (to) if it can be included or omitted.** B

1 I've always wanted to go white-water rafting, but I've never had the opportunity .... before.
2 Luka had to admit that he'd failed, even though he obviously hated ....
3 When the police officer told the crowd to leave the square they refused ....
4 I don't have to walk to work. I do it because I choose ....
5 We didn't want Alina to leave college, but she was determined ....
6 Spain won 3–0, and deserved ...., after a fine performance.
7 A: Shall we ask Dad before we borrow the car? B: Yes, it might be a good idea ....
8 A: Would you present the prizes for the competition? B: I'd be delighted ....
9 A: Would you like to travel first class? B: Well, yes, I'd certainly prefer ....
10 I was hoping to go to Russia this year, but I can't afford ....

65.3 **If necessary, correct B's responses. If they are already correct, write ✓.** C

1 A: Can I have a biscuit? B: Take more than one if you like to.
2 A: When shall we start playing the music? B: Whenever you'd like.
3 A: Will Sara be able to play? B: I asked her, but she says she doesn't want.
4 A: I can't come out tonight, I'm seeing Emma. B: She can join us, if she'd like to.
5 A: Where are you going to in Norway? B: I haven't decided yet. I'll just go where I want.
6 A: I don't think I'll go after all. B: That's okay. You don't have to if you don't want.
7 A: Can the children come too? B: Yes, of course, if they want.
8 A: Shall we go out walking tomorrow? B: Yes, I'd like very much.
9 A: Could I ask you a personal question? B: Of course. Ask anything you like to.
10 A: Did you ask Dr Mori to help you? B: No, he was very busy, so I didn't like.

→ Additional exercise 12 (page 248)

Unit 66

Position of adjectives

A

Many adjectives can be used either before the noun they describe, or following linking verbs such as **appear**, **be**, **become**, **feel**, **get**, and **seem** (see Unit 21). Compare:

- ☐ The **high** *price* surprised him. *and* ☐ The price **seemed** *high*.

B

Some adjectives are seldom or never used before the noun they describe. These include –

☆ some '**a-**' adjectives:

- ☐ The horse *was* **alone** in the field. (*but not* The alone horse ...)

> *Also*: **afraid, alike, alive, ashamed, asleep, awake, aware**

Some have related adjectives that can be used before a noun or after a linking verb. Compare:

- ☐ The animal was **alive**. *and* A **living** animal. (*or* A **live** animal. / The animal was **living**.)

> *Also*: **afraid – frightened, alike – similar, alone – lone, asleep – sleeping**

☆ some adjectives used to describe health and feelings:

- ☐ My son *felt* **unwell**. (*but not* My unwell son ...)

These are sometimes used between an adverb and noun e.g. 'a terminally **ill** patient'.

> *Also*: **content, fine, glad, ill** (but 'ill health'), **sorry, (un)sure, upset** (but 'an upset stomach'), **well** (but 'He's really not a well man')

C

Emphasising adjectives are used to emphasise your feelings about something. Compare:

- ☐ I felt a fool. *and* ☐ I felt a **complete** fool. (for emphasis)

Some emphasising adjectives (such as **complete**, and also **absolute, entire, mere, sheer, total, utter**) are seldom or never used after a linking verb:

- ☐ It was a **total** failure. (*but not usually* The failure was total.)

Classifying adjectives are used to say that something is of a particular type. Like emphasising adjectives, classifying adjectives are seldom or never used after a linking verb:

- ☐ a **nuclear** explosion (*but not usually* 'The explosion was nuclear', unless we particularly want to emphasise a contrast with other kinds of explosion)

> *Also*: **atomic, chemical, digital, domestic, environmental, medical; general, occasional, northern** (etc.), **maximum, minimum, underlying**

Qualitative adjectives are used to give the quality that a thing or person has. We use them either directly before a noun or after a linking verb. Compare:

- ☐ a **beautiful** sunset ☐ The sunset was **beautiful**.

Note that some classifying adjectives can also be used with different meanings as qualitative adjectives and placed after a linking verb. Compare:

- ☐ The country's **economic** *reforms*. *and*
- ☐ The process isn't **economic**. (= not profitable)

> *Also*: **academic, conscious, educational, (il)legal, scientific**

D

Many adjectives can be used immediately after a noun, at the beginning of a reduced relative clause (see Unit 69B). For example –

☆ adjectives before a **to-infinitive**, or a prepositional phrase as part of the adjective phrase:

- ☐ It was a *speech* **calculated** *to appeal* to the unions.
- ☐ He is a *manager* **capable** *of making* difficult decisions.

☆ some **-ible** and **-able** adjectives such as **available**, **imaginable**, **possible**, **suitable**. However, we use these adjectives immediately after a noun *only* when the noun follows **the** or when the noun is made definite by what follows in a relative clause:

- ☐ This was *the* most difficult *decision* **imaginable**.
- ☐ It is a *treatment* **suitable** *for all children with asthma*.

☆ the adjectives **concerned**, **involved**, **opposite**, **present**, **proper**, **responsible**. These words have different meanings when they are used *before* a noun and immediately after it. Compare:

- ☐ All the *people* **present** (= who were there) approved of the decision. *and*
- ☐ I was asked for my **present** *address*. (= my address now)

Exercises

66.1 **If necessary, correct these sentences, or write ✓ if they are already correct.** B

1 After the accident I tried to comfort the upset driver of the car.
After the accident I tried to comfort the driver of the car, who was upset.
2 In the distance I could see an alone figure walking towards me.
3 It wasn't a great surprise when Rahim died as he hadn't been a well man for years.
4 I remember her as a glad person who was always smiling.
5 He stood at the bedroom door, looking at his asleep daughter.
6 The fire on the ship is under control, but there are still many afraid passengers on board.
7 She spent most of her life nursing seriously ill children in the hospital.
8 The two children were of an alike age.
9 We were unsure which way to go.
10 The sorry girls apologised to their teacher for their behaviour.

66.2 **Complete each pair of sentences using one pair of adjectives from the box. If an adjective can be used in both sentences, write it in both; if not, write it only in one. (Use a dictionary if necessary.)** C

domestic – unsafe	**educational – entertaining**	
inevitable – utter	**legal – stupid**	**serious – underlying**

1 a The experiment was a / an .... failure.
  b After Dr Owen left the project, its failure was ....
2 a None of the equipment in the warehouse is ....
  b The shop doesn't sell .... equipment.
3 a The trip to the wildlife park was a / an .... experience.
  b The toys were .... and the children played with them for hours.
4 a The computer fault was .... enough to disrupt all the work in the office.
  b The .... problem has not yet been solved.
5 a He was involved in a .... argument with his neighbour over a tree in the garden.
  b It's completely .... to charge a fee for entry into the museum.

66.3 **Write the word in brackets in one of the spaces in each sentence, either before or after the noun (or both if possible). (Use a dictionary if necessary.)** D

1 The party was excellent, and I'd like to thank all the .... people .... (*concerned*)
2 As the .... minister .... for the health service, I think he should resign. (*responsible*)
3 The new machinery was intended to increase output, but it seems to have had the .... effect .... (*opposite*)
4 Children are only admitted when accompanied by a / an .... adult .... (*responsible*)
5 It's the only .... room .... in the hotel that night. (*available*)
6 The pond on the village green was filled in with the .... approval .... of local residents. (*apparent*)
7 Cars drive too fast past the school and .... parents .... have complained to the police. (*concerned*)
8 For those who need it, there is .... financial advice .... (*available*)

→ Additional exercise 13 (page 248)

Unit 67

Gradable and non-gradable adjectives 1

A

Gradable adjectives can be used with *grading adverbs* such as **very** or **extremely** to say that a thing or person has more or less of a particular quality. Here are some examples of adjectives used as gradable in their most common meanings:

Grading adverbs		+		Gradable adjectives
Grading adverbs	**a bit**, **dreadfully**, **extremely**, **hugely**, **immensely**, **intensely**, **rather**, **reasonably**, **slightly**, **very**	+	**angry**, **big**, **busy**, **clever**, **common**, **different**, **fast**, **friendly**, **happy**, **important**, **low**, **popular**, **quiet**, **rich**, **strong**, **weak**, **young**	*Gradable adjectives*

- She was *extremely* **rich**.
- It's *hugely* **popular**.
- The people there are *reasonably* **friendly**.
- They're *slightly* **different**.

Non-gradable adjectives are not used with adverbs such as **very** or **extremely** because these adjectives do not refer to qualities which have different degrees. With non-gradable adjectives we can use *non-grading adverbs* which emphasise their extreme or absolute nature, such as **absolutely**, **completely**, etc. Many classifying adjectives (see Unit 66) are usually non-gradable. Adverbs such as **almost**, **exclusively**, etc., which indicate the extent of the quality, are commonly used with classifying adjectives. Here are some examples of non-gradable adjectives in their most common meanings:

Non-grading adverbs	**absolutely**, **completely**, **entirely**, **perfectly**, **practically**, **simply**, **totally**, **utterly**, **virtually**; **almost**, **exclusively**, **fully**, **largely**, **mainly**, **nearly**, **primarily**	+	**awful**, **excellent**, **huge**, **impossible**, **superb**, **terrible**, **unique**, **unknown**, **wrong**; **domestic**, **environmental**, **agricultural** (see Unit 66C)	*Non-gradable adjectives*

- She's *completely* **wrong**.
- He was *practically* **unknown** to the public.
- It was *absolutely* **superb**.
- The region is *largely* **agricultural.**

Gradable adjectives are sometimes used with non-grading adverbs, and non-gradable adjectives with grading adverbs to give special emphasis or to be humorous:

- What you're asking isn't just difficult – it's *extremely* **impossible**! (*grading adverb + non-gradable adjective*)
- You've won a hundred pounds? Wow, you're *virtually* **rich**! (*non-grading adverb + gradable adjective*)

Note that not all the adverbs can go with all the adjectives given in each of the tables above. For example, we can say 'absolutely huge', but we wouldn't usually say 'completely huge' unless it was for particular emphasis or for humour.

B

The adverbs **fairly** (= to quite a large degree, but usually less than 'very'), **really** (= 'very [much]') and **pretty** (= similar to 'fairly'; used in informal contexts) are commonly used with both gradable and non-gradable adjectives:

- She's *fairly* **popular** at school.
- I'm *really* **busy** at the moment.
- It's a *pretty* **important** exam.
- It was a *fairly* **awful** film.
- The flooding was *really* **terrible**.
- The bill was *pretty* **huge**.

However, note that we don't generally use **fairly** (or **very**) with non-gradable adjectives which indicate that something is very good or necessary:

- Experience is *really / pretty* **essential** for the job. (*not* … fairly essential …)
- The weather was *really / pretty* **perfect**. (*not* … fairly perfect.)

Also: **invaluable, superb, tremendous, wonderful**

Exercises

67.1 Complete the four sentences which contain gradable adjectives using very. Complete the remaining sentences with the adverbs from the box. Try to use a different one each time. A

absolutely	almost	completely	exclusively	mainly	practically

1 The bridge is now .... complete.
2 The material is .... cotton.
3 The food was .... excellent.
4 Her explanation was .... clear.
5 Their actions were .... illegal.
6 The new restaurant is .... popular.
7 I was in a / an .... permanent state of suspense.
8 I thought she was .... attractive.
9 Until last year the club was .... male.
10 Small black cars are not .... visible.

67.2 Answer the questions using an adverb + adjective. A **How would you feel if …**

1 … a friend said s/he had just won a million pounds? *I'd be absolutely delighted.*
2 … your best friend told you s/he was emigrating to Australia?
3 … someone broke a window in your house or flat?
4 … a complete stranger told you that you were very beautiful / handsome?
5 … you lost some airline tickets you had just bought?

67.3 If necessary, correct the italicised parts of this email. If they are already correct, write ✓. A

Dear Nathan,

I'm writing this email in my new flat in Stratford. It's in an (1) *absolutely old* building which was (2) *totally renovated* last year. Fortunately, I didn't have to do much decorating when I moved in. As you know, I'm (3) *hugely useless* at DIY so I was (4) *absolutely happy* about that. The building is (5) *reasonably unique* in this part of Stratford, as most others around are (6) *rather modern*, and the view across the river from my sitting room is (7) *simply superb*. The flat's (8) *simply small*, but (9) *completely comfortable* for me.

My neighbours are (10) *very friendly* and usually (11) *fully quiet*. The only problem is that the woman upstairs plays the trumpet and I find it (12) *a bit impossible* to read when she's playing. I get (13) *slightly angry* about this, but she doesn't play for long each time, so it's not an (14) *extremely terrible* problem.

I know that the weather has been (15) *dreadfully awful* recently, so it's been difficult for you to get here, but you must come over one evening. There's an (16) *absolutely marvellous* restaurant nearby that we could go to.

Hope all is well,

Lea

67.4 Cross out any incorrect or unlikely alternatives. B

1 Her advice was *fairly / really* invaluable.
2 Our neighbours are *really / fairly* friendly.
3 I thought his performance as Hamlet was *fairly / really* tremendous.
4 The children kept *pretty / very* quiet during the concert.
5 The view from the window was *very / pretty* wonderful.
6 Their cooperation is *pretty / very* essential if we want the project to go ahead.
7 The weather was *really / fairly* perfect for a long walk.
8 In this photograph she looked *really / very* young.
9 The workmanship in the furniture was *pretty / very* superb.
10 The disease is *fairly / pretty* common in this part of the country.

Unit 68

Gradable and non-gradable adjectives 2

A

Some adjectives have both gradable and non-gradable senses.

(i) Some adjectives have different senses when they are gradable and non-gradable. Compare:

- Smith is a *very* **common** name. (= frequently found; gradable) *and*
- We have a lot of **common** interests. (= shared; non-gradable; not *very*)
- The house is *very* **old**. (= existed many years; gradable) *and*
- I met my **old** politics professor the other day. (= former; non-gradable; not *very*)

Also: **civil, clean, critical, electric** (= 'exciting' when gradable), **empty, false, late, odd, original, particular, straight**

(ii) Some adjectives have similar meanings when they are gradable and non-gradable. However, when they are gradable we talk about the quality that a person or thing has (i.e. they are *qualitative* adjectives and therefore can be used with an adverb), and when they are non-gradable we talk about the category or type they belong to (i.e. they are *classifying* adjectives). Compare:

- I don't know where he came from, but he sounded *slightly* **foreign**. (= not from this country; gradable) *and*
- She is now advising on the government's **foreign** policy. (= concerning other countries; non-gradable)
- They had a *very* **public** argument. (= seen / heard by a lot of people; gradable) *and*
- He was forced to resign by **public** pressure. (= from many people in the community; non-gradable)

Also: **academic, adult, average, diplomatic, genuine, guilty, human, individual, innocent, mobile, private, professional, scientific, technical, true, wild**

B

In spoken English in particular, we can use **good and ...**, **lovely and ...**, and **nice and ...** followed by another gradable adjective in order to emphasise the second adjective. Possible patterns include –

☆ **good and ready** and more colloquially **good and proper / relaxed / strong** (*but not usually* good and beautiful / rich / tall):

- If you're all feeling **good and relaxed** after the break, let's get on with the meeting.

☆ **lovely and dry / soft / sunny / warm** (*but not usually* lovely and decent / empty / short):

- It's **lovely and warm** in here. Freezing outside, though.

☆ **nice and bright / clean / cold / comfortable / early / fresh / quiet / simple / soft / tidy / warm** (*but not usually* nice and interesting / handsome / exciting):

- 'Shall we get some strawberries?' 'Yes, they look **nice and fresh**.'

We can also link comparative adjectives (see Unit 72) with **and** to talk about an increasing degree of the quality described in the adjective. We use **more and more + adjective** in a similar way:

- As she got **more and more excited**, her voice got **higher and higher** and **louder and louder**.
- The taxi driver just drove **faster and faster and faster** until I told him to stop, and I got out.

Exercises

68.1 **Complete the sentences using each of the adjectives from the box twice, once with a gradable sense (adding very) and once with a non-gradable sense. (Use a dictionary if necessary.)** Ai

critical	**false**	**late**	**original**	**straight**

1 The novel was praised by the judges for its ...very original... use of language.
2 The train is .... again. I wonder if the bad weather has delayed it.
3 The report was .... of the police officers involved in the investigation.
4 I had a / an .... choice between working for my father and having no job at all.
5 She was accused of giving .... information during the trial.
6 The driver of the overturned lorry was in a / an .... condition in hospital last night.
7 I was given the oil painting by my .... uncle Simon.
8 The .... fireplaces had been removed and replaced by more modern ones.
9 The path to the summit of the hill was .... and steep.
10 Many of the people I met were quite sincere, but some seemed .... , so that I could never be sure if they meant what they said.

68.2 **Complete each pair of sentences using the adverb + adjective pairs from the box. Use the adjective in both sentences, but include the adverb in only one.** Aii

(largely) academic	~~**(fairly) average**~~	**(extremely) diplomatic**
(very) human	**(intensely) private**	**(highly) technical**

1 a The ...average... temperature on the island is a pleasant 23.4 °C.
b Brecston is a / ~~an~~ ...fairly average... town in the south of England.
2 a The instructions were .... and clearly meant for an expert.
b Fiona got a job providing .... support for people having computer problems.
3 a Being frightened in this situation is a .... response and nothing to be ashamed of.
b Near the top of the mountain there were signs of .... habitation, perhaps centuries old.
4 a I found it difficult to understand the .... talk that Professor Downs gave.
b The .... standards at the school are very high.
5 a He worked hard to afford a .... education for his three children.
b She was a / an .... person and had few close friends.
6 a After Mara left university she worked in the .... service for a number of years.
b When he was asked to comment on the French President's decision he gave a / an .... answer, not wanting to appear critical.

68.3 **Complete the sentences with phrases beginning with good / lovely / nice + and + an appropriate adjective.** B

1 Now that the room is painted yellow, it looks ...lovely and bright....
2 I've put you in the spare room at the back of the house, so it'll be ....
3 A: Have you felt the material my new coat's made of? B: Oh, it's ....
4 The oranges looked quite old, but when I cut into them they were ....
5 There's no point in trying to persuade Gustavo. He won't make up his mind until he's ....

Unit 69

Participle adjectives and compound adjectives

A

Participle adjectives

Some **-ing forms** (present participles) and **-ed forms** (past participles) of verbs can be used as adjectives. Most of these *participle adjectives* can be used before the noun they describe or following linking verbs (see Unit 21):

- The hotel had a **welcoming** *atmosphere*.
- I found this **broken** *plate* in the kitchen cupboard.
- The students' tests results *were* **pleasing**.
- My mother *seemed* **delighted** with the present.

B

We can use many participle adjectives *immediately* after nouns when they identify or define the noun. This use is similar to *defining relative clauses* and they are often called 'reduced relatives':

- We had to pay for the *rooms* **used**. (*or* ... the *rooms* **that were used**.)

Some of these are rarely used before the noun:

- My watch was among the *things* **taken**. (*but not* ... the taken things.)

Also: **applying, caused, found, included, provided**

Others can be used before *or* immediately after nouns:

- The *crowd* **watching** grew restless. *or*
- The **watching** *crowd* grew restless.

Also: **affected, alleged, allocated, broken, chosen, identified, infected, interested, remaining, resulting, stolen**

C

In formal English, **that** and **those** can be used as pronouns before a participle adjective:

- The flour is of a higher quality than **that produced** by other varieties of wheat. (= the flour which is produced)
- The touchscreens perform less well than **those manufactured** elsewhere. (= the touchscreens which are manufactured elsewhere)
- Here is some advice for **those** (= people) **preparing** to go on holiday.

D

Compound adjectives

Many *compound adjectives* include a participle adjective. Common patterns are:

adverb + ***-ed*** *participle*	They are **well-behaved** children.
adverb + ***-ing*** *participle*	Social networking is a **fast-growing** activity.
adjective + ***-ed*** *participle*	She seems to live on **ready-made** meals.
adjective + ***-ing*** *participle*	He's the **longest-serving** employee in the company.
noun + ***-ed*** *participle*	The public square was **tree-lined**.
noun + ***-ing*** *participle*	I hope it will be a **money-making** enterprise.
-ed *participle* + *particle*	Did it really happen, or was it a **made-up** story? (from two-word verbs)

We can use some participle adjectives **only** in adjective compounds. For example, we can't say '... behaved children' or '... a making enterprise' as the sense is incomplete without the adverb or noun.

Also: **New York-based, Paris-born, brick-built, easy-going, peace-keeping, long-lasting, good-looking, home-made, hair-raising, far-reaching, well-resourced, sweet-smelling, strange-sounding, soft-spoken, sour-tasting, nerve-wracking**

Note that many other compound adjectives do not include participle adjectives:

- The problem is **short-term**.
- It was just a **small-scale** project.

Exercises

69.1 Replace the italicised parts of these sentences with present or past participle adjectives formed from the verbs in the box. Give alternative positions for the adjective if possible. B

~~cause~~ | identify | include | interest | provide | remain | result

1 I offered to pay for any damage *that was the result.* caused (*not* ... any caused damage.)
2 Steps are being taken by telephone engineers to solve the problems *which have been noticed.*
3 Visitors *who want to find out more* can buy a booklet with further information.
4 Please answer the questions on the sheet *that has been given to you*.
5 The holiday cost £1,200, with flights *which were part of the total*.
6 I didn't want to be on TV but the publicity *that was the consequence* was good for business.
7 Just before serving the pasta, sprinkle over any cheese *that is left over*.

69.2 Write a sentence to describe each set of information using either **that** or **those** followed by one of the participle adjectives from the box. C

earned | found | grown | manufactured | ~~recorded~~

1
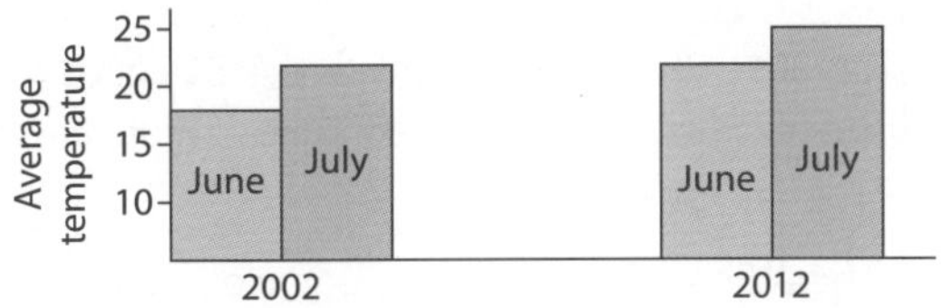

Average temperatures in June and July 2012 were higher than those recorded in June and July 2002. (or ... in the corresponding months in 2002.).

2

3

4
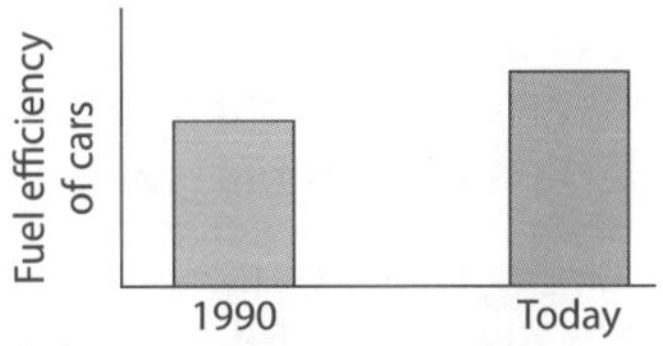

5

69.3 Complete each second sentence using a compound adjective from D to replace the italicised information in each first sentence. D

1 The company *is organised from New York*. It is a New York-based company.
2 The school *has all the things it needs*, with sufficient books and computers. The school is ...., with sufficient books and computers.
3 I found that the whole experience *made me tense and worried*. I found the whole experience ....
4 The proposed changes will *have a major influence on a large number of people*. The proposed changes will be ....

69.4 Match the words to form compound adjectives and use them to rewrite the italicised parts of these sentences. D

clean | eye | ~~ill~~ | wide

catching | ~~equipped~~ | ranging | shaven

1 At the age of 16 children *do not have the ability or experience* to take on the role of parents. are ill-equipped .
2 The discussions *dealt with a great variety of topics*. ....
3 When I last saw him he had a beard, but now he *has no beard*. ....
4 The advertisements for the new car are *very noticeable*. ....

→ Additional exercise 13 (page 248)

Unit 70

Adjective + **to-infinitive, -ing, that-clause, wh-clause**

A

When an adjective comes after a linking verb (e.g. **appear**, **be**, **become**, **seem**; see Unit 21) we can use a number of patterns after the adjective including a **to-infinitive**, **-ing**, **that-clause**, and **wh-clause**. (For **It** + **linking verb** + **adjective**, see **B**.)

	adjective +	*example adjectives used in this pattern*
i	**to-infinitive** ◯ You're **free** *to leave* at any time you want.	**(un)able**, **careful**, **crazy**, **curious**, **difficult**, **easy**, **foolish**, **free**, **good**, **hard**, **impossible**, **inclined**, **mad**, **nice**, **prepared**, **ready**, **stupid**, **welcome**, **willing**
ii	**-ing** ◯ He was **busy** *doing* his homework.	**busy**, **crazy**, **foolish**, **mad**, **stupid**; (after the verb **feel**) **awful**, **awkward**, **bad**, **good**, **guilty**, **terrible**
iii	**that-clause** ◯ He became **worried** (*that*) she might fall down.	**afraid**, **alarmed**, **amazed**, **angry**, **annoyed**, **ashamed**, **astonished**, **aware**, **concerned**, **disappointed**, **glad**, **(un)happy**, **pleased**, **shocked**, **sorry**, **upset**, **worried**; **certain**, **confident**, **positive**, **sure**
iv	**wh-clause** ◯ I'm not **certain** (of / about) *why* he wants to borrow the money	**afraid**, **not aware / unaware**, **not certain / uncertain**, **doubtful**, **not sure / unsure**, **worried**
v	**to-infinitive** *or* **that-clause** ◯ She was **afraid** *to say* anything. ◯ I was **afraid** *that* I would be late.	the adjectives in (iii) above, except **aware**, **confident** and **positive**
vi	**to-infinitive** *or* **-ing** ◯ He'd be **stupid** *to leave* now. ◯ He'd be **stupid** *giving up* the job.	**crazy**, **foolish**, **mad**, **stupid**
vii	**-ing** *or* **that-clause** ◯ She felt **awful** *leaving* him with all the clearing up. ◯ She felt **awful** *that* she was late.	(after the verb **feel**) **awful**, **awkward**, **bad**, **good**, **guilty**, **terrible**

B

It + linking verb + adjective

We can sometimes use **it + linking verb + adjective + to-infinitive** as an alternative to **subject + linking verb + adjective + to-infinitive** (see also Units 96 and 97):

◯ The fireworks were **amazing** *to watch*. *or*
◯ **It was amazing** *to watch* the fireworks.

> *Also*: **annoying, awkward, easy, good, interesting, lovely, simple, terrific, wonderful**

In informal speech we can use an **-ing** form instead of a **to-infinitive**:

◯ **It is easy** *understanding* her.
◯ **It was amazing** *watching* the fireworks.

We can use a similar pattern with **adjective + wh-** or **that-clause** (see Unit 96A):

◯ It is not **clear** *why* he did it.
◯ It was **odd** *that* she left so suddenly.

After certain adjectives we often include **of + subject** between the adjective and a **to-infinitive**:

◯ It was rude **(of them)** to criticise her. *or*
◯ They were rude to criticise her.

> *Also*: **brave, generous, kind, mean, thoughtful, unprofessional, unreasonable**

When we talk about how somebody reacts to a situation we can use **it + make** with an adjective and **to-infinitive**, **-ing** or **that-clause**:

◯ **It made me angry** (*to discover*) *that* so much money was wasted. (*or* **It made me angry** *discovering* that ... *or* I was angry to discover that ...)

> *Also*: **ashamed, furious, glad, happy, miserable, nervous, sad, tired, uncomfortable**

Exercises

70.1 Complete the sentences with a **to-infinitive** or an **-ing** form of the verbs in the box. Give alternatives where possible. A

cheat	**know**	**leave**	**open**	**panic**	**reduce**
resign	**talk**	**turn**	**underestimate**		

1 I'm afraid I can't afford that much. Would you be prepared .... the price if I pay cash?
2 Kenzo was stupid .... in the exam. He was bound to get caught.
3 He felt good .... that he had helped solve the problem.
4 Don't feel that you need to stay to the very end. You're free .... at any time.
5 Anyone trying to climb the mountain would be foolish .... the challenge facing them.
6 People said I was crazy .... a shop in the village, but it's been a success so far.
7 She was too busy .... on the phone to notice that Roya had come into the room.
8 It's so difficult to get a job at the moment you'd be mad ....
9 Some people would be inclined .... if they smelt smoke in the house.
10 I felt awful .... people away from the concert, but there just wasn't any more room.

70.2 Correct any mistakes in the italicised parts of this email about a holiday in Thailand. A

... After a couple of days Mark announced that he was going walking in the hills near the hotel. I thought he was (1) *stupid that he would go* alone and that it was dangerous. But he said that he was (2) *confident not to get lost*. We ended up arguing and finally he stormed off, saying he (3) *wasn't sure when* he'd be back. I went into town, but I felt a bit (4) *guilty to shop* all day. On the bus on the way back to the hotel I got talking to a local woman and (5) *was concerned learning* that it got very cold in the hills at night. I started (6) *to get worried* that he might be in danger, but I (7) *wasn't certain what* to do. But when I got back to the hotel, there was Mark (8) *busy to drink* orange juice by the pool. He'd decided not to go walking after all! He said he (9) *was sorry upsetting me*. At first I was angry and said he was stubborn and that he just (10) *wasn't prepared admitting* that I'd been right. But really I was just (11) *pleased that* he was safe ...

70.3 Rewrite these sentences using **It + be + adjective**. If possible, use **of + a personal pronoun** after the adjective. B

1 She was brave to spend the night in the old house alone. *It was brave of her to spend the night in the old house alone.*
2 Such a magnificent performance was wonderful to hear.
3 You were mean to eat all the cake and not leave any for me.
4 They were unreasonable to complain about the exam results.
5 The top of the jar was awkward to get off.
6 The shelves were simple to put up.
7 He was unprofessional to criticise the headteacher in front of the staff.
8 You were kind to give birthday presents to the children.

70.4 Complete these sentences with **It made me +** any appropriate adjective. B

1 *It made me angry* to hear how she had been insulted.
2 .... listening to his lies.
3 .... that we wouldn't be working together again.
4 .... to learn how badly we treated immigrants in the 1950s.
5 .... hearing the dentist's drill as I sat in the waiting room.

Unit 71

Adjectives and adverbs

A

Reminder ➜ L5–L6

Some adverbs of manner (saying how something is done) are formed from an **adjective + -ly**: **sudden** → **suddenly**, **happy** → **happily**, etc. When an adjective already ends in **-ly** (e.g. **cowardly**, **elderly**, **friendly**, **kindly**, **lively**, **lonely**, **lovely**) we don't add **-ly** to it to make an adverb. Instead we can use a prepositional phrase with **fashion**, **manner**, or **way**:

- He smiled at me in a **friendly way**.
- She waved her hands around in **a lively fashion**.

Most participle adjectives ending in **-ed** (see Unit 69) don't have an adverb form and so we use a prepositional phrase instead:

- They rose to greet me in **a subdued manner**. (*not* ... subduedly.)

or we use a preposition and a related noun if there is one:

- She looked at me **in amazement**. (*not* ... amazedly.)

However, some do have an adverb form with **-ly**. Compare:

- The storm was **unexpected**. *and*
- The weather turned **unexpectedly** stormy.

Also: **agitatedly, allegedly, deservedly, determinedly, disappointedly, excitedly, hurriedly, pointedly, repeatedly, reportedly, reputedly, supposedly, worriedly**

B

Some adverbs have two forms, one ending in **-ly** and the other not. We can sometimes use either form without changing the meaning, although the form ending in **-ly** is grammatically correct and more formal:

- She ran **quick** / **quickly** towards the door.

and must be used if the adverb comes immediately before the verb:

- She **quickly** *ran* towards the door. (*not* She quick ran ...)

Also: **cheap(ly), clean(ly), clear(ly), fine(ly), loud(ly), thin(ly), slow(ly)**

C

Some adverbs have different meanings with and without **-ly**. Compare:

- She gave her time **free**. (= for no money) *and* She gave her time **freely.** (= willingly)
- I arrived **late** for the concert. (= not on time) *and* I haven't seen Amy **lately**. (= recently)

Compare also:

He wandered **deep** into the forest and got lost. (= a long way)	He felt **deeply** hurt by her criticisms. (= very) They loved each other **deeply**. (= very much)
You don't have to change trains. You can go **direct**. (= without stopping)	I'll be with you **directly**. (= very soon) He saw Hassan **directly** ahead. (= straight)
It sounded awful – one of the choir members was singing **flat**.	This time I **flatly** refused to lend him any money. (= definitely; completely)
He kicked the ball **high** over the goal.	Everyone thinks **highly** of her teaching. (= they think her teaching is very good)
'Is Emil here yet?' 'He's **just** arrived.' She looks **just** like her mother.	You can be **justly** proud of your musical achievements. (= rightly; justifiably)
Which of these cheeses do you like **most**?	Her novels are now **mostly** out of print. (= most of them) We **mostly** go on holiday to France. (= usually)
They cut **short** their holiday when Lina fell ill. (= went home early)	The speaker will be arriving **shortly** (= soon). Please take your seats.
The door was **wide** open so I just went straight in. (= completely)	You won't have any problems getting the book. It's **widely** available. (= in many places)

Exercises

71.1 **Rewrite the italicised words using a -ly form of the participles in the box. If a -ly form isn't possible, use a prepositional phrase or a preposition + related noun.** A

agitated	**anticipated**	**despaired**	**determined**	**disappointed**
organised	**relaxed**	**repeated**	**reputed**	**satisfied**

1 I warned him *again and again* of the dangers on the mountain, but he insisted on going on.
2 The class was out of control and he put his head in his hands *feeling that he could do nothing*.
3 As his mother took the roast chicken out of the oven, Rod licked his lips *because he was looking forward to eating it*.
4 It is *said to be, although no one knows for certain*, the smallest post office in the country.
5 'Still no news from Paul,' she said *in a sad way*.
6 He ran the company *in a calm way* and rarely let anything annoy him.
7 She shook her head *as if she had made a firm decision*.
8 When he had finished the painting, he looked at it *in a way that showed he was happy*.
9 Vicky runs the office *carefully and tidily*, so I don't think we should change things now.
10 Sofia paced about *in an anxious way* as she waited to go into the interview.

71.2 **Complete the sentences with suitable pairs of adverbs from C. Use the form with -ly in one sentence and the form without -ly in the other.** C

1 a What she hated .... was having to get up at 5:30 every morning.
  b We don't go out much in the evening. We .... watch television.
2 a The firm paid compensation, but stopped .... of admitting they were to blame.
  b The book is due to be published ....
3 a I'm not in my office at the moment, but if you leave your name and number I'll get back to you .... *[Message on a telephone answering machine]*
  b I used to have to change in Amsterdam to get to Moscow, but now I can fly ....
4 a I got very little sleep on the flight, but I felt .... awake when I arrived in Tokyo.
  b French is .... spoken in North Africa.
5 a She is one of the most .... regarded researchers in the university.
  b We could just see the plane flying .... overhead.

71.3 **Correct any mistakes in these sentences. If there are no mistakes, write ✓.** A–C

1 The rise in car crime in the area is deeply worrying.

2 She waved friendlily to me.
3 Cut the onions up finely and fry them with garlic.
4 I asked the boys to move their bicycles off the football pitch but they flat refused.
5 I couldn't understand what he was saying. He didn't speak very clearly.
6 He was accused of behaving cowardlily in the battle.
7 Pierre Evene manufactured the glass for which the town became just renowned.
8 I called Elena and she slow turned to face me.
9 Spread some butter on the bread as thin as possible.
10 The prime minister was loud applauded by her audience.

Unit 72

Adjectives and adverbs: comparative and superlative forms

A

Comparatives: -er vs more / less ... than

Reminder ➔ L7–L8

We usually add **-er** to one-syllable adjectives and adverbs to make their comparative form. However, we use **more** + **adjective** –

☆ with one-syllable past participle adjectives (see Unit 69) such as **bored**, **creased**, **pleased**, **worn**:

- After I'd ironed my shirt it looked **more creased** than before. (*not* ... creaseder ...)

☆ with **fun**, **real**, **right** and **wrong**:

- I expected the film to be rather dull, but I couldn't have been **more wrong**. (*not* ... wronger.)

☆ when we are comparing two qualities:

- 'Wasn't he brave to swim across?' 'I think he was **more mad** than **brave**.'
- Although the paint was called 'Sky Blue', I thought it was **more green** than **blue**.

We can also use '... he was**n't so much** *brave* **as mad**' and '... it was *blue* **rather than** *green*'.

We can sometimes use **more** as an alternative to the **-er** form to emphasise the comparison:

- You might think it's dark here but it's **more dark** in the cellar. (*or* ... **darker** ...)

> *Also*: **clear**, **cold**, **deep**, **fair**, **rough**, **soft**, **true**.

B

Some adjectives with two syllables are most commonly used with **more** / **less**, particularly:

- **participle adjectives** (e.g. **worried**, **boring**)
- **adjectives ending in -ful** and **-less** (e.g. **careful**, **careless**)
- **afraid**, **alert**, **alike**, **alone**, **ashamed**, **aware**
- some other adjectives, including **active**, **cautious**, **certain**, **complex**, **direct**, **eager**, **exact**, **formal**, **frequent**, **modern**, **special**, **recent**

Most two-syllable adjectives ending **-y**, **-ow**, **-er** and **-ure** can take either an **-er** or the **more** + **adjective** form, although the **-er** form is more frequently used.

Some adjectives (e.g. **complete**, **equal**, **favourite**, **ideal**, **perfect**, **unique**) have a comparative or superlative meaning so are not often used with **-er** / **more** / **less** or **–est** / **most** / **least**. However, we can use comparative or superlative forms for special emphasis:

- The weather today was good, but **less perfect** than yesterday.

C

Superlatives

We usually use **the**, a possessive form (with **-'s**), or a possessive pronoun before a superlative adjective or adverb. In informal contexts we sometimes leave out **the** before an **-est** or **most** + **adjective** superlative after a linking verb, particularly at the end of a sentence:

- 'Why did you go by bus?' 'It was (**the**) **cheapest**.'
- Which was (**the**) **most expensive**?

However, we can't leave out **the** when we go on to say what group of things is being compared:

- 'Why did you buy these oranges?' 'They were **the cheapest** *ones I could find*.' (*not* They were cheapest ones ...)

When **most** + **adjective** / **adverb** is used without **the**, **most** means something like 'very':

- I checked the form **most carefully** (= very carefully) but didn't notice the mistake.

D

After a superlative we use **of** + **a plural noun phrase** to name the objects being compared:

- Adam's *the oldest* **of my three brothers**.

Note that we can put the **of-phrase** at the beginning to emphasise it:

- **Of my three brothers**, Adam's *the oldest*.

When we give the location or context within which the comparison is made we usually use **in** + **a singular noun phrase**:

- It was *the tallest tree* **in the forest**. (*not* ... the tallest tree of the forest.)

Exercises

72.1 Complete the sentences with a comparative adjective from the box, using an -er or more + adjective form. Use both if possible. A

deep	hard	long	naughty	pretty	scared	strong	true

1 It was almost as if the wolf was .... of us than we were of it.
2 The river was .... than I expected so I decided to turn back.
3 I think I'd describe her as .... than beautiful.
4 I bought this tennis racket because it's ....
5 Sam isn't a bad boy really. He's .... than dishonest.
6 The exam was .... than I thought it would be.
7 We need to take responsibility for elderly neighbours, and in a cold winter like this it is .... than ever.
8 We took the .... path up the hill as the other one was very steep.

72.2 If necessary, correct or improve the comparative adjectives. B

1 I may not be much of a cook, but Nina is even ~~uselesser~~ in the kitchen than I am.
more useless
2 When I took the washing out of the machine it looked *dirtier* than when it went in.
3 A: The painting is from the 17th century.
B: Really? It looks *recenter* than that.
4 The film starts slowly, but gets *excitinger* after the first half hour.
5 Louis is already rich, but his aim in life seems to be to become even *more wealthy*.
6 All of us are unique, but some of us are *more unique* than others.
7 Most research in this area uses simple interviews, but we used a *complexer* methodology.
8 I didn't do well at school, and my fellow students all seemed *cleverer* than me.
9 For an extra $500 you could buy a much *powerfuler* motorbike.
10 Curiously, many people say they feel mentally *alerter* if they eat very little for a day.

72.3 Put brackets around the if it can be omitted in these sentences. C

1 It was the sweetest orange I'd eaten for ages.
2 Anna, Beth and Clara were all excellent musicians, but Clara was the most creative.
3 He's the fastest runner in his class.
4 We get lots of birds in our garden, but blackbirds are the most common.
5 A: Shall we go by train, bus or car?
B: Well, going by bus is actually the easiest.

72.4 Complete the sentences with in or of. D

1 The building is said to be the highest .... Europe.
2 The Democrats are the smallest .... the four main political parties.
3 Parmesan is perhaps the most famous .... all Italian cheeses.
4 For many people, it is the most important day .... the whole year.
5 She's without doubt the best swimmer .... my school.

Unit 73

Comparative phrases and clauses

A

We use **as + adjective / adverb + as** to say that something or someone is like something or someone else, or that one situation is like another:

- Was the film **as funny as** his last one?
- I came round **as quickly as** I could.

Negative forms of sentences like this can use either **not as** or **not so**. In formal speech and writing it is more common to use **less + adjective + than**:

- The gap between the sides is **not as / so wide as** it was. (*or* … is **less wide than** it was.)

B

If we put a singular countable noun between an adjective and the second **as**, we use **a / an** in front of the noun:

- Despite his disability, he tried to lead **as normal a life as** possible. (*not* … as normal life as …)

The negative form of sentences like this can use either **not as** or sometimes **not such**:

- It's **not as quiet a place** (*or* ... **not such a quiet place** …) **as** it used to be.

Note that we use **not as + adjective + a / an + noun** but **not such a / an + adjective + noun**.

We can use **so**, **too** and **how** followed by an adjective in a similar way:

- It's not quite **so straightforward a problem as** it might at first seem.
- 'Conspiracy' is perhaps **too strong a word**.
- **How big a piece** do you want?

C

We also use **as much / many as** or **as little / few as** to say that a quantity or amount is larger or smaller than expected. **Many** and **few** are preferred before numbers; **much** and **little** are preferred with amounts (e.g. $5, 20%) and distances (e.g. 3 metres):

- There are a small number of people involved, possibly **as few as** twenty.
- Prices have increased by **as much as** 300%.

D

We can use **not + adjective / adverb + enough + to-infinitive** to mean that there isn't as much as is necessary to do something:

- I'm not **tall enough** *to reach*.
- He didn't speak **loudly enough** *to be heard*.

We can use **sufficiently** before adjectives to express a similar meaning to **enough**. **Sufficiently** is often preferred in more formal contexts:

- She didn't play **sufficiently well** to qualify. (*or* … **well enough** to qualify.)

E

We can use **too + adjective / adverb + to-infinitive** to mean 'more than necessary, possible, etc.' to do something:

- They arrived **too late** *to get* seats.
- It moved **too fast** *to see* it clearly.
- The suitcase was **too small (for him)** *to get* all his clothes in.

In rather formal English we can use **too + adjective + a / an + noun**:

- I hope you haven't had **too tiring a day**. (*not* … a too tiring day.)

(In a less formal style we might say 'I hope your day hasn't been too tiring.')

F

We can use **so + adjective / adverb + that-clause** to say that something existed or happened to such a degree that a specified result occurred (see also Unit 81):

- It's **so simple** *that* even I can do it.
- He came in **so quietly** *that* I didn't hear him.

Less often we use **so + adjective / adverb + as + to-infinitive** with a similar meaning. Compare:

- The difference was **so small** *that* it wasn't worth arguing about. *and*
- The difference was **so small as** *to not be* worth arguing about. (= Because the difference was so small, it wasn't worth arguing about)

We can use **go so / as far as + to-infinitive** to talk about actions that are surprising or extreme:

- One furious woman **went so / as far as** *to throw* tomatoes at the minister.

Exercises

73.1 **Complete these sentences with as … as or not as / such … as (or both if possible). Use the words in brackets and add any other necessary words.** B

1 It's *not such a polluted city now as / not as polluted a city now as* it was ten years ago. (*not / polluted / city now*)
2 The Downtown Hotel is .... Strand Hotel. (*not / pleasant / place to stay*)
3 The President's address to the nation is .... he is ever likely to make in his career. (*important / speech*)
4 It was .... I first thought. (*not / big / problem*)
5 Theresa's dog is .... I've ever seen. (*ferocious / animal*)
6 She's .... she claims to be. (*not / fluent / Greek speaker*)

73.2 **Complete these sentences with as much as, as many as, as little as, or as few as.** C

1 When it was really hot I was having .... four showers a day.
2 The elephant population may soon fall to .... 1,000 from 5,000 ten years ago.
3 At the end of the 200-metre race there was .... 50 metres between the first and second runners.
4 .... 5,000 people phoned in to complain about last night's TV programme.
5 Lit continuously, the life of a light bulb varies from .... two weeks to three months.
6 Some days there were .... three or four students at his lectures.
7 We don't use much electricity. Sometimes our bill is .... £40 a month.
8 The country spends .... 25% of its income on defence.

73.3 **Join the sentences using so + adjective + as + to-infinitive.** F

1 The noise from the factory was loud.
2 Her handwriting was untidy.
3 The bookcase was heavy.
4 The CD was badly scratched.
5 The plot of the novel was complicated.
6 The difference between the results was small.

a It was nearly illegible.
b It was insignificant.
c It was unplayable.
d ~~It prevented me sleeping.~~
e It was almost impossible to move it.
f It was completely incomprehensible.

1 + d *The noise from the factory was so loud as to prevent me sleeping.*

73.4 **Correct any mistakes in the italicised parts of this interview with a football manager.** A–F

INTERVIEWER: (1) *How serious injury* is it? Is it (2) *so serious as* has been claimed in the newspapers? Some people are saying Franz Kahn will never play international football again.

MANAGER: Well, it's certainly (3) *enough bad to* keep him out of football for at least six months. He's obviously (4) *not so fit as* he used to be and even he would admit that he's (5) *not such good player as* he was in his twenties. But I wouldn't (6) *go so far to say* that he'll never play for the national team again. I know him (7) *sufficiently well enough* to say that he will consider his future carefully before making any major decisions.

INTERVIEWER: Well, we all wish him (8) *as speedy recovery as* possible …

Unit 74

Position of adverbs 1

A

There are three main positions for adverbs which modify a verb: *end*, *front* and *mid* position –

☆ In *end position*, the adverb comes after the verb – either immediately after it or later in the clause.	They *played* **quietly** all day. He *tried to leave* **quietly**. He *sat* in the corner **quietly**.
☆ In *front position* the adverb comes before the subject.	**Finally** *he* could stand the noise no longer. **Sometimes** *I* feel like leaving.
☆ In *mid position* the adverb comes between the subject and verb, immediately after **be** as a main verb, or after the first auxiliary verb.	*He* **usually** *plays* better than this. She *is* **usually** here by ten. They *would* **usually** *come* by car.

Many adverbs can go in any of these positions, depending on context or style. For example:

- He turned round **slowly**. (*end*)
- **Slowly** he turned round. (*front*)
- He **slowly** turned round. (*mid*)

B

End position

In end position, we usually put an adverb *after* an object rather than immediately after the verb:

- We considered *the problem* **briefly**. (*not* We considered briefly the problem.)

However, if an object is very long other positions are possible:

- We considered **briefly** *the long-term solution to the problem*. (*or* We **briefly** considered ...)

C

We avoid putting an adverb between a main verb and a following **-ing** form or **to-infinitive**:

- He began running **quickly**. *or* He **quickly** began running. (*not* He began quickly running.)
- She tried to leave **quietly**. *or* She **quietly** tried to leave. (*not* She tried quietly to leave.)

The position of the adverb can change the meaning of the sentence (see Unit 75A). Compare:

- I recall telling him **clearly** that he had won. (= I told him clearly; 'clearly' modifies 'telling him') *and*
- I **clearly** recall telling him that he had won. (= I clearly recall it; 'clearly' modifies 'recall'.)

'I recall **clearly** telling him that he had won' is also possible, but is ambiguous; it can have either of the two meanings given above. In speech, the meaning intended is usually signalled by intonation.

D

When there is more than one adverbial in end position, the usual order in written English is **adverbial of manner** (= saying *how* something is done), **place**, and then **time**:

- In the accident she was thrown **violently forwards**. (= manner + place)
- We arrived **here on Saturday**. (= place + time)

For special emphasis we can move an adverbial to the end:

- In the accident she was thrown **forwards**, **violently**.

If one adverbial is much longer than another then it is usually placed last:

- They left **at three with a great deal of noise**. (= time + manner)

An adverb usually comes before a prepositional phrase when these have the same function (i.e. when they both describe manner, or place, or time):

- She went **downstairs to the cellar**. (= place + place)

E

End position is usual for many adverbials of **place**, **definite frequency**, and **definite time**:

- They live **upstairs**. (*not* They upstairs live.)
- She goes **weekly**. (*not* She weekly goes.)
- Have you heard the good news? Eva had a baby **in May**. (*not* Eva in May had a baby.)

However, adverbs of indefinite time usually go in mid position (see Unit 75).

Note that in journalism, other adverbs of time are often used in mid position, where we would normally place them in end (or front) position:

- The government **yesterday** announced an increase in education spending.

Exercises

74.1 **Put the adverb in brackets in an appropriate position in each sentence. In some cases both positions are possible.** C

1 I .... expect Catalina to win the race .... (*easily*)
2 He .... regretted missing the concert .... (*greatly*)
3 I .... hated playing the piano .... , although my parents thought I loved it. (*secretly*)
4 He .... started to walk .... across the bridge over the gorge. (*calmly*)
5 She .... offered to do the work .... (*kindly*)
6 Bruno .... finished speaking .... and sat down. (*hurriedly*)
7 I .... don't remember putting it down .... (*simply*)
8 We .... look forward to hearing from you .... (*soon*)
9 They .... tried to ignore me .... (*deliberately*)
10 I don't .... pretend to understand the instructions .... (completely)

74.2 **Complete this email using the words and phrases from the box below in the correct order.** B & D

Delete Junk Reply Reply All Forward Print To Do

We had a great time driving (1) ..around Switzerland in July.. . We flew into Zurich and hired (2) .... We drove (3) .... , and stayed (4) .... Every morning we got up (5) .... and went down to the nearby lake for a swim – freezing, but wonderful! The next week we drove east and stayed (6) .... It's in a spectacular part of the country, but we had to drive (7) .... Finally, we drove back to Zurich and caught (8) .... We enjoyed (9) .... and we're looking forward to going back (10) ....

1 ~~in July / around Switzerland~~	2 a car / at the airport
3 towards the lakes / south	
4 in a beautiful cottage belonging to some friends of Kim's mother / for a week	
5 early / at about six o'clock	
6 in the village where Kim had spent some time when she was a student / briefly	
7 carefully / on the narrow winding roads	8 home / the train
9 in Switzerland / enormously / ourselves	10 before too long / there

74.3 **If necessary, rewrite these sentences putting the italicised word or phrase in a more appropriate position. If the sentence is already correct, write ✓.** B–E

1 I try to visit *every week* my parents. ..I try to visit my parents every week.. / ..Every week I try to visit my parents..
2 Next, beat the eggs *vigorously* in a small bowl.
3 I thought I'd locked *securely* the luggage.
4 I stopped *regularly* playing tennis after I broke my wrist.
5 Lee was *easily* beaten in the final.
6 Matias never eats in the canteen at work. He always brings *from home* sandwiches.
7 A: Do the Patel family still live next door? B: No, they moved last year *away*.
8 The local residents welcomed the decision to introduce a new bus service from their village into the nearby town *warmly*.
9 We have to hand the homework in *on Tuesday*.

→ **Additional exercise 13** (page 248)

Position of adverbs 2

A Front position

Most types of adverb commonly go in front position in a clause (see Unit 74A). In particular –

☆ *connecting adverbs*, which make immediately clear the logical relation to the previous sentence.	◯ The value of the yen has fallen. **As a result**, Japan faces a crisis.
☆ *time* and *place adverbs*, which give more information about a previous reference to a time or place.	◯ The last few days have been hot. **Tomorrow** the weather will be much cooler.
☆ *comment* and *viewpoint adverbs*, which highlight the speaker's attitude to what they are about to say (see Unit 78).	◯ She has just heard that her sister is ill. **Presumably**, she will want to go home.

Note, however, that other positions are possible for these adverbs.

Some words can be used both as comment adverbs or adverbs of manner. As comment adverbs they usually go in front position (but can go in other positions) and relate to the whole of the clause; as adverbs of manner they usually go in end position and modify the verb. Compare:

◯ **Naturally**, I'll do all I can to help. *and*
◯ The radioactive gas *occurs* **naturally** in many areas.

Also: **clearly, curiously, frankly, honestly, oddly, plainly, seriously**

Note that for special emphasis or focus, adverbs that usually go in mid position (see **B**) and end position (see also Units 74 and 76) can sometimes be put in front position:

◯ **In May**, Maxine had a baby. ◯ **Regularly**, Helena works on several paintings at once.

B Mid position

The following types of adverb usually go in mid position (see Unit 74A) –

☆ *degree adverbs* (e.g. **almost**, **hardly**, **nearly**, **quite**, **rather**, **scarcely**):

◯ The street lighting was so bad that *we* **almost** *missed* the turning.

although some (e.g. **completely**, **enormously**, **entirely**, **greatly**, **slightly**) can go in end position:

◯ I *admire* your work **greatly**. (*or* I **greatly** *admire* your work.)

Note that some degree adverbs are not usually used in mid position with some verbs. For example, **enormously** is not usually used in mid position with **develop**, **differ**, **go up** or **vary**; **greatly** is not normally used in mid position with **care** or **suffer**.

☆ *adverbs which indicate the order of events*, such as **first**, **last** and **next**. These can also go in end position, but if there is a phrase giving the time of an event they usually go before this:

◯ I **first** *met* her in 1997. (*or* I met her **first** in 1997.)

We don't usually put these in front position, except to list actions (see also Unit 76B):

◯ **Next**, add three teaspoons of sugar.

☆ *adverbs of frequency* which say in an indefinite way how often something happens, including **hardly ever**, **often**, **rarely**, **regularly**, **seldom** (see also Unit 76B); and also the frequency adverbs **always** and **never**:

◯ We **hardly ever** *see* Kaspar nowadays, he's so busy at the office.

Note, however, that adverbial phrases of indefinite frequency (e.g. **as a rule**, **on many occasions**, **from time to time**, **every so often**) usually go in front or end position:

◯ **As a rule**, I go every six months. (*or* … every six months, **as a rule**; *not* I as a rule go …)

C

We rarely put long adverbials (including clauses; see Units 58 and 59), and prepositional and noun phrases in mid position. Usually they go in end position or front position for emphasis:

◯ She phoned home, **anxious for news**. (*or* **Anxious for news**, she phoned home.)
◯ He picked up the vase **with great care**. (*or* **With great care** he picked up the vase.)
◯ I'd seen Tarik **the day before**. (*or* **The day before**, I'd seen Tarik.)

Exercises

75.1 **Complete each pair of sentences using one adverb from the box. Put the adverb in front position (as a comment adverb) in one sentence, and in end position (as an adverb of manner) in the other.** A

clearly	~~curiously~~	frankly	honestly	plainly	seriously

1 a ....Curiously.... , the house has two chimneys .... , although there's only one fireplace.
  b .... , Esther looked at him ....curiously.... , trying to work out whether he was being serious or not.
2 a .... , I was brought up to earn money .... , not to steal it from others.
  b .... , I'm perfectly capable of putting up the shelf myself ....
3 a .... , she admitted .... that she felt she wasn't doing a good job.
  b .... , I went to sleep during his lecture .... , it was so boring.
4 a A: Thanks for looking after the children for me.
  B: That's okay.
  A: .... , I don't know what I'd have done if you hadn't been around to help.
  b .... , I tried to speak .... to him about his bad behaviour, but he kept making me laugh.
5 a The chief executive of Eclom has phoned me every day this week to ask whether I've made my mind up. .... , he wants me to take the job ....
  b .... , I'd had very little sleep and was having difficulty thinking ....
6 a Lucas fidgeted in his seat and kept looking nervously at the door. .... , he was feeling ill at ease ....
  b .... she always dressed .... at work in a white blouse and grey skirt.

75.2 **Cross out any adverbs or adverbials that are incorrect / unlikely in these sentences.** B & Unit 74E

1 Asthma rates in cities do not *enormously / significantly* differ from those in rural areas.
2 Now that Lorna has moved to Kuala Lumpur, I *from time to time / rarely* see her.
3 I could see them *easily / scarcely* in the bright sunshine.
4 It was snowing and I was *almost / by an hour* late for the interview.
5 Carmen had *often / on many occasions* spoken at meetings before, so it was no surprise when she stood up.
6 I play chess with Lorenzo *hardly ever / every week*.
7 Although he had to lift heavy boxes in the factory, he *greatly / rarely* suffered from backache.
8 I forgot about the meeting *nearly / entirely* and my boss was really angry with me.

75.3 **Which of the positions [1], [2] or [3] can the adverb or adverbial in brackets go in?** A–C

1 [1] He [2] moved to New Zealand [3]. (*the following year*)
2 [1] The children [2] walked along the road [3]. (*in single file*)
3 [1] We [2] see Alex [3] any more. (*seldom*)
4 [1] He [2] complained to his physics teacher [3] . (*unhappy with the result*)
5 [1] I [2] agree with you [3]. (*entirely*)
6 [1] I [2] meet [3] Emma at school. (*often*)

→ Additional exercise 13 (page 248)

Unit 76 Adverbs of place, direction, indefinite frequency, and time

A

Adverbs of **place** and **direction** (or adverbials, particularly prepositional phrases) usually go in end position, but we can put them in front position to emphasise the location. The effect may also be to highlight what comes at the end (e.g. 'a body' in the example below). This order is found mainly in formal descriptive writing and reports. Compare:

- The money was eventually found **under the floorboards**. (= end) *and*
- The police searched the house. **Under the floorboards** they found a body. (= front)

If we put an adverb of place in front position we put the subject *after* the verb **be** (see also Unit 99A):

- **Next to the bookshelf** *was* a fireplace. (*or less formally* **Next to the bookshelf** there *was* a fireplace; *not* Next to the bookshelf a fireplace was.)

We can also put the subject after the verb with intransitive verbs (except with a pronoun subject) used to indicate being in a position or movement to a position:

- Beyond the houses **lay** *open fields*. *but*
- Beyond the houses *they* **lay**. (*not* … lay they)

Note that '... open fields lay' might be used in a literary style.

Also: **hang, live, sit, stand; come, fly, go, march, roll, run, swim, walk**

However, we don't usually put the subject after the verb when we talk about actions: if one of these intransitive verbs is followed by an adverb of manner; with other intransitive verbs; or with transitive verbs:

- Through the waves the boy **swam** *powerfully*. (*rather than* … swam the boy powerfully.)
- Outside the church the choir **sang**. (*rather than* … sang the choir.)
- In the garden Nik **built** *a play house* for the children. (*not* In the garden built Nik …)

B

When we put certain adverbs of time in front position the subject must come *after* an auxiliary verb or a main verb **be** (see also Unit 100):

- **At no time** would *he* admit that his team played badly. (*not* At no time he would admit …)
- **Not once** was *she* at home when I phoned. (*not* Not once she was …)

If the main verb is not **be** and there is no auxiliary, we use **do**, although inversion is not necessary in this case:

- **Only later did** *she* realise how much damage had been caused. (*or* Only later she realised …)

Adverbs like this include negative time adverbials such as **at no time**, **hardly ever**, **not once**, **only later**, **rarely**, and **seldom**. Note also that we can put **first**, **next**, **now** and **then** in front position with the verb **come** to introduce a new event, when the subject follows the verb. But if a comma (or an intonation break in speech) is used after **first** (etc.) the verb follows the subject. Compare:

- At first there was silence. **Then** *came* a voice that I knew. (*not* Then a voice came …) *and*
- At first there was silence. **Then**, a voice *came* that I knew.

C

Adverbs of **time** which indicate a definite point or period in time or a definite frequency usually go in end position, or front position for emphasis, but not in mid position. Note that when these adverbs are in front position there is no inversion of subject and verb:

- I went to Paris **yesterday**. (*or* **Yesterday** I went to Paris.)
- We meet for lunch **once a week**. (*or* **Once a week** we meet for lunch.)

The adverbs **daily**, **hourly**, **monthly**, **weekly**, **annually**, **quarterly** (= four times a year), etc. only go in end position:

- I pay my subscription **annually**. (*not* Annually I pay …; *not* I annually pay …)

Exercises

76.1 Rewrite the sentences putting the italicised adverbs of place or direction at the front of the clause. If possible, invert the order of subject and verb. A

1 A dark wood was *at the bottom of the garden.*
At the bottom of the garden was a dark wood.
2 The car stopped suddenly and Daniel jumped *out*.
3 Two small children stood *outside the door*.
4 The boys were playing cricket *in the park*, despite the muddy conditions.
5 A jade necklace hung *around her neck*.
6 The man released the monkey and it climbed *up the tree*.
7 The door burst open and a delegation from the striking workers marched *in*.
8 While Marko was looking around for his net the fish swam *away*.
9 Most of the furniture was modern, but a very old grandfather clock was *in the corner*.
10 Lea found it difficult to concentrate *in the office*, but she worked more efficiently *at home*.

76.2 If possible, rewrite the italicised parts of these sentences putting the time adverbial in front position. Where you can, invert subject and verb, and make any other necessary changes. B & C

1 I trusted Dan completely, and *I realised only later that he had tricked me.*
I trusted Dan completely, and only later did I realise that he had tricked me.
2 After working so hard all summer, *I had a holiday last week*.
3 Professor Coulson was to give the initial paper at the conference, but *a welcoming address came first by the head of the organising team*.
4 The area was cleared before the explosion, and *members of the public were in danger at no time*.
5 I've got high blood pressure and *I have to take tablets daily* for it.
6 When it became clear that he was in danger of losing the election, *a politician can seldom have changed his views so quickly as Beckett*.
7 After a few days of relative calm, *a blizzard came next, preventing us from leaving the hut*.
8 It's hard to imagine that *we'll be in Japan by next Friday*.
9 You won't have long to wait as *trains for Rome leave hourly*.
10 My grandfather was a gentle man, and *I hardly ever heard him raise his voice in anger*.

76.3 If necessary, correct the word order in these sentences. A–C

1 I walk to work for the exercise, and I twice a week play squash.
2 If you take the job, monthly your salary will be paid into your bank account.
3 Down the hill the horse ran quickly.
4 Through the window Megan watched sadly.
5 Around the town drove she for hours looking for the gallery, until she spotted in a side street the place.
6 I tripped over the cat, dropped the tray, and across the room flew it.

Unit 77

Degree adverbs and focus adverbs

A

Degree adverbs can be used before adjectives, verbs, or other adverbs to give information about the extent or level of something:

- They're **extremely** *happy*.
- I **really** *hate* coffee.
- He **almost** *always* arrived late.

Some degree adverbs, such as **almost**, **largely**, **really** and **virtually**, are usually used before the main verb, and others, such as **altogether**, **enormously**, **somewhat**, and **tremendously**, are usually used after the main verb. Degree adverbs are rarely used in front position (see Unit 75B).

Focus adverbs draw attention to the most important part of what we are talking about. Some (e.g. **especially**, **even**, **mainly**, **mostly**, **particularly**, **specifically**) make what we say more specific:

- There is likely to be snow today, **particularly** in the north.

and others (e.g. **alone**, **just, only**, **simply**, **solely**) limit what we say to one thing or person:

- Many people offered to help me invest the money, but I **only** trusted Rick.

B

Much and very much

In affirmative sentences in formal contexts, **much** can be used as a degree adverb before the verbs **admire**, **appreciate**, **enjoy**, **prefer** and **regret** to emphasise how we feel about things:

- I **much** *enjoyed* having you stay with us.
- Their music *is* **much** *admired*.

Much is used in this way particularly after **I** and **we**. Note that we don't usually use this pattern in questions (e.g. *not* Did you much enjoy ...?).

We can use **very much** in a similar way before the verbs above and also before **agree**, **doubt**, **fear**, **hope**, **like** and **want**. Note, however, that we don't use **much** before this last group of verbs. Compare:

- I **much** *prefer* seeing films at the cinema than on DVD. (*or* I **very much** prefer ...) *and*
- We **very much** *agree* with the decision. (*or* We agree very much ...; *but not* ... much agree ...)

We can also use **much** or **very much** before a past participle which is part of a passive:

- The new by-pass *was* (**very**) **much** *needed*.

We don't use **much** but can use **very much** before past participle adjectives (see Unit 69A):

- I was **very much** *surprised* by her news. (*or* I was *surprised* ...; *but not* I was much surprised ...)

and we don't use either **much** or **very much** before present participle adjectives:

- The hotel was (very) *welcoming*. (*but not* The hotel was (very) much welcoming.)

In negative sentences in informal contexts we can use (**very**) **much** before verbs such as **appreciate**, **enjoy**, **like**, and **look forward to** to emphasise a negative feeling about something:

- I didn't (**very**) **much** *enjoy* the film.

C

Very and too

Before an adjective or another adverb we use **very** when we mean 'to a high degree', and **too** when we mean 'more than enough' or 'more than is wanted or needed'. Compare:

- The weather was **very** hot in Majorca – perfect for swimming. (*not* ... too hot ...) *and*
- It's **too** hot to stay in this room – let's find somewhere cooler. (*not* ... very hot ...)

In negative sentences in informal spoken English we can use **not too** to mean 'not very':

- I'm **not too** bothered about who wins. (*or* I'm **not very** bothered ...)

D

Even and only

Even and **only** usually go in mid position (see Unit 75), but if they refer to the subject they usually come before it. Compare:

- My mother has **only** brought some food. (= She hasn't brought anything else) *and*
- **Only** my mother has brought some food. (= My mother and nobody else)
- Aya can **even** speak French. (= in addition to everything else she can do) *and*
- **Even** Aya can speak French. (= you might not expect her to) (*rather than* Aya even ...)

Exercises

77.1 Cross out any incorrect answers. B

1 We *very / much / very much* hope that the striking workers will now resume negotiations.
2 Thanks for organising the quiz night. Your help was *very / much / very much* appreciated.
3 I felt *very / much / very much* intimidated by some of the questions in the interview.
4 I had always *very / much / very much* admired her work, and it was great to meet her.
5 As a child, I *very / much / very much* wanted to be an artist.
6 I would *very / much / very much* prefer to be remembered as kind rather than wealthy.
7 It was *very / much / very much* thrilling to get Marie's news.
8 When I was travelling in India I became *very / much / very much* interested in regional foods.
9 Kristof says that he wants to go into politics, but I *very / much / very much* doubt that he's serious.
10 I *very / much / very much* regret not being able to hear Dr Greco when she gave her lecture.

77.2 Write very, too, or very / too if either is possible. C

1 Leo was in a wheelchair as he was still .... weak to walk far.
2 Ellie has agreed to start work earlier, but she's not .... enthusiastic about it.
3 The instructions are .... easy. You'll have no trouble understanding them.
4 It was .... alarming to learn that one of the plane's engines had stopped.
5 We'll be at the cinema well before the film starts. It won't take .... long to get there.
6 It was snowing .... heavily for us to climb further up the mountain.
7 He revised .... hard and did well in his exams.
8 The old bridge in town was .... narrow for the coach to drive across, so we had to go an extra 50 miles to the new one.

77.3 Put even or only in the most appropriate place in each sentence. D

1 Ben offered to let me stay with him while I was in Glasgow, and .... he .... offered to pick me up from the station.
2 .... I will .... be in my office on Monday next week as I'm going to Poland for a business meeting on Tuesday.
3 Every penny the charity raises helps the homeless, and .... the smallest donation .... can make a vital difference.
4 Jan seems to have invited everyone to the party. .... he has .... asked Ann, and they haven't spoken to each other for years.
5 .... Louis .... knew where the keys were kept, and nobody else.
6 I don't get home from work until late, so .... I .... cook at the weekend.

Unit 78 Comment adverbs and viewpoint adverbs

A

We use some adverbs to make a *comment* on what we are saying.

some comment adverbs:	*examples*
☆ indicate how likely we think something is	**apparently**, **certainly**, **clearly**, **definitely**, **obviously**, **presumably**, **probably**, **undoubtedly**
☆ indicate our attitude to or opinion of what is said	**astonishingly**, **frankly**, **generally**, **honestly**, **interestingly**, **luckily**, **naturally**, **sadly**, **seriously**, **surprisingly**, **unbelievably**
☆ show our judgement of someone's actions	**bravely**, **carelessly**, **foolishly**, **generously**, **kindly**, **rightly**, **stupidly**, **wisely**, **wrongly**

Comment adverbs often apply to the whole sentence and are most frequently used in front position (see Unit 75A), although they can also be used at the end of the sentence and in other positions. At the beginning and end of sentences we usually separate them from the rest of the sentence by a comma in writing or by intonation in speech:

- **Presumably**, he didn't hear me when I called.
- The book was based on his experience in China, **apparently**.
- If you practise continuously, you will **undoubtedly** get better.

Comment adverbs which show judgement usually follow the subject, although they can be put in front position for emphasis:

- He **kindly** offered to give me a lift. (*or* **Kindly**, he offered … *to emphasise* 'Kindly')

If comment adverbs apply to only part of the sentence they can be used in other positions. Compare:

- **Astonishingly**, she did well in the exam. (= I was surprised that she did well) *and*
- She did **astonishingly** well in the exam. (= she did extremely well)
- You've had a major operation. **Obviously**, it will be very painful for a while. (= I expect you to know this already) *and*
- When he stood up it was **obviously** very painful. (= the pain was clear to see)

B

Some adverbs are used to make clear what *viewpoint* we are speaking from; that is, identifying what features of something are being talked about:

- **Financially**, the accident has been a disaster for the owners of the tunnel.
- The brothers may be alike **physically**, but they have very different personalities.

Also: **biologically**, **environmentally**, **financially**, **ideologically**, **industrially**, **logically**, **medically**, **morally**, **outwardly**, **politically**, **technically**, **visually**

A number of phrases are used in a similar way:

- **Politically / In political terms**, this summer is a crucial time for the government.

Also: politically **speaking**, **in terms of** politics, **from a** political **point of view**, **as far as** politics **is / are concerned**

Some adverbs or phrases are used to say *whose* viewpoint we are expressing:

- The head of National Bank is to receive, **according to reports**, a £1 million bonus.
- **In my view**, the foreign minister should resign immediately.

Also: **to my / his / her** (etc.) **knowledge**, **from my / his / her** (etc.) **perspective**, **personally**, **in my / his / her** (etc.) **opinion**

Exercises

78.1 **Rewrite the italicised words using an adverb from the box. Choose the most likely position for the adverb.** A

~~astonishingly~~	bravely	carelessly	generously
interestingly	obviously	presumably	rightly

1 *It was very surprising indeed that* no paintings were destroyed by the fire in the gallery.
Astonishingly, no paintings were destroyed by the fire in the gallery.
2 As you drive off the ferry, there are lots of different flags flying by the side of the road. *It seems likely that* the idea is to welcome visitors from other countries.
3 *Acting more kindly than they needed to*, the builders agreed to plant new trees to replace the ones they had dug up.
4 Most people believe *in a correct way* that the prisoners should be released.
5 *It was easy to see that* she knew more about the robbery than she told the police.
6 He broke the window when he was painting *because he wasn't paying attention to what he was doing*.
7 She picked up the spider and put it outside, *showing no fear*.
8 *I found it strange that* the road didn't appear on the SATNAV.

78.2 **Complete the sentences with an appropriate viewpoint adverb from (i) and an ending from (ii).** B

(i)

environmentally	financially
industrially	~~medically~~
outwardly	politically
technically	visually

(ii)

... we'd be much better off if we moved there.
... the performance was stunning.
... it is relatively undeveloped.
... she looked remarkably calm.
... she could be sent to prison.
~~... the doctors can't find anything wrong.~~
... it is no longer the problem it once was.
... he claims to be a socialist.

1 Thomas says that he is still getting severe headaches, although ...
medically the doctors can't find anything wrong.
2 As she stepped onto the stage she felt terrified, but ...
3 Now that lead is no longer added to most petrol, ...
4 The country earns most of its income from agriculture and ...
5 The band didn't play terribly well, and the singing was awful, but ...
6 The cost of living is much lower in the north, so ...
7 Hansen is one of the richest men in the country, although ...
8 Julie is likely to be fined for failing to pay her gas bill, although ...

78.3 **Complete the sentences using the phrases from B either with the words from the box (or adjectives or adverbs formed from them) or your own words.** B

architecture	democracy	geology	grammar	~~history~~

1 Historically speaking, in what ways has disease affected the development of Western civilisation?
2 .... limestone is a relatively new rock.
3 The building is similar to the opera house in Milan ....
4 .... the essay was well written, but its style was inappropriate.
5 The election was clearly rigged and the result is a severe blow to the country ....

Adverbial clauses of time

A As, when and while

Reminder ➜ M1 & M8

We can often use **as**, **when** or **while** to mean 'during the time that', to talk about something that happens when something else takes place:

- **As / When / While** Miguel was eating, the doorbell rang.

We use **when** (*not* **as** or **while**) to introduce a clause which talks about –

☆ an event that takes place at the same time as some longer event (in the main clause):

- They were playing in the garden **when** they heard a scream.

☆ the circumstances in which the event in the main clause happens:

- **When** they are fully grown these snakes can be over two metres long.

We also use **when** to mean 'every time', and we prefer **when** to talk about past periods of our lives:

- I still feel tired **when** I wake up in the morning. (= 'every time')
- His mother called him Robbie **when** he was a baby. (= a past period)

We prefer **when** if one event happens immediately after another, particularly if one causes the other:

- You'll see my house on the right **when** you cross the bridge.
- **When** the lights went out, I lit some candles.

In the first sentence, 'as' or 'while' would suggest 'during the time that' and the continuous would be more likely ('… as / while you are crossing …'). In the second sentence 'as' or 'while' would be very unlikely because lights usually go out instantaneously.

We prefer **as** to say that when one thing changes, another thing changes at the same time:

- **As** the cheese matures, its flavour improves. (*rather than* When the cheese …)

We can also use 'While …', particularly with a continuous tense: 'While the cheese is maturing …'.

We prefer **while** or **as** (rather than **when**) to talk about two longer actions that go on at the same time, although **while** is more common than **as** in informal speech:

- I went shopping **while** Liam cleaned the house. (*or* … **as** Liam cleaned …)

We use **while** or **when** (rather than **as**) to avoid ambiguity where 'as' could mean 'because':

- **While** you were playing golf, I went to the cinema. (As you were playing … = Because …)

B Before, after and until

We use **before** or **after** to talk about an event happening earlier or later than another event:

- I put on my coat **before** I went out.
- The message arrived **after** I'd left.

We can often use either **until** or **before** when a situation continues to happen up to a time indicated in the adverbial clause:

- I had to wait six weeks **until / before** the parcel arrived.

However, we use **until** to talk about an action that continues to a particular time and then stops:

- They sat on the beach **until** the sun sank below the horizon, and then they went home.

and when the adverbial clause describes the *result* of an action in the main clause:

- He cleaned his shoes **until** they shone. ('shining' is the result of 'cleaning'.)

C Hardly, no sooner, scarcely

When we say that one event happened immediately after another we can use sentences with **hardly**, **no sooner**, and **scarcely** (see also Unit 100). After **hardly** and **scarcely** the second clause begins with **when** or **before**; after **no sooner** it begins with **than** or **when**:

- The concert had **hardly** begun *before* all the lights went out.
- I had **no sooner** lit the barbecue *than / when* it started to rain.

We often use a past perfect in the clause with **hardly** (etc.), **no sooner** or **scarcely** and a past simple in the other.

Exercises

79.1 **Complete these sentences with as, when or while. If possible, give alternative answers and notice any differences in meaning.** A

1 She fell over .... she kicked the ball.
2 .... we were younger our parents had to pay for our music lessons.
3 .... I speak Spanish, I talk slowly to help people understand me.
4 .... I packed all the books away, Lana made a note of their titles on her laptop.
5 She stayed at home watching television .... her brother was at school.
6 Where did you live .... you got married?
7 .... the results started to come in, it became clear that President Como had lost the election.
8 The humidity started to increase .... the day wore on.
9 The snow was getting deeper and deeper .... we waited for the train to arrive.
10 .... the paint dries it changes colour from a light to a deep red.

79.2 **If necessary, correct or improve these sentences.** A

1 As I'm older I'd love to be a dancer.
2 When the boy watched in fascination, the ants picked up the dead beetle and carried it off to their nest.
3 The disk drive makes a buzzing sound while I switch my PlayStation on.
4 As the car went by, someone waved to me from the back seat.
5 While Kasem had finished, he tidied up the room and left.
6 I was in the shower as the phone rang.

79.3 **Complete this talk about the life and work of a professor with before or until or both if possible.** B

1 He continued to work at London University .... he retired in 2007.
2 .... he left his native country, he learned English by listening to the radio.
3 It wasn't long .... he was appointed Professor of Chemistry.
4 He married Martha .... he moved to England in 1960.
5 .... he came to England he worked in his father's grocery shop.
6 He applied for research positions .... he was appointed to a post at London University.
7 He was almost unknown outside his field .... he was awarded the Nobel Prize.
8 He would work in his lab for days at a time .... he had completed an experiment.

79.4 **Complete the sentences in any appropriate way.** C

1 The paint on the sitting room wall had scarcely dried ...
before my daughter put her dirty hands all over it.

2 Martin had no sooner recovered from a broken ankle ...
....

3 He had hardly put down the phone ...
....

4 We had no sooner eaten ...
....

5 Lisa had hardly finished speaking ...
....

6 I had scarcely driven to the end of the street ...
....

→ Additional exercise 14 (page 249)

Unit
80 Giving reasons: **as**, **because**, etc.; **for** and **with**

A

We can begin a clause with **as**, **because**, **seeing that**, **seeing as**, or **since** to give a *reason* for a particular situation:

- **As** *it was getting late*, I decided I should go home.
- We must be near the beach, **because** *I can hear the waves*.
- **Since** *he was going to be away on his birthday*, we celebrated before he left.
- We could go and visit Natalia, **seeing that** *we have to drive past her house anyway*.

Note that –

☆ it is common and acceptable for **because** to begin a sentence, as in:

- **Because** *everything looked different*, I had no idea where to go.

☆ to give reasons in spoken English, we most often use **because**. **So** is also commonly used to express a similar meaning (see also Unit 81). Compare:

- **Because** *my mother's ill*, I won't be able to come. ('because' introduces the reason) *and*
- *My mother's ill*, **so** I won't be able to come. ('so' introduces the result.)

☆ when it means 'because', **since** is rather formal. It is uncommon in conversation, but is frequently used in this way in academic writing:

- I had to go outside **because** I was feeling awful. ('since' is unlikely in an informal context)
- The results of this analysis can be easily compared to future observations **since** satellite coverage will remain continuous. (more likely than 'because' in this formal context.)

☆ **seeing that** is used in informal English. Some people also use **seeing as** in informal speech:

- Joel just had to apologise, **seeing that / as** he knew he'd made a mistake.

B

In formal or literary written English we can also introduce a reason in a clause beginning **for**, **in that**, or, less commonly, **inasmuch as**. **For** is a formal alternative to 'because'; **in that** and **inasmuch as** introduce clauses which clarify what has been said by adding detail:

- We must begin planning now, **for** *the future may bring unexpected changes*. (*not* For the future …, we must …)
- The film is unusual **in that** *it features only four actors*. (*or* **In that** …, the film is …)
- Clara and I have quite an easy life, **inasmuch as** *neither of us has to work too hard but we earn quite a lot of money*. (*or* **Inasmuch as** …, Clara and I …)

C

The prepositions **because of**, **due to**, and **owing to** can also be used before a noun or noun phrase to give a reason for something:

- We were delayed **because of** an accident.
- She was unable to run **owing to / due to** a leg injury. (= because of a leg injury.)
- We have less money to spend **owing to / due to** budget cuts. (= because of budget cuts.)

Note that we don't use **because** alone before a noun or noun phrase:

- We were delayed **because** there was an accident. (*not* … because an accident.)

In current English we usually avoid **owing to** directly after a form of **be**:

- The company's success *is* **due to** the new director. (*not* ... is owing to ...)

However, **owing to** is used after **be + a degree adverb** such as **entirely**, **largely**, **mainly**, **partly**:

- The low election turnout *was partly* **due to / owing to** the bad weather.

We can often use either **it was due to … that** or **it was owing to … that**:

- *It was* **owing to** his encouragement *that* she applied for the job. (*or It was* **due to** … *that*)

D

We can use **for** and **with** followed by a noun phrase to give a reason (compare **B** above):

- She was looking all the better **for** her stay in hospital. (= 'as a result of')
- **With** so many people ill, the meeting was cancelled. (= 'as a result of there being')

Exercises

80.1 Complete the sentences by putting an item from (i) and one from (ii), in the correct order. A

(i)	(ii)
1 ~~passengers were given a full refund~~	a it's your birthday
2 Andrea agreed to book tickets for us all	b it was her idea to go to the theatre
3 I'll buy you lunch	c Dr Gomez spoke about his research instead
4 I've given up dairy products	d a new copy would be very expensive
5 we were recommended to buy the textbook second-hand	e I suggested we all go on holiday together
6 the guest lecturer was late	f ~~the train was delayed for more than an hour~~
7 we get on so well	g it's supposed to be unlucky
8 you should never walk under a ladder	h I'm trying to lose weight

1 + f **Since** the train was delayed for more than an hour, passengers were given a full refund.

2 .... **as** ....

3 **Seeing as** ....

4 **Because** ....

5 .... **since** ....

6 **As** ....

7 .... **seeing that** ....

8 .... **because** ....

80.2 Complete the sentences using **due to** or **owing to** with one of the phrases from the box. If both **due to** and **owing to** are possible, write both. C

lack of interest ~~**stress at work**~~ **heavy cloud** **its central location** **human error**

1 She claims her illness is entirely due to / owing to stress at work.

2 The cancellation of the competition is ....

3 The popularity of the restaurant is largely ....

4 It's likely that the mistake was ....

5 We couldn't see last night's eclipse of the moon ....

Now complete these sentences using **because** or **because of** + a phrase from the box. C

his age **his mobile was switched off** **local opposition** **the bright sunlight** **there was a fly in it**

6 I had to drive in dark glasses ....

7 I couldn't speak to Jacob ....

8 The council had to withdraw its plan to close the swimming pool ....

9 My grandfather couldn't do a sponsored parachute jump ....

10 He sent the soup back ....

80.3 Rewrite these sentences using **for** or **with** instead of **because (of)**. Give alternatives where possible. D

1 I got a job as a street sweeper because my money was running out.
With my money running out, I got a job as a street sweeper. / I got a job as a street sweeper, with my money running out.

2 I couldn't hear what Isabella was saying because of the noise.

3 Olivia went to stay with her aunt because her father was in hospital.

4 I felt a lot fitter because of all the exercise I was doing.

5 Because the train drivers are on strike tomorrow, I don't think I'll go to town after all.

➜ **Additional exercise 14** (page 249)

Unit 81

Purposes and results: **in order to, so as to**, etc.

A In order / so as + to-infinitive

To talk about the purpose of an action we can use **in order / so as + to-infinitive**:

- He took the course **in order to get** a better job.
- Trees are being planted by the roadside **so as to reduce** traffic noise.

In spoken English in particular it is much more common simply to use a **to-infinitive** without 'in order' or 'so as' to express the same meaning:

- He took the course **to get** a better job.

We rarely use just **not + to-infinitive**, but instead use **so as not to** or **in order not to**:

- He kept the speech vague **in order not** *to commit* himself to one side or the other. (*not* … vague not to commit himself …)
- I wrote down her name **so as not to** *forget* it. (*not* … name not to forget …)

However, in contrastive sentences we can use **not + to-infinitive, but + to-infinitive** as in:

- I came to see you **not** (*in order / so as*) **to complain**, **but** (*in order / so as*) **to apologise**.

Note that we can put **in order / so as** before the **to-infinitives** in sentences like this.

B In order that and so that

We also use **in order that** and **so that** to talk about a purpose. Compare:

- She stayed at work late **in order / so as** to complete the report. *and*
- She stayed at work late **in order that / so that** she could complete the report. (*not* … *in order that / so that* to complete the report.)

So that is more common than **in order that**, and is used in less formal situations. Note that informally we can leave out **that** after **so**, but we always include it after **in order**.

A present tense verb in the main clause is usually followed by a present tense verb (or a modal with present or future reference – **can**, **will**, etc.) in the clause beginning **in order that / so that**. A past tense verb in the main clause is usually followed by a past tense verb (or a modal with past reference – **could**, **would**, etc.) in the clause beginning **in order that / so that**. Modal verbs are very often used after **in order that / so that**:

- Regular checks *are made* **in order that** safety standards *are maintained*.
- Advice *is given* **in order that** students *can* choose the best course.
- *Did* you give up your job **so that** you *could* take care of your mother?
- I *hid* the presents **so that** Marianna *wouldn't* find them.

C Such that and in such a way that / as to; such … that

In formal contexts, such as academic writing, we can use **such that** to introduce a result:

- The model was designed **such that** the value of *x* could be calculated. (= 'in a way that has the result that …'; *or* … **in order that** …; *or* … **so that** …)

Less formally we can also use **in such a way that** or **in such a way as + to-infinitive** with a similar meaning:

- The advertisement is printed **in such a way that** two very different pictures can be seen depending on how you look at it.
- Our business is managed **in such a way as to minimise** its environmental impact.

We can also use **such + noun phrase + that** to introduce a result:

- It is **such** *a popular play* **that** all the performances were sold out after the first day.
  (For **so + adjective / adverb + that**, see Unit 73.)

Exercises

81.1 **Combine the two sentences in the most appropriate way using in order (not) + to-infinitive or so as (not) + to-infinitive.** A

1 I had to borrow money from the bank.
2 He packed his suitcase with the books at the bottom.
3 Bus fares in the city were being cut.
4 We crept quietly towards the deer.
5 I walked around the outside of the field.
6 We put up a fence.
7 She looked down at the book in front of her.
8 The roadworks were carried out at night.

a This was done to encourage people to use public transport.
b We wanted to prevent people walking across the grass.
c I didn't want to damage the growing crops.
d ~~I did this to set up the business.~~
e They didn't want to disrupt traffic too much.
f We didn't want to frighten them away.
g She wanted to avoid his gaze.
h He didn't want to crush his clothes.

1 + d I had to borrow money from the bank in order to set up the business.
(*or* ... so as to set up ...)

81.2 **Look again at the sentences you wrote in 81.1. Is it also possible to use only a to-infinitive, without in order or so as? Write ✓ or ✗.** A

1 I had to borrow money from the bank to set up the business. ✓

81.3 **Complete the sentences with the correct versions of the phrases from the box.** B

it *will / would* receive the new channels
it *won't / wouldn't* take up a lot of computer memory
mosquitoes *can't / couldn't* get in **nobody *will / would* know it was there**
~~**people *can / could* walk around the gardens**~~ **we *can / could* see the view over the city**

1 They have an open day at their house each year so that people can walk around the gardens.
2 I put a rug over the stain on the carpet so that ....
3 There were screens on all the windows so that ....
4 The software is designed so that ....
5 We went up to the top floor so that ....
6 The TV needs to be retuned so that ....

81.4 **Rewrite each sentence less formally in two ways; once using in such a way that and once using in such a way as to.** C

1 The factory demolition was planned such that any risk to the public was avoided.
The factory demolition was planned in such a way that any risk to the public was avoided. / The factory demolition was planned in such a way as to avoid any risk to the public.

2 The meeting room is designed such that everyone's voice can be heard without the use of microphones. ....
3 The website is organised such that it is easy to navigate. ....
4 If the dial is rotated such that the number 1 is at the top, the valve opens.
....

→ Additional exercise 14 (page 249)

Unit 82 Contrasts: **although** and **though**; **even though / if**; **while**, **whilst** and **whereas**

A Although and though

We use **although** or (less formally) **though** to say that there is a surprising contrast between what happened in the *main clause* and what happened in the *adverbial clause*:

- **Although / Though** Reid failed to score himself, he helped Jones to score two goals.

With a similar meaning, we can use **despite the fact that / in spite of the fact that** (e.g. **Despite the fact that / In spite of the fact that** Reid failed to score ...), **despite / in spite of** + **-ing** (e.g. **Despite / In spite of** Reid **failing** to score ...), or **despite / in spite of his / her + noun** (e.g. **Despite / In spite of his failure** to score ...).

Note that we can use **though**, but not **although**, at the end of a clause:

- I eat most dairy products. I'm not keen on yogurt, **though**.

We can give special emphasis to an adjective by putting it before **though** in the pattern **adjective** + **though** + **noun / pronoun** + **verb** (usually a linking verb such as **appear**, **be**, **become**, **feel**, **look**, **seem**, **sound**, **prove**, etc.). **As** (but not **although**) can be used instead of **though**. Compare:

- **Hot though** (*or* **as**) **the night air was**, they slept soundly. *and*
- **Although / Though** the night air **was** hot, they slept soundly.

B Even though and even if

We can use **even though** (*but not* 'even although') to mean 'despite the fact that' and **even if** to mean 'whether or not'. Compare:

Even though Matt doesn't speak Spanish, I think he should still visit Madrid.	= Despite the fact that he doesn't speak Spanish	i.e. the speaker knows that Matt doesn't speak Spanish
Even if Matt doesn't speak Spanish, I think he should still visit Madrid.	= Whether or not he speaks Spanish	i.e. the speaker doesn't know definitely whether Matt speaks Spanish or not

C While, whilst and whereas

In formal contexts we can use **while** or **whilst** with a meaning similar to 'although' to introduce something that qualifies what is said in the main clause or something that may seem to conflict with it. In this case, the **while / whilst** clause comes before or within the main clause, but not after it:

- **While / Whilst** there is no evidence that Rob cheated, we were all astonished that he passed the exam. (*not* We were all astonished that he passed the exam, while ...)
- The diesel model of the car, **while / whilst** more expensive, is better value for money.

Note that **whilst** is a rather literary word and some people avoid using it.

We can use **while** or **whereas** (or less often **whilst**) to say that something contrasts with something in the main clause. The **while / whereas** clause may come before or after the main clause:

- Juan gets lots of homework from school, **while / whereas** Mia gets very little.
- **While / Whereas** I always felt I would pass the exam, I never thought I would get an A grade.

We don't use **whereas** if what is said in the subordinate clause makes what is said in the main clause unexpected:

- **Although / While** Sophie's father is from Spain, she doesn't speak Spanish. (*not* Whereas ...)

We can use **-ing** and **past participle** (**-ed**) clauses after **although**, **though**, **while** and **whilst**, and also clauses with the subject and verb left out (see Unit 59D).

Exercises

82.1 **Join the sentence halves and give special emphasis to the adjective by moving it to the front of the sentence. Use either though or as.** A

1 it may seem amazing
2 she was frightened
3 food became scarce
4 the climbers were experienced
5 the instructions first appeared confusing
6 it looked disgusting
7 she felt confident
8 their new products have proved successful

a they were very useful when I looked at them in detail
b she forced herself to pick up the snake
c they had never faced such severe conditions before
d the company is still in financial difficulties
e they always found enough to share with me
f she knew the examination would not be easy
g ~~my brother Johan has just won the lottery~~
h it was actually quite tasty

1 + g Amazing though it may seem, my brother Johan has just won the lottery.
(*or* Amazing as it may seem ...)

82.2 **Expand the notes in brackets and rewrite the sentences using In spite of + -ing in 1–3 and In spite of his / her + noun in 4–6.** A

1 Although she has to cope with three small children, ... (*taking – part-time MBA course*)
In spite of having to cope with three small children, she is taking a part-time MBA course.
2 Although he was much younger than the others, ... (*was – most outstanding rider – team*)
3 Although he ate a big lunch, ... (*had – three-course meal – evening*)
4 Although he was frightened, ... (*allowed – huge spider – placed in his hands*)
5 Although she is obviously intelligent, ... (*finds – it difficult – express – ideas in writing*)
6 Although she was ill, ... (*went – walking holiday – Nepal*)

Now rewrite the sentences you have written beginning Despite the fact that ...

1 Despite the fact that she has to cope with three small children, she is taking a part-time MBA course.

82.3 **Underline the correct phrase.** B

1 The driver stopped to let on more passengers *even though / even if* the bus was already full.
2 I wouldn't tell you where Mariam lives *even though / even if* I knew.
3 *Even though / Even if* I only play one match for my country, I'll be happy.
4 *Even though / Even if* he had just had lunch, Thomas bought a hamburger.
5 He plays for France *even though / even if* he was born in Algeria.
6 You won't see all the animals in the zoo *even though / even if* you stay for the whole day.
7 *Even though / Even if* I'm quite old, I still miss my parents.
8 I still couldn't afford to go to Taipei, *even though / even if* I took the cheapest route.

82.4 **Rewrite these sentences with a similar meaning. Begin the sentence with Whereas if possible and While if not.** C

1 Horse riding is an expensive pastime, but more and more people are taking it up.
While horse riding is an expensive pastime, more and more people are taking it up.
(*Whereas* ... is not possible)
2 A decade ago only 5% of students dropped out of college, but the figure today is 25%.
3 The temperature is below freezing, but it actually feels quite warm when the sun is out.
4 The cost of rail travel has increased, but the number of train passengers has grown.
5 I've always wanted to visit Australia, but I've never had any wish to go to Canada.

→ **Additional exercise 14** (page 249)

Unit 83

If 1

A Real conditionals

Reminder → M9–M17

In real conditionals we usually use a present tense verb in the **if-clause** to talk about the future:

- If you **leave** now, you'll be able to catch the 5 o'clock train. (*or* If you**'re leaving** now ...)

However, in conversation we can use **be going to** instead of a present tense verb:

- If I**'m going to** catch the train, I'll have to leave now.
- We'll need more chairs if we**'re going to** invite so many people to the performance.

When we make offers, and give instructions or advice we can use an imperative in the main clause:

- **Take** another sandwich if you're hungry.
- If you have a mobile phone, **check** that it is turned off.

B

We can use **if-clauses** with a present tense verb to introduce certain conditions under which something is true. In this case, 'if' has a meaning similar to 'when':

- The video pauses **if** you *click* on this button.
- **If** age-related changes *are taken* into account, the conclusion remains the same.

C

We can talk about possible future events with a present perfect verb in the **if-clause** and a future form (**will**, present continuous, or **be going to**) in the main clause. Sometimes present perfect or present simple can be used with a similar meaning:

- I*'ll* lend you *War and Peace* if I**'ve finished** it before you go on holiday. (*or* ... if I **finish** ...)
- If you **haven't paid** the bill by Friday, we*'re taking* the carpets back. (*or* If you **don't pay** ...)

However, to focus on the future consequences of a past event, we use the present perfect. Compare:

- If **I've failed** my exam again, I'm giving up the course. (suggests I have already taken the exam; I don't know the result) *and*
- If I **fail** my exam again, I'm giving up the course. (I may or may not have taken the exam)

D Unreal conditionals

In unreal conditionals we can use **if ...were + to-infinitive** rather than **if + past simple** to talk about imaginary future situations, particularly when it is unlikely that the situation in the **if-clause** will happen (see also Unit 14):

- **If** the technology **were to become** available, we would be able to expand the business.

However, note that we don't usually use this pattern with verbs such as **belong**, **doubt**, **enjoy**, **know**, **like**, **remember,** and **understand** when they describe a state:

- **If** I **knew** they were honest, I'd gladly lend them the money. (*not* If I were to know ...)

We sometimes use this pattern to make a suggestion sound more polite:

- Would it be too early for you **if we were to** meet at 5:30?

E

We use **if it was not for + noun phrase** (or more formally **if it were not for + noun phrase**) to say that one situation is dependent on another situation or on a person (see also Unit 85A). When we talk about the past we can also use **if it had not been for + noun phrase**:

- **If it wasn't / weren't for** *Nina*, the conference wouldn't be going ahead.
- **If it hadn't been for** *Dad*, I wouldn't have gone to college. (*or* **If it wasn't / weren't for** ...)

In formal language we can also use **Were it not for ...** and **Had it not been for ...** (see Unit 84A):

- **Were it not for** Nina ...
- **Had it not been for** Dad...

We can use **but for + noun** with a similar meaning, particularly in formal contexts:

- The village school would have been closed years ago **but for** *the determination* of teachers and parents to keep it open. (= ... if it hadn't been for the determination ...)

Exercises

83.1 **Complete these sentences with an imperative (1–3) or an if-clause (4–6).** A

1 There have been a lot of thefts from cars in the city centre. If you leave your car there, make sure it's locked. / don't leave any valuables in it.

2 If you have any more problems with the computer, ...

3 If you see Ned today, ...

4 .... keep well away from them.

5 .... don't hesitate to get in touch with me again.

6 .... get off at the stop near the library.

83.2 **Complete the sentences using the verb pairs from the box. Use the present simple or present perfect in the if-clause, and give alternatives. Notice any differences in meaning.** C

not fill in – need	**not help – go**	**leave – meet**
not arrive – give	~~**study – know**~~	**break – have to**

1 If you have studied / study *Macbeth*, you'll know the scene with the witches.

2 If you .... home before I get there, I'll .... you at the airport.

3 If you .... the window, you'll .... pay for it.

4 If the taxi .... by 10 o'clock, I'll .... you a lift to the station.

5 If you .... an application form, you will .... to do so before you can be considered for the job.

6 If the antibiotics .... by the end of the week, I'll .... back to the doctor.

83.3 **If necessary, correct the italicised part of the sentence using a past simple form of the same verb.** D

1 I'd sell the house immediately if it *were to belong* to me.

2 If they *were to hold* an election now, the Democrats would undoubtedly win.

3 I'd go back to the restaurant if I *were to like* sushi more.

4 If I *were to doubt* his honesty, I wouldn't employ him.

5 There would be no cinema in the town if the Odeon *were to close*.

6 If I *were to understand* Chinese, I'd do the translation myself.

83.4 **Complete these rewritten sentences with similar meanings.** E

1 The weather was terrible. Otherwise, we would have gone walking this weekend. *If it had* ... not been for the terrible weather, we would have gone walking this weekend.

2 His happiness would have been complete except for his anxiety over Carla. *If it were* ....

3 The strike would probably still be going on if the government hadn't intervened. *Were it* ....

4 The fight could have got out of hand if the police hadn't arrived. *Had it* ....

5 Everything was quiet except for the sound of birds singing. *But for* ....

6 There would have been far more wars in the last 50 years without the United Nations. *If it was* ....

7 We would have been here two hours ago except for the roadworks. *If it had* ....

If 2

A

When the first verb in a conditional **if-clause** is **should**, **were**, or **had** we can leave out **if** and put the verb at the start of the clause (see Units 99 and 100 for more on inversion). We do this particularly in formal or literary English, and only in hypothetical conditionals (a type of unreal conditional which answers the question 'What would happen if ...?'):

Reminder ➔ M9–M17

- **Should** any of this **cost** you anything, send me the bill. (= If any of this should **cost** ...)
- It would be embarrassing, **were** she **to find out** the truth. (= ... if she were to **find** out ...)
- **Had** they **not rushed** Jo to hospital, she would have died. (= If they **hadn't rushed** Jo ...)

B

We don't usually use **if ... will** in conditional clauses. However, we can use **if ... will** –

☆ when we talk about a *result* of something in the main clause. Compare:

- Open a window **if** it **will help** you to sleep. (*or* ... **if** it **helps** you to sleep; 'Helping you to sleep' is the result of opening the window) *and*
- I will be angry **if** it **turns out** that you are wrong. (*not* ... if it will turn out ...; 'Turning out that you are wrong' is **not** the result of being angry)

☆ in requests or with the meaning 'if you are willing to' (*or* **if ... would** to be more polite):

- **If** you **will** / **would** take your seats, ladies and gentlemen, we can begin the meeting.

☆ in real conditionals when we want to show that we disapprove of something. In this case, **will** is stressed in speech (see also Unit 16B):

- A: I'm tired. B: Well, **if** you <u>**will**</u> go to bed so late, I'm not surprised.

Note that we can use **if ... won't** when we talk about a refusal to do something:

- There's no point in trying to teach the class **if** they **won't** pay attention.

C

In a *real* conditional sentence, we use **if ... happen to**, **if ... should**, or **if ... should happen to** to talk about something which may be possible, but is not very likely. **If ... happen to** is most common in spoken English:

- **If** you **happen to** be in our area, drop in and see us. (*or* **If** you **should** [**happen to**] be ...)

Note that we don't usually use this pattern in *unreal* conditionals talking about states or events in the **if-clause** which the speaker perceives as highly unlikely or impossible:

- **If** the North Sea **froze** in winter, you could walk from London to Oslo. (*but probably not* If the North Sea happened to freeze / should (happen to) freeze in winter ...)

D

In *comparison clauses* we can use **as if** followed by a **noun phrase**, **-ing** clause, **past participle (-ed)** clause, or **to-infinitive** to introduce a comparison with a situation described in the main clause. We do this to give an explanation or to say that something appears to be the case but is not:

- Magnus walked in **as if** *nothing* had happened.
- His hands made a circular motion, **as if** *steering* a bus through a sharp bend.
- When he caught the ball, Lee fell to the floor **as if** *hit* by a bullet.
- **As if** *to convince* herself that Luis was really there, she gently touched his cheek.

Note that we can use **as though** instead of **as if**, and in informal speech some people use **like** with the same meaning:

- The crowd reacted **as though** they were watching a boxing match. (*or* ... **as if** ...)
- He walked into the room **like** nothing had happened. (*or* ... **as if** ...)

Exercises

84.1 **Rewrite these sentences with similar meanings. Begin with the word given.** A

1 Consult your doctor again if the symptoms remain 72 hours after starting the course of medicine. *Should* ... the symptoms remain 72 hours after starting the course of medicine, consult your doctor again.

2 You would know what you have to do for homework, if you had not been absent from school on Friday. *Had* ....

3 Clare would have been able to stay with her friends if they were still living in Brussels. *Were* ...

....

4 The factory would not have had to shut down if the workers were prepared to accept a wage cut. *Were* ....

5 We shall have to reduce the number of employees if the financial performance of the company doesn't improve in the near future. *Should* ....

6 I might have considered taking the job if the salary had been higher. *Had* ....

84.2 **If necessary, correct the italicised parts of these sentences.** B

1 *If I will press this button*, will it start to record?
2 You're welcome to borrow my old bike, *if you think it will be of any use to you.*
3 *If he won't resign*, the Prime Minister should sack him.
4 *If the disease will be untreated*, it can lead to brain damage.
5 *If you'll tell me where the vacuum cleaner is*, I'll do some cleaning.
6 *If you'll complain about me*, I'll get into trouble with my teacher.
7 *If it'll save money*, I'm willing to go by public transport.

84.3 **If possible, rewrite the italicised parts of these sentences with happen to. If it is unlikely, write ✗ after the sentence.** C

1 *If I see Georgia when I'm in Rome*, I'll send her your regards.

....

2 *If a UFO landed in the centre of New York*, there would be mass panic.

....

3 The plan for a new airport to be built outside London is bad news *if you live nearby*.

....

4 *If I was the President*, I would order our nuclear weapons to be destroyed.

....

5 *If you are in the south of Spain next week*, there is a good chance of seeing a total eclipse of the sun.

....

84.4 **Complete the sentences using your own words or the notes if you prefer.** D

(agree – everything Julia said) ~~**(I – say – shocking)**~~ **(it – reverse – wall)**
(try – imagine – contained) **(overcome – great weariness)**

1 My father raised his eyebrows as if I had said something shocking.
2 He folded his arms on the table and laid his head on them, as if ...
3 She stared hard at the parcel as if ...
4 He nodded his head slowly as if ...
5 The back of the car looked as if ...

Unit 85 If I were you ...; imagine he were to win

A

In *unreal* conditional sentences we can use **were** after any subject in the **if-clause**, including singular first and third person subjects (e.g. **I / she / he / it**). This use of **were** is sometimes called the *past subjunctive*, and is generally preferred only in formal contexts. Note that although the verb has a past form, reference is to the imagined present or future:

Reminder ➔ M13–M17

- **If your mother were** here, I'm sure she wouldn't let you eat all those chocolates.
- My job would not exist **if it were not for** government funding.

Was can be used instead of **were** with the same meaning ('If your mother was here ...', etc.). However, we prefer **were** rather than **was** when we give advice with **If I were you ...**:

- **If I were you**, I'd take it back to the shop. It's got a hole in it. (*rather than* If I was you ...)

B

Were is used in this way in other patterns when we talk about *imaginary situations* –

(i) when we use **were + subject + to-infinitive** or **were + subject** as a more formal alternative to **if + subject + was / were** (see also Unit 84A):

- **Were the election to be** held today, the Liberals would win easily. (*or* **If the election was / were** held today ...)
- **Were I not** in my seventies and rather unfit, I might consider taking up squash. (*or* **If I wasn't / weren't** in my seventies and rather unfit ...)

(ii) after **wish**:

- I enjoy my job enormously, but I *wish* **it were** closer to home. (*or* ... I *wish it* **was** ...)
- Of course I'm pleased that Jan has been given the award. I only *wish* **he weren't** so boastful about it. (*or* ... I only *wish* **he wasn't** ...)

(iii) after **if only** when we express our regret that a situation isn't different:

- 'If your job is so bad, why don't you leave?' '*If only* **it were** that simple.' (*or If only* **it was** ...)
- I'd really like to do accounting. *If only* **I weren't** so poor at maths. (*or If only* **I wasn't ...**)

(iv) after **would ('d) rather** and **would ('d) sooner** when we talk about preferences:

- I feel embarrassed about what happened and *would rather* **the event were** forgotten. (*or* ... **was** forgotten.)
- 'I've arranged a meeting for the end of July.' 'I*'d sooner* **it were** earlier, if possible. (*or* ... **it was** earlier.)

(v) in sentences or clauses beginning with **suppose**, **supposing** and **imagine**:

- *Suppose* **I were** to lower the price by £100. Would you consider buying the car then? (*or Suppose* I **was** to lower ...)
- I know it looks rather dirty now, but *imagine* **the house were** (to be) repainted. It would look a lot more attractive. (*or* ... *imagine* **the house was** (to be) repainted.)

And in *comparisons* we can use **were** –

(vi) after **as if** and **as though** (see Unit 84D) and **even if**:

- I remember stepping off the boat in New York *as if* **it were** yesterday.
- Despite losing the election, she continues to act *as though* **she were** prime minister.
- It's too late to start the work this year *even if* **it were** possible to find the money for it.

Exercises

85.1 **Match an item from (i) with an ending from (ii) to form a sentence. Begin Were ... (not).** Bi

(i)
1 ... found guilty of libel ...
2 ... government to increase university fees ...
3 ... anyone to lean against the window ...
4 ... not already busy in August ...
5 ... to see the conditions in which the refugees are living ...

(i)
a the glass would certainly break
b you would be horrified
c I would gladly accept your invitation
d there would be an outcry from students
e ~~the newspaper would face huge legal costs~~

1 + e *Were it to be found guilty of libel, the newspaper would face huge legal costs.*

85.2 **Expand the notes to write a sentence to go before each question below. Use Suppose, Supposing, or Imagine, followed by a pronoun, noun or noun phrase and then were.** Bv

1 (miss / last train) *Supposing we were to miss the last train.* How would we get home?
2 (inherit / million dollars) ....
How would it change your life?
3 (parents / tell you / emigrating to Canada) ....
How do you think you would react?
4 (Spain / win / World Cup) ....
How would you celebrate?
5 (population of Britain / all Buddhist) ....
How would its society be different?

85.3 **Complete the sentences with either as if or even if followed by an appropriate pronoun and then were.** Bvi

1 Muller spoke slowly *as if it were* a great physical effort.
2 Every day Mrs Demir would walk around the park .... snowing.
3 She knew she wouldn't be able to eat rabbit meat .... starving.
4 Theo completely ignored me .... not standing next to him.
5 He picked Natasha up .... no heavier than a two-year-old.
6 I don't think I would have got the job .... better qualified.
7 When Martina saw that I was stuck she laughed out loud .... a joke.
8 I wouldn't accept the job .... to offer it to me.

85.4 **Complete the sentences using one of the phrases in (i) with expanded notes from (ii).** A & B

(i)

~~if it were not for~~	if I were you
wish he were	if only it were
'd rather it were	'd sooner she were

(ii)

forgotten ... classmates	going ... friends
not so critical ... employees	
~~long nights ... winter~~	as easy ... that
breakfast before ... leave	

1 I would be happy to live in the north of Sweden *if it were not for the long nights in winter*.
2 I'm not happy about Jess going to Thailand alone. I ....
3 A: If you're unhappy with your new car, why don't you ask for your money back?
B: Well, ...
4 I know you haven't got much time, but ....
5 Wearing odd shoes to school was embarrassing and I ....
6 I'm very fond of Paul, but I ....

Unit 86

If ... not and unless; if and whether; etc.

A If ... not and unless

Unless is used in conditional sentences with the meaning 'except if':

- You can't travel on this train **unless you have** a reservation.

With **unless** we use present tenses when we talk about the future:

- **Unless it rains**, I'll pick you up at six. (*not* Unless it will rain ...)

B

In *real* conditional sentences, we can often use either **unless** or **if ... not** with a similar meaning:

- **Unless** the theatre is able to raise £100,000, it will have to close. (*or* **If** the theatre is**n't** able to ...; implies 'it will have to close *only if* it can't raise the money')

However, we use **if ... not** but not **unless** –

☆ when we say in the main clause that an event or action in the **if**-clause is unexpected:

- I'll be amazed **if** Christie does**n't** win.

☆ usually in questions:

- **If** you do**n't** pass the test, what will you do?

☆ when the 'only if' implication does not apply:

- **If** it was**n't** the best performance of *Hamlet* I've seen, it was certainly the strangest.

We usually use **if ... not** rather than **unless** in *unreal* conditional sentences:

- **If** I were**n't** so tired, I'd give you a hand.

However, **unless** can be used in *unreal* conditional sentences when the main clause is negative:

- She wouldn't have gone to university **unless** her parents had insisted.

C If and whether

We can use **if** or **whether** to say that two possibilities have been talked or thought about, or to say that people are not sure about something:

- They couldn't decide **if / whether** it was worth resitting the exam.
- Do you know **if / whether** Ben's at home?

Whether can usually be followed immediately by **or not**. Compare:

- I didn't know **if** Aya was coming **or not**. (*not* ... if or not Aya was coming.) *and*
- I didn't know **whether or not** Aya was coming. (*or* ... **whether** Tom was coming **or not** ...)

D

We use **whether** rather than **if** –

☆ after a **preposition** (although **if** is sometimes used informally) and before a **to-infinitive**:

- We argued *about* **whether** butter or margarine was better for you. (*informally* ... **if** ...)
- I couldn't decide **whether** *to buy* apples or bananas.

☆ in the pattern **noun / adjective + as to whether** to mean 'about' or 'concerning':

- There was some *disagreement* **as to whether** he was eligible to play for France.

Also: **conflict**, **confusion**, **debate**, **discussion**, **doubt, question**, **speculation**, **uncertainty**; **concerned**, **indifferent**, **uncertain**, **undecided**, **unsure**

and we prefer **whether** rather than **if** –

☆ after the verbs **advise**, **choose**, **consider**, **depend on**, **discuss**, **talk about**, and **think about**:

- You should *consider* **whether** the car you are interested in is good value.

☆ in a clause acting as a subject or complement:

- **Whether the minister will quit over the issue** remains to be seen.
- The first issue is **whether he knew he was committing a crime**.

Exercises

86.1 **Match the sentence halves and write a new sentence with the same meaning, beginning each one with Unless … .** A

1 We'll never get to the meeting …
2 Alternative sources of funding must be found …
3 If the roads haven't changed in that part of town …
4 The weather must start improving soon …
5 If it isn't ridiculously expensive …
6 You are only entitled to state benefit …

a … or the farmers will lose their crops.
b ~~… if the train doesn't leave within five minutes.~~
c … I'm sure I'll be able to find my way there.
d … or the research will not be able to continue.
e … I think I'll buy that painting.
f … if you have been unemployed for six months.

1 + b *Unless the train leaves within five minutes, we'll never get to the meeting.*

86.2 **If necessary, correct the italicised phrase using if … not.** B

1 *Unless she had gone* to university, she would have gone into the army. *If she hadn't gone*
2 *Unless the infection is treated* urgently, there is a real danger that she will die.
3 *Unless he was* so clumsy, he'd be the best person to do the work.
4 You won't be allowed into the country *unless you have* a visa.
5 It'll be surprising *unless Anya passes* her piano exam.
6 *Unless you get* a loan from the bank, how will you pay for the house?
7 They'll go on strike *unless they get* a pay rise.
8 Where will you stay *unless Louise is at home*?
9 The police can't prosecute me *unless they can prove* I intended to steal the ring.
10 She'd be a really good teacher *unless she was* so disorganised.

86.3 **Write whether or if / whether (if both are possible) in these sentences.** C & D

1 I was wondering ………… you'd had your exam results yet.
2 She was undecided as to ………… to fly or go by train.
3 Police have refused to confirm ………… or not they have arrested anyone for the theft.
4 It is unclear ………… the new regulations will affect all buildings or just new ones.
5 A: How much will the laptop cost?
B: That depends on ………… I get one with a 15 or 17-inch screen.
6 Danny said that he was leaving home, but I didn't know ………… to believe him.
7 Have you any idea ………… Steve will be at the meeting?
8 Can you remember ………… the door was open or closed when you got to the house?
9 There was considerable debate as to ………… chess was a game or a sport.
10 I don't know ………… Andrea's going to wait for us or not.
11 The government is considering ………… to hold an enquiry into the accident.
12 Everyone in the village was very friendly. It didn't matter ………… you'd lived there for a short or a long time.

Unit 87 Connecting ideas in a sentence and between sentences

A

Some words and phrases (*sentence connectors*) are used to connect one sentence with a previous sentence or sentences. Often (but not always) these go at the beginning of the sentence:

- There was no heating in the building. **As a result**, the workers had to be sent home.

Other words and phrases (*conjunctions*) are used to connect clauses *within* a single sentence:

- **While** I was waiting, I read a magazine.
- I stood up **so that** I could see better.

type of connection	*sentence connectors*	*conjunctions*
comparing, contrasting, and indicating that a situation (in the main clause) is unexpected	after all, all the same, alternatively, anyway, by contrast, even so, however (*but see* **C**), in any case, in contrast, instead, nevertheless, on the contrary, on the other hand	although, even though, though, whereas, while, yet
reasons and results	as a consequence, as a result, consequently, for one thing, so; hence, in consequence, therefore, thus (*the last four are rather formal*)	as, because, for, in that, since, insofar as, so, so that
adding information	above all, after all, also, besides, furthermore, in addition, likewise, moreover, similarly, what's more; as well, too (*the last two are not used at the beginning of a sentence*)	
condition	if not, if so, otherwise	as long as, assuming (that), if, on condition that, provided (that), so long as, supposing (that), unless
time: one event at the same time as another	at that time, at the same time, meanwhile	as, when, whenever, while
time: one event before or after another	after, after that, afterwards, before, before that, earlier, later, previously, soon, subsequently, then	after, as soon as, before, since, until

Note that **after**, **before** and **so** can be both connectors and conjunctions.

We can't use a sentence connector on its own with a comma to connect clauses *within* one sentence (e.g. *not* I expect to be promoted, if not I'll leave).

However, a sentence connector can be used to connect two clauses in one sentence if the clauses are joined with **and**, **but**, **or**, **so**, or a **semi-colon** (;), **colon** (:), or **dash** (–):

- The building was extremely well constructed **and, as a result**, difficult to demolish.
- You could fly via Singapore; **however**, this isn't the only way.

B

Even though is a conjunction used to say that a fact doesn't make the rest of the sentence untrue (see also Unit 82B). It connects ideas *within* a sentence:

- **Even though** it was midday, I put on the light.

Even so is a sentence connector used to introduce a fact that is surprising in the context of what was just said. It connects ideas *between* sentences:

- It was midday. **Even so**, I put on the light.

C

However is often used as a sentence connector, but it can also be used –

☆ as an adverb when it is followed by an **adjective**, **adverb**, or **much / many**:

- We just don't have the money to do the work, **however necessary** you think it is.

☆ as a conjunction when it means 'in whatever way':

- **However** she held the mirror, she couldn't see the back of her neck.

Exercises

87.1 **Choose items from (i) and from (ii) to complete these texts in an appropriate way. Note the punctuation at the ends of the sentences and phrases already given.** A & B

(i)	(ii)
alternatively	~~everybody had their fair share~~
as long as	you could poison them
for one thing	his face seemed familiar
meanwhile	it's too expensive
otherwise	the rent was paid on time
~~so that~~	the street was deserted
while	the volcano continues to erupt
yet	we were on holiday

1 Mara cut the cake carefully into slices *so that everybody had their fair share.*
2 A small boy was kicking a ball against a wall; ....
3 I couldn't remember meeting him before, ...
4 A mass evacuation of islanders is taking place. ....
5 A: Why don't you like that new French restaurant?
B: ....
6 Ingrid came down with flu ....
7 My landlady didn't mind me having parties in my room ....
8 One way of getting rid of weeds is to dig them out. ....

87.2 **Underline the correct option.** A–C

1 Your essay is badly organised and full of spelling mistakes. *Though / Nevertheless*, it contains some very interesting ideas.
2 To the east the trees were left standing, *while / in contrast* to the west they were cut down.
3 I felt guilty about leaving the company *even so / even though* I knew it was the right decision.
4 The course taught me a lot about astronomy. *Even though / Even so*, there is still a lot to learn.
5 I expected my mother to be happy with the news. *Instead / Although* she started to cry.
6 Herbs are usually grown in temperate climates, *whereas / on the other hand* spices are mainly from tropical areas.
7 We were very short of money *so / as a consequence* we had to spend the night on a park bench.
8 I turned the ignition, but the car wouldn't start. *As / Meanwhile* the lions were getting ever closer.
9 She wrote the questions on the whiteboard *while / at the same time* the students copied them into their books.
10 *Previously / Before* I went to Australia, I'd never seen a koala.
11 I'll have to buy some ladders *unless / if not* I can borrow a pair from Harry.
12 I first met Connor in the 1970s. *At that time / When* he had long hair and a beard.

87.3 **Use your own ideas to complete the sentences. Begin however + adjective / adverb / many / much.** C

1 She is determined to be a successful artist, *however difficult it might be to achieve.*
2 .... , it is difficult to lose weight without cutting down on the amount you eat.
3 .... , it is important to spend some time apart.
4 Professor Malcolm is always happy to spend time with his students, ...
5 .... , it never fails to impress me.
6 Some people never seem content, ...

➜ **Additional exercise 14** (page 249)

Unit 88

Prepositions of position and movement

A Across, over

We can use **across** or **over** to talk about a *position* on the other side of, or *moving* to the other side of a road, bridge, border, river, etc.:

- ▢ Antonio lives in the house **across / over** *the road* from ours.
- ▢ Once she was **across / over** *the border*, she knew she would be safe.

We use **over** rather than **across** when we talk about reaching the other side of something that is high, or higher than it is wide. Compare:

- ▢ He jumped **over** *the fence* into the garden. *and*
- ▢ He jumped **across** *the stream*.

When we are talking about something we think of as a flat surface, or an area such as a country or sea, we prefer **across** rather than **over**:

- ▢ He suddenly saw Eva **across** *the room*.
- ▢ The programme was broadcast **across** *Canada*.

We prefer **all over** rather than **all across** to mean 'to or in many different parts of an area'. However, we commonly use **across**, or **right across** for emphasis:

- ▢ The disease has now spread **all over** the world. (*or* … (**right**) **across** the world.)

B Along, through

When we talk about following a line of some kind (a road, a river, etc.), we use **along**:

- ▢ They walked **along** the footpath until they came to a small bridge.

We use **through** to emphasise that we are talking about movement in a three dimensional space, with things all around, rather than a two dimensional space, a flat surface or area:

- ▢ He pushed his way **through** the crowd of people to get to her.

Through often suggests movement from one side or end of the space to the other. Compare:

- ▢ She walked **through** the forest to get to her grandmother's house. *and*
- ▢ She spent a lot of her free time walking **in** the forest.

C Above, over; below, under; beneath, underneath

We can use either **above** or **over** when we say that one thing is at a higher level than another:

- ▢ **Above / Over** the door was a sign saying, 'Mind your head'.

However, we prefer **above**, when one thing is not directly over the other. Compare:

- ▢ They lived in a village in the mountains **above** the lake. (not directly over) *and*
- ▢ The bird hovered just a few metres **above / over** the lake. (directly over)

We use **over**, not **above**, when something covers something else and touches it:

- ▢ She put a quilt **over** the bed.

and usually when we are talking about horizontal movement at a higher level than something:

- ▢ I saw the helicopter fly out **over** the water, near the fishing boat.

Below is the opposite of **above**; **under** is the opposite of **over**. The differences in the uses of **below** and **under** are similar to those between **above** and **over** (see above):

- ▢ It's hard to believe that there is a railway line **below / under** the building. (at a lower level)
- ▢ Her head was **below** the level of the table so nobody noticed her. (not directly under)
- ▢ She hid the presents **under** a blanket. (the blanket covers and touches the presents)
- ▢ Zara ran **under** the bridge. (horizontal movement at a lower level)

We can use **underneath** as an alternative to **under** as a preposition of place. **Beneath** is sometimes used as a more formal alternative to **under** or **below**.

Exercises

88.1 **Complete the sentences with across or over, whichever is correct or more likely. If both are possible, write across / over.** A

1 After I'd finished work I walked .... the car park to where Mona was waiting.
2 They own a house .... the river in the old town.
3 The gate was locked so we had to climb .... the wall.
4 You're not allowed to walk .... the railway line. You have to use the bridge.
5 Julie Wafaei was the first woman to row alone .... the Atlantic.
6 Nuclear waste is transported .... the country, despite objections from campaigners.
7 The traffic was busy on the main road so we walked .... the pedestrian crossing.
8 She leaned out .... the balcony rail and looked for Omar in the square below.

88.2 **Underline the correct or most appropriate option(s) in each sentence.** A & B

1 It took several minutes to walk *across / over / along / through* the corridor to the exit.
2 *Across / Over / Along / Through* the table I could see Oliver looking at his watch.
3 He fell *across / over / along / through* the floor into the cellar below.
4 I could see Lisa *across / over / along / through* the other side of the river.
5 He cycles thousands of miles each year all *across / over / along / through* the country.
6 Hotels have been built *across / over / along / through* the beach for about 25 kilometres.

88.3 **Correct the prepositions (above, over, below, under) if necessary, or write ✓.** C

1 He slept with his wallet below his pillow.
2 He broke his leg just below his knee.
3 The town stood at the top of the hill, and stretching into the distance under it were green fields.
4 She threw a coat above her shoulders and stepped out into the cold.
5 He lived in a first-floor flat above a greengrocer's in Leyton.
6 When the police got to the car they found the driver slumped above the steering wheel.
7 He always wore a vest below his shirt, even in summer.
8 I could hear the plane flying high over the clouds.

88.4 **A number of common idioms include the prepositions in this unit. Match the idioms in italics to their meanings below.**

1 A: What's wrong?
B: I'm just feeling rather *under the weather*.
2 A: You never arrive on time. You'd be late for your own funeral, you would!
B: That's a bit *below the belt*, isn't it?'
3 She already has 18 books on gardening *under her belt* and she is now working on number 19.
4 He had never played well for the club and left *under a cloud*.
5 She lost her temper and went completely *over the top*, accusing him of cheating.
6 They received a bonus in December *over and above* their monthly salary.

a in addition to
b successfully completed
c ill
d cruel or unfair
e with some people's disapproval
f extreme behaviour; indicating disapproval

Unit 89

Between and among

A

As prepositions of *place* we use **between** with two or more people or things that we see as individual or separate, and we use **among** when we see the people or things as part of a group or mass. **Among** is only used with three or more people or things:

- She held the diamond **between** her thumb and forefinger.
- Zimbabwe is situated **between** Zambia to the north, Mozambique to the east, Botswana to the west, and South Africa to the south.
- He stood **among** all his friends at the party and felt very happy.
- She eventually found her passport **among** the clothes in the drawer.

Note that **amongst** is sometimes used instead of **among**, but in more literary contexts.

B

Between and **among** are not only used as prepositions of place. For example, we can use either to talk about something divided or shared between people:

- The money is to be divided **between / among** the towns in the area.
- The prize will be shared **between / among** the first six finishers in the race.

We also use **between** –

☆ to talk about comparisons and relationships:

- There should be a better *balance* on the committee **between** the various ethnic groups.
- They are wrong to claim that there is a *link* **between** unemployment and crime.

Also: **association**, **comparison**, **connection**, **contrast**, **correlation**, **difference**, **distinction**, **relationship**

☆ to talk about choices:

- I have to choose **between** the universities of Leeds, York and Manchester.
- He felt torn **between** his family and his friends.

☆ to talk about discussions or the results of discussions when we specify the two or more people or groups involved:

- There was a disagreement **between** Emma, Jade and Zoe.
- The treaty was signed **between** Great Britain and France.

☆ to say that people or things share an amount of something:

- **Between** them, Will and Alice must earn about €100,000 a year.
- Last year the three companies built 30,000 houses **between** them.

We also use **among** –

☆ when we mean 'existing or happening in a particular group':

- The disease has now broken out **among** the hill tribes.
- Their music is still very popular **among** teenagers.

☆ when we mean 'included in a particular group':

- They are **among** the best hockey players in the world.
- **Among** the capital cities of South America, Quito is the second highest.

C

There are a number of common expressions using **between** and **among**:

- The concert features, **among others**, Karl Frisk and the Johnsons. (= other singers / groups are featured, too)
- I later found out that he had been a carpenter and a plumber, **among other things**. (= he had had other jobs, too)
- **Between ourselves / Between you and me** (= keep this a secret), I don't think Jack is as honest as he should be.

Exercises

89.1 Underline the correct option. A

1 For a couple of days I've had a pain *between / among* my shoulder blades.
2 He couldn't find a microphone *between / among* all the recording equipment he had with him.
3 It would be easier to read if you put a line space *between / among* the paragraphs.
4 In the photograph Anna is standing *between / among* her parents.
5 The lost manuscript was discovered *between / among* the thousands of books in the cellar.
6 The buffet is towards the middle of the train *between / among* the first and second class sections.
7 She carried trays of drinks and food *between / among* the crowd of guests in the room.
8 I couldn't see Robbie *between / among* the audience, although he said he would be there.
9 Rebecca commutes *between / among* her flat in Paris and her office in Brussels.

89.2 Complete the sentences with between or among and the most likely words or phrases from the box. If you can use either, write between / among. B

amateur **its clients** **my closest friends** **cooking**
intake of refined sugar **the pupils** **his remaining relatives**
the striking dockers **teenagers** ~~**us**~~

1 I wasn't feeling very hungry, so Daniel and I shared a bowl of noodles ..between us.....
2 I bought four bars of chocolate and divided them .... in the class.
3 The distinction .... and professional athletes is becoming less clear.
4 It has become fashionable .... to dye their hair in various colours.
5 When Malik died, his daughter inherited the house and the rest of his money was split
....
6 The advertising company is very successful, numbering most of the big banks
....
7 Researchers have found a striking correlation .... and arthritis.
8 Given a choice .... and washing up, I know which I'd prefer to do.
9 Luka and Ivan are .... , so I'll invite them to the wedding, of course.
10 Late last night the talks .... and their employers broke down.

89.3 Complete this email with between or among. A & B

Send Save Now Discard

« Plain Text Check Spelling ▾

Hi Mum and Dad!

Rome must be (1) .... the most fascinating cities in the world. Yesterday we visited, (2) .... other places, the Foro Romano – the centre of ancient Rome – and the Vatican. There is such an incredible contrast (3) .... the old parts of the city built up to 2,000 years ago and the more recent parts. In the Vatican we climbed the long stairs to the top of St Peter's church. The view from the top must be (4) .... the most incredible over any city in the world. But (5) .... you and me, I'm a bit scared of heights and was glad to get back to ground level. Later we went to the Pantheon, an ancient Roman temple, which is (6) .... the Vatican and the Foro Romano. The Italian king Umberto I and the artist Raphael are (7) .... the people buried there. In the evening there was a bit of an argument (8) .... us over where we should eat – Jo wanted pizza, but I wanted to try some of the special local food. Eventually we found a place that did excellent pasta, (9) .... other things. The only problem then was choosing (10) .... the many different types!

Will be in touch again when I can.

Love, Keira

Unit 90

Prepositions of time

A During, in, over, throughout

We use **during** or **in** to talk about a period of time within which an event or activity occurs. The activity may continue for the whole of the period of time:

- I stayed at home **during** the summer. (*or* … **in** the summer.)
- The population of the city has actually fallen **during** the last decade. (*or* … **in** the last …)

or the event may happen at some time, or be repeated a number of times, in the period of time:

- We went to Turkey **during** the summer. (*or* … **in** the summer.)
- He suffered a number of injuries **during** his career as a jockey. (*or* … **in** his career …)

We use **during**, rather than **in**, to mean 'at some time in the period of' before nouns such as **illness**, **holiday**, **meal**, **stay**, **treatment**, and **visit**, when we refer to an event which lasts some time:

- The President made the speech **during** *a visit* to Madrid.

and also with the phrase **the whole** (**of**), emphasising duration of an entire period:

- No one was allowed to leave the ship **during** *the whole of* its time in port.

We can use **throughout** to emphasise that something happens over the whole of a period of time:

- We had enough firewood to keep us warm **throughout** the winter. (*or* … warm **during** / **through** the winter.)

B

We can use **over** or **during** when we talk about something that goes on for a length of time within a *period of time*, either for some of that period or for the whole of it:

- Weather conditions have been improving **over** / **during** *the past few days*.
- I hit my head and can't remember anything that happened **over** / **during** *the next hour or so*.

However, if we talk about a short event that happens within a period of time, we prefer **during**:

- *She sneezed* **during** the performance. (= once or a few times; *not* … over the performance.)
- **During** a pause in the conversation, *she left the room*. (*not* Over a pause …)

C Until, by, up to

There are a number of ways of saying when something that has continued for some time stops –

☆ We use **until** (or informally **till**) to say that something continued or will continue to a particular time, and **by** to say that something happened or will happen either before a particular time or at that time at the latest. Compare:

- We have to be at home **until** 2:30. (We must not leave home before 2:30) *and*
- We have to be at home **by** 2:30. (We must arrive home either before or at 2:30)

☆ In informal contexts we can use **up to** or **up till** instead of **until**. We commonly use **up to** / **till** with **now** and with **then**:

- I've just bought a tablet computer. I've always used a laptop **up to** *now*. (*or* … **up till** now …)

☆ We can use **until now** to talk about a situation that will not continue beyond now:

- Supermarkets say that **until now** there has been little consumer interest in buying organic produce. (The situation has changed or is going to change)

Note, however, that we don't use **until now** for a situation that will or may continue into the future. Instead we can use **so far** or, in formal contexts, **to date**:

- It was certainly the best match of the football season **so far**.
- When the contract is signed it will be the building company's biggest order **to date**.

Exercises

90.1 **In which of the sentences can the word in brackets replace during? Write ✓ if it can replace it and ✗ if it can't.** A & B

1 I'm going to get a cup of coffee *during* the break. (*in*)
2 She lost more than 15 kilos *during* her illness and she was off work for two months. (*in*)
3 He twisted his ankle *during* the match and had to retire injured. (*over*)
4 The weather was terrible here *during* December. (*in*)
5 The meeting will be some time *during* January. (*over*)
6 People no longer expect to be employed in the same place *during* the whole of their working lives. (*in*)
7 Do you think standards of numeracy have fallen *during* the last 20 years? (*over*)
8 She sang in a choir *during* her childhood. (*throughout*)
9 The town was rebuilt *during* the early 16th century. (*over*)
10 It was impossible to buy bananas *during* the war. (*in*)
11 Karl had a phone call *during* the meal and had to leave early. (*in*)
12 My stomach ache got steadily worse *during* the evening. (*over*)

90.2 **Complete the pairs of sentences with by and until. Use by in one sentence and until in the other.** C

1 a I was feeling really hungry .... the time dinner was served.
  b We sat around the fire talking .... the time dinner was served.
2 a Sorry I'm late. I've been in a meeting .... now.
  b I thought Lars would have been here .... now.
3 a I've got to pay the money back .... the end of the month.
  b I've got .... the end of the month to pay the money back.
4 a I put on an extra pair of socks. .... then my feet were freezing cold.
  b I stood outside the cinema for an hour. .... then my feet were freezing cold.
5 a She was already a leading economist .... her early twenties.
  b She studied economics .... her early twenties and then moved into law.
6 a I hope to finish the decorating .... the weekend.
  b It will take me .... the weekend to finish the decorating.

90.3 **Underline the correct or more likely option (or both if possible) in this email.** A–C

Send | Save Now | Discard

Hi Pete

(1) *Over / During* the last three weeks we've covered thousands of kilometres by train. (2) *So far / Until now* we've been to Stockholm, Berlin and Rome, and now we're in Amsterdam. (3) *So far / Until now* I thought Rome was the best city we'd been to, but I think I love Amsterdam even more. We've been here for three days, and have been very impressed with what we've seen (4) *so far / until now*. We spent the first two days in galleries, looking particularly at Van Gogh's paintings. I didn't know much about his work (5) *so far / until now*. Incidentally, we bumped into your friend Eleni (6) *in / during* our visit to the Van Gogh museum. We're staying here (7) *until / by* Saturday and then we're going to Paris. Must go now. We're off to The Hague for the day and have to be at the station (8) *until / by* 9:30.

Hope all is well with you.

Love, Keira

Unit 91

Talking about exceptions

A

We use **except (for)** to introduce the only thing(s) or person / people that a statement does not include:

- The price of the holiday includes all meals **except** (**for**) lunch.
- Everyone seemed to have been invited **except** (**for**) Mrs Woodford and me.
- I had no money to give him **except** (**for**) the few coins in my pocket.

We use **except**, not **except for**, with **to-infinitives**, and **that-clauses**:

- I rarely need to go into the city centre **except** *to do* some shopping.
- They look just like the real thing, **except** *that* they're made of plastic.

We usually use **except** before **prepositions**, **bare infinitives**, and **that-clauses** including those where the word *that* is left out (see Unit 53). However, informally **except for** is sometimes also used, although this is grammatically incorrect:

- There is likely to be rain everywhere today **except** *in* Wales.
- There is nothing more the doctor can do **except** *keep* an eye on him.
- They look just like the real thing, **except** (*that*) they're made of plastic.

We can use **except for**, but not **except**, with the meaning 'but for' (see **C** below).

B

We use **except** (**for**) to mean that something is not included in a particular statement, but we use **besides** to mean 'as well as' or 'in addition to'. Compare:

- I don't enjoy watching any sports **except** (**for**) cricket. (= I enjoy only cricket) *and*
- **Besides** cricket, I enjoy watching football and basketball. (= I enjoy three sports)
- I haven't read anything by her, **except** (**for**) one of her short stories. *and*
- **Besides** her novels and poems, she published a number of short stories.

Apart from can be used with the same meanings as both **except** (**for**) and **besides**:

- I don't enjoy watching any sports **apart from** cricket. (= except for)
- **Apart from** cricket, I enjoy watching football and basketball. (= besides; as well as)

C

We can use **but** with a similar meaning to **except** (**for**), particularly after negative words such as **no**, **nobody**, and **nothing**:

- After the operation he could see *nothing* **but** / **except** (**for**) / **apart from** vague shadows.
- There was *no* way out **but** / **except** / **apart from** upwards, towards the light.

But for has a different meaning from **except for**. We use it to say what would or might have happened if the thing introduced by **but for** had not happened:

- The country would now be self-sufficient in food **but for** the drought last year. (= if there hadn't been the drought ...)
- **But for** the leg injury he suffered last year, he would probably have been picked for the national team by now. (= if he hadn't injured his leg ...)

However, some people use **except for** in the same way as **but for**, particularly in informal spoken English:

- I'd have got there on time **except for** the taxi being late. (*or* ... **but for** the taxi being late.)
- **Except for** the problems with my computer, I would have got the book finished weeks ago. (*or* **But for** the problems with my computer ...)

Note that we can use **excepted**, **apart** or **aside** after mentioning a person or thing to say that they are not included in the statement we make:

- It has been, *1984* **excepted** / **apart** / **aside**, the hottest July for the last 100 years.

Exercises

91.1 Complete the sentences with **except** or **except for**. Indicate where both are possible. A & C

1 He was dressed very smartly .... that his shoes were dirty.
2 I liked everything in the meal .... the cabbage.
3 I had nothing to do .... sit by the pool and relax.
4 We would have gone walking last week .... the terrible weather.
5 She had no choice .... to wait for the next train.
6 There are very few wolves left in the country .... in the northern forests.
7 All the puddings on the menu cost €6 .... the ice cream, which was €4.
8 I'm in the office all the time .... at lunchtimes.
9 She might have won the race .... hitting the last fence.
10 The plant is found on every continent .... Africa.
11 He gave no excuse for turning up late .... that he was tired.
12 I drove all the way without stopping .... to buy petrol.

91.2 If necessary, correct these sentences with **besides** or **except (for)**. If the sentence is already correct, write ✓. B

1 She had never been out of the country besides a week in Ireland as a child.
2 Besides being small, Denmark is very flat, with villages linked by country roads.
3 The new road will increase traffic in the area except for damaging an area of woodland.
4 Except for his novels, Campbell wrote a number of biographies.
5 There was nothing in the fridge besides a rather mouldy piece of cheese.
6 He was unhurt in the crash except for a bruise on his forehead.

91.3 Match pairs of sentences and rewrite them as single sentences beginning **But for the ...** . C

1 Katerina gave me excellent directions.
2 The bad weather caused interruptions.
3 The charity supplied food and medicines.
4 The trees provided shelter.
5 The EU threatened sanctions.
6 The bank gave me a loan.

a If it hadn't, the building would have been completed by now.
b Without this, human rights would not have improved in the country.
c Otherwise, many more people would have died in the famine.
d If it hadn't, I would not have been able to set up my business.
e ~~Without these, I would have got totally lost.~~
f Otherwise, the wind would have caused even more damage to the house.

1 + e *But for the excellent directions Katerina gave me, I would have got totally lost.*
....
....
....
....
....

Prepositions after verbs

A

Some verbs are frequently followed by particular prepositions:

	about	*for*	*of*	*on*	*with*
agree	✓			✓	✓
argue	✓	✓			✓
ask	✓	✓	✓		
care	✓	✓			
know	✓		✓		
learn	✓		✓		
talk	✓		✓	✓	✓

B

about usually means 'concerning a particular thing':

- They began to **learn about** nutrition when they were at primary school.

We use **care about** to talk about something we are (not) concerned about:

- He doesn't seem to **care about** the effect a poor diet has on him.

for is used with **ask** to talk about what people want:

- He finished the drink quickly and **asked for** another.

with **argue** when we talk about giving reasons why something is true or right:

- Many people **are arguing for** a big tax cut.

and with **care** to talk about doing the necessary things for someone or something in order to keep them in good health or condition:

- Jo **cared for** her disabled mother until her death last year. (*or* Jo **took care of** ...)

or to mean 'like', particularly in negative sentences, and to mean 'want' in offers. Both of these uses of **care for** are rather formal:

- I don't **care for** the theatre much.
- Would you **care for** a cup of coffee?

of is used with **talk**, **know**, and **learn** to talk about discussing, having or getting information:

- Mira went recently to Laos and can **talk of** nothing else. (*or less formally* ... **talk about** ...)
- The whole country **knew of** Churchill's love of cigars. (*or less formally* ... **knew about** ...)
- I have just **learnt of** the death of Dr Ramirez. (*or less formally* ... **learnt about** ...)

We use **ask of** when we make or talk about requests:

- I have a favour to **ask of** you and your sister.

on is used with **talk** and **agree** to mean 'concerned with a particular topic':

- I was asked to **talk on** my research. (*or* ... to **talk about** ...)
- We **agreed on** a time to meet. (usually there has been previous discussion or disagreement.)

Note that we use **agree to** to say that someone allows something to happen:

- Once the government **agreed to** the scheme it went ahead without delay.

with is used with **argue** and **talk** when we go on to mention the person involved:

- I used to **argue / talk with** Pedro for hours.

We use **agree with** to say that two people have the same opinion:

- Adam thinks we should accept the offer, and I **agree with** him.

and to say that we approve of a particular idea or action:

- I **agree with** letting children choose the clothes they wear. (*or* I **agree about / on** ...)

or to say that two descriptions are the same:

- Stefan's story **agreed with** that of his son.

Exercises

92.1 Cross out any incorrect prepositions. A

1 I only advertised the car for sale on Wednesday, but by the end of the week ten people had phoned to ask *of / for / about* it.
2 We can learn a great deal *after / about / for* the oceans by studying even a small piece of coral.
3 I didn't agree *about / for / with* a word of what she said.
4 Professor Owen is giving a talk *of / with / on* the Romans in Lecture Hall 1.
5 I had to care *for / after / about* my elderly parents when they both became ill.
6 For many years we have been arguing *for / on / with* changes in the way the college is managed.
7 She didn't know *of / about / on* her stepbrother's existence until her mother died.

92.2 Complete the sentences using the correct or most appropriate preposition from section A. Sometimes two answers are possible. A & B

1 On the website they ask .... your email address.
2 I first learnt .... his decision to resign on the radio last night.
3 We're going to talk .... the council about planting some new trees in the park.
4 I don't care .... pop music at all. I much prefer classical music.
5 The teacher says we've got to do the test, so there's no point in arguing .... it.
6 Scientists do not agree .... the origin of the universe.
7 If you know .... any reasons why you should not be given medical insurance, you must declare them here.
8 A: Josh can be really stupid sometimes.
B: You shouldn't talk .... your brother like that.
9 She's always arguing .... her parents about what to watch on television.
10 I know it's a lot to ask .... you, but would you look after the children while I'm in Japan on business?
11 The course was brilliant. We learnt .... using the Internet in teaching writing.
12 A: Dan said he'll try to fix my car.
B: What does he know .... cars?
13 I don't think the government cares enough .... nursery education to fund it properly.
14 After days of discussion, the committee agreed .... the amount of money to donate.

92.3 These pairs of sentences include more verbs that are commonly followed by the prepositions in A. Can you explain the difference in meaning? Use a dictionary if necessary.

1 a The police *acted on* the information very quickly.
b I couldn't be at the meeting, so my solicitor *acted for* me.
2 a I've been *thinking* a lot *about* your idea, and I've decided I'd like to support you.
b What do you *think of* the colour in the bedroom?
3 a Doctors have *called on* the Health Minister to resign.
b Campaigners have *called for* a referendum on the issue.
4 a They say he *worked for* the CIA in the 1980s.
b She *works with* computers.
5 a We're *counting on* Julia to supply the food for the party.
b Playing exciting basketball *counts for* little if the team isn't winning.

→ **Additional exercise 15** (page 249)

Unit 93

Prepositions after nouns

A

Many nouns are followed by the same prepositions as their related adjective or verb. Compare:

- Are you **satisfied** *with* the way that the business is being run? *and*
- The shareholders have expressed **satisfaction** *with* the way the business is being run.

A few nouns are followed by different prepositions. Compare:

- They became **fond** *of* each other at school. *and*
- Their **fondness** *for* each other grew and many years later they married.

Also: **proud of / pride in, ashamed of / shame about / at**

Some nouns take a preposition where their related verb does not. Compare:

- I **respect** Louis enormously. *and*
- I have enormous **respect for** Louis.

Also: **admiration for, ban on, discussion about / on, improvement in, influence on, interview with, lack of, respect for**

Note that many other nouns are commonly followed by *of* phrases which indicate possession, a property, or classify the noun by describing what it relates to. Compare:

- He **described** the conductor as moving his arms like a windmill. *and*
- His **description** *of* the conductor was very funny.

B

Some nouns can be followed by **of + -ing** but not usually **to-infinitive**:

- He's got into the **habit** *of biting* his nails when he's nervous.

Also: **cost, effect, fear, likelihood, possibility, probability, problem, prospect, risk, sign**

Some nouns can be followed by a **to-infinitive** but not usually **of + -ing**:

- His unhappy childhood explains his **reluctance** *to talk* about his parents.

Note that many of these nouns can also be used with other prepositions **+ -ing** (e.g. **attempt at -ing, reason for -ing,** etc.).

Also: **ability, attempt, concern, decision, desire, determination, failure, inability, permission, proposal, reason, refusal, (un)willingness**

C

Some nouns can sometimes be followed either by **of + -ing** or a **to-infinitive** with a similar meaning, usually after **the**:

- Do staff have *the* **opportunity** *of taking* unpaid leave? (*or* … *the* **opportunity** *to take* …)
- *The* **aim** *of providing* clean drinking water has been achieved. (*or The* **aim** *to provide* …)

Also: **ambition, idea, option, plan**.

However, some nouns, such as **chance**, **sense** and **way**, have more than one meaning and are followed either by **of + -ing** or a **to-infinitive** depending on which meaning is used. Compare:

- What's the **chance** *of getting* five heads when you toss a coin five times? (= likelihood; *not* … chance to get …) *and*
- Will you get the **chance** *to visit* Miki in Japan? (= opportunity; *not* … of visiting …)
- He didn't have the **sense** *to move* away from the puddle of water as the bus went past. (= good judgement; *not* … sense of moving …) *and*
- Everyone was very friendly and she had a **sense** *of belonging* within a few days of moving to her new school. (= feeling; *not* … sense to belong …)
- I've got a new **way** *to cook* rice. (= method; *or* … **way** *of cooking* …) *and*
- She has a really funny **way** *of speaking*. (= manner; *not* … way to speak)

Note also that **of + -ing** usually follows **no / every / the sole / the slightest / (not) any / with the + intention**, but that we can use either **of + -ing** or a **to-infinitive** in most other cases. Compare:

- I have **no intention** *of lending* Dan any more money. (*not* … no intention to lend …) *and*
- He announced his **intention** *to stand* in the election. (*or* … **intention** *of standing* …)

Exercises

93.1 **Rewrite the italicised words with a similar meaning using a noun related to the underlined verb. Add an appropriate preposition after the noun.** A

1 I *greatly admire* people who work full time and also study for a university degree.
  have great admiration for
2 Yasemin is still in hospital but over the last couple of days *her condition has improved*.
3 Rashid *is very proud of* his cooking, and is always eager to talk about his recipes.
4 The website *advises on* how to lose weight.
5 I hate *it when people are cruel to* animals, and would support a ban on hunting.
6 We *discussed* the relative merits of CDs and records *for a long time*.
7 I had to *be vaccinated against typhoid* before entering the country.
8 Benny Carter *significantly influenced* the development of British jazz.
9 *The city lacks affordable housing* and many people are homeless.
10 There is widespread support for *fireworks to be banned*.

93.2 **Complete the sentences with a noun from (i) and either of + -ing or the to-infinitive form of a verb from (ii).** B

(i)

ability	**cost**	**decision**
failure	**~~fear~~**	**possibility**
reason	**risk**	**sign**
unwillingness		

(ii)

acknowledge	**allow**	**buy**
~~fly~~	**get**	**protect**
remember	**stop**	**transmit**
worry		

1 My mother recently overcame her fear of flying and had a holiday in South Africa.
2 The snow has been falling now for two days and shows no ....
3 The government has defended its .... coal mining in the national park.
4 Your blood pressure is a little high, but there is no .... about it.
5 She was kept in isolation to reduce the .... the virus to other people in the hospital.
6 The exercise tests children's .... a random sequence of numbers.
7 The government has been criticised for its .... the region from flooding.
8 The .... a new car in Europe is expected to fall in the next year.
9 I knew that there was little .... the job with so many applicants.
10 It's hard to work with Nik because of his .... that he ever makes mistakes.

93.3 **Complete the sentences with an appropriate verb using either of + -ing or a to-infinitive. Give both forms if both are possible.** C

1 Although Mia said she would think about it, she never had the slightest intention of accepting my suggestion.
2 It's going to be cloudy tonight so there is only a fifty-fifty chance .... the eclipse of the moon.
3 It's pouring with rain. I hope David had the sense .... an umbrella with him.
4 The head of the company repeated his intention .... on his 65th birthday.
5 When the History Department closed she was given the option .... another job.
6 Katrin had a very unusual way ...., keeping her feet firmly on the floor and waving her arms around her head.

→ **Additional exercise 15** (page 249)

Unit 94

Two- and three-word verbs: word order

A

The meaning of some verbs commonly used with a particular *preposition* or *adverb* (or *particle*) is often different from the meaning of their separate parts. We can call these *two-word verbs*:

- I'll quickly **go over** the main points of the report again. (= summarise)
- She had to **let** her dress **out** because she'd put on weight. (= make it larger)

Other *three-word verbs* are commonly used with an *adverb* + *preposition*.

- Do you think he's really likely to **go through with** his threat? (= do it)
- The team has failed to **live up to** earlier expectations. (= achieve what was expected)

These two- and three-word verbs are sometimes also called *phrasal verbs*.

B

Many two-word verbs are usually *intransitive*:

- He **grew up** on a farm.
- When she **came to** she found herself in hospital.

Also: **crop up, fall through, get up, move off, shop around, splash out**

However, some two-word verbs can be used transitively or intransitively with the same meaning:

- I'll **call back** later.
- I'll **call** *you* **back** when I get home.

Also: **answer back, clear away, cover up, help out, take over, tidy up, wash up**

and other two-word verbs can be used transitively or intransitively with a different meaning:

- The engine **cut out** and the car came to a stop.
- I **cut** *the picture* **out** and kept it.

Also: **break in, hold out, look out, look up, pick up, split up, turn in, wind up**

C

With many *transitive* two-word verbs, the object can come before or after the adverb:

- I want to **try out** *the local food. or*
- I want to **try** *the local food* **out**.

Also: **bring about, clean up, count out, drink up, gather up, get down, leave out, make up, mess up, shoot down, sort out, throw away, use up**

However, if the object is a pronoun it must come between the verb and the adverb:

- I won't be able to go to the party. You'll have to **count** *me* **out**. (*not* ... count out me.)

and we prefer to put the object after the adverb when the object is long. Compare:

- She had to **clean** *the kitchen* **up**. (*or* ... **clean up** *the kitchen.*) *and*
- She had to **clean up** *the mess in the kitchen*. (*rather than* ... clean the mess in the kitchen up.)

D

With some transitive two-word verbs, the object comes between the verb and the adverb:

- I just couldn't **tell** *the twins* **apart**. (*not* ... tell apart the twins)

Also: **catch out, hear out, order about, pull to, push to, shut up** (= to silence), **stand up**

E

With some transitive two-word verbs, the object follows the preposition:

- She **takes after** *her mother*.
- I **flicked through** *a magazine* while I was waiting.

Also: **account for, act on, approve of, call on, check into, look after, provide for, result from, run into, take against**

F

With most three-word verbs, the object goes after the preposition:

- He really **looks up to** *his older brother*.

Also: **come in for, come up against, cut back on, look down on, put up with**

However, a few three-word verbs usually have the object immediately after the verb. A second noun or noun phrase goes after the preposition:

- She tried to **talk** *me* **out of** *the plan*.

Also: **do out of, help on with, let in on, put down as, put up to, take up on**

Exercises

94.1 If possible or necessary, add an appropriate noun or pronoun in the space. B

1 The same problem kept cropping .... up, even though I thought I'd fixed it.
2 I'm not sure how you spell it. I'll look .... up in the dictionary.
3 I'm busy at the moment, but I can help .... out this evening.
4 If you tidy .... up, I'll do the cleaning.
5 The deal fell .... through because we couldn't agree a price.

94.2 Show where the word or phrase in brackets should go in each sentence with a ⋀. If it is possible to put it in more than one place, mark these two possibilities. C

1 The house is untidy, but I haven't got time to sort ⋀ out now. (*it*)
2 We've introduced a training scheme to bring about. (*some improvement*)
3 The strike by airline pilots messed up. (*the holiday I'd spent months planning*)
4 I decided to try out for a couple of months. (*the diet*)
5 I used up to buy the car. (*all my savings*)
6 A: I must get my shoes repaired again.
B: But they're so old – why don't you just throw away ? (*them*)

94.3 Complete each sentence using a two-word verb from (i) and a noun phrase from (ii). If two word orders are possible, give both. C & D

(i)

get down	**leave out**	**make up**
~~push to~~	**hear out**	**shut up**

(ii)

the general ideas	**me**	**my mind**
her name	**the thing**	**~~the window~~**

1 It's freezing in here. Can you push the window to?
2 When she filled the form in she ...., so they sent it back to her.
3 The alarm started when I opened the car door, and now I can't ....
4 There were so many desserts on the menu, I couldn't ....
5 I ...., but the lecturer spoke so quickly I couldn't follow the details.
6 I know you suspect me of cheating, but you've got to give me a chance to explain myself. At least .... before making up your mind.

94.4 If necessary, correct the word order or give a more likely word order in these sentences. If they are already correct, write ✓. D, E & F

1 He was always ordering about everyone, getting them to do his work for him.
2 It is assumed that parents will provide their children for until they are 18.
3 She wouldn't let in me on the secret, however hard I tried to persuade her.
4 The snow was so heavy that the police called motorists on to avoid unnecessary journeys.
5 I checked into the hotel at about four.
6 I took up Emre on his offer and stayed in his flat while I was in Ankara.
7 The government has come in for a lot of criticism over its decision to increase spending on defence.
8 My parents didn't approve of our engagement.
9 I had always looked Mr Gao up to, so I was shocked to discover what he had done.

→ Additional exercise 15 (page 249)

Unit 95

There is, there was, etc.

A

When we introduce a new person or thing – to say that this person or thing exists, happens, or is found in a particular place – we can use a sentence beginning **There** + **be**:

- **There was** a loud bang from upstairs. (*not* A loud bang was from upstairs.)
- **There's** nothing to eat. (*not* Nothing is to eat.)

We invert this pattern in questions to ask about the existence etc. of people and things:

- **Is there** anybody in here?

We can also use **there** with auxiliary and modal verbs with **be** (e.g. **has been**, **can be**):

- **There** *must be* some way of contacting her.

with **verb + to be** (e.g. **used to be**, **is supposed to be**, **tends to be**, **appears to be**, **seems to be**):

- **There** *appears to be* a major disagreement between the two presidents.

and some other verbs that indicate existence (e.g. **arise**, **emerge**, **exist**, **remain**):

- During the 1990s **there** *arose* a demand for organic food.

Because we use **there** in this way to *introduce* topics, the noun after **there** + **be** often has an indefinite or non-specific meaning. So we often use **a / an**, **zero article**, **any**(**one**) (+ noun), or **some**(**thing**), **no**(**body**), etc. rather than **the**, **this**, **my**, **your** (+ noun), or a **name**, which give the noun a more definite or specific meaning. Compare:

- **There's** *nobody* here.
- **There was** *something* strange about her. *and*
- *The cat* was in the kitchen. (*more usual than* There was the cat in the kitchen.; *but compare* **There was** *a cat* in the kitchen.)
- *Jan* is waiting for me outside. (*more usual than* There is Jan waiting for me outside.)

When we use **there** + **be** + **the**, this is often done to show a change of topic. Choosing **the**, **that**, etc. + **noun** indicates that we think the topic is already known to the listener or reader:

- ... And then **there is the** question of who is going to pay.

B

The verb **be** should agree with the noun that comes after it:

- **There is** a very good *reason* for my decision.
- **There were** too many *people* trying to get into the football stadium.

However, in informal speech we sometimes use **there's** before a plural noun:

- 'Anything to eat?' 'Well, **there's** *some apples* on the table.'

If the noun phrase consists of two or more nouns in a list, we use a singular verb if the first noun is singular or uncountable, and a plural verb if the first noun is plural:

- When I opened the fridge **there was** only *a bottle of milk*, some eggs, and butter.
- When I opened the fridge **there were** only *some eggs*, a bottle of milk, and butter.

C

There + **be** is also used with nouns followed by a **that-**, **wh-**, **to-infinitive** or **-ing** clause:

- **Is there** *a chance* (*that*) Kim could arrive this afternoon?
- **There is** *no reason* (*why*) I can't see you tomorrow.
- **There is** *a small stream which / that* runs at the bottom of the garden.
- **There was** *an attempt to resolve* the dispute at the factory.
- **There was** *a taxi waiting* outside the hotel.

We don't usually leave out a relative pronoun when it is the *subject* of the following finite verb, but can leave it out when it is the *object* (see Unit 53).

D

In formal English we can use a clause with **there being** to introduce a reason for something:

- **There being** no evidence against him, he was released. (= Because there was no evidence).
- **There being** no reports of adverse reactions, the drug is to be sold more widely.

Exercises

95.1 **Rewrite these sentences using there *only* if the answer is likely. Consider why some answers are not likely.** A

1 Coffee was spilt on the table. *There was coffee spilt on the table.*
2 Your dinner is in the oven. *(A sentence with 'There ...' is unlikely.)*
3 Is something bothering you?
4 A barrier was across the road.
5 The doctor is free to see you now.
6 The problem of what to do with nuclear waste remains.
7 My son is at university.
8 A video is supposed to be on the website, but it doesn't work.
9 No petrol was available anywhere in the city.
10 Can anyone help me?
11 You can follow some general rules.
12 An art gallery used to be around here.

95.2 **The sentences below are all taken from written English. Which is correct or more likely in the space – is or are?** A

1 There .... two pubs and a church on the village green.
2 There .... other possible locations for the car park, but the central one is preferred.
3 There .... no direct rail link between the cities.
4 There .... further rain and strong winds forecast for the next three days.
5 There .... chocolate bars, crisps, and a bottle of cola in the bag if you get hungry.
6 There .... substantial evidence to suggest that the Robinsons lied to the police.
7 There .... no easy answers to the problem of climate change.
8 There .... a shower, television, and two single beds in each room.

95.3 **Join the matching sentence halves using an appropriate relative pronoun (that, which, or who). Write the relative pronoun in brackets if it can be left out.** C & Unit 53

1 There were a lot of people at the party
2 There's a cake in the kitchen
3 There was never any doubt
4 There have been suggestions
5 There aren't many people alive today
6 There are still some old houses in the village
7 There was absolutely nothing
8 There are few people in the company

a an election will be held next month.
b are harder-working than Kristin.
c I've made especially for your birthday.
d I could do to prevent him falling.
e ~~hadn't been invited.~~
f haven't watched TV.
g don't have electricity.
h Bruno would get the job.

1 + e *There were a lot of people at the party who / that hadn't been invited.*

95.4 **Write new sentences with similar meanings beginning There being ... .** D

1 As there was no food in the house, they went to a local restaurant.
There being no food in the house, they went to a local restaurant.
2 There was no further business, so the meeting closed at 12:30.
....
3 The patients were sent home because there was no doctor available.
....
4 Because the facilities were inadequate at the hotel, the conference was relocated to a nearby university.
....

It ... 1

A

We can use an introductory **it** at the beginning of a sentence –

☆ to place long or grammatically complex sentence elements at the end (the usual place for them in English). Compare:

- *To drive without a licence* is illegal. *and*
- **It is illegal** to drive without a licence.

☆ to focus attention on something by putting it at the end (the usual place for new or important information in English). Compare:

- *That she wasn't hurt* is a miracle. *and*
- **It's a miracle** *that she wasn't hurt*.

Introductory **it** is commonly used when the subject is a **to-infinitive** or **that-clause** (as in the examples above), and also when the subject is a **wh-** or **-ing clause** (see also Unit 25):

- **It is clear** *why* Diego decided to leave Spain.
- **It is useless** *asking* Sophie to help.

B

We often use introductory **it** with **be + adjective / noun** (as in the examples above), but other patterns with an introductory **it** are possible. Here are some common examples–

☆ **it + verb + to-infinitive**

- 'I've got a terrible headache.' '**It helps** *to lie down*.'
- If you want someone to help you, **it doesn't do** *to annoy* them just before you ask. ('[not] do' = (not) advisable, acceptable or enough)

> *Also*: **hurt, pay** (= give an advantage or benefit)

☆ **it + verb + object + to-infinitive**

- **It shocked** *him to see* her looking so ill.
- It **means** *a lot to get* a place at university.

After these verbs the object usually refers to a person.

> *Also*: **amaze**, **annoy**, **astonish**, **concern**, **cost**, **frighten**, **hurt**, **scare**, **surprise**, **upset**, **worry** (most are to do with feelings)

We can also use **it + take + object + to-infinitive** when we say what is or was needed in a particular activity; for example, time, resources or characteristics needed. Compare:

- **It takes** *a lot of effort to play* the flute. *and*
- To play the flute takes a lot of effort.

☆ **it + verb + that-clause**

- **It seems** *that* she has lost her memory.
- **It emerged** *that* he already had a criminal record.

> *Also*: **appear, come about, follow, happen, transpire**

☆ **it + verb + object + that-clause**

- **It** suddenly **hit** *me that* Sara wanted to borrow money. (*less likely is* That Sara wanted to borrow money suddenly hit me.)

The object in this pattern usually refers to a person.

> *Also*: **dawn on, not bother, strike** (= occur to), **turn out**, and the highlighted verbs above

C

We don't usually use an **it ...** pattern as an alternative to a **noun** as subject:

- **Their success** was unexpected. (*not* It was unexpected their success.)

However, in informal contexts, particularly in speech, this is quite common in order to give special emphasis to the information immediately following **it ...**:

- **It tastes really good**, this new ice cream.

and also to place a longer noun phrase at the end in order to focus attention on it:

- **It's ridiculous**, all the bureaucracy involved in running a school these days.

Exercises

96.1 **Rewrite these sentences beginning It ... but only if they would be correct written English; otherwise write ✓ and consider why an It ... sentence would be inappropriate.** A & C

1 That we continue to monitor the situation is important.
It is important that we continue to monitor the situation.
2 How he stared straight at me was unsettling.
3 Francesco's excellent exam result was surprising.
4 To be a qualified driver is an advantage in the job.
5 Her proposal is quite radical.
6 To put carpet on walls is highly unusual.
7 Robin's new car is a Ferrari.
8 Finding a good plumber is hard these days.

96.2 **Complete the sentences using it ... followed by a verb from (i) and an expanded form of the notes in (ii). Include an appropriate object where necessary.** B

(i)

~~appear~~	astonish
not bother	concern
hurt	not do
pay	strike
upset	scare

(ii)

pedal / bicycle	~~seriously injured / back~~
see / carrying knives	plan your journey ahead
criticise / too much	hadn't even told / when / going away
everyone / see in	discover / also / successful novelist
he / jealous	hear / offended

1 When Laura fell heavily and lay completely still,
it appeared that she had seriously injured her back
2 I knew that Lotta was a journalist for the local paper, but ...
3 Since I broke my ankle last year, ...
4 I told Peter that I had invited Hugo, too. When he became angry ...
5 My comment about Ben's baldness was only meant as a joke and ...
6 There were no curtains in his house, but ...
7 I didn't mind Amy not asking me to go on holiday with her, but ...
8 Children need a lot of praise and ...
9 The boys walked towards me in a threatening way, and ...
10 You can save money by booking tickets in advance, so ...

96.3 **What personal or physical characteristics are needed to ...? Use It takes ... in your answers.** B

1 play a musical instrument well
It takes a lot of determination to play a musical instrument well.
2 build your own house
3 make a speech in front of a group of strangers
4 explain the rules of cricket to someone who doesn't know the game

Now suggest completions for these sentences.

5 It takes bravery ...
6 It takes a lot of organisation to ...
7 It takes a great deal of time ...

Unit 97

It ... 2

A

We can use a pattern with **it** as the object of a verb where **it** refers forward to a clause. **It** can sometimes be followed directly by a **that-**, **if-** or **when-clause** after **can't bear, hate, like, love, resent** and **can't stand**, and by an **if-** or **when-clause** after **dislike, enjoy, prefer** and **understand**:

- I *hate* **it** *that* you can swim so well and I can't. (*not* I hate that you can swim ...)
- We always *enjoy* **it** *when* they stay with us. (*not* We always enjoy when they ...)

Some verbs can be followed by **it** and a **that-clause**, particularly in spoken English, or directly by a **that-clause** without **it**:

- You've just got to **accept (it)** *that* Emil's gone and won't be coming back.

Also: **admit, deny, guarantee, mention**

Many other verbs that can be followed by a **that-clause** or **wh-clause** are not used with **it** in this way:

- I can't **remember** *when* I last saw her. (*not* ... remember it when ...)

Also: **argue, discover, emphasise, notice, predict**

B

With other verbs used to indicate how we see a particular event or situation, **it** is followed first by an adjective or noun phrase and then a **that-clause**, **to-infinitive clause**, or clause beginning **when**:

- Officials said they **believe it unlikely** *that* any lasting damage to the environment has been done. (*or* ... they **believe it is unlikely** *that* ...; *not* ... they believe unlikely that ...)

Also: **consider, feel, find** (= discover something from experience), **think**

When we use **leave** and **owe** (= have a responsibility to) with **it** we can use **to somebody + to-infinitive** after **it:**

- Don't bother to arrange anything. Just **leave it to me to sort out.**
- She **owed it to her parents to do** well at college.

C

With the verbs **accept**, **regard**, **see**, **take** (= interpret something in a particular way), or **view** we use **it** + **as** + **noun** (or **adjective**) + **clause**:

- We **see it as an insult** *to have received no reply to our letter*.
- **I take it as encouraging** *when students attend all my lectures*.

D

It is / was no ... vs There is / was no ...

Here are some common expressions including **It is / was no ...** and **There is / was no ...**:

- **It's no secret** that he wants a new job.
- **It's no surprise** that his latest film has been so successful.
- **It's no use** telling me now. I needed to know a week ago.
- **It's no good** getting angry. That won't help solve the problem.
- **It's no coincidence** (*or* **accident**) that they left the party at the same time.
- **It's no longer** necessary to have a visa to visit the country.

- **There's no denying** that he's intelligent.
- I'm afraid **there's no alternative** (*or* **choice**) but to ask her to leave.
- **There's no hope** of getting more money.
- **There's no need** to explain how it works; I'll read the manual.
- **There's no point** in buying an ice-cream maker unless you plan to use it a lot.
- **There's no question** of agreeing to his demands.
- **There's no reason** to be pessimistic.
- **There's no chance** of finding a cure if we don't fund more research.

The sentences with **It is / was no ...** have alternatives in which the **that-**, **-ing** or **to-infinitive** clause is placed at the front, but the sentences with **There is / was no ...** do not. Compare:

- **It's no secret** that he wants a new job. (*or* That he wants a new job is no secret.) *and*
- **There's no denying** that he's intelligent. (*but not* That he's intelligent is no denying.)

Exercises

97.1 **Complete each sentence with an appropriate form of a verb from the box. If necessary, add it.** A & B

~~can't bear~~	consider	discover	enjoy	find
leave	owe	predict	prefer	remember

1 She *can't bear it* when people criticise her work, and she gets very upset.
2 I .... hard to understand why the film was made in black and white and not colour.
3 If you .... that you can't get to the meeting on the 16th I'll try to rearrange it.
4 We .... to our supporters to play to the best of our ability in the match.
5 I .... that the camera was on the table when I left the house.
6 I really .... when the weather's hot like this. I'd hate to live in a cold climate.
7 I can't stop you dismantling your motorbike in the kitchen, but I'd .... if you didn't.
8 I think we should .... to the children to do the washing up.
9 I .... that Randa will withdraw from the course within a month.
10 I .... a privilege to have known Mark Jennings.

97.2 **Here are some notes a managing director made for his first speech to the board of directors. In the speech he expanded the notes beginning I + (verb) + it as ..., using the verbs in brackets. Write what he said.** C

1 great honour – asked to become – managing director – Rexco (*take*)
I take it as a great honour to be asked to become managing director of Rexco.

2 part of my role – significantly reduce Rexco's carbon footprint – next 5 years (*see*)

3 necessary evil – some people – may redundant – in next year (*accept*)

4 important for relations with workforce – make available information – managers' salaries (*view*)

5 unacceptable – modern company – exclude workforce – major decision-making (*regard*)

6 fundamental principle of company – suppliers of raw materials – given fair price for products (*take*)

97.3 **Complete the sentences with an appropriate it ... or there ... phrase from section D opposite. Suggest alternatives where possible.** D

1 *It's no coincidence* that Karlsbad has won the ice hockey tournament for the last three years. It is a very rich club and its training facilities are excellent.
2 My contact lens must have fallen out in the snow, so .... of finding it.
3 .... that Julia and Jakub have split up. Everyone in the office knows.
4 I know your exam result wasn't good, but .... getting depressed about it.
5 Your broken arm will take some time to mend, but .... why you shouldn't be playing tennis again by the summer.
6 As the car ferry isn't running because of the high winds, ... but to drive 100 kilometres around the lake.
7 .... possible to buy tickets at the theatre. You have to buy them online.
8 Bungee jumping might be dangerous, but .... that it's very exciting.

Unit 98

Focusing: **it-clauses** and **what-clauses**

A

Focusing with it-clauses

We can use an **it-clause** with **be** to focus attention on the information that immediately follows **it + (be)**. A sentence like this is sometimes called a *cleft sentence*. The clause after the **it-clause** (usually a **that-clause**) contains information that is already known or considered to be less important:

- 'Lea bought the car from Olav.' 'No, **it was Olav** *that* bought the car from Lea.'
- I don't mind her criticising me, but **it's how she does it** *that* I object to.
- **It was to show how much I cared for her** *that* I bought her the necklace.

We sometimes use **which** or **who** instead of **that**; **when** and **where** can also be used, but usually only in informal English; and note that **how** or **why** can't replace **that**:

- Karl was always there to help her, and **it was to him** *that / who* she now turned for support.
- 'Ida's seriously ill in hospital.' 'But **it was only last Sunday** *when / that* I was playing tennis with her.'
- **It was in Warsaw** *where / that* the film was made.
- 'Was it by cutting staff that he managed to save the firm?' 'No, **it was by improving distribution** *that* he made it profitable.' (*not* … how he made it profitable.)

B

Focusing with what-clauses

We can also use a **what-clause** followed by **be** to focus attention on certain information in a sentence (= another form of *cleft sentence)*. This pattern is particularly common in conversation. The information we want to focus attention on is outside the **what-clause**. Compare:

- We gave them some home-made cake. *and*
- **What we gave them** *was* some home-made cake.

We often do this if we want to introduce a new topic; to give a reason, instruction or explanation; or to correct something that has been said or done. In the following examples, the information in focus is in italics:

- **What I'd like you to work on is** *the revision exercise on the website.*
- Isa arrived two hours late: **what had happened was** that *his bicycle chain had broken*.
- 'We've only got this small bookcase – will that do?' 'No, **what I was looking for was** *something much bigger and stronger*.'

We can often put the **what-clause** either at the beginning or the end of the sentence:

- **What upset me most was** *his rudeness. or*
- *His rudeness was* **what upset me most**.

To focus attention on an *action* performed by someone, we use a sentence with **what** + **subject** + **do** + **be** + **to-infinitive** clause. We can't use an **it-clause** to do this (see **A**):

- Luis lost his job and was short of money, so **what he did was (to) sell** his flat and move in with his brother. (*not* … so it was (to) sell his flat that he did.)

C

The pattern in **B** is only usually used with **what-clauses**. Instead of placing other **wh-clauses** (beginning **how**, **when**, **where**, **who**, **why**) at the beginning of the sentence we prefer to use a noun which has a meaning related to the **wh-word** (e.g. **reason** rather than **why**; **place** rather than **where**) followed by a **that-** or **wh-clause.** Here are some examples:

- **The** only **reason** (**why / that**) I left the party early was that I was feeling unwell. (*rather than* Why I left the party early was …)
- **The place** (**where / that**) you should play football is the playground, not the classroom.
- **Somebody** (**who / that**) I enjoy reading is Peter Carey.
- **The time** (**when / that**) I work best is early morning.

Exercises

98.1 Complete the rewritten sentences to focus attention on the underlined information. Start with it + be and use an appropriate wh-word or that. A

1 Mark's known for ages that his parents are coming to stay with us this weekend, but he only told me yesterday. *Mark's known for ages that his parents are coming to stay with us this weekend, but …* it was only yesterday that / when he told me.

2 Helena has been feeling a bit depressed for some time, so I booked a holiday in Amsterdam to cheer her up. *Helena has been feeling a bit depressed for some time, so …*

3 It's not that I don't want to have dinner with you tonight; I can't come because I've got so much work to do. *It's not that I don't want to have dinner with you tonight; …*

4 I had my wallet when I went into the sports hall, so I lost it somewhere in there. *I had my wallet when I went into the sports hall, so …*

5 She doesn't find learning languages very easy, and she improved her Spanish only by studying very hard. *She doesn't find learning languages very easy, and …*

6 I have had a great deal of help from my parents and two brothers in my research, and I dedicate this thesis to my family. *I have had a great deal of help from my parents and two brothers in doing my research, and …*

98.2 Write B's responses beginning No, what …, correcting what was said in A's question. Use the notes in brackets. B

1 A: Did you say that Rudi was going to live in Austria? (*holiday / Austria*)
B: No, what I said was that he was going on holiday to Austria.

2 A: Do you hope to sell your Picasso paintings? (*be put into / public art gallery*)
B: ……………………………………………………………………………… .

3 A: Did it annoy you that Carla came so late? (*not apologise*)
B: ……………………………………………………………………………… .

4 A: Did you mean to give Ella your bike? (*could borrow it / until needed again*)
B: ……………………………………………………………………………… .

Now give similar responses which focus on the action.

5 A: Did you watch the football on TV last night? (*get brother / record it / watch tonight*)
B: No, what I did was (to) get my brother to record it and I'll watch it tonight.

6 A: This steak tastes delicious. Did you fry it? (*put oil and soy sauce on / grill*)
B: ……………………………………………………………………………… .

7 A: Did you buy Megan the coat she wanted? (*give / money towards it*)
B: ……………………………………………………………………………… .

8 A: Did you fly from Sydney to Brisbane. (*hire a car / drive all the way*)
B: ……………………………………………………………………………… .

98.3 Complete B's responses using one of the phrases from section C opposite and the information in brackets. Put the information in the right order and add an appropriate form of be. C

1 A: I suppose Paul got the job because of his qualifications. (*uncle owns company*)
B: *Well, actually, I think …* the reason why / that Paul got the job was that his uncle owns the company.

2 A: Do you know anyone who could mend my computer? (*might be able / help / Petra*)
B: *I don't know if she's free, but* ………………………………………………………
……………………………………………………………………………… .

3 A: You grew up in this village, didn't you? (*between this village and next*)
B: *In fact* ………………………………………………………
……………………………………………………………………………… .

4 A: In what period of your life do you think you were happiest? (*lived Australia*)
B: *I suppose* ………………………………………………………
……………………………………………………………………………… .

Unit 99

Inversion 1

A

In statements it is usual for the verb to follow the subject, but sometimes this word order is reversed. We can refer to this as *inversion*. There are two main types of inversion: when the verb comes before the subject (inversion is often optional), and when the auxiliary comes before the subject and the rest of the verb phrase follows the subject (inversion is usually necessary):

- *Alex* **stood** in the doorway. → In the doorway **stood** *Alex*. (*or* … Alex stood.)
- *I* **had** rarely **seen** such a view. → Rarely **had** *I* **seen** such a view. (*not* Rarely I had seen …)

Inversion brings about *fronting*, the re-ordering of information in a sentence to give emphasis in a particular place. Often this causes an element to be postponed until later in the sentence, focusing attention on it.

B

In conversation we use **Here comes + noun** and **There goes + noun**, with inversion of verb and subject, to talk about things and people moving towards or away from the speaker:

- **Here comes** the bus.
- **There goes** Per Alvin, the conductor.

Here comes … is also used to say that something is going to happen soon, and **There goes …** is used to talk about things (particularly money) being lost and to say that something (such as a phone or door bell) is ringing:

- **Here comes** lunch.
- My bike's been stolen! **There goes** £100!
- **There goes** the phone. Can you answer it?

We also put the verb before the subject when we use adverbs expressing direction of movement, such as **along**, **away**, **back**, **down**, **in**, **off**, **out**, **up** with verbs such as **come**, **fly**, **go**. This pattern is found particularly in narrative, to mark a change in events:

- The door opened and **in came** the doctor. (*less formally* … and the doctor came in.)
- As soon as I let go of the string, **up went the balloon**, high into the sky. (*less formally* … the balloon went up …)

For more on inversion after adverbs of place and direction, see Unit 76A.

C

We can use clauses with inversion instead of certain kinds of **if-clause** (see Unit 83). Compare:

It would be a serious setback, **if** *the talks* **were to fail**.	It would be a serious setback, **were** *the talks* **to fail**.
If *you should* **need** more information, please telephone our main office.	**Should** *you* **need** more information, please telephone our main office.
If *Andy* **had asked**, I would have been able to help.	**Had** *Andy* **asked**, I would have been able to help.

The sentences with inversion are rather more formal than those with 'if'. Note that in negative clauses with inversion, we don't use contracted forms:

- **Had** *the plane* **not been diverted**, they would have arrived early. (*not* Hadn't the plane …)

D

In formal written language we commonly use inversion after **as** and **than** in comparisons:

- Paper was invented in China, **as** *was* **the process of printing**.
- Most young people did not vote in the election, **as** *was* **the case in 2010**.
- I believed, **as** *did* **my colleagues**, that the plan would work.
- Research shows that parents watch more television **than** *do* **their children**.

Note that we don't invert subject and verb after **as** or **than** when the subject is a pronoun:

- We now know a lot more about the universe **than** *we* **did** ten years ago. (*not* … than did we ten years ago.)

Exercises

99.1 **Complete the sentences with an appropriate adverb and a form of either come or go.** B

1 We'd just got to the top of the hill when ...down came... the rain and we got soaked.
2 Just when you've bought a computer that you think will last a lifetime, ... some new software that needs an even bigger hard drive.
3 Whenever I ask the class a question, ... their hands and they sit patiently until I choose one of them to answer.
4 I asked Ryan to get three kilos of potatoes from the supermarket and he only bought one kilo, so .... he .... to get some more.
5 After I'd been waiting for an hour, the door opened and .... the nurse, who said the dentist would be able to see me now.
6 I'd lost hope of getting the cat out of the tree, when .... a man with a ladder.
7 As soon as I'd given Daisy some pocket money, ... she .... to buy sweets.

99.2 **Match the sentence halves and write new sentences beginning Were ..., Should ..., or Had ... .** C

1 If Kahn had not resigned as party leader, ...
2 If you do not wish to receive further information about our products, ...
3 If the plane were ever to be built, ...
4 If the ice hockey team wins again today, ...
5 If I were offered the job, ...
6 If a car had been coming the other way, ...
7 If there had been a referendum on the issue, ...
8 If you are not able to afford the SXL3, ...
9 If Charles Dickens were alive today,...

a it would cut the journey time from New York to Tokyo by four hours.
b there are less expensive models in the range.
c ~~he would have been sacked.~~
d I would have no hesitation in accepting.
e he would be writing novels about the homeless in London.
f it is unlikely that the electorate would have supported the government.
g it will be their tenth consecutive victory.
h click on the box below.
i I might have been seriously injured.

1 + c ...Had Kahn not resigned as party leader, he would have been sacked....

99.3 **Report the information in the table. Write three sentences using sentence frame (i) and three using sentence frame (ii).**

Household expenditure (% of total income)

	Housing	Food and drink	Clothing	Transport	Recreation
Europe 1970	22	12	3	8	10
America 1970	15	14	2	6	12
Europe Today	17	8	5	12	9
America Today	16	15	3	7	13

(i) *Europeans / Americans* *spend / spent* *more / less* of their income on ... *today / in 1970* than *do / did* *Europeans / Americans*
1 ...Americans spend more of their income on food and drink today than do Europeans....

(ii) *Europeans / Americans* *spend / spent* *more / less* of their income on ... than on ... *today / in 1970*, as *is / was* the case *today / in 1970*.

99.4 **Rewrite these sentences with a similar meaning using as or than + be or do.** D

1 I was opposed to the new road. Everyone else in the village was opposed to it, too.
...I was opposed to the new road, as was everyone else in the village....
2 Kamal went to Oxford University. His sister went there, too. *Kamal went ...*
3 Compared with people in developed nations, people in poorer countries consume a far smaller proportion of the earth's resources. *People in poorer countries ...*
4 Compared to five years ago, he is a much better teacher. *He is ...*
5 Dan is a keen golfer. His wife is a keen golfer, too. *Dan is ...*

→ **Additional exercise 16** (page 250)

Unit 100

Inversion 2

A Inversion after negative adverbials

In formal and literary language in particular, we use negative adverbials at the beginning of a clause. The subject and first auxiliary are inverted, and **do** is used with a simple tense verb after –

☆ the time adverbials **never (before)**, **rarely**, **seldom**; **barely / hardly / scarcely ... when / before**; **no sooner ... than**:

- **Seldom do** *we* **have** goods returned to us because they are faulty.
- **Hardly had** *everybody* **taken** their seats when Dr Lee began her lecture.

☆ **only + a time expression**, as in **only after**, **only later**, **only if**, **only once**, **only then**, **only when**:

- She bought a newspaper and some milk at the shop on the corner. **Only later did** *she* **realise** that she'd been given the wrong change.
- **Only when she apologises will** / **speak** to her again.

☆ **only** + other prepositional phrases beginning **only by ...**, **only in ...**, **only with ...**, etc.:

- **Only by chance had** *Carl* **discovered** where the birds were nesting.
- Maria had to work in the evenings. **Only in this way was** *she* **able to complete** the report.

☆ expressions such as **at no time**, **in no way**, **on no account**, **under / in no circumstances**:

- **At no time did** *they* actually **break** the rules of the game.
- **Under no circumstances are** *passengers* **permitted** to open the doors themselves.

☆ expressions with **not ...**, such as **not only**, **not until**, **not since**, **not for one moment** and also **not a + noun**:

- **Not until August did** *the government* **order** an inquiry into the accident.
- **Not a word had** *she* **written** since the exam had started.

☆ **little** with a negative meaning:

- **Little do** *they* **know** how lucky they are to live in such a wonderful house. (= 'they don't know' or 'they don't know sufficiently')

Note that inversion can occur after a clause beginning **only after / if / when** or **not until**:

- **Only when the famine gets worse will** *world governments* **begin** to act.
- **Not until the train pulled into the station did** *Miguel* **find** that his coat had gone.

B Inversion after so + adjective ... that; such + be ... that; neither ... / nor ...

We can use **so + adjective** at the beginning of a clause to emphasise the adjective. When we do this, the subject and first auxiliary are inverted, and **do** is used with a simple tense verb:

- **So successful** *was* **her business**, that Lana was able to retire at the age of 50.
- **So dangerous** *did* **weather conditions** *become*, that all mountain roads were closed.

We can use **such + be** at the beginning of a clause to emphasise the extent or degree of something:

- **Such** *is* **the popularity** of the play that the theatre is likely to be full every night.

We use inversion after **neither** and **nor** when these words begin a clause to introduce a negative addition to a previous negative clause or sentence:

- For some time after the explosion Jack couldn't hear, and **neither** *could* **he** *see*.
- The council never wanted the new supermarket to be built, **nor** *did* **local residents**.

Note that we also use inversion in **Neither / Nor do I**, **Neither / Nor does Diane** (etc.) and in **So do I**, **So does Maya** (etc.).

Exercises

100.1 **Rewrite the sentences with a similar meaning beginning with a word / phrase from the box.** A

only if **barely** **only with** **~~rarely~~** **at no time** **little**

1 A new film has not often before produced such positive reviews.
Rarely has a new film produced such positive reviews.
2 The public was never in any danger.
3 He only felt entirely relaxed with close friends and family.
4 The match won't be cancelled unless the pitch is frozen.
5 I didn't know then that Carmen and I would be married one day.
6 He had only just entered the water when it became clear he couldn't swim.

Now do the same using these words and phrases. A

only once **only in** **on no account** **hardly** **not only** **not for one moment**

7 You must not light the fire if you are alone in the house.
8 There was never any rivalry between the three brothers.
9 I wasn't only wet through, I was freezing cold.
10 I had only ever climbed this high once before.
11 The audience had only just taken their seats when the conductor stepped onto the stage.
12 He has only been acknowledged to be a great author in the last few years.

100.2 **Complete these sentences in any appropriate way using the words from the box.** B

alike **boring** **complicated** **dominance** **~~interest~~** **strength**

1 Such *is the interest in Dr Lowe's talk* that it will be held in a bigger lecture theatre.
2 Such .... that few buildings were left standing.
3 Such .... that she hasn't lost a match for over three years.
4 So .... that even their parents couldn't tell them apart.
5 So .... that it even took a computer three days to solve it.
6 So .... that most of the students went to sleep.

100.3 **Correct any mistakes in this news article.** Units 99 & 100

NEWSONLINE

TOWN EVACUATED AS FOREST FIRES APPROACH

The people of Sawston were evacuated yesterday as forest fires headed towards the town. Such the heat was of the oncoming inferno that trees more than 100 metres ahead began to smoulder. Only once in recent years, during 2004, a town of this size has had to be evacuated because of forest fires. A fleet of coaches and lorries arrived in the town in the early morning. Into these vehicles the sick and elderly climbed, before they headed off to safety across the river. Residents with cars left by mid morning, as all non-essential police officers did.

Hardly the evacuation had been completed when the wind changed direction and it became clear that the fire would leave Sawston untouched. Soon after that were heard complaints from some residents. 'At no time the fires posed a real threat,' said one local man. 'I didn't want to leave my home, and nor most of my neighbours did.' So upset some elderly residents are that they are threatening to complain to their MP. But Chief Fire Officer Jones replied, 'Hadn't we taken this action, lives would have been put at risk. Only when the fires have moved well away from the town residents will be allowed to return to their homes.'

→ Additional exercise 16 (page 250)

Appendix 1
Irregular verbs

bare infinitive	*past simple*	*past participle (-ed form)*
arise	arose	arisen
awake	awoke	awoken
be	was / were	been
bear	bore	borne
beat	beat	beaten
become	became	become
begin	began	begun
bend	bent	bent
bet	bet	bet
bind	bound	bound
bite	bit	bitten
bleed	bled	bled
blow	blew	blown
break	broke	broken
bring	brought	brought
broadcast	broadcast	broadcast
build	built	built
burn[1]	burnt	burnt
burst	burst	burst
buy	bought	bought
cast	cast	cast
catch	caught	caught
choose	chose	chosen
cling	clung	clung
come	came	come
cost	cost	cost
creep[1]	crept	crept
cut	cut	cut
deal	dealt	dealt
dig	dug	dug
dive	dived	dived
do	did	done
draw	drew	drawn
dream[1]	dreamt	dreamt
drink	drank	drunk
drive	drove	driven
dwell[1]	dwelt	dwelt
eat	ate	eaten
fall	fell	fallen
feed	fed	fed
feel	felt	felt
fight	fought	fought

bare infinitive	*past simple*	*past participle (-ed form)*
find	found	found
fit[1]	fit	fit
flee	fled	fled
fling	flung	flung
fly	flew	flown
forbid	forbade[2]	forbidden
forecast[1]	forecast	forecast
forget	forgot	forgotten
forgive	forgave	forgiven
freeze	froze	frozen
get	got	got
give	gave	given
go	went	gone
grow	grew	grown
hang[1]	hung	hung
have	had	had
hear	heard	heard
hide	hid	hidden
hit	hit	hit
hold	held	held
hurt	hurt	hurt
keep	kept	kept
kneel[1]	knelt	knelt
knit[1]	knit	knit
know	knew	known
lay	laid	laid
lead	led	led
lean[1]	leant	leant
leap[1]	leapt	leapt
learn[1]	learnt	learnt
leave	left	left
lend	lent	lent
let	let	let
lie[4]	lay	lain
light[1]	lit	lit
lose	lost	lost
make	made	made
mean	meant	meant
meet	met	met
mow[3]	mowed	mown
pay	paid	paid
prove	proved	proven

bare infinitive	*past simple*	*past participle (-ed form)*
put	put	put
quit	quit	quit
read	read[5]	read[5]
ride	rode	ridden
ring	rang	rung
rise	rose	risen
run	ran	run
saw[3]	sawed	sawn
say	said	said
see	saw	seen
seek	sought	sought
sell	sold	sold
send	sent	sent
set	set	set
sew[3]	sewed	sewn
shake	shook	shaken
shear[3]	sheared	shorn
shed	shed	shed
shine	shone	shone
shoot	shot	shot
show	showed	shown
shrink	shrank	shrunk
shut	shut	shut
sing	sang	sung
sink	sank	sunk
sit	sat	sat
sleep	slept	slept
slide	slid	slid
sling	slung	slung
smell[1]	smelt	smelt
sow[3]	sowed	sown
speak	spoke	spoken
speed[1]	sped	sped
spell[1]	spelt	spelt
spend	spent	spent
spill[1]	spilt	spilt

bare infinitive	*past simple*	*past participle (-ed form)*
spin	spun	spun / span
spit	spat	spat
split	split	split
spoil[1]	spoilt	spoilt
spread	spread	spread
spring	sprang	sprung
stand	stood	stood
steal	stole	stolen
stick	stuck	stuck
sting	stung	stung
stink	stank	stunk
strike	struck	struck
strive	strove	striven
swear	swore	sworn
sweep	swept	swept
swell[3]	swelled	swollen
swim	swam	swum
swing	swung	swung
take	took	taken
teach	taught	taught
tear	tore	torn
tell	told	told
think	thought	thought
throw	threw	thrown
thrust	thrust	thrust
tread	trod	trodden
understand	understood	understood
wake[1]	woke	woken
wear	wore	worn
weave[1]	wove	woven
weep	wept	wept
wet[1]	wet	wet
win	won	won
wind	wound	wound
wring	wrung	wrung
write	wrote	written

[1] These verbs have two past simple and two past participle forms, both the ones given and regular forms (e.g. burn; burnt / burned; burnt / burned).

[2] 'forbad' is also sometimes used, but is old fashioned.

[3] These verbs have two past participle forms, the one given and a regular form (e.g. mow; mowed; mown / mowed).

[4] When *lie* means 'deliberately to say something untrue' it is regular ('lie / lied / lied').

[5] Pronounced /red/ .

Appendix 2
Passive verb forms

If an agent is mentioned, it goes in a prepositional phrase with **by** after the verb (see also Unit 24).

Present simple		
Active:	**tell(s)**	John **tells** me that you're thinking of leaving.
Passive:	**am / is / are told**	**I'm told** (by John) that you're thinking of leaving.
Past simple		
Active:	**told**	John **told** me that you were leaving.
Passive:	**was / were told**	I **was told** (by John) that you were leaving.
Present perfect		
Active:	**have / has told**	John **has told** me that you are leaving.
Passive:	**have / has been told**	I **have been told** (by John) that you are leaving.
Past perfect		
Active:	**had told**	John **had** already **told** me that you were leaving.
Passive:	**had been told**	I **had** already **been told** (by John) that you were leaving.
Present continuous		
Active:	**am / is / are telling**	John **is** always **telling** me that you are leaving.
Passive:	**am / is / are being told**	I **am** always **being told** (by John) that you are leaving.
Past continuous		
Active:	**was / were telling**	John **was** always **telling** me that you were leaving.
Passive:	**was / were being told**	I **was** always **being told** (by John) that you were leaving.
Future simple		
Active:	**will tell**	I **will tell** John that you are leaving.
Passive:	**will be told**	John **will be told** (by me) that you are leaving.
Future perfect		
Active:	**will have told**	By tomorrow I **will have told** John that you are leaving.
Passive:	**will have been told**	By tomorrow John **will have been told** (by me) that you are leaving.
Present perfect continuous (rare in the passive)		
Active:	**has / have been telling**	John **has been telling** me for ages that you are leaving.
Passive:	**has / have been being told**	I **have been being told** (by John) for ages that you are leaving.

Modal verbs with passives

Active:	**should / could / might / ought to** (etc.) **tell**	You **should tell** John.
Passive:	**should / could / might / ought to** (etc.) **be told**	John **should be told**.
Active:	**should / could / might / ought to** (etc.) **have told**	You **should have told** John.
Passive:	**should / could / might / ought to** (etc.) **have been told**	John **should have been told**.
Active:	**should / could / might / ought to** (etc.) **have been telling**	You **should have been telling** John while I was outside.
Passive:	**should / could / might / ought to** (etc.) **have been being told**	John **should have been being told** while I was outside.

Other passive verb forms are very rare.

active
In an active clause or active sentence, the grammatical subject is the person or thing that performs the action given in the verb (e.g. Dan wrote the book). Compare PASSIVE.

adjective
A word that describes a noun (e.g. an *interesting* book) or a pronoun (e.g. a *red* one). **Gradable adjectives** can be used to say that a person or thing has more or less of this quality (e.g. She's very *happy*), while **non-gradable adjectives** can't (e.g. It's *impossible*. We can't say 'It's very impossible'). **Classifying adjectives** say that something is of a particular type (e.g. *atomic*, *initial*). **Emphasising adjectives** stress how strongly we feel about something (e.g. *complete* nonsense). **Qualitative adjectives** say what qualities a person or thing has (e.g. *big*, *rich*). See also **grading** ADVERBS and **non-grading** ADVERBS.

adjective phrase
A group of words where the main word is an adjective (e.g. it's *extremely important*; it wasn't *strong enough*).

adverb
A word that describes or gives more information (when, how, where, etc.) about a verb (e.g. He ran *quickly*), adjective (e.g. an *extremely* expensive car), another adverb (e.g. She did it *very* easily), or phrase (e.g. They live *just* across the road.). Types of adverb include: **adverbs of manner** (e.g. *slowly*, *violently*) which we use to say how something is done; **connecting adverbs** (e.g. *consequently*, *similarly*); **time adverbs** (e.g. *tomorrow*, *already*); **place adverbs** (e.g. *upstairs*, *outside*); **direction adverbs** (e.g. *backwards*, *through*); **comment adverbs** (e.g. *apparently*, *personally*) which we use to make a comment on what we are saying; **viewpoint adverbs** (e.g. *financially*, *politically*) which we use to make clear from what point of view we are speaking; **adverbs of indefinite frequency** (e.g. *always*, *never*); **degree adverbs** (e.g. *completely*, *quite*) which give information about the extent or degree of something; **focus adverbs** (e.g. *just*, *even*) which we use to focus on a particular word or phrase. **Grading adverbs** (e.g. *extremely*, *very*) are used with **gradable** ADJECTIVES. **Non-grading adverbs** (e.g. *completely*, *mainly*) are used with **non-gradable** ADJECTIVES.

adverbial
A word or group of words that says when, how, where, etc. something happens. They may consist of an ADVERB (e.g. *quietly*), a PREPOSITIONAL PHRASE (e.g. *through the door*), a NOUN PHRASE (e.g. *next week*), or an ADVERBIAL CLAUSE (e.g. *after she left*).

adverbial clause
A type of **subordinate** CLAUSE that says when, how, where, etc. something happens (e.g. *Before I went to school this morning*, I did my homework).

affirmative sentence
A statement (i.e. not a question) that is positive, not negative.

agent
The person or thing that performs the action described in a verb. Usually it is the subject in an active clause and comes after 'by ...' in a passive clause.

article
The word *the* is the **definite article** and the word *a* (*an* before vowels) is the **indefinite article**. When there is no article before a noun we refer to this as the **zero article**.

auxiliary verbs
The verbs *be*, *have* and *do* when they are used with a main verb to form questions, negatives, tenses, passive forms, etc. MODAL VERBS are also auxiliary verbs.

clause
A group of words that contains a verb. A clause may be a complete sentence or a part of a sentence. A **main clause** can exist as a separate sentence, while a **subordinate clause** cannot (e.g. *If I see Matt at work* [= subordinate clause], *I'll invite him over this evening* [= main clause]). Types of clause include: **to-infinitive clause** (e.g. *To become a doctor* takes years of study); **present participle(-ing) clause** (e.g. *Feeling hungry*, I went into the kitchen); **past participle (-ed) clause** (e.g. *Built during the 1970s*, the building is now in need of repair); **being + past participle (-ed) clause** (e.g. *Being unemployed*, Tom had a lot of time on his hands); **having + past participle (-ed) clause** (e.g. *Having seen the doctor*, I went straight home). See also CONDITIONAL CLAUSE, RELATIVE CLAUSE.

cleft sentence
A sentence in which focus is given to either the subject or object using a pattern beginning 'It ...' (e.g. It was my brother who lent me the money) or 'What ...' (e.g. What you need is a holiday).

complement
A word or phrase that follows a LINKING VERB and describes the SUBJECT (e.g. Linda is a *lawyer*) or OBJECT (e.g. I found the food *inedible*). A complement may also be an ADVERBIAL or PREPOSITIONAL PHRASE which completes the meaning of a verb. Some verbs need a complement (e.g. The disease originated *in Britain*; 'The disease originated' would be incomplete).

compound
A **compound noun** consists of two or more words together used as a noun (e.g. a *language school*). A **compound adjective** consists of two or more words together used as an adjective (e.g. They were *well-behaved*).

conditional
A **conditional clause** usually starts with 'if', but other patterns are possible (e.g. *Had it not rained*, Spain would have won). A **conditional sentence** contains a conditional clause. A distinction can be made between **real conditionals**, which suggest that the situation is or was true, or may have been or may become true (e.g. If she makes a promise, she keeps it) and **unreal conditionals**, which suggest that the situation is imaginary or untrue (e.g. If you had asked me, I would have helped).

conjunction
A word such as *and*, *but*, *if*, *while*, *after*, *because* which connects words, phrases, or clauses in a sentence. Compare SENTENCE CONNECTOR.

countable
A **countable noun** can be both singular and plural (e.g. *cup / cups*). An **uncountable noun** doesn't have a plural form (e.g. *electricity*, but not 'electricities').

determiner
A word that goes in front of a noun to identify what the noun refers to (e.g. *this*, *some*, *the*, *a / an*, *each*, *all*, *my*). **Possessive determiners** (also called **possessive adjectives**) are words such as *my*, *your* and *their*.

direct speech
Speech that is written using the exact words of the speaker, without any changes. Compare REPORTED SPEECH.

imperative
An **imperative clause** uses the **bare** INFINITIVE form of a verb for such things as giving orders and making suggestions (e.g. *Go to bed!*).

infinitive
The form of a verb that usually goes after 'to'. The form can be either the **to-infinitive** (e.g. *to sing*, *to eat*) or the **bare infinitive** (e.g. *sing*, *eat*).

intransitive verb
A verb that doesn't take an object (e.g. She *smiled*). Compare TRANSITIVE VERB.

inversion
Changing the usual word order so that the verb comes before the subject (e.g. Up *went the balloon*).

linking verb
A verb (e.g. *be*, *become*, *appear*) that connects a SUBJECT with its COMPLEMENT.

modal verbs
A group of verbs (*can*, *could*, *may*, *might*, *must*, *ought to*, *shall*, *should*, *will*, *would*) that give information about such things as possibility, necessity, and obligation. **Semi-modal verbs** (*used to*, *need*, *dare*, *had better*, *have* (*got*) *to*, *be able to*) have similar meanings to modal verbs.

non-affirmative
Referring to a lack of positive, affirmative meaning; for example, in most questions and negatives. However, questions which expect a positive reply are affirmative. The terms 'non-assertive' and 'assertive' are sometimes used for 'non-affirmative' and 'affirmative'.

noun
A word that refers to a person, place, thing, quality, etc. A **collective noun** refers to a group of people or things (e.g. *audience*, *crowd*, *herd*). See also COUNTABLE NOUN.

noun phrase
A group of words where the main word is a noun (e.g. I've been talking to *the woman across the road*; We spoke to *several small children*).

object
The **direct object** is the person or thing affected by the action of the verb (e.g. I put *the book* [= direct object] back on the shelf). The **indirect object** is the person or thing who benefits from the action or who receives something (e.g. I gave *my mother* [= indirect object] some flowers [= direct object]). Compare SUBJECT.

participle
The **present participle** is the **-ing form** of a verb (e.g. *walking*, *singing*, *eating*) used, for example, in continuous tenses. The **past participle** is the **-ed** form of a verb (e.g. *walked*, *sang*, *eaten*) used, for example, in perfect tenses. A **participle adjective** is one formed from the present or past participle of a verb (e.g. the candidates *applying*, a *broken* plate). A **participle clause** has a present participle or past participle verb form (e.g. *Feeling unwell*, he went to bed; The person *appointed to the post* will have a difficult job to do).

particle
An adverb or preposition that follows a verb in TWO-WORD VERBS and THREE-WORD VERBS (e.g. What time did you *get in*? [in = adverb]; I *flicked through* the magazine [through = preposition]; She *looks up to* her mother [up = adverb, to = preposition]).

passive
In a passive clause or passive sentence, the grammatical subject is the person or thing that experiences the effect of the action given in the verb (e.g. The book was written by Dan). Compare ACTIVE.

performative
A performative is a verb which states the action that is performed when a speaker uses the verb (e.g. I *promise* I'll do it tomorrow; I *apologise*).

phrasal verb
A verb together with a following adverb and / or a preposition that has a single meaning (e.g. *set off*, *look up to*). Compare 'I *ran across* Tanya at the concert' (= met unexpectedly; a phrasal verb) and 'She *ran across* the road' (= a PREPOSITIONAL VERB).

possessive
The possessive form of a noun ends in either *-'s* (e.g. *Marta's* car) or *-s'* (e.g. the *girls'* changing room).

preposition
A word such as *in*, *on*, or *by* that comes before a noun, pronoun, noun phrase or **-ing** form (e.g. *in* March, *above* my uncle's head, *by* investing).

prepositional phrase
A group of words that consists of a PREPOSITION and its **prepositional object** (a noun, pronoun, noun phrase or **-ing** form) (e.g. *behind our house*, *across it*).

prepositional verb
A verb and a following preposition (e.g. *believe in*, *consist of*, *look after*). Compare PHRASAL VERB.

pronoun
A word that is used instead of a noun or noun phrase. Pronouns include **personal pronouns** (e.g. *I*, *she*, *me*), **reflexive pronouns** (e.g. *myself*, *herself*), **possessive pronouns** (e.g. *mine*, *yours*), and RELATIVE PRONOUNS (e.g. *who*, *which*).

quantifier
A word or phrase that goes before a noun or noun phrase to talk about the quantity of something (e.g. *a little* water, *many of* the women in the room).

question
A **wh-question** begins with a WH-WORD (e.g. *Where are you going?*). A **yes / no question** is one that can be answered with 'yes' or 'no' (e.g. *Do you like coffee?*). An **echo question** repeats part of a previous utterance and asks for a repetition of all or part of it (e.g. 'I'm moving to Alaska.' '*You're moving where?*'). We can ask an **indirect question** by putting it into a **subordinate** CLAUSE beginning with a WH-WORD or with *if* or *whether* (e.g. Can you tell me *where you live*?).

relative clause
A kind of **subordinate** CLAUSE that describes a noun that comes before it in a **main** CLAUSE. A **defining relative clause** says which person or thing is being talked about (e.g. A friend *who lives in London* is getting married). A **non-defining relative clause** gives more information about the noun (e.g. My bicycle, *which I've left outside your house*, is over 20 years old). A **nominal relative clause** begins with a WH-WORD or *whatever*, *whenever*, etc. and functions as a NOUN PHRASE in a sentence (e.g. *What I need now* is a long, hot bath). A **reduced relative clause** usually begins with an **-ing** (present participle) or **-ed** (past participle) form and has a similar meaning to a relative clause (e.g. I met the people *living in our old house* [= ... who live in our old house], The new rules only affect people *born before 1960* [= ... who were born before 1960]).

relative pronoun
A pronoun such as *who*, *which*, or *that* which is used at the beginning of a relative clause.

relative word
Words including RELATIVE PRONOUNS and others (e.g. *whereby*, *why*) that can begin a RELATIVE CLAUSE.

reported speech
Speech that is reported without using the exact words of the speaker. Sometimes called 'indirect speech'.

reporting clause & reported clause
A statement that reports what people think or say is often divided into a **reporting clause** and a **reported clause** (e.g. *She said* [= reporting clause] *that the building was unsafe* [= reported clause]).

reporting verb
A verb used in a REPORTING CLAUSE that describes what people say or think (e.g. *ask*, *claim*, *say*).

sentence connector
A word or phrase that shows a connection between two separate sentences (e.g. My car isn't very comfortable. *However*, it's very cheap to run.; The house is large and has a beautiful garden. *What's more*, it's very close to the station.). Compare CONJUNCTION.

state verb
A verb that is used to describe a state (e.g. *believe*, *think*) rather than an action.

subject
The person or thing that does the action of the verb (e.g. *Luca* went home). Compare OBJECT.

subjunctive
The subjunctive is a set of verb forms used mainly in rather formal English to talk about possibilities rather than facts. The **present subjunctive** uses the base form of the verb (e.g. We suggest that she *leave* immediately) and the **past subjunctive** uses *were* (e.g. If I *were* you, I'd go home now).

transitive verb
A verb that takes an object (e.g. She *was holding* a bunch of flowers). Compare INTRANSITIVE VERB.

two-word verbs & three-word verbs
Verbs that are commonly used with a particular PARTICLE (adverb or preposition) are referred to here as **two-word verbs** (e.g. She *looked after* her elderly parents). Verbs that are commonly used with two particular particles (adverb + preposition) are referred to here as **three-word verbs** (e.g. He *looked up to* his older brothers). See also PREPOSITIONAL VERB and PHRASAL VERB.

verb
A **finite verb** has a tense (e.g. She *waited*; She *is waiting* for you). **Non-finite** verb forms are INFINITIVE (e.g. He came *to see* me) and PARTICIPLE forms (e.g. *Shouting* loudly, I was able to make myself heard; *Built* in 2011, the tower is still the tallest construction in Europe).

verb phrase
A group of words consisting of one or more verbs (e.g. *gives*, *is giving*, *has been giving*).

wh-words
A group of words (*who*, *whom*, *whose*, *where*, *when*, *why*, *how*) that are used in **wh**-QUESTIONS.

Study planner

Use this study planner if you need help in deciding which units you should study, or which part of the *Grammar reminder* you should read first.

Which of the four multiple-choice options, A, B, C or D, completes the sentences in the correct or most likely way? Sometimes more than one option is possible. If you are not sure which options are correct, you may need to study any related sections of the *Grammar reminder* first and then the corresponding unit(s) listed on the right in the table below. You will find the full correct version of each sentence either in the section of the *Grammar reminder* or in the unit highlighted.

Tenses		Grammar reminder	Unit
1.1	'Who .... ?' '.................. to get through to Misaki.' **A** do you phone ... I'm trying **B** are you phoning ... I'm trying **C** are you phoning ... I try **D** do you phone ... I try	A1	1, 2
1.2	.... to Turkey every year for your holidays? **A** Are you going **B** Were you going **C** Have you gone **D** Do you go	A5	1, 2
1.3	I .... you park outside the city and get the bus to the centre. **A** am suggesting **B** suggests **C** suggest **D** was suggesting		1, 2
1.4	Sophia .... me that you're thinking of emigrating. **A** told **B** tells **C** is telling **D** tell		2, 1
1.5	Aisha .... a few minutes ago. **A** has left **B** leaves **C** left **D** had left	A6	3, 4, 5
1.6	We .... to the tennis club since we moved here. **A** have belonged **B** belong **C** belonged **D** are belonging	A11	3, 6
1.7	After she .... hospital, she had a long holiday. **A** leaves **B** is leaving **C** has left **D** left		3, 4, 5
1.8	When he realised I .... at him, he .... away. **A** looked ... was turning **B** was looking ... turned **C** was looking ... was turning **D** looked ... turned	A13	4, 7
1.9	When the builders were here I .... them cups of tea all the time. **A** was making **B** am making **C** made **D** make		4, 7
1.10	When I went into the bathroom, I found that the bath.................................... . **A** overflows **B** overflowed **C** had overflowed **D** is overflowing	A14	5, 7
1.11	I was sure that I .... him before. **A** had met **B** am meeting **C** meet **D** met		5, 7
1.12	Your eyes are red – .... ? **A** did you cry **B** have you been crying **C** have you cried **D** do you cry	A17	6

		Grammar reminder	Unit
1.13	.... this holiday for ages. **A** We're looking forward to **B** We've been looking forward to **C** We look forward to **D** We've looked forward to		6, 3
1.14	When I saw the vase on the website, I knew it was exactly what I .... **A** looked for **B** look for **C** had been looking for **D** have looked for	A18	7
1.15	.... hard all year, so I felt that I deserved a holiday. **A** I work **B** I'd been working **C** I'd worked **D** I'm working		7, 4, 5

The future

		Grammar reminder	Unit
2.1	I .... one of my special desserts for dinner, if you like. **A** make **B** 'm going to make **C** 'll make **D** 'm making	B3	9
2.2	If Erik phones I .... you know. **A** 'm going to let **B** let **C** 'm letting **D** 'll let		9
2.3	'Has anybody offered to look after the children?' 'Sophia .... it.' **A** is to do **B** 's going to do **C** does **D** will do	B5	9
2.4	The next train to Dublin .... at 3:45. (*station announcement*) **A** will leave **B** is leaving **C** is going to leave **D** leaves	B6	10
2.5	When you .... Ben, tell him he still owes me some money. **A** are going to see **B** are seeing **C** see **D** will see		10
2.6	We .... a party next Saturday. Can you come? **A** 're to have **B** 're having **C** have **D** 'll have	B7	10
2.7	After the operation you .... any sport for a while. **A** won't be doing **B** aren't doing **C** don't do **D** won't to do	B8	11
2.8	When the race starts later this afternoon the drivers .... for drier weather than last year. **A** were hoping **B** are hoping **C** hope **D** will be hoping		11
2.9	In the next few years, thousands of speed cameras .... on major roads. **A** are appear **B** will appear **C** are to appear **D** are appearing		12
2.10	.... to Bangkok by the end of June. **A** I aim getting **B** I'm aiming getting **C** I aim to get **D** I'm aiming to get		13
2.11	We .... each other later that day, but I had to phone and cancel. **A** see **B** are seeing **C** were seeing **D** saw		14

Modals and semi-modals		Grammar reminder	Unit
3.1	Despite yesterday's snowfalls, we .... home in less than an hour. **A** could drive **B** can drive **C** were able to drive **D** are able to drive	C5	15
3.2	She swam strongly and .... cross the river easily, even though it was swollen by the heavy rain. **A** can **B** was able to **C** could **D** is able to		15
3.3	.... me to get you some water? **A** Would you like **B** Should you like **C** Shall you like **D** Will you like	C12	16
3.4	We .... Switzerland four times during the 1990s. **A** would visit **B** used to visit **C** visit **D** visited		16
3.5	'While we're in Moscow shall we go and see Dariya?' 'But it's been nearly 20 years since we last saw her. She .... remember us.' **A** can't **B** couldn't **C** may not **D** might not	C17	17
3.6	During the war, the police .... arrest you for criticising the government. **A** may **B** might **C** should **D** could		17
3.7	'I'm seeing Dr Evans next week.' 'That .... be right. He's on holiday then.' **A** mustn't **B** can't **C** hasn't to **D** hasn't got to	C23	18
3.8	I can't access the database. You .... a password. **A** must have got to put in **B** must've to put in **C** must have to put in **D** must put in		18
3.9	I .... an interview because I'd worked there before. **A** didn't have to have **B** needn't have had **C** didn't need to have **D** needn't have	C27	19
3.10	Nowadays it .... cost a fortune to own an e-book reader. **A** hasn't to **B** needn't **C** doesn't have to **D** mustn't		19
3.11	Walking under a ladder..................................be unlucky. **A** is suppose to **B** should **C** ought to **D** is supposed to	C32	20
3.12	It's the third time she's been skating this week. She .... really enjoy it. **A** must **B** should **C** ought to **D** had better		20

Linking verbs, passives, questions		Grammar reminder	Unit
4.1	The traffic lights .... green and I pulled away. **A** got **B** became **C** turned **D** went		21
4.2	The building .... the earthquake but then .... by a fire. **A** was survived ... destroyed **B** survived ... was destroyed **C** survived ... destroyed **D** was survived ... was destroyed	D1	22, 23, 24

		Grammar reminder	Unit
4.3	I'm really disappointed. I .... for the team again. **A** wasn't picked **B** didn't pick **C** didn't get picked **D** wasn't got picked	D2	22, 23, 24
4.4	When I asked what was wrong, ... **A** I was explained the problem **B** he explained the problem to me **C** the problem was explained to me **D** he explained me the problem		22
4.5	The children .... to the zoo. **A** were enjoyed taken **B** enjoyed being taken **C** were enjoyed taking **D** enjoyed taking		23 App.2
4.6	The new computer system .... next month. **A** is being installed by people **B** is be installed **C** is being installed **D** is been installed		24 App.2
4.7	.... that we have to leave. **A** They have informed us **B** It has been informed **C** It has been informed us **D** We have been informed		25
4.8	He just turned away when I asked him. .... he meant? **A** Which do you think **B** How do you think **C** What you think **D** What do you think	E4, E1	26
4.9	.... to see in the town? **A** What there are **B** What is there **C** What are there **D** What there is		26
4.10	.... was in the box? **A** What did you think that **B** What you thought **C** What did you think **D** What you did think		27

Verb complementation: what follows verbs

		Grammar reminder	Unit
5.1	I always associate .... **A** pizza **B** pizza by Italy **C** Italian pizza **D** pizza with Italy		28
5.2	She described .... **A** the situation **B** the situation to me **C** me the situation **D** the situation me		29
5.3	Stevens .... the wallet. **A** admitted to steal **B** admitted steal **C** admitted stealing **D** admitted him stealing	F5	30, 31
5.4	My parents wouldn't .... to the party. **A** allow me go **B** allow me to go **C** allow me going **D** allow to go	F9	30, 31
5.5	She felt the mosquito .... her. **A** bites **B** to bite **C** bite **D** biting	F13	30, 31

		Grammar reminder	Unit
5.6	You don't object .... late tonight, do you? **A** to working **B** to work **C** work **D** working		30
5.7	They arranged .... in London. **A** for Rania to stay **B** Rania to stay **C** by Rania to stay **D** for Rania staying		31

Reporting

		Grammar reminder	Unit
6.1	Georgia .... she would be late for the meeting. She .... she was feeling ill. **A** told that ... said that **B** told that ... said me that **C** told me that ... said that **D** told me that ... said me that	G4/5	32
6.2	She .... her holiday in Finland. **A** told me about **B** said about **C** said me about **D** told about	G7	32
6.3	'I suppose you've heard the latest .... to me. **A** news,' said she **B** news.' she said **C** news', she said **D** news,' she said		32
6.4	I notified .... I had changed my address. **A** with the bank that **B** the bank that **C** that **D** to the bank that		33
6.5	She reminded .... **A** what to do **B** me what I had to do **C** what I had to do **D** me what to do		34
6.6	Police said that they .... the missing girl. **A** had found **B** have found **C** find **D** were finding		35
6.7	She encouraged .... the job. **A** to take the job **B** that Fran should take **C** Fran to take **D** to Fran to take		36
6.8	He asked where he .... put the box. **A** shall **B** ought to **C** will **D** should		37
6.9	She asked my advice .... subject she should study at university. **A** on to what **B** as to what **C** on what **D** to what		38
6.10	They directed that the building .... **A** be pulled down **B** to be pulled down **C** should be pulled down **D** should pull down		39

Nouns

		Grammar reminder	Unit
7.1	The .... faulty. **A** equipments are **B** equipment was **C** equipments were **D** equipment were	H1	

		Grammar reminder	Unit
7.2	The company .... doing a lot of .... in South America. **A** is ... businesses **B** are ... business **C** are ... businesses **D** is ... business	H2	40
7.3	The .... shoes were covered in mud, so I asked them to take them off before they got into .... car. **A** girl's ... Leon's **B** girls'... Leons' **C** girls'... Leon's **D** girl's ... Leons'	H7	43
7.4	The council .... postponed a decision on the new road, and many leading members of the opposition party .... criticised the delay. **A** has ... have **B** has ... has **C** have ... has **D** have ... have		40
7.5	.... thinks that Phil should be given the job. **A** Neither of us **B** The majority of my colleagues **C** Practically everyone **D** A number of people		41
7.6	Police .... that Thomas is in Brazil, although his exact whereabouts ....unknown. **A** believes ... are **B** believe ... are **C** believes ... is **D** believe ... is		42
7.7	A new .... is being built outside the town. **A** golf course **B** golfcourse **C** golf's course **D** golf-course	H5	
7.8	The government has introduced .... **A** a children's clothes tax **B** a tax on children clothes **C** a children clothes tax **D** a tax on children's clothes		43
7.9	.... has improved enormously. **A** David's guitar playing **B** David guitar playing **C** Davids' guitar playing **D** The guitar playing of David	H11	40

Articles, determiners and quantifiers

		Grammar reminder	Unit
8.1	I'll be with you in .... **A** one quarter of an hour **B** a quarter of an hour **C** a quarter of one hour **D** a quarter of hour		44
8.2	Look at .... It's very bright tonight. **A** the moons **B** moon **C** the moon **D** a moon	I5	45–47
8.3	Sydney is .... **A** a beautiful city **B** beautiful city **C** the beautiful city **D** the beautiful cities	I7	45–47
8.4	.... of the present continuous tense on page 32. **A** There are example **B** There are examples **C** There are the examples **D** There is example	I9	45–47

		Grammar reminder	Unit
8.5	.... is one of the many factors involved in changing farming methods. **A** Climate **B** A climate **C** Climates **D** The climate		45
8.6	Against her parents' wishes, she wants to be .... **A** the journalist **B** journalist **C** a journalist **D** journalists		46
8.7	'You look upset.' 'Yes, I've had ....' **A** the terrible morning **B** terrible morning **C** some terrible morning **D** a terrible morning		47
8.8	I haven't been here for .... **A** some years **B** any years **C** years **D** the years	I14	48
8.9	We haven't got .... left. **A** a butter **B** any butter **C** the butter **D** some butter	I15	48
8.10	'Where were you last week?' 'I was visiting ....' **A** any friends **B** friends **C** the friends **D** some friends		48 49–51
8.11	.... my jewellery is missing. **A** Some of **B** Any of **C** Some **D** Any	I23	49
8.12	.... the furniture .... arrived yet. **A** None ... has **B** None ... have **C** None of ... has **D** None of ... have	I34, I22–28	49
8.13	I phoned Sarah at home, but .... **A** there were no answers **B** there were no answer **C** there was no answers **D** there was no answer		49
8.14	There isn't .... traffic along the street where I live. **A** many **B** much **C** much of **D** many of	I38, I22–28	50
8.15	.... the food was inedible. **A** A large amount of **B** Many of **C** Much of **D** A large number of		50
8.16	.... waiting to hear the results. **A** Everyone was **B** All was **C** Everyone were **D** All were	I44	51
8.17	Following the flood, ... in the area .... major repair work. **A** each of building ... need **B** every building ... needs **C** every building ... need **D** each buildings ... need	I46, I22–28	51
8.18	.... to Athens during the vacation. **A** All they are going **B** They are all going **C** They all are going **D** They are going all		51
8.19	There is .... evidence to support his claim. **A** little of **B** few **C** a few **D** little	I48, I22–28	52
8.20	We should use .... time we have available to discuss Jon's proposal. **A** the little of **B** the little **C** the few **D** little		52

Relative clauses and other types of clause	Grammar reminder	Unit
9.1 My mother ………… enjoys hill walking. **A** who is in her seventies **B** , that is in her seventies, **C** , which is in her seventies, **D** , who is in her seventies,	J2	53
9.2 She's one of the kindest people ………… . **A** that I know **B** I know **C** who I know **D** which I know		53
9.3 Do you know the date ………… we have to hand in the essay? **A** which **B** on which **C** by which **D** when		54
9.4 The valley ………… the town lies is heavily polluted. **A** in that **B** in which **C** in **D** which		55
9.5 The prisoners ………… are all women. **A** who being released **B** are being released **C** being released **D** who are being released		56
9.6 She lives in the house ………… . **A** which has the red door **B** has the red door **C** with the red door **D** which with the red door		57
9.7 'Wait a minute,' said Amy, ………… . **A** running through the door **B** run through the door **C** ran through the door **D** runs through the door	J8	58, 59
9.8 ………… by the boys' behaviour, she complained to the head teacher. **A** She annoyed **B** Annoyed **C** She was annoyed **D** Annoying	J10	58, 59
9.9 ………… at the party, we saw Ruth standing alone. **A** Arrived **B** We arrived **C** Arriving **D** We were arriving		58
9.10 Josh was the first person I saw ………… hospital. **A** by leaving **B** on leaving **C** in leaving **D** on to leave		59

Pronouns, substitution and leaving out words	Grammar reminder	Unit
10.1 'What did you do to your hand?' 'I ………… when I was chopping vegetables.' **A** cut me **B** cut **C** myself cut **D** cut myself	K1	60
10.2 The scheme allows students from many countries to communicate ………… . **A** each other **B** with each other **C** themselves **D** with one another	K7	
10.3 We are confident that both sets of fans will ………… at the match. **A** behave itself **B** behave them **C** behave themselves **D** behave		60
10.4 'We need new curtains.' 'Okay, let's buy ………… .' **A** ones with flowers on **B** some **C** ones **D** one		61

		Grammar reminder	Unit
10.5	The two children .... for breaking the window. **A** each blamed other **B** blamed other **C** blamed each other **D** each blamed the other	K9	
10.6	I had a racing bike when I was young, and .... **A** my brother did so **B** so did my brother **C** so my brother **D** did my brother	K10	62
10.7	'I don't suppose there'll be any seats left.' 'No, I ....' **A** don't suppose **B** suppose **C** don't suppose so **D** suppose not		62
10.8	They needed someone who was both an excellent administrator and manager. .... was not easy to find. **A** Such person **B** A such person **C** Such **D** Such a person		63
10.9	'They could have been delayed by the snow.' 'Yes, they ....' **A** could have **B** could **C** could been **D** could have been		64
10.10	Leon was frightened – or maybe he just .... **A** pretended to be **B** pretended to **C** pretended **D** pretend to be		65

Adjectives and adverbs

		Grammar reminder	Unit
11.1	He is a .... **A** capable of making difficult decisions manager **B** manager capable of making difficult decisions **C** capable manager of making difficult decisions **D** manager capable to make difficult decisions		66
11.2	Our teacher gave us .... problem to solve. **A** a very impossible **B** a completely impossible **C** an absolutely impossible **D** an extremely impossible	L2	67, 68
11.3	Experience is .... for the job. **A** really essential **B** fairly essential **C** pretty essential **D** very essential		67
11.4	I met my .... professor the other day. She is now advising on the government's .... **A** old politics ... very foreign policy **B** very old politics ... foreign policy **C** very old politics ... very foreign policy **D** old politics ... foreign policy		68
11.5	I drank some .... coffee. **A** good very Brazilian **B** Brazilian very good **C** very good Brazilian **D** very Brazilian good	L3	
11.6	I was .... to find that the film was quite .... **A** surprised ... frightening **B** surprised ... frightened **C** surprising ... frightening **D** surprising ... frightened	L4	

		Grammar reminder	Unit
11.7	My watch was among the .... **A** things taken **B** taken things **C** things stolen **D** stolen things		69
11.8	He was busy .... his homework. **A** to do **B** doing **C** that he was doing **D** he was doing		70
11.9	It was .... as we went into the room. **A** strange quiet **B** strange quietly **C** strangely quiet **D** strangely quietly	L6	71
11.10	She .... towards the door. **A** quick ran **B** ran quick **C** ran quickly **D** quickly ran		71
11.11	It was the .... thing to say. **A** most ridiculous **B** ridiculous **C** ridiculousest **D** most ridiculousest	L8	72
11.12	'Why did you buy these oranges?' 'They were ....' **A** cheapest **B** the cheapest **C** the cheapest ones I could find **D** cheapest ones I could find		72
11.13	Despite his disability he tried to lead .... as possible. **A** as normal life **B** a normal a life **C** as normal as life **D** as normal a life		73
11.14	Have you heard the good news? .... **A** In May, Eva had a baby. **B** Eva had a baby in May. **C** Eva in May had a baby. **D** Eva had in May a baby.		74, 75
11.15	.... Kaspar nowadays, he's so busy at the office. **A** We see hardly ever **B** We hardly see ever **C** We hardly ever see **D** Hardly we ever see		75
11.16	Only later .... how much damage had been caused. **A** she realised **B** she did realised **C** did she realise **D** realised she		76, 99, 100
11.17	We .... with the decision. **A** agree very much **B** much agree **C** agree much **D** very much agree		77
11.18	.........., this summer is a crucial time for the government. **A** Politics speaking **B** Politically **C** In political terms **D** In a political point of view		78

Adverbial clauses and conjunctions

		Grammar reminder	Unit
12.1	I .... unwell when I .... this morning. **A** felt ... get up **B** felt ... got up **C** feel ... get up **D** feel ... got	M2	
12.2	Have something to eat before you .... **A** leave **B** left **C** will leave **D** had left	M3	

		Grammar reminder	Unit
12.3	I still feel tired .... in the morning. **A** when I wake up **B** as I wake up **C** when I will wake up **D** while I wake up		79
12.4	We were delayed .... an accident. **A** because **B** because of there was **C** because there was **D** because of		80
12.5	I wrote down her name .... forget it. **A** so as not to **B** so not to **C** not to **D** in order not to		81
12.6	..................................they slept soundly. **A** Hot though was the night air **B** Hot though the night air was **C** Hot as the night air was **D** Hot although the night air was		82
12.7	I'll give you a lift if it .... **A** is raining **B** will rain **C** rained **D** rains	M9	83, 84
12.8	If I had known how difficult the job was, I .... it. **A** won't have taken **B** wouldn't have taken **C** won't take it **D** mightn't have taken	M14	83, 84
12.9	If I .... a more reliable car, I .... to Spain rather than fly. **A** would have ... would drive **B** had ... had driven **C** had ... would drive **D** would have had ... would drive	M17	83, 84
12.10	If the technology .... available, we would be able to expand the business. **A** would become **B** were become **C** were to become **D** became		83
12.11	If the North Sea .... in winter, you could walk from London to Oslo. **A** happened to freeze **B** froze **C** should freeze **D** should happen to freeze		84
12.12	.... in my seventies and rather unfit, I might consider taking up squash. **A** Were I not **B** Was I not **C** Weren't I **D** If I wasn't		85
12.13	They couldn't decide .... it was worth re-sitting the exam. **A** if **B** whether or not **C** whether **D** if or not		86
12.14	It was midday. ...., I put on the light. **A** Even so **B** Although **C** Even **D** Even though		87

Prepositions

		Grammar reminder	Unit
13.1	He suddenly saw Eva .... the room. He pushed his way .... the crowd of people to get to her. **A** across ... through **B** over ... through **C** across ... across **D** over ... along		88

		Grammar reminder	Unit
13.2	The concert features, ... others, Karl Frisk and the Johnsons. Their music is still very popular ...... teenagers. **A** between ... among **B** between ... between **C** among ... between **D** among ... among		89
13.3	...... a pause in the conversation, she left the room. **A** In **B** During **C** Over **D** By		90
13.4	...... cricket, I enjoy watching football and basketball. **A** Apart from **B** Except **C** Except for **D** Besides		91
13.5	Jo ...... her disabled mother until her death last year. **A** cared after **B** cared for **C** took care of **D** cared about		92
13.6	What's the chance ...... five heads when you toss a coin five times? **A** of getting **B** to get **C** of get **D** get		93
13.7	She tried to .... **A** talk me the plan out of **B** talk out of me the plan **C** talk me out of the plan **D** talk out me of the plan		94

Organising information

		Grammar reminder	Unit
14.1	...... people trying to get into the football stadium. **A** There were too much **B** There were too many **C** It was too many **D** There was too many		95, 96
14.2	...... Sara wanted to borrow money. **A** Suddenly hit me that **B** It suddenly hit **C** It suddenly hit me that **D** Suddenly hit me		96
14.3	I ...... you can swim so well and I can't. **A** hate **B** hate it that **C** hate that **D** hate it		97
14.4	Luis lost his job and was short of money, so ...... his flat and move in with his brother. **A** that he did was to sell **B** what he did was to sell **C** what he did sold **D** what he did was sell		98
14.5	...... been diverted, they would have arrived early. **A** Had the plane not **B** Hadn't the plane **C** The plane had not **D** The plane not had		99
14.6	...... that Lana was able to retire at the age of 50. **A** So successful her business was, **B** So successful was her business, **C** Her business was so successful **D** So was her successful business		100

Grammar reminder

The *Grammar reminder* summarises basic information about some important areas of grammar. References within the main units point you to the sections of the *Grammar reminder* that are relevant to those units. Read these sections to refresh your understanding before you start work on the advanced grammar points in the unit.

A Tenses

→ Units 1–8

Present continuous (→ Units 1, 2 & 8)

A1 ☐ 'Who *are you phoning*?' '*I'm trying* to get through to Misaki.'
We use the present continuous to talk about particular events or activities that have begun but have not ended at the time of speaking. The event or activity is in progress at the present time, but not necessarily at the moment of speaking.

A2 ☐ She*'s doing* voluntary work with young children until she starts her university course.
We use the present continuous to suggest that an event or activity is or may be temporary. (For the present continuous for the future, see B7 & Unit 10.)

Present simple (→ Units 1, 2 & 8)

A3 ☐ Trees *grow* more quickly in summer than in winter.
We use the present simple with verbs describing states or situations that are always true or continue indefinitely.

A4 ☐ This cake *tastes* wonderful. Where did you buy it?
We use the present simple with states or situations (thoughts, feelings) that exist at the present moment.

> Verbs describing states include ***agree**, **appreciate**, **attract**, ***desire**, ***doubt**, **expect**, **hate**, **hope**, **like**, **love**, ***prefer**, ***regret** (*to do with emotions, attitudes, and preferences*); **anticipate**, **assume**, ***believe**, **consider**, **expect**, **feel**, **find**, **imagine**, ***know**, **realise**, **think**, **understand** (*mental states*); **ache**, **hear**, ***notice**, **see**, ***smell**, **sound**, ***taste** (*senses and perception*); ***belong to**, ***consist of**, ***constitute**, ***contain**, **cost**, ***differ from**, **have**, **look**, ***mean**, **measure**, ***own**, ***possess**, ***resemble**, ***seem**, **weigh** (*to do with 'being', 'having'*, etc.).

The verbs marked * are rarely used with continuous tenses (but can be if we mean actions rather than states).

A5 ☐ *Do* you *go* to Turkey every year for your holidays?
We use the present simple to talk about habits or regular events or actions. (For the present simple for the future, see B6 & Unit 10.)

Past simple (→ Units 3, 4, 5 & 8)

A6 ☐ Aisha *left* a few minutes ago.

A7 ☐ Mikhail *continued* the course even though it was proving very difficult.
We use the past simple to refer to a completed action or event in the past or to talk about situations that existed over a period of time in the past, but not now. We can either say when something happened, using a time adverbial (e.g. *a few minutes ago*: A6), or assume that the listener or reader already knows when it happened or can understand this from the context (A7).

A8 ☐ I *saw* my grandparents every week as a child.
We use the past simple to talk about repeated past actions.
(For the past simple in conditionals, see M12 & M13 and Unit 83.)

Present perfect (→ Units 3, 6 & 8)

A9 ☐ We can't have a meeting, because so few people *have shown* any interest.

A10 ☐ My ceiling *has fallen* in and the kitchen is flooded. Come quickly!

A11 ☐ We *have belonged* to the tennis club since we moved here.

A12 ▢ Lee *has represented* his country on many occasions, and hopes to go on to compete in the next Olympics.
We use the present perfect to talk about a past action, event or state, when there is some kind of connection between what happened in the past, and the present time. Often we are interested in the way something that happened in the past affects or is relevant to the situation that exists now (A9). However, the connection with the present may also be that the action happened recently with a consequence for the present (A10), that it continues until the present time (A11), or that a repeated event in the past may (or may not) happen again (A12).

Past continuous (➜ Units 4, 7 & 8)

A13 ▢ When he realised I *was looking* at him, he turned away.
We use the past continuous to talk about a situation (… I *was looking at him* …) that started before a particular point in the past (… *he turned away*) and was still in progress at that point.

Past perfect (➜ Units 5, 7 & 8)

A14 ▢ When I went into the bathroom, I found that the bath *had overflowed*.
A15 ▢ By 10 o'clock most people *had gone* home.
We use the past perfect to talk about a past event that took place before another past event (A14), or before or up to a particular time in the past (A15).
(For the past perfect in conditionals, see M14 & Unit 83.)

Present perfect continuous (➜ Units 6 & 8)

A16 ▢ Since the operation two months ago, Samuel *has been learning* to walk again. He can already take one or two steps unaided.
A17 ▢ Your eyes are red – *have* you *been crying*?
We use the present perfect continuous to talk about an activity in progress in the past for a period until now, which is still in progress (A16) or has recently finished (A17).

Past perfect continuous (➜ Units 7 & 8)

A18 ▢ When I saw the vase on the website, I knew it was exactly what I *had been looking* for.
We use the past perfect continuous to talk about a situation or activity that was in progress over a period up to a particular past point in time.

B The future

➜ Units 9–14

Will + infinitive (➜ Unit 9)

B1 ▢ It's late. I think I*'ll* go to bed now.
B2 ▢ I think you*'ll* enjoy the film.
We use **will** when we state a decision made at the moment of speaking (B1) and when we say that we think something is likely to happen in the future (B2).
B3 ▢ I*'ll* make one of my special desserts for dinner, if you like.
B4 ▢ I've asked her to join us this evening, but she *won't*.
We use **will** (or **'ll**) when we talk about *willingness* to do something in the future (e.g. in offers (B3), invitations, requests, and orders) and **will not** (or **won't**) when we talk about *unwillingness* to do something in the future (e.g. reluctance, refusal (B4)).

Be going to + infinitive (➜ Unit 9)

B5 ▢ 'Has anybody offered to look after the children?' 'Sophia*'s going to* do it.'
We use **be going to** when we state a decision made some time before we report it. **Going to** is often preferred in informal spoken English (where it is often pronounced /gənə/) and **will** is preferred in more formal contexts.

Present simple for the future (→ Unit 10)

B6 ▢ The next train to Dublin *leaves* at 3.45. (*station announcement*)
We use the present simple to talk about future events that are part of some official arrangement such as a timetable or programme. A time expression is usually used with the present simple for the future (... *at 3.45*) unless the time referred to is already clear from the context.

Present continuous for the future (→ Unit 10)

B7 ▢ We*'re having* a party next Saturday. Can you come?
We use the present continuous to talk about future activities and events that are intended or have already been arranged. Usually a personal pronoun is used (*We* ...) and a future time is mentioned (... *next Saturday*) or already understood.

Future continuous (→ Unit 11)

B8 ▢ After the operation you *won't be doing* any sport for a while.
We use the future continuous to talk about an activity or event happening at a particular time or over a particular period in the future. We usually mention the future time (*After the operation* ...).

C Modals and semi-modals

→ Units 15–20

The modal verbs are: **will**, **would**, **can**, **could**, **may**, **might**, **shall**, **should**, **must**

Modal verbs have meanings relating to ideas such as possibility, likelihood, prediction, necessity, permission and obligation. They do not have **to-infinitive**, **-s**, **-ing** or past participle forms. They are often followed by the **bare infinitive** of another verb (e.g. *She might go*) but can also be used on their own (e.g. *Yes, I can*). They cannot be followed directly by a **to-infinitive**, an **-ing** form, a **past participle**, or another **modal verb**. In questions they come before the subject (e.g. *Could you help?*) and before *not* in negatives (e.g. *He won't* [= will not] *help*).

The semi-modals are: **ought to**, **used to**, **need**, **dare**, **had better**, **have** (**got**) **to**, **be able to**

These have meanings like modal verbs but not the same formal features: for example, some can be marked for tense (e.g. *have / had* [*got*] *to*); some have non-modal uses (e.g. *She needs a rest*).

Can, could and be able to (→ Unit 15)

C1 ▢ A polyglot is someone who *can* speak several different languages.
C2 ▢ Anita *could* speak three languages before she was six.
C3 ▢ Olivia *couldn't* swim until she was ten.
When we say that someone or something has or doesn't have the ability to do something, we use **can('t)** (for the present; C1) or **could(n't)** (for the past; C2, C3).

C4 ▢ 'Why isn't Ben here yet?' 'It *could* be because his mother's ill again.'
We use **could**, not **can**, to say there is a possibility of something happening or being true.

C5 ▢ Despite yesterday's snowfalls, we *were able to* drive home in less than an hour.
We can use **be able to** instead of **can** or **could** to talk about ability. We prefer **be able to** when we talk about a specific achievement (particularly if it is difficult, requiring some effort; C5) rather than a general ability. Where there is a choice, in speech we generally prefer **can** or **could** rather than **be able to**.

C6 ▢ After the trees have been cut back, we *will be able to* see more of the garden from the sitting room.
We use **will be able to**, not **can**, to say that something is possible in the future on condition that something is done first.

C7 ▢ We *can / are allowed to* stay up late on Fridays and Saturdays because we don't have to go to school the next day.
We use **can** for the present or the future and **could** for the past to report permission. We can also use **be allowed to**.

Will, would and used to (→ Unit 16)

C8 ◯ *Will / Won't* you have another biscuit? ('Won't you ...?' is a very polite and rather formal offer)

C9 ◯ 'Luka wants to borrow the car.' 'He *will not*.' (a firm refusal)

C10 ◯ You *will* now put your pens down and pay attention. (a firm instruction)
We use **will** and **will not** (**won't**) to talk about (un)willingness (see B3–4) and also to make offers (C8), requests, refusals (C9), and to give instructions (C10).

C11 ◯ You should apply for the job. You *would* have a good chance of getting it.
We can use **would** to make a prediction about an imaginary situation; that is, about something that may or may not happen (see also M13).

C12 ◯ *Would* you like me to get you some water?
We can use **Would you like ...** when we make an offer, but not 'Will you like ...'. In requests, too, we can say **I would like ...**, but not 'I will like ...'. We can use **should** (with **I** or **we**) instead of **would** in requests like this, but this is formal.

C13 ◯ We *would / used to* lend him money when he was unemployed.

C14 ◯ I *used to* live in a flat in Paris.
To talk about things that happened repeatedly in the past, but don't happen now, we can use **would** or **used to** + **infinitive** (C13). **Used to** is more common in informal English. We can use **used to** but not **would** to talk about permanent past states (C14). Note how we normally make questions and negatives with **use to** in spoken English: '*Did* your children *use to* sleep well when they were babies?'; 'I *didn't use to* like visiting the dentist when I was young.' Many people avoid using **used to** in questions and negatives without **do** ('Used you to ...?', 'I usedn't to ...') and in question tags (..., usedn't you?) because it sounds very formal and old-fashioned.

May, might, can and could (→ Units 15 & 17)

C15 ◯ If the drought goes on much longer, there *may / might / could* be a hosepipe ban before the end of the month.

C16 ◯ Her parents *may / might / could have influenced* her decision to resign.
In affirmative sentences (that is, sentences which are not questions or negatives) we use **may**, **might**, or **could** with a similar meaning to say that there is a possibility of something happening or being true (C15). **Can** is not used in this way. We sometimes prefer **could** to show that we are giving an opinion about which we are unsure. We use **may / might / could** + **have** + **past participle** to say that it is possible that something happened in the past (C16).

C17 ◯ 'While we're in Moscow shall we go and see Dariya?' 'But it's been nearly 20 years since we last saw her. She *may not / might not* remember us.'

C18 ◯ I definitely saw her go out, so she *can't / couldn't* be at home.
In negative sentences, including sentences with words like **only**, **hardly**, or **never**, we use **may not** or **might not** to say it is possible that something is not true (C17), and **can't** or **couldn't** to say that it is not possible that something is true (C18).

C19 ◯ Coats *may* be left in the cloakroom.
May (not 'might') is used in formal contexts to say that something is allowed. **May not** is used to say that things are not allowed (e.g. Calculators *may not* be used in the examination.).

Must and have (got) to (→ Unit 18)

C20 ◯ That's really good news. I *must* tell Marco straight away.

C21 ◯ 'Can we meet on Thursday morning?' 'Sorry, no. I *have to* go to the dentist at eleven.'
When we say that it is necessary to do something, we use **must** or **have** (**got**) **to**. Sometimes it doesn't matter which we use, although **have got to** is less formal than either **must** or **have to** and is particularly common in spoken English. However, we use **must** when we want to indicate that the *speaker* decides that something is necessary (C20) and we use **have** (**got**) **to** to suggest that *someone else* or some outside circumstances or authority makes something necessary (C21).

C22 ◯ She was bruised quite badly in the accident. It *must* hurt a lot.
We normally use **must**, not **have** (**got**) **to**, when we conclude that something (has) happened or that something is true .

C23 ◯ 'I'm seeing Dr Evans next week.' 'That *can't* be right. He's on holiday then.'
When we give a negative conclusion we rarely use **must not** or **have** (**got**) **to**. Instead, we use **can't** (**cannot**) or **couldn't**.

C24 ◯ When my father went to school he *had to* learn Latin.
To say that something was necessary in the past we use **had to**, not **must**.

Need(n't), don't have to and mustn't (→ Units 18 & 19)

C25 ◯ He didn't cook the meal himself so you *needn't / don't have to* eat it all. He won't be offended.

C26 ◯ You *mustn't* put anything on the shelves until the glue has set hard.
We use **needn't** (or **don't need to**) or **don't have to** to say that something is not necessary (C25) and **mustn't** to say that something is not allowed (C26).

C27 ◯ I *didn't need to / didn't have to* have an interview because I'd worked there before.

C28 ◯ I *needn't have* cooked dinner. Just as it was ready, Pablo and Daniela phoned to say that they couldn't come to eat.
When we say that it was not necessary to do something in the past, and it wasn't done, we use **didn't need to** or **didn't have to** (C27). To show that we think something that *was* done was not in fact necessary we use **need not** (**needn't**) **have** (C28).

Should, ought to and be supposed to (→ Unit 20)

C29 ◯ You'll catch cold if you go out like that. I think you *should / ought to* take a hat.

C30 ◯ I enjoyed her first novel, so the new one *should / ought to* be good.
We can often use **should** or **ought to** with little difference in meaning when we talk about obligation (e.g. in giving advice, making recommendations, or talking about a responsibility, (C29) and the probability of something happening or being true (C30).

C31 ◯ The work was *supposed to start / should have started / ought to have started* last week.

C32 ◯ Walking under a ladder *is supposed to* be unlucky.
(**Be**) **supposed to** can be used instead of **should / ought to** to express a less strong obligation than **should** (C31). It is also used to report what many people think is true, but **should / ought to** are not used in this way (C32).

D Passives

→ Units 22–25

Passive verb forms have one of the tenses of the verb **to be** and a **past participle**. Passive verb forms are summarised in Appendix 2. The choice between an active and passive sentence allows us to present the same information in two different orders. Compare:

active ◯ The storm damaged the roof.	*passive* ◯ The roof was damaged. ◯ The roof was damaged by the storm.
This sentence is about *the storm*, and says what it did. The subject (*The storm*) is the 'agent' and the object (*the roof*) is the 'done to'.	These sentences are about *the roof* and say what happened to it (in the first sentence) and what did it (in the second). The subject (*The roof*) is the 'done to'. If it is mentioned, the agent (*the storm*) goes in a prepositional phrase with *by* after the verb.

D1 ◯ The building *survived* the earthquake but then *was destroyed by* a fire.
Verbs which take an object (*transitive verbs*) can have a passive form (... *was destroyed*).
Verbs which *do not* take an object (*intransitive verbs*) do not have passive forms (The child *vanished* ..., but not 'The child was vanished ...').

However, many verbs can be used at different times with and without objects – that is, they can be both transitive and intransitive. Compare: '**Are they meeting him** at the airport?' (*transitive*) and '**Is he being met** at the airport?' (*passive*); 'When shall we **meet**?' (*intransitive*; no passive possible)

D2 ▢ I'm really disappointed. I *didn't get picked / wasn't picked* for the team again.

D3 ▢ The house *was owned* by an elderly couple before I bought it.

In spoken language we often use **get** + **past participle** (... *didn't get picked* ...) instead of a passive form (... *wasn't picked* ...) to talk about actions or events that we see as negative (D2). Note, however, that we can also use it to talk about positive actions and events (e.g. Great news – I **got picked** for the team again!). We don't normally use **get** + **past participle** to describe states (D3).

E Questions

→ Units 26–27

E1 *Basic question forms*

If a verb phrase includes an auxiliary verb, the auxiliary verb comes before the subject.	▢ **Are they** leaving soon? ▢ Where **will you** stay?
If a verb phrase includes more than one auxiliary verb, only the first comes before the subject.	▢ **Has she** *been* doing her homework? ▢ What **should we** *have* told Nina?
In present and past simple tenses of verbs (apart from **be**), we use **do** or **did**.	▢ **Does he** *enjoy* school? ▢ Where **did you** *go* on holiday?
If **be** is used in a verb phrase without another verb, the form of **be** comes before the subject.	▢ **Are you** happy at work? ▢ Where **was Lars** today?
If we use **what**, **which**, **who** or **whose** as the subject, we use the same word order as in a statement; i.e. the subject goes before the verb phrase.	▢ **What made** that noise? ▢ **Who can tell** me the answer to question 5?

E2 ▢ *What happened* to your eye?

If we use **what**, **which**, **who** or **whose** as the subject, we don't use **do** in the question (E2). However, note that we can sometimes use **do** when **what**, **which**, **who** or **whose** is the subject if we want to add emphasis, or to contrast with what has been said or implied. **Do** is stressed in spoken English: 'Come on, be honest – who *did* tell you?' Don't confuse **whose** with **who's** (short for either **who is** or **who has**), which are pronounced the same.

E3 ▢ I've got orange juice or apple juice. *Which* would you prefer?

E4 ▢ He just turned away when I asked him. *What* do you think he meant?

In these questions the **wh-word** is the object. We prefer **which** when we are asking about an identified group or range of things or people (E3), and we use **what** when the possible range of reference is open (E4). Sometimes, however, we can use either **which** or **what** with little difference in meaning (e.g. *What / Which* towns do we go through on the way?).

E5 ▢ *Haven't you finished* your homework yet?

E6 ▢ *Why didn't* she pay for the meal?

E7 ▢ *Who wouldn't like* to own an expensive sports car?

We can use negative **yes / no** or **wh-questions** to make a suggestion, to persuade someone, to criticise, or to show that we are surprised, etc. We make a negative **yes / no** or **wh-question** with an auxiliary verb (*have*, *did*, *would*, etc.) + **-n't** (E5, E6, E7). We can also ask a negative question using a negative statement and a positive 'tag' at the end (e.g. We do*n't* have to leave just yet, *do we*?). Negative questions can be used to sound polite when giving an opinion (e.g. Should*n't* we offer her a lift?).

F Verb complementation: what follows verbs

→ Units 28–31

F1 ◯ She described the attacker to the police.
F2 ◯ They arrived at the restaurant an hour late.
F3 ◯ He gave me a biscuit.

Some verbs (e.g. *describe* in F1) are followed by an object ... *the attacker* ...). These are called *transitive verbs*.

Also: **arrest**, **avoid**, **do**, **enjoy**, **find**, **force**, **get**, **grab**, **hit**, **like**, **pull**, **report**, **shock**, **take**, **touch**, **want**, **warn**

Some verbs (e.g. *arrive* in F2) are not usually followed by an object. These are called *intransitive verbs*. If a verb can't be followed by an object, it can't be made passive.

Also: **appear**, **come**, **fall**, **go**, **happen**, **matter**, **sleep**, **swim**, **wait**

Some verbs (e.g. *give* in F3) are commonly followed by two objects (*me* and *a biscuit* in F3).

Also: **lend**, **offer**, **pay**, **sell**, **tell**, **throw**

A good dictionary will list the meanings of verbs and tell you whether each meaning is intransitive, transitive and, if transitive, whether it is followed by one or by two objects.

F4–13 Many verbs can be followed by another verb in the form of a **to-infinitive** (e.g. refuse *to eat*), **-ing** (e.g. avoid *working*), **bare infinitive** (e.g. help *carry*). Note that when **to** comes after a verb it can be part of a **to-infinitive** (= *to* + the base form of a verb; e.g. He wants *to go*, She hopes *to win*) or it can be a **preposition** followed by a noun phrase (e.g. He went *to the theatre*) or by an **-ing** form (e.g. He admitted *to having* a gun). An **-ing** form often behaves like an object (e.g. I regret *leaving*).

Here is a summary of common patterns together with examples of verbs that are used in this pattern. Note that many verbs can be used in several different patterns, and that some of the verbs given can be used just with an object, and may also be used intransitively (e.g. He failed to stop, He failed the test, He failed).

Verb + to-infinitive	F4 ◯ They won't *agree to pay* for the damage. *Also*: **aim, ask, decline, demand, fail, hesitate, hope, hurry, manage, offer, plan, prepare, refuse, want, wish**
Verb + -ing	F5 ◯ Stevens *admitted stealing* the wallet. *Also*: **avoid, consider, delay, deny, detest, dread, envisage, feel like, finish, imagine, miss, recall, resent, risk, suggest**
Verb + to-infinitive *or* **-ing** (little difference in meaning)	F6 ◯ Before we *began eating / to eat* my father thanked everyone for coming. *Also*: **cease, continue, start**
Verb + to-infinitive *or* **-ing** (difference in meaning)	F7 ◯ She *came hurrying* up the path to bring us the news. F8 ◯ How did you *come to buy* the car? *Also:* **go on, mean, regret, remember, stop, try**
Verb + object + to-infinitive (= there must be an object)	F9 ◯ My parents wouldn't *allow me to go* to the party. *Also*: **believe, cause, command, consider, enable, encourage, entitle, force, invite, order, persuade, show, teach, tell, warn**

Verb + (object) + to-infinitive (= there may be an object)	**F10** ◯ I would *hate* (*her*) *to give* the job up. *Also*: **help, like, love, need, prefer, want, wish**
Verb + object + -ing (= there must be an object)	**F11** ◯ The police *caught him driving* without a licence. *Also*: **discover, feel, find, hear, leave, notice, observe, overhear, see, spot**
Verb + (object) + -ing (= there may be an object)	**F12** ◯ I *can't stand* (*him*) *wearing* a suit. *Also*: **detest, dislike, dread, envisage, hate, imagine, like, love, mind** (in questions and negatives)**, miss, recall, regret, remember, resent, risk, start, stop**
Verb + object + bare infinitive *or* **-ing** (sometimes a difference in meaning)	**F13** ◯ She *felt the mosquito bite / biting* her. *Also*: **hear, notice, observe, overhear, see, watch**

G Reporting

➜ Units 32–39

When we report speech in a different context from the one in which it was originally produced, we sometimes need to make changes to the original words. Of course, differences between the original speech context and the one in which it is reported will influence whether changes are needed and what they should be. Here are some possible changes:

G1 ◯ 'Dan*'s arriving* later *today*.' ◯ She said that Dan *was arriving* later *that day*.
G2 ◯ 'I was sure *I'd* left it *here*.' ◯ He said that he was sure *he'd* left it *there / on the table*.
G3 ◯ '*I grew these* carrots *myself*.' ◯ He told me that he *had grown those* carrots *himself*.

The tense we choose for a report is one that is appropriate *at the time that we are reporting* what was said or thought. This means that we sometimes use a different tense in the report from the one that was used in the original statement (G1 & G3) and change pronouns, references to time and place, and words such as **this**, **that**, and **these** (G1–G3).

G4 ◯ Georgia *told me* (that) she would be late for the meeting.
G5 ◯ She *said* (that) she was feeling ill.
G6 ◯ I *said to Ivan* (that) he had to work harder.
G7 ◯ She *told me about* her holiday in Finland.

Say and **tell** are the verbs most commonly used to report statements. We use an **object** after **tell** (... *me* ..., G4), but not after **say** (G5). Note, however, that we can use **to** + **object** after **say** (... *to Ivan* ..., G6), but not after **tell,** and that we can report what topic was talked about using **tell** + **object** + **about** (G7).

G8 ◯ 'It's a pity you can't come this weekend.'
G9 ◯ "I'm really hungry. I fancy a cheese sandwich."

When we quote what people think or what they have said, we put single ('...') (G8) or double ("...") (G9) quotation marks at the beginning and end of a report of their exact spoken or written words. This is often referred to as *direct speech*

G10 Here are more examples of direct speech. Note the punctuation used:
◯ 'I think we should go to India while we have the opportunity,' argued Oliver.
◯ 'Can I make an appointment to see the doctor?' asked Maxim.
◯ 'You must be mad!' yelled her brother.
◯ 'It tastes horrible,' said Anna, 'but it's supposed to be very good for you.'
◯ 'You should go home,' Maria advised. 'You're looking really ill.'
◯ Daniel said, 'Put them all on the top shelf.'
◯ She stood up and shouted to the children: 'It's time to go home!'

G11 ◯ 'Why did she look at me like that?' wondered Julia.
◯ Perhaps the door is open, thought Omar.
◯ Suddenly she thought: Could they be trying to trick me?

To quote what a person *thinks*, we use the conventions shown in the examples above, or separate the quotation from the reporting clause with a comma (or colon) and leave out quotation marks.

H Nouns

→ Units 40–43

Countable and uncountable nouns

H1 ▢ The *equipment* was faulty.

Nouns can be either **countable** or **uncountable**. Countable nouns are those which can have the word **a / an** before them or be used in the plural. Uncountable nouns are not used with **a / an** or in the plural. Some nouns in English are normally uncountable (like *equipment* in H1), while in many other languages they are countable, e.g. accommodation, advice.

Also: **applause**, **assistance**, **baggage**, **camping**, **cash**, **chaos**, **chess**, **clothing**, **conduct**, **courage**, **cutlery**, **dancing**, **dirt**, **employment**, **evidence**, **fun**, **furniture**, **harm**, **health**, **homework**, **housing**, **housework**, **information**, **jewellery**, **leisure**, **litter**, **luck**, **luggage**, **machinery**, **money**, **mud**, **music**, **news**, **nonsense**, **parking**, **pay**, **permission**, **photography**, **poetry**, **pollution**, **produce**, **progress**, **publicity**, **research**, **rubbish**, **safety**, **scenery**, **shopping**, **sightseeing**, **sunshine**, **transport**, **underwear**, **violence**, **weather**, **work**

H2 ▢ The company is / are doing a lot of *business* in South America.

Sometimes a noun is used uncountably when we are talking about the whole substance or idea (e.g. *business*), but countably when we are talking about units or different kinds (e.g. *businesses*).

Also: **beer**, **coffee**, **water**; **fruit**, **toothpaste**, **washing powder**; **cake**, **chicken**, **land**, **paint**, **space**, **stone**; **abuse**, **(dis)agreement**, **difficulty**, **fear**, **improvement**, **language**, **life**, **pain**, **protest**, **responsibility**, **success**, **thought**, **war**

Compare:

- ▢ Three coffees and a lemonade, please. – Brazil is a major producer of coffee.
- ▢ Most toothpastes contain colourings. – Don't forget to buy some toothpaste.
- ▢ The chickens have escaped. – I don't eat chicken.
- ▢ I have a fear of spiders. – He was trembling with fear.

H3 ▢ The use of recycled *paper* is saving thousands of trees from being cut down each year.

Some nouns (e.g. *paper*) usually have different meanings when they are used countably and uncountably.

Also: **competition**, **glass**, **grammar**, **iron**, **jam**, **lace**, **property**, **room**, **sight**, **speech**, **time**, **tin**, **work**

Compare:

- ▢ I just don't understand grammar. – I looked the answer up in a grammar (= a reference book)
- ▢ I got held up in a jam (= traffic jam). – This jam is really sweet. (Note that 'jams' can also be used to mean types of jam)
- ▢ She made a wonderful speech at the wedding. – His speech has been affected by the illness.

Compound nouns (→ Unit 43)

H4 ▢ How much *pocket money* do you give to your children?

H5 ▢ A new *golf course / golf-course* is being built outside the town.

A *compound noun* (e.g. *pocket money*) is an expression made up of more than one word, which functions as a noun in a sentence. For example, we can use a **noun + noun** combination to say what something is made of, where something is, when something happens, or what someone does.

Examples: **rice pudding**, **a glasshouse**, **the kitchen cupboard**, **hill fog**, **a night flight**, **a morning call**, **a language teacher**, **a window-cleaner**

We sometimes make compounds from nouns, which consist of more than two nouns.

Examples: **a milk chocolate bar**, **an air-traffic controller**, **a dinner-party conversation**

Some compound nouns are usually written as one word (e.g. **a tablecloth**), some as separate words (e.g. **waste paper**), and others with a hyphen (e.g. **a house-sitter**). Some compound nouns can be written in more than one of these ways (e.g. **a golf course** *or* **a golf-course**; H5). A good dictionary will tell you how a particular compound noun is usually written.

H6 ▢ She got some *chewing gum* stuck on her shoe.

-ing + **noun** compound nouns (the *-ing* form usually says what purpose the following noun has)	*Examples*: **chewing gum**, **a living room**, **drinking water**, (**a pack of**) **playing cards**, **a dressing gown**, **a turning-point**, **a working party**
noun + **-ing** compound nouns (usually refer to actions or processes)	*Examples:* **fly-fishing**, **film-making**, **sunbathing**, **risk-taking**, **life-saving**

The possessive form of nouns

H7 ▢ The *girls'* shoes were covered in mud, so I asked them to take them off before they got into *Leon's* car.

To make the possessive form of nouns in writing – referring to people or groups of people (e.g. *companies*), other living things, places, times, etc. – we add **'s** ('apostrophe s') to singular nouns and to irregular plurals that don't end in *-s* (e.g. **Leon's** car; the **college's** administrators; **women's** issues) and add **'** (an apostrophe) to regular plurals (e.g. the **girls'** shoes; the **companies'** difficulties). To make the possessive form of names ending in -s pronounced /z/ we can add either **'** or **'s** (e.g. It's Leon **Jones'** [*or* Leon **Jones's**] new sports car).

H8 ▢ That *old car of Zara's* is falling apart.

H9 ▢ It belongs to a *friend of his*.

We can use the pattern **noun** + **of** + **'s** (H8) or a *possessive pronoun* (H9) to talk about something that someone owns, or about a relationship. Note that when we are talking about relationships between people we can also use a noun without **'s** (e.g. an uncle **of** Emil**'s** (*or* an uncle of Emil)).

H10 ▢ We're going to *Mona's* (house) for the evening.

The noun following a possessive form can be left out when we talk about someone's house. We don't use 'shop' when we talk about, for example, **the newsagent's / the chemist's** or **the newsagent / the chemist** (but not 'the newsagent's shop' / 'the chemist's shop') where the name of the shop includes the profession of the person who works there (compare 'the sweet shop', but not 'the sweet's shop').

H11 ▢ *David's guitar playing* has improved enormously.

H12 ▢ *The construction of the office block* was opposed by protestors.

Often we can use the possessive **'s** or ... **of** + **noun** ... with very little difference in meaning. However, in general, we are more likely to use the **possessive** form of a noun when the noun refers to a particular person or group of people (H11); and when we are talking about time (e.g. **next year's** holiday prices, *rather than* the holiday prices of next year).

We are more likely to use the **... of** + **noun ...** form with an inanimate noun (H12); when we are talking about a process, or a change over time (e.g. *the establishment* **of the committee**, *rather than* the committee's establishment); and when the noun is a long noun phrase (e.g. She is *the sister* **of someone I used to go to school with**. *rather than* She is someone I used to go to school with's sister.).

I Articles, determiners and quantifiers

→ Units 44–52

Determiners are words such as **this**, **her**, and **your** which determine or specify what a noun or noun phrase refers to. They come before the noun and at the front of the noun phrase. *Quantifiers* are words such as **some**, **much**, and **few** which identify the quantity of something. Some words can be both determiners and quantifiers (e.g. 'I sent out invitations to a *few* friends' [few = determiner] and 'A *few* of my friends came to the party' [few = quantifier]) while some are determiners only (e.g. 'This is *my* friend Andrew' [my = determiner]). Many determiners and quantifiers can be *pronouns*, taking the place of a noun phrase (e.g. I've invited all my friends and *most* are coming [most = pronoun]). *Articles* (**a / an** and **the**) are determiners. They also specify what the noun refers to and come at the beginning of the noun phrase. However, they cannot be quantifiers or pronouns.

The (→ Units 45–47)

I1 ○ Lisa took a cake and some biscuits to the party, but only *the* biscuits were eaten.
I2 ○ Can you shut *the* door after you, please?
I3 ○ We had a good time on holiday. *The* beaches were all beautifully clean.
I4 ○ Give it to *the* man wearing the red coat.
I5 ○ Look at *the* moon. It's very bright tonight.

We use **the** with singular, plural or uncountable nouns when we expect the listener or reader to be able to identify the thing or person we are referring to in the following noun. It may be that the thing has already been mentioned (I1); that it is clear from the situation which person or thing we mean (I2); that it is in some other way understandable from the context which thing or person we mean (I3; 'the beaches' = 'the beaches we went to'); that the thing or person is identified in what is said after the noun (I4; 'wearing the red coat'); or that there is only one of a particular thing (I5 and also, for example, the Great Wall of China, the North Pole, the USA, the world).

A / an (→ Units 44–47)

I6 ○ Helen's just bought *a* house on Wilson Street.
I7 ○ Sydney is *a* beautiful city.

We use **a / an** with singular nouns when we don't expect the listener or reader to be able to identify the thing or person we are referring to in the following noun. We often use **a / an** to introduce a new specific person or thing (I6); or when the noun refers to a class of people or things generally – for example, when we describe someone or something or say what type of thing someone or something is (I7).

Zero article (→ Units 45–47)

I8 ○ *[–]* Water has got into my camera and damaged it.
I9 ○ There are *[–]* examples of the present continuous tense on page 32.

We use **zero article** *[–]* with uncountable and plural nouns when we talk generally about people or things rather than about specific people or things. We might talk about a whole class of things in a general way (I8) or about an indefinite number or amount (I9).

Some (→ Unit 48)

Some and **any** are used with plural and uncountable nouns, usually when we are talking about limited, but indefinite or unknown, numbers or quantities of things.

I10 ○ Peter gave me *some* advice.
I11 ○ Hasn't *some* information about the proposal been sent out already? I thought I read about it last week.
I12 ○ Shall I send you *some* details?

We generally use **some**: in affirmative sentences (sentences which are not negatives or questions) (I10); in questions where we expect agreement or the answer 'Yes' (I11); in offers and requests in order to sound positive, expecting the answer 'Yes' (I12). If it is used in this way **some** is pronounced with its weak form /səm/.

I13 ☐ *Some* teachers never seem to get bored with being in the classroom.
We use **some** to talk about particular, but unspecified, people or things with the implication 'some, but not all'. If it is used in this way **some** is pronounced with its strong form /sʌm/.

I14 ☐ I haven't been here for *some* years.
We use **some** (pronounced /sʌm/) when we mean quite a large amount of, or a large number of something. Note that we can say '*some* years, months, weeks, etc.' or just 'years, months, weeks, etc.' with a similar meaning.

Any (➔ Unit 48)

I15 ☐ We haven't got *any* butter left.
I16 ☐ Do you have *any* better ideas?
I17 ☐ *Any* student could have answered the question.
We generally use **any**: in sentences with a negative meaning (I15); in questions where we don't necessarily expect agreement or the answer 'Yes' (I16); when we mean 'all (of them), and it's not important which' (I17).

I18 ☐ If you see *any* cherries in the shop, can you buy them?
I19 ☐ *Any* questions should be sent to the manager.
We commonly use **any**: in 'if' clauses (I18; note that 'some' is possible, but would seem to expect that you will see cherries); when **any** means 'if there is / are' (I19; = If there are questions ...).

Anyone, someone, etc.

I20 ☐ Isabella lives *somewhere* in Denmark.
I21 ☐ I've never seen *anybody* that tall before.
The rules for the use of the following words are generally the same as those given in I10–I19 for **some** and **any**: the pronouns **someone / anyone**, **somebody / anybody**, **something / anything**, (note that **somebody** = **someone**, and **anybody** = **anyone**), and the adverbs **somewhere / anywhere**. For example, **some-** words are generally used in affirmative sentences (I20), and **any-** words are generally used in sentences with a negative meaning (I21).

Quantifiers with and without 'of': any (of), some (of), much (of), many (of), both (of), all (of) each (of), none (of), few (of), little (of) (➔ Units 48–52)

I22 ☐ *Many of* Liam's closest friends are women.
I23 ☐ *Some of* my jewellery is missing.
I24 ☐ Have you seen *any of* these new light bulbs in the shops yet?
I25 ☐ Are you going to eat *all* (*of*) that cake, or can I finish it?
I26 ☐ *Both of* us were exhausted after flying to Japan.
I27 ☐ I polished *each* trophy with a soft cloth.
I28 ☐ Is there *much* orange juice left?
We usually need to put **of** after quantifiers when there is a **possessive form** (I22), **pronoun** (I23) or **determiner** (I24) before a noun. Note, however, that in informal contexts after **both** and **all** we can leave out **of** before **the**, **these**, **those** (and **this** or **that** with **all**; I25); **my**, **your**, **her**, **his**, etc.; and **mine**, **yours**, etc., but not before **them**, **you**, or **us** (I26) (or **it** with **all**). We don't use **of** after a quantifier immediately before a noun (I27 & 28).

No, none (of), neither (of), either (➔ Unit 49)

I29 ☐ There's *no* train until tomorrow.
I30 ☐ *No* information was given about how the study was conducted.
I31 ☐ She had *no* shoes on.
I32 ☐ *None of* my clothes fit any more.

I33 ▢ 'How many children have you got?' '*None.*'
We use the determiner **no** to mean 'not a' or 'not any' before a singular (I29), uncountable (I30), or plural noun (I31). Before **the**, **my**, **this**, etc. we use the quantifier **none (of)** to mean 'not any' (I32). If it is clear from the context what we mean, we can use the pronoun **none** (I33).

I34 ▢ *None of* the furniture has arrived yet.
When we use **none of** with an uncountable noun the verb must be singular. However, when we use **none of** with a plural noun the verb can be either singular or plural (e.g. **None of** *the parcels* **have / has** arrived yet), although the singular form is more grammatical.

I35 ▢ *Neither of* his parents could drive.
We use **neither of** instead of **none of** when we are talking about two people or things.

I36 ▢ You could catch the 10:05 or the 10:32. *Either* train gets you there in good time.

I37 ▢ Has *either of* them passed their driving test yet?
When we use **either** as a determiner (I36), it is followed by a singular countable noun. If this is the subject of the sentence, it is followed by a singular verb. We use **either of** with plural nouns and pronouns (I37). Note that **either** can also be used as an adverbial as in 'We can **either** take the train or go by bus' and 'I had no wish to go, and Lev didn't want to go **either**'.

Much (of), many (of), a lot of, lots (of) (→ Unit 50)

I38 ▢ There isn't *much* traffic along the street where I live.

I39 ▢ Will you be taking *many* suitcases on the trip?
Much and **many** are used to talk about quantities and amounts. **Much** is used with uncountable nouns (I38) and **many** with plural nouns (I39). Before **the**, **my**, **this**, etc. we use **much of / many of**. **Much of** can also be used with a singular countable noun to mean 'a large part of' (e.g. *Much of* the national park was destroyed in the fire.). We can use **much** and **many** without a noun if the meaning is clear (e.g. Can you get some sugar when you go shopping? There isn't *much* left.). **Much** and **many** are often used after **as**, **how**, **so**, and **too** (e.g. I'd say there were twice *as many* women at the meeting as men.).

I40 ▢ She didn't show *much* interest in what I said.

I41 ▢ Mariam offered me *a lot of* money for the car.

I42 ▢ *Many of* my relatives live around Auckland.
Much (**of**) and **many** (**of**) are used in *negative sentences* to emphasise that we are talking about small (or smaller than expected) quantities or amounts (I40) and in *questions* to ask about quantities or amounts (e.g. Have you got *much* homework to do?). In *affirmative sentences* we often use **a lot of**, **lots of** or **plenty of** rather than **much** (**of**) and **many** to talk about large amounts and quantities, particularly in conversation and informal writing (I41). However, **many of** is common in affirmative sentences in both formal and informal contexts (I42).

All (of) (→ Unit 51)

I43 ▢ There is heating in *all* (*of*) the holiday cottages.
We use **all** or **all of** when we are talking about the total number of things or people in a group, or the total amount of something. In informal contexts we can leave out **of**.

I44 ▢ *Everyone* was waiting to hear the results.
In modern English we don't use **all** without a noun to mean 'everyone' or 'everything'. However, **all** can mean 'everything' when it is followed by a *relative clause* (e.g. I don't agree with *all* that he said. (= everything that he said)). We can also use **all** without a noun to mean 'the only thing' (e.g. *All* she wants to do is help.).

Each / every (→ Unit 51)

I45 ▢ *Every* newspaper had the same front page story.

I46 ▢ Following the flood, *every* building in the area needs major repair work.
We can use **each** and **every** with singular countable nouns (I45), and **each of** with plural nouns, to mean all things or people in a group of two or more (**each** (**of**)) or three or more

(**every**). We use a singular verb (... *needs* ...) after **each** (**of**) and **every** (I46). However, when **each** follows the noun or pronoun it refers to, the noun / pronoun and verb are plural (e.g. *Every* student *is* tested twice a year. They *are each* given a hundred questions to do.).

(A) few (of), less (of), (a) little (of) (→ Unit 52)

I47 ▢ *A few of* the boys were very good computer gamers.
I48 ▢ There is *little* evidence to support his claim.
We use (**a**) **few** (**of**) with plural countable nouns (I47) and (**a**) **little** (**of**) with uncountable nouns (I48).
I49 ▢ There's a lot *less* water in the lake than last year.
I50 ▢ The holiday cost *less* than I thought it would.
We use **less** (**of**) with uncountable nouns (I49) or in a general sense (I50).
I51 ▢ I've got *a few* close friends that I meet regularly.
I52 ▢ He has *few* close friends and often feels lonely.
We often use **a few** and **a little** in a 'positive' way (I51); for example, to suggest that a small amount or quantity is enough, or to suggest that it is more than we would expect. We often use **few** and **little** in a 'negative' way (I52); for example, to suggest that the amount or quantity is not enough, or is surprisingly low. Compare '*A few of* her songs were popular and she was very well known' (= 'positive') and '*Few of* her songs were very popular and eventually she gave up her musical career' (= 'negative'). This use of **few** and **little** is often rather formal.

J Relative clauses and other types of clause

→ Units 53–59

Relative clauses have a similar function to adjectives in that they give more information about someone or something referred to in a main clause. Participle clauses (**-ing** and **-ed** clauses) can be used like relative clauses, but can also have an adverbial function, giving information about time, cause, etc.

Relative clauses (→ Units 53–55)

J1 ▢ Magnus stopped the police car *that was driving past*.
J2 ▢ My mother, *who is in her seventies*, enjoys hill walking.
Defining relative clauses (e.g. ... *that was driving past*; J1) are used to specify *which* person or thing we mean, or which *type* of person or thing we mean. Note that we don't put a comma between the noun and a defining relative clause.
Non-defining relative clauses (e.g. ..., *who is in her seventies*, ...; J2) are used to add extra information about a noun, but this information is not necessary to explain which person or thing we mean. We don't use them often in everyday speech, but we do use them frequently in written English. Note that we often put a comma before and after a non-defining relative clause.
J3 ▢ The house, *which is to the north of the road*, is owned by a rock star.
After a relative clause, we don't repeat the subject with a pronoun; so, for example, we wouldn't say 'The house which is to the north of the road it is owned by a rock star'. However, this is sometimes found in informal speech; for example, 'A friend of mine who is a solicitor – she helped me.'
J4 ▢ I have *a friend* **who** / **that** *plays guitar*. (a friend = subject, plays = verb, guitar = object)
J5 ▢ He showed me *the rocks* (**which** / **that**) *he had collected*. (the rocks = object, he = subject, had collected = verb)
When we use *a defining relative clause*, the relative pronoun can be either the subject or the object of the relative clause. When it is the *subject* the word order is subject + verb + object (J4). When the relative pronoun is the *object* the word order is object + subject + verb (J5).

-ing clauses (= present participle clauses) (→ Units 58 & 59)

J6 ▢ *Glancing over his shoulder*, he could see the dog chasing him.
J7 ▢ *Pushing her way through the crowds*, she just managed to get on the bus as it pulled away.

J8 ▢ 'Wait a minute,' said Amy, *running through the door*.
We can use an **-ing** clause to talk about something that takes place at the same time as (J6) or just before (J7) an action in the main clause. We often use an **-ing** clause in written narrative after quoted speech, when we want to say what someone was doing while they were talking (J8).
Note that the understood subject of **-ing** and **-ed** (see J10) clauses should be the same as the subject of the main clause. For example, in J6, 'he' is the unstated subject of 'Glancing over his shoulder ...'.

J9 ▢ *Knowing exactly what I wanted*, I didn't spend much time shopping.
-ing clauses can be used to talk about reasons and results. This sentence has a similar meaning to 'Because I knew exactly what I wanted, I didn't spend much time shopping'.

-ed clauses (= past participle clauses) (→ Units 58 & 59)

J10 ▢ *Annoyed by the boys' behaviour*, she complained to the headteacher.
We can use an **-ed** clause to talk about something that happened before an action in the main clause. Often the event in the **-ed** clause causes the event in the main clause.

K Pronouns, substitution and leaving out words

→ Units 60–65

Reflexive pronouns (→ Unit 60)

K1 ▢ 'What did you do to your hand?' 'I cut *myself* when I was chopping vegetables.'
When the subject and object of a sentence refer to the same person or thing, we use a **reflexive pronoun** as the object of a sentence rather than a personal pronoun. The singular forms of reflexive pronouns are **myself**, **yourself**, **herself**, **himself**, **itself**; the plural forms are **ourselves**, **yourselves**, **themselves**.

K2 ▢ We phoned the plumber and he came *himself*.

K3 ▢ My sister drew the picture *herself*.

K4 ▢ I was given this book by the author *herself*.
We can use reflexive pronouns for emphasis: for example, after an intransitive verb (K2) to emphasise the subject; after a transitive verb (K3) to emphasise that something is done without help; or after a noun to emphasise that noun (K4).

Each other / one another

K5 ▢ They tried to avoid *each other* / *one another* at the party.

K6 ▢ John and Carmen first met (*each other* / *one another*) when they were working in Spain.
Some verbs, such as **avoid** (K5), can be used to describe actions in which two or more people or things do the same thing to the other(s). We use **each other** or **one another** with these.

> *Also*: **attract**, **complement**, **face**, **help**, **repel**

After other verbs such as **meet** (K6), we can use **each other** or **one another**, but this may be omitted when the subject is plural or has the form '... and ...' .

> *Also*: **embrace**, **fight**, **kiss**, **marry**

K7 ▢ The scheme allows students from many countries to communicate *with each other* / *with one another*.

K8 ▢ We *looked at each other* / *one another* and started to laugh.
With some verbs (e.g. *communicate*) we have to use a preposition, often **with**, before **each other** / **one another** (K7 & K8).

> *Also*: **agree**, **coincide**, **collaborate**, **compete (against)**, **contrast**, **co-operate**, **disagree**, **joke**, **look at**, **quarrel**, **talk to / with**

K9 ▢ The two children *each* blamed the *other* for breaking the window.
For emphasis we can separate **each** and **other**. This sentence is more emphatic than 'The two children blamed each other ...'.

Substitution (→ Units 61–63)

K10 ☐ I had a racing bike when I was young, and *so did my brother*.
K11 ☐ 'Emma loves ice cream.' '*So do I.*'
K12 ☐ 'I didn't think much of the restaurant.' '*Neither did I.*'
We can use **so + auxiliary verb + subject** to say that a second person does the same things as the person already mentioned (K10 & K11). The corresponding negative form uses **neither** (K12), **nor** ('Nor did I'), or **not ... either** ('I didn't either'). We often use this to avoid repetition (e.g. in K12 we use 'Neither did I' rather than 'I didn't think much of the restaurant either').

L Adjectives and adverbs

→ Units 66–78

Gradable and non-gradable adjectives (→ Units 67–68)

L1 ☐ They live in a very *large* house.
L2 ☐ Our teacher gave us an absolutely *impossible* problem to solve.
Most adjectives describe qualities that can be measured or graded, and so can be used in comparative and superlative forms and with words such as 'very' or 'extremely'. These are referred to as **gradable** adjectives (for example, 'large' in L1). Some adjectives are not gradable because they refer to qualities that are completely present or completely absent. These **non-gradable** adjectives (e.g. 'impossible' in L2) are not usually used in comparative and superlative forms or with words such as 'very' or 'extremely'. They can often, however, be used with words such as 'absolutely' or 'completely'.

Order of adjectives

L3 ☐ I drank some *very good Brazilian* coffee.
When we use more than one adjective before a noun, there is often a *preferred* (although not fixed) order for these adjectives depending on what type of adjective they are:

opinion + size / physical quality / shape / age + colour + participle adjectives + origin + material + type + purpose + NOUN	
Examples:	
an old plastic container	= age + material + noun
a hard red ball	= quality + colour + noun
a frightening Korean mask	= opinion + origin + noun
a round biscuit tin	= shape + purpose (for holding biscuits) + noun
a small broken plate	= size + participle adjective + noun
a useful digital alarm clock	= opinion + type + purpose + noun

To help you to learn this order, it can be useful to remember that *gradable* adjectives (describing *opinion*, *size*, *quality*, *shape*, and *age*) usually precede *ungradable* adjectives (*participle adjective* and adjectives describing *origin*, *material*, *type* and *purpose*).

Easily confused adjectives

L4 ☐ I was *surprised* to find that the film was quite *frightening*.
Some adjectives that are used to describe feelings about something or someone else have both an **-ed** and **-ing** form. Generally, the **-ed** form describes how the person feels (e.g. I was *surprised* ...), and the **-ing** form gives an evaluation of the thing or other person (e.g. ... the film was quite *frightening*.)

> *Also*: **alarmed – alarming**, **amazed – amazing**, **bored – boring**, **excited – exciting**, **interested – interesting**, **pleased – pleasing**, **tired – tiring**, **worried – worrying**

Adjectives and adverbs: use (→ Unit 71)

L5 ☐ The staff in the shop always speak *politely* to customers.
L6 ☐ It was *strangely* quiet as we went into the room.
We use an *adverb*, not an *adjective*, to say how something happened or was done (L5), or to modify adjectives (L6).

Adjectives and adverbs: comparative and superlative forms (→ Unit 72)

L7 ▢ The building was *bigger* than I'd expected.

L8 ▢ It was the *most ridiculous* thing to say.

We usually add the ending **-er** to one-syllable adjectives and adverbs to make their comparative forms (L7) and **-est** to make their superlative forms. With three or more syllables we usually add **more / less** and **most / least** (L8). With two syllables we can usually use either.

Quite

L9 ▢ I was *quite* satisfied with the result.

L10 ▢ No, you're *quite* wrong!

L11 ▢ The food here is *quite* superb.

Quite has two meanings: to a particular degree, but not 'very' (= 'fairly') (L9); and to a large degree, or 'very much' (= 'completely') (L10). When **quite** is used with non-gradable adjectives it means 'completely' (L11).

M Adverbial clauses and conjunctions

→ Units 79–87

An adverbial clause is a type of subordinate clause, linked to a main clause. An adverbial clause adds extra information to the main clause about such things as time and conditions. Most adverbial clauses begin with a conjunction that indicates their link with the main clause. Example conjunctions are **after**, **before**, **when** and **until** (time conjunctions); and **if** and **unless** (conditional conjunctions).

Tenses in adverbial and main clauses: general

M1 ▢ Because I'*m* overweight, my doctor *has put* me on a diet.

M2 ▢ I *felt* unwell when I *got* up this morning.

The verb in the adverbial clause is usually the same tense as the verb in the main clause. In M1 they are both present (present simple + present perfect), and in M2 they are both past (past simple + past simple).

Time clauses: tenses (→ Unit 79)

M3 ▢ Have something to eat before you *leave*.

To refer to the future after a time conjunction (... *before* ...) we use present tenses.

M4 ▢ As soon as you *see / have seen* her, come and tell me.

M5 ▢ She wrote to me after she *spoke / had spoken* to Carlos.

To talk about an action in the adverbial clause that is completed before another action described in the main clause, we can use either simple or perfect tenses (present as in M4 or past as in M5), but not **will** or **will have** + **-ed** (the future perfect).

M6 ▢ When I *saw* Kim, I asked her over for dinner.

If the actions in the main clause and the adverbial clause take place at the same time, we use simple, not perfect tenses.

M7 ▢ While the children *were swimming*, their mother kept a watchful eye on them.

M8 ▢ I read a book while I *waited*.

While is mainly used with continuous tenses (M7) and also with simple tenses (M8).

Conditional clauses (→ Units 83–86)

Real and unreal conditionals (→ Units 83 & 84)

Some conditional clauses beginning with **if** suggest that a situation is *real* – that is, the situation is or was true, or may have been or may become true (e.g. *If anyone phones*, tell them I'll be back at eleven; *If you really want to learn Italian*, you need to spend some time in Italy). Others suggest that a situation is *unreal* – that is, the situation is imaginary or untrue. (e.g. What would you do *if you won the lottery*?; *If you had started out earlier*, you wouldn't have been so late).

Compare: *If I go to Berlin*, I'll travel by train. (= *real* conditional) and *If I went to Berlin*, I'd travel by train. (= *unreal* conditional). In the first, the speaker is thinking of going to Berlin (it is a real future possibility), but in the second, the speaker is not thinking of doing so. The second might be giving someone advice.

Real conditionals: tenses (➜ Units 83 & 84)

M9 ▢ I'll give you a lift if it *rains*.
M10 ▢ If you *leave* now, you'll be home in two hours.
M11 ▢ If water *freezes*, it expands.
M12 ▢ If I *made* the wrong decision then I apologise.
In real conditionals we use a present tense to talk about the future (M9), the present (M10) or unchanging relationships (M11), and past tenses to talk about the past (M12).

Unreal conditionals: tenses (➜ Units 83 & 84)

M13 ▢ *If* my grandfather *was / were* still alive, he *would* be a hundred today.
To talk about *present* or *future* situations in unreal conditionals, we use a past tense (either simple or continuous) in the **if-clause** and **would** + **bare infinitive** in the main clause.
In *unreal* conditionals we don't use the past simple or past perfect in the main clause. In *unreal* conditionals, we can also use **could / might** (**have**) instead of **would** (**have**) (e.g. If my grandfather *was / were* still alive, he *might have* enjoyed looking after our garden; If I *lived* out of town, I *could* take up horse riding.). Note that we sometimes use **if ... were** instead of **if ... was** (see Unit 85).
M14 ▢ *If* I *had known* how difficult the job was, I *wouldn't have taken* it.
When we talk about something that might have happened in the *past*, but didn't, then we use **if** + **past perfect** and **would have** + **past participle** in the main clause. We can also use **might / could have** instead of **would have** in the main clause (e.g. They *might have found* a better hotel *if* they *had driven* a few more kilometres.).
M15 ▢ *If* Bruno *wasn't* so lazy, he *would have passed* the exam easily.
M16 ▢ *If* the doctor *had been called* earlier, Paula *would* still *be* alive today.
In some *unreal* conditionals we use mixed tenses. That is, a past tense in the **if-clause** and **would have + past participle** in the main clause (M15), or a past perfect in the **if- clause** and **would** + **infinitive** in the main clause (M16). We can use these patterns to talk about possible consequences if situations were or had been different. We can also use **might / could** (**have**) in the main clause instead of **would** (**have**) (e.g. ... he *could have* passed the exam easily.; ... Paula *might* still *be* alive today.).
M17 ▢ If I *had* a more reliable car, I'd drive to Spain rather than fly.
In *unreal* conditional sentences we don't normally use **would** in an **if-clause** (but see Unit 84).

Other adverbial clauses

Other types of *adverbial clause* give information about *place* (M18), *contrast* (M19 and Unit 82), *cause* or *reason* (M20 and Unit 80), *purpose* (M21 and Unit 81), and *result* (M22 and Unit 81):

M18 ▢ Can you put it back *where you found it*, please?
M19 ▢ My sister is blonde, *whereas my brother has dark hair*.
M20 ▢ He wasn't allowed in *because he was too young*.
M21 ▢ We got up early *so that we could watch the sunrise*.
M22 ▢ He played so badly *that he was easily beaten*.

Additional exercises

These additional exercises provide further practice of important areas from the book; each exercise covers grammar from two or more units. References to the relevant exercises are given at the bottom of the main unit exercise pages. The key can be found on p.278.

List of exercises:

Present and past; simple and continuous tenses

Units 1, 2 & 4

1 **Complete each pair of sentences with a positive or negative form of the same verb from the box. Use the present simple, present continuous, past simple or past continuous. Give all possible answers. Use ⋌ to add any words outside the gap.**

consider	**expect**	**own**	**phone**	**prefer**
~~promise~~	**put**	**read**	**tell**	**weigh**

1 a If I'm not too busy, I ......*promise*...... to help you in the garden later today.
  b I'll try to get over on Saturday, but I .... to be there.
2 a I made a cup of coffee while she .... the letter.
  b As soon as the teacher told us to start, I .... through all the questions quickly.
3 a They .... to reach the mountain summit by evening, but the weather was too bad.
  b We .... Luisa to visit us in June if she can get a cheap flight.
4 a Over 90% of the population now .... a mobile phone.
  b I grew up in Beijing, where my father .... a bookshop.
5 a I .... selling my house and buying a flat.
  b Many people .... her to be the finest violinist in the country at the moment.
6 a Leo .... me that you're getting married. Congratulations!
  b Apparently Angela is very ill. They .... me that she never leaves her house now.
7 a I .... the theatre four times this morning, but there was no answer.
  b I .... my mother twice a day when my father was in hospital.
8 a He always .... his feet up on the chairs. It's really unhygienic.
  b I find it annoying that she constantly .... empty milk cartons back in the fridge.
9 a A survey has found that, surprisingly, most children .... to walk to school than be taken by car.
  b I swam across the river, but my friends .... to walk to the nearest bridge.
10 a Nathan .... over 100 kilos and really needs to take more exercise.
  b He held the fish in his hands as if he .... it and then said, 'It's about 3.5 kilos.'

Present perfect, past simple, and present perfect continuous

Units 3 & 6

2 **Match the beginnings and endings. Sometimes there is more than one possibility.**

1 a I haven't had time to phone Hugo today, b I didn't have time to phone Hugo today,	(i) but I'll certainly contact him before I leave work. (ii) but I'll certainly contact him some time tomorrow.
2 a When she was prime minister, Mrs Perez b Since she became prime minister, Mrs Perez	(i) has often been accused of ignoring the advice of her colleagues. (ii) was often accused of ignoring the advice of her colleagues.
3 a I've watched *Mamma Mia* b I've been watching *Mamma Mia*	(i) and now I keep humming the songs to myself. (ii) at least ten times already.
4 a I'd always wanted to own a Porsche b I won't know if I can afford a Porsche	(i) until I've found out how much they cost. (ii) until I found out how much they cost.
5 a Unemployment has risen b Unemployment has been rising	(i) by 58% since the present government came to power. (ii) ever since the present government came to power.
6 a As soon as I've finished the book b As soon as I finished the book	(i) I'm going to have a holiday. (ii) I started writing another one.
7 a I've been playing squash b I've played squash	(i) since my doctor advised me to lose weight. (ii) a couple of times before, but I can't get the hang of it.
8 a I haven't been back to London b I haven't eaten really good pasta	(i) since I lived in Italy. (ii) since I've lived in Italy.

Past perfect, past perfect continuous, and past simple

Units 5 & 7

3 **Complete each sentence (b) so that it has a similar meaning to sentence (a). Use a verb related to the italicised word in an appropriate tense (active or passive): past perfect, past perfect continuous or past simple. Give alternatives where possible.**

1 a The proposed new library had been under *discussion* for almost three years at the time an appropriate site became available.
b At the time an appropriate site became available, they had been discussing the proposed new library for almost three years.

2 a There had been a considerable *improvement* in his condition when I saw him in hospital last night.
b His condition ……

3 a It was announced that there was a ten-minute *delay* to the Toulouse train.
b It was announced that the Toulouse train ……

4 a Thomas had been on a *diet* for a month when he came to stay with us, and we noticed immediately that he had already lost a lot of weight.
b Thomas ……

5 a There was an *expectation* that Victoria would win comfortably, but she finished third.
  b Victoria ....
6 a When I reversed the car out of the garage, I did some *damage* to the rear number plate.
  b When I reversed the car out of the garage, I ....
7 a Andrei received a *promotion* last week.
  b Andrei ....
8 a Rentpool had been under *investigation* by the tax authorities for a number of months when they arrested the chairman.
  b The tax authorities ....
9 a The Minister made her colleagues *angry* when she criticised them during her speech yesterday.
  b The Minister ....
10 a There had already been a *suggestion* from Emilia that the money should be spent on new tablet computers for the school.
  b Emilia ....

The future

Units 9 & 10

4 **If necessary, correct or improve the italicised verbs in these dialogues, using will, shall, going to, present continuous for the future, or present simple for the future.**

A A: Careful, (1) you*'re going to* spill your coffee.
  B: Oh, no! Too late. Now (2) I*'m going to* have to change my trousers.
B A: What have you got all that wood for?
  B: (1) I*'ll* build a bird table in the garden.
  A: If you need any help, let me know and (2) I*'m going to* give you a hand.
C A: (1) *Shall* you be able to come over on the 3rd? We (2) *have* a barbecue.
  B: Just a minute, (3) I*'m going to* have a look in my diary. No, I'm sorry. (4) I*'m meeting* some friends in town that day.
D A: Did you know that David (1) *is going to go* to New Zealand this summer?
  B: Yes, I heard. I'm really sorry he (2) *doesn't come* to see us.
  A: I wonder when we (3) *see* him again?
  B: Well, he certainly (4) *won't* be back before Christmas.
E A: I (1) *take* Aunt Lucy to the station later. Do you want a lift into town, too?
  B: What time (2) *does* her train *go*?
  A: It (3) *will be* at 4:15. It (4) *takes* us about half an hour to get there if there isn't too much traffic.
  B: Well you should start out early. Apparently, (5) we*'ll* have heavy snow this afternoon. In fact, thanks for your offer, but I think (6) I*'m going to* stay at home in the warm.

Modals and semi-modals

Units 15–20

5 **Underline the best answer from each group in italics.**

1 A: I've spent most of the morning trying to fix my washing machine, but I seem to have made it worse.
  B: You *ought to ask / may ask / ought to have asked* me to come over and take a look at it. I *would have been / should be / would be* happy to help. But I suppose it's too late now!
2 The taxi *needs to / should / would* be here in a couple of minutes. We*'d better / 've better / 'd better to* get ready to go.
3 My daughter *wouldn't / won't / may not* eat carrots. She hates the taste of them. I *don't have to / 'm not able to / can't* think of any way of getting her to eat them. But to tell the truth, I *could / would / used to* hate them when I was young, too.

4 A: We're completely lost! I*'m not able to* / *can't* / *mustn't* find any of the street names around here on the map.
B: We *must have* / *have got to have* / *can have* taken the wrong turning at the traffic lights about a kilometre back.

5 You *haven't got to* / *needn't* / *mustn't* go on the beach when the tide's coming in. It's very dangerous. You *can* / *might* / *would* play in the playground instead.

6 I was beginning to be concerned that I *won't* / *mustn't* / *wouldn't* get to the station for my train. But I *didn't need worry* / *needn't have worried* / *needn't worry*; Aisha turned up in good time to give me a lift.

7 Most headteachers today feel that parents *need* / *should* / *had better* play a more active part in the running of schools. There was a time when parents *would* / *will* / *should* put a lot of effort into fundraising for schools, but those days seem to have gone.

8 A: These trousers shrank the first time I washed them.
B: If I were you, I *ought to* / *should* / *can* take them back.
A: Yes, I suppose they *can* / *need* / *may* give me my money back.

9 Preliminary research suggests that the bones *must* / *have got to* / *used to* be at least 100,000 years old, but they *would* / *could* / *can* be considerably older than that.

10 Apparently, in the future, we *will be able to* / *can* / *could* to get holograms of the people we're talking to on our mobile phones. Of course, by the time this is common, we *can* / *must* / *might* have started using other ways of communicating.

11 Both candidates for the job were very strong and it was hard to choose between them. I certainly *couldn't* / *mustn't* / *had got to* have decided which one to appoint. But fortunately, we *hadn't got to* / *didn't have to* / *mustn't* make a final decision; the management found enough money to allow us to appoint both of them.

12 You *needn't* / *don't need to* / *mustn't* be very fit to play badminton well. It *can* / *is able to* / *could* be played by anyone who is reasonably fit and who has a good sense of timing.

Passives

Units 22–25

6 **Some extracts from radio news reports are given below. Rewrite them using passive forms in which the italicised word is the subject of each clause. If that is italicised, use a passive construction with it or there.**

Examples:
Picasso encouraged *her* to paint. → **She was encouraged** to paint by Picasso.
People believe *that* the Prime Minister will resign tomorrow. → **It is believed** that the Prime Minister will resign tomorrow.

A People are encouraging *the Prime Minister* to sack the Environment Minister, Maria Long, after someone revealed *that* she had received payments from a major oil company. However, in a statement today, the Prime Minister said: 'My advisors tell *me* that the company paid *Mrs Long* the money before she joined the government. I have no intention of dismissing her.'

B A tropical storm has caused severe flooding in the city of Chittagong in southern Bangladesh. Although we understand *that* there are no casualties, the floods have made *many thousands of people* homeless, and people estimate the *damage to property* as running into millions of dollars.

C Protesters have continued to block the construction of the new ring road by tying themselves to trees along the proposed route. Police say that they have given *the protesters* two days to leave the area or they will arrest *them*.

D Conservation groups have demanded that the government should close down *the nuclear power station* after a report which said that investigators have found *unacceptable levels of radiation* in the local area.

E The Commissioner of the Dublin police force has revealed that they have received *a death threat* against the life of President Nabon, who is visiting the capital this weekend. He says that they are taking *the threat* very seriously. People expect *that* security levels will be increased during the President's visit.

F Someone found *a man* injured on a Scottish hillside this morning. People think *that* he fell while coming down a hillside in bad weather. Medical staff are treating *him* in hospital for leg and head injuries. Someone reported *him* missing last night when he failed to return home after a day's walking.

G And now football. People expect *that* there will be a record crowd at tonight's match between Barcelona and Real Madrid. People report *that* the club will give *the Barcelona players* a huge financial bonus if they win and people have even suggested *that* the club might pay *them* as much as €50,000 each.

Verb complementation: what follows verbs

Units 30 & 31

7 **Underline the correct option. Sometimes both are possible.**

1 He insisted *to pay / on paying* for the meal.
2 The interviewer started off *to ask / by asking* me why I wanted the job.
3 I can clearly recall *his saying / him saying* that he was meeting Sarah at eight o'clock.
4 The university has *arranged / appointed* Dr Lopez to be head of the new Medical Institute.
5 I knew I could *ask / count* on Hannah if I needed any help.
6 My parents are always going on *at me to tidy / for to tidy* up my bedroom.
7 The ticket enables you *visiting / to visit* both the museum and the art gallery.
8 Fatima is so small that she often has to resort to *wearing children's clothes / children's clothes* to get the right size.
9 We objected to *their cat / their cat's* digging up our garden.
10 The government plans to bring in new laws *forcing / making* parents to take more responsibility for the education of their children.
11 I don't approve of *her wearing / wearing* outdoor shoes in the house.
12 Ramos was arrested when he failed *him to appear / to appear* in court.
13 If you have any problems with the computer, contact Simon. It's best if you *allow / let* him deal with them.
14 I've heard a lot about Dr Lau, and I'm looking forward *to hearing / to hear* his talk tomorrow.
15 Although Carmen is a doctor herself, it doesn't *entitle her to / entitle for her to* special treatment, and she will have to join the waiting list like everyone else.
16 We *waited / waited for* the storm to pass before we continued.
17 When I was in the supermarket I *noticed a man to take / noticed a man take* a packet off the shelf and hide it inside his coat.
18 We *invited / refused* Lisa to come to the party.
19 I overheard her *tell / telling* Aleksi that she was seriously ill.
20 She gave up work so that she could focus on *looking / look* after her children.
21 We were unhappy in England, and even *discussed / talked* of emigrating to New Zealand.
22 The lizard is amazingly well adapted *to live / to living* in very dry and windy conditions.
23 Another increase in the price of petrol would discourage *me from using / from using* my car.

Reporting

Units 33, 35, 36 & 38

8 Complete each report using a noun from the box followed by a **that-clause** or **to-infinitive clause**. Give both alternatives if possible.

advice	**complaint**	**conclusion**	**confession**	**decision**	**prediction**
promise	**refusal**	**reply**	~~**statement**~~	**threat**	**warning**

1 'The government has decreased taxation every year since we came to power,' stated the President.
Opposition leaders have challenged *the President's statement that the government have / had decreased taxation every year since they came to power.*

2 Karen said, 'I've decided not to go to university next year.' We were disappointed with *Karen's decision* ....

3 'The Earth will pass through the tail of a comet within the next five years,' predicted Professor Adams.
Considerable media attention has been focused on ....

4 'We said that we would dismiss the strikers if they didn't return to work, and we have now done that.'
The company has carried out ....

5 'You should delegate more of your work to your secretary,' Nicky was advised by her boss.
Nicky decided to follow ....

6 'I'll pick you up at ten,' Jason promised.
Jason didn't turn up until eleven, despite ....

7 'Professor Jones doesn't know what he's talking about,' Rob concluded.
I wasn't surprised by ....

8 'My dinner is cold!'
We decided to ignore Dan's ....

9 'We will not negotiate over the ownership of the land!'
I was astonished by ....

10 'Small children should be kept indoors until pollution levels have decreased,' the Health Minister has warned.
The Health Minister has issued ....

11 'I've never used a computer before,' she confessed.
I was surprised by ....

12 'Where's Bethany?' I asked Zeb. 'I don't know,' he replied.
When I asked Zeb where Bethany was ....

Nouns

Units 40–43

9 **Complete each sentence with an appropriate present simple form (singular or plural) of the verb in brackets. If both singular and plural forms are possible, give both.**

1 I've been trying to sell my car for ages, but nobody ...... to buy it. (*want*)
2 A lettuce and a carrot ...... all I need to make the salad. (*be*)
3 A lot of students ...... in the old houses near the university. (*live*)
4 All of the scientific evidence ...... to the conclusion that increasing use of pesticides in farming is damaging our health. (*point*)
5 The university ...... to appoint lecturers who already have a PhD. (*prefer*)
6 She's one of those people who ...... just sitting in the sun on holiday. (*love*)
7 The office staff ...... that they have been treated badly by management. (*claim*)
8 All of my children ...... to the same school. (*go*)

9 A lot of cheaper furniture nowadays .... in pieces inside a flat box for you to build yourself. (*come*)
10 In France, the media .... more respectful of the privacy of celebrities than in Britain. (*be*)
11 Currently, 16% of the workforce .... jobless. (*be*)
12 It's a really quiet town at night. Everything .... at around 10 o'clock. (*shut*)
13 The police .... that the fire was caused deliberately. (*suspect*)
14 The majority of the children in the class .... under five years old. (*be*)
15 Although the bracelet might be worth something, none of the other jewellery .... to be of great value. (*appear*)
16 The stairs .... quite steep, so be careful how you go down. (*be*)
17 What worries me about the car .... the problems we've been having with the brakes. (*be*)
18 The United Nations .... to send a team of doctors to investigate the outbreak of TB. (*plan*)
19 One of the arguments in favour of the new airport .... that it will bring jobs to the area. (*be*)
20 Many people have speculated on the reasons for the southern population movements in the Indian subcontinent during the 15th century, but none of the historical records identified so far .... an answer. (*provide*)
21 It's a charity performance, so none of the actors .... a fee for taking part. (*get*)
22 Every letter and parcel .... carefully checked before posting to make sure it has the correct address. (*be*)
23 My parents want to move to Spain, but neither of them .... Spanish. (*speak*)
24 A: Where are the scissors? B: I think either Leyla or Miguel .... borrowed them. (*have*)
25 Most people would agree that the criteria .... not of equal importance. (*be*)
26 The economics of nuclear power .... become more and more difficult in the last decade. (*have*)
27 Whoever had contact with the patient .... to be found and vaccinated against polio. (*have*)
28 A: I've got to walk all the way to my uncle's house, and he lives about two miles away.
B: But two miles .... far. (*be / not*)
29 A recent survey shows that around 10% of all cars .... dangerous to drive. (*be*)
30 Phonetics .... one of the options you can take in the second year of the course. (*be*)

Articles, etc.

Units 44–48

10 **Complete the sentences using the words from the box. Which *one* option can complete *all* three sentences a, b and c?**

a / an   one   some   the   'zero article' (–)

1 a Could you look after my cat while I'm away on holiday? It's only for .... week.
b Jules lives less than .... mile from school, so he can get up at eight o'clock and still be at school by nine.
c When I arrived, Alice was sitting in .... corner of the room and Jake was sitting in the other. I could tell that they had been arguing.
2 a .... vulture feeds primarily on dead animals.
b Eleni has arthritis, and her doctor has suggested that she should spend as much time as possible in .... warm climate.
c Fiona has decided she wants to be .... accountant.
3 a A: How should I get to the town centre from here?
B: Well, you could walk, but catching a bus is probably .... quickest.
b The World Wide Fund for Nature organised a major campaign to save .... tiger.
c .... washing machine has had a huge impact on people's lives since it was invented.

4 a A: Rafael Nadal is visiting our school next week to talk about tennis.
B: You mean .... Rafael Nadal – the famous tennis player? Can you get his autograph for me?
b It was hot in the house, so she opened all the windows to let in .... fresh air.
c Large areas of Canada are still covered by .... forest.
5 a She was made .... Chief Executive Officer in 2002.
b Do you want .... sugar in your coffee?
c You can buy .... mobile phones for as little as £10.
6 a .... 500 people were at the meeting.
b Despite years of research, we still don't understand the significance of .... dreams.
c It is a sad fact that .... money buys political power in many societies.
7 a .... earthquake in the south of the country has left thousands homeless.
b I love having holidays at .... seaside.
c Do you remember .... Wilmotts? They used to live opposite us.
8 a .... bicycle is an important means of transport for many people with no access to public transport.
b We only stayed in Oslo for .... night, but we really liked the place.
c Juan owns a painting that he claims is .... Picasso.
9 a I felt fine when I woke up, but by .... evening I had a fever.
b The temperature at .... midday reached over 40 °C.
c It's probably easiest to contact me by .... email.
10 a My history teacher at school – .... Mrs Bullenski – was always giving us advice on how to improve our examination skills.
b I'll just spend .... day or two in Singapore and then go on to Australia for three weeks.
c It was .... day that would remain in my memory forever.

Relative clauses

Units 53–55

11 **Rewrite each sentence including the information in brackets in a relative clause. Give all possible relative pronouns, but if you can leave them out, put them in brackets. Use commas where necessary.**

1 Later in the programme we have an interview with Laura Dekker. (in 2012 she became the youngest solo round-the-world sailor) *Later in the programme we have an interview with Laura Dekker, who in 2012 became the youngest solo round-the-world sailor.*
2 Carla's restaurant is very good value. (it serves a range of Mediterranean dishes)
3 The New Zealand rugby team are clear favourites to win the match. (all of its members weigh over 100 kilos)
4 Chloe brought home a kitten. (she'd found it in the park)
5 The story is about a teenage boy. (his ambition is to become an astronaut)
6 Paul has got a job with Empirico. (its main product is electric light bulbs)
7 Politicians should give more consideration to the working people. (they represent them)
8 Among the group of people was Professor Fischer. (I had last seen him in Munich 20 years earlier)
9 I live on a small road. (it leads down to the river)
10 Monet's earlier paintings are in a new exhibition in New York. (many have never been seen in the USA before)
11 Ian McIver has become managing director of Europe's largest food retailer. (his first job was selling vegetables in a market)
12 Kaspar has a new girlfriend. (she works in the library)
13 My Volkswagen Golf is a very reliable car. (I bought it in 2006)
14 Bronwen Brookes will be present at its official opening. (the Brookes art gallery is named after her)

Substitution and leaving out words

Units 62–65

12 **Underline the appropriate alternatives. Sometimes both are possible.**

1 He has a shave every morning, but you wouldn't think he *did / had*.
2 The developers pulled down the clock tower to make way for the new road. In *doing so / so doing*, they destroyed one of the finest examples of 17th century architecture in the country.
3 A: Ben won't be coming this weekend. B: But he *promised so / promised he would*.
4 A: It looks like Vettel is going to win again. B: It *appears / appears so*.
5 A: I didn't know you cycled to work. B: Yes, I always *do / do so*.
6 I don't like eating shellfish, and never *have / have done*.
7 They asked me to go fishing with them, but I *didn't want / didn't want to*.
8 A: Will it take you long to fix it? B: Well, it might *do / do so*. I'm not sure yet.
9 A: Do you think Fred will be up by now? B: I *doubt that he will / doubt so*.
10 A: Dad won't mind us borrowing the car, will he? B: No, I *don't suppose so / suppose not*.
11 Just park the car wherever you *want to / want*.
12 A: Has Rachel arrived yet? B: No, I don't think she *has done / has*.
13 Karl had to choose between working much longer hours and moving to another part of the country. He had never faced *such a dilemma / a such dilemma* before.
14 He owns much more land than I *do so / do*.
15 We'd like to go to Canada to see Ellie, but we can't *afford to / afford*.
16 A: I imagine the information is kept on computer somewhere. B: I would *expect so / expect*.
17 I don't know whether my parents want me to go to Norway, but I *suspect not / don't suspect*.
18 A: Will she expect us to get the job finished by the weekend?
B: I certainly *don't hope so / hope not*.
19 A: There's no answer. I suppose she might have left home by now.
B: Yes, I suppose she *might have / might*.
20 The car's in good condition. They *told so / told me so* at the garage.
21 I didn't want Luca to climb the mountain, but he was *determined to / determined*.
22 A: My mother was really angry. B: But didn't you expect her *to / to be*?
23 A: It doesn't look like the rain's going to stop soon. B: I *don't guess / guess not*.
24 A: Are you going to the library today? B: I *might do / might be*.

Position of adjectives, adverbs and adverbial phrases

Units 66, 69, 74 & 75

13 **Are the italicised words and phrases in the correct position? If not, suggest a change of position or rewrite the text if necessary.**

a I *every so often* leave work *early* and go to a performance in the local concert hall. It's very close to my office, in the *opposite* building. *Usually* they *rather* are good, but yesterday's, given by a singer and pianist, was a *total* disaster. The singer *with wonderful control* began to sing. But when the pianist started to play, it sounded awful. At first I thought he was *badly* playing, but then it became obvious that the piano *completely* was out of tune. They stopped and discussed *briefly* the problem. They couldn't continue *clearly*, and they left the stage *unhappily*. *Naturally*, all the *present* people felt sorry for them. I'm sure the *responsible* person for tuning the piano will be severely reprimanded.

b I *just* was going out to work this morning when the postman pushed *through my letterbox* a letter. It was from Mara, who writes *from time to time*. The letter said that she has to come to Bristol to visit her *unwell* uncle. She is one of his few *remaining* relatives. She wants us to meet and asked if I could suggest a time *possible*. Well, I *for a couple of years* haven't seen her, so I was really pleased. We *first* met at university. We have *alike* interests, so *always* we find a lot to talk about. The *included* photos in the letter showed that she hadn't changed since I *last* saw her. I spent so long reading the letter that I *nearly* was late for work.

Adverbial clauses and conjunctions

Units 79–82 & 87

14 **Match the ideas in (i) and (ii) and use the word in brackets to write either a single sentence (as in 1) or two sentences (as in 2), as appropriate. Note that you can put the idea in (ii) first in the sentence.**

(i)	(ii)
1 I knew there was something wrong	a I found the film boring
2 prepare the remaining vegetables	b Johan must weigh over 120 kilos
3 his wife is really small	c to prepare for the marathon
4 only about 100 people attended	d ~~she said she was feeling fine~~
5 I can't afford a coat like that	e I don't like the style
6 I'm determined to finish the report	f ~~leave the carrots to cool for a few minutes~~
7 you'll have to walk all the way from the station	g make sure you catch the last bus at 11:00
8 I stayed until the end	h I have to stay at work until midnight
9 her husband would never find it	i she hid the letter between the pages of a book
10 I've been running about 200 kilometres a week	j there had been a lot of publicity about the meeting

1 (even though) (+ d) I knew there was something wrong, even though she said she was feeling fine. or Even though she said she was feeling fine I knew there was something wrong.
2 (meanwhile) (+ f) Leave the carrots to cool for a few minutes. Meanwhile, prepare the remaining vegetables.
3 (whereas)
4 (even so)
5 (besides)
6 (even if)
7 (otherwise)
8 (although)
9 (so that)
10 (in order to)

Prepositions

Units 92–94

15 **Add the missing prepositions in the correct places after the italicised words.**

1 Personally, I don't *agree* with fox hunting, although I know that you *approve* it.
2 There seems to be little *likelihood* Williamson winning Wimbledon because of her *inability* play well on grass tennis courts.
3 Our plan is to *split* the organisation into a number of small units. This will improve our *prospects* competing with more specialised companies.
4 I *ran* Danny in town the other day. He *asked* your email address, so he'll probably be in touch with you.
5 Jack takes great *pride* never *throwing* anything. He always says that one day he'll find a use for things.
6 Although Professor Martinez *knows* a great deal meteorology, even he can't *account* the unusual weather we have been having over the last few weeks.
7 There has been a great *improvement* the behaviour of children in the school. This has *resulted* the headteacher's idea involving them in decision-making.
8 Even though Charlotte didn't *act* my advice and follow a career in medicine, I'm full of *admiration* her *determination* train to be a vet.

Inversion

Units 99 & 100

16 **Rewrite each sentence with a similar meaning starting with a word / phrase from the box followed by inversion of the verb and the subject.**

Had	**Hardly**	~~**Little**~~	**Not for one moment**	**Only if**	**Only in**
Seldom	**Should**	**So**	**Under no circumstances**	**Such**	**Were**

1 I didn't imagine that the boss had called me into her office to fire me. *Little did I imagine that the boss had called me into her office to fire me.*

2 The police will only investigate the matter further if an official complaint is made.

3 The instructions were so complicated, that it was impossible to assemble the machine.

4 If we had known how ill Rob was, we would have taken him straight to the hospital.

5 The wind was so strong that all the trees in the park were blown down.

6 She didn't often regret her lack of formal education, although she was sometimes aware of gaps in her knowledge.

7 You should only phone for an ambulance in an emergency.

8 There was never any disagreement between us.

9 If it were not for financial assistance from the government, the museum would have closed long ago.

10 They had only just finished eating before a waiter started to clear away the plates.

11 Children should never be allowed into the room without adult supervision.

12 If the bridge is ever built, it will be welcomed by the local community.

Key to Exercises

UNIT 1

1.1

2 a 'm (am) measuring
b measures
3 a doubt
b doubt
4 a is currently attracting ('attracts' is also possible)
b attract
5 a doesn't like
b 'm (am) not liking ('don't like' is also possible)
6 a 're (are) fitting
b doesn't fit
7 a feels
b 'm (am) not feeling ('don't feel' is also possible)
8 a consists of ('consists only of' would also be possible)
b consists of
9 a 's (is) sounding ('sounds' is also possible)
b sounds
10 a 's (is) having
b has

1.2

1 apologise / ~~'m apologising~~
2 admit / ~~'m admitting~~
3 don't suggest / 'm not suggesting (both possible)
4 now realise / 'm now realising (both possible)
5 confess / ~~'m confessing~~
6 ~~consider~~ / 'm considering
7 do you find / are you finding (both possible)
8 know / ~~'m knowing~~
9 don't guarantee / 'm not guaranteeing (both possible)
10 promise / ~~'m promising~~

UNIT 2

2.1

1 shoots, are attacking
2 arrives, is waiting, says
3 is playing, stands, starts

2.2

Possible answers

2 I gather Vegecorp are going to sack a thousand workers.
3 I understand we're going to have a new public holiday for the President's birthday.
4 Ed tells me Bruno's crashed his car again.
5 Julia says she's got a new job.
6 They say they've identified a gene which causes some people to overeat.

2.3

2 You're forever asking me for money.
3 You're constantly criticising my driving.
4 You're continually changing your mind.
5 You're forever moaning about (your) work.

2.4

The most likely verbs are given:

1 a we're (are) usually eating ('we usually eat' is also possible)
b don't eat
2 a plays ('is playing' is also possible)
b 're (are) constantly playing ('constantly play' is also possible)
3 a I'm normally taking ('I normally take' is also possible. It would suggest, however, that this is the time they leave home. Present continuous suggests that they are on the way to school at 8:30.)
b takes

UNIT 3

3.1

1 went
2 've (have) had
3 wore
4 've (have) spent
5 overslept
6 haven't read

3.2

1 hasn't wanted – fell
2 has worked – hasn't had
3 rescued – has been
4 has happened – spoke
5 have been able – have felt
6 has improved – has been

3.3

1 a ~~signed~~ 've (have) signed
b signed ✓
2 a ~~finished~~ 've (have) finished
b finished ✓
3 a got ✓
b ~~got~~ have got
4 a heard ✓
b ~~heard~~ 've (have) heard

3.4

The most appropriate tenses are given

1 has visited
2 has closed (*or* has been closed; present perfect passive) – died
3 has dropped – has fallen
4 have been stolen (present perfect passive) – insisted – held

UNIT 4

4.1

2 was hoping – gave
3 lived – was spending / was living – spent
4 started – was checking in
5 was looking – saw
6 came – was showing
7 was playing – broke
8 went off – lit
9 wasn't listening ('didn't listen' is also possible) – was explaining ('explained' is also possible)
10 added – tasted
11 wasn't watching ('didn't watch' is also possible) – was dreaming ('dreamt' is also possible)
12 pushed – ran

4.2

1 'was getting' and 'got' are both possible. The past simple suggests that one event followed the other: I got in and then the lights went off. The past continuous suggests that the lights went off as I was in the process of getting ready to get into the bath.
4 'was checking in' or 'checked in' are both possible with a similar meaning. Using the past continuous presents 'checking in' as the background event which was going on as the couple started to chat to him.
7 'was playing' and 'played' are both possible. The past continuous suggests that this was a temporary rather than a regular arrangement.
11 'didn't watch' and 'dreamt' are also possible. However, the past continuous emphasises that 'not watching' and 'dreaming' went on at the same time and seems more likely here.

4.3

1 was buying
2 saw
3 turned
4 was slowly putting (Past simple in 3 and past continuous in 4 seem most likely here as 'turned round' describes a completed action and 'was slowly putting' describes the action that was going on at that time. However, past continuous is also possible in 3 and past simple is also possible in 4.)
5 was carrying
6 walked
7 picked up
8 thought
9 was looking

10 dropped
11 had
12 noticed
13 was watching
14 hurried
15 were walking / walked (similar meaning)
16 ran

UNIT 5

5.1

events	order events are mentioned in text	order of events
I moved...	2	2
I learnt...	5	6
The property developer decided...	9	8
I heard...	8	9
I first saw the old house	1	3
A property developer bought it	6	4
I nearly gave up...	7	7
I put together enough money...	4	5
It was empty	3	1

The first past 'point of reference' is 'When I first saw the old house'. Events before this are in the past perfect: 'I had just moved'... 'It had been empty'.
The second past 'point of reference' is when 'I learnt...'. Events before this are in the past perfect: 'I had put together' ... 'had bought'. Notice that we could use 'I put together' here as the order of events is made clear by 'By the time...'.
The third past 'point of reference' is '... when I heard that the house was for sale again'. Events before this are in the past perfect: 'I had nearly given up'... 'The property developer had decided...'.

5.2

1 had met
2 had been / went
3 had taken / took
4 had seen
5 had lost
6 had found
7 had cheated / cheated
8 had made up
9 had gone / went
10 hadn't heard
11 had finished / finished
12 had eaten (Note: In North American English 'ate' would also be possible.)

5.3

2 Lara hadn't intended to become a dentist ...
3 I had expected the operation to be painful ...
4 I hadn't thought of cooking rabbit ...
5 He hadn't meant to insult her ... (*or* He hadn't meant it to be an insult to her ...)

UNIT 6

6.1

1 a 's (has) been staying ('has stayed' is also possible)
b 've (have) stayed
2 a have been stopping ('have stopped' is also possible)
b has stopped
3 a haven't read
b 've (have) been reading ('have read' is also possible)
4 a has been giving ('has given' is also possible)
b has given
5 a haven't swum
b 've (have) been swimming
6 a have been putting ('have put' is also possible)
b has (or 'have') put
8 a has disappeared
b have been disappearing ('have disappeared' is also possible)

6.2

a
1 ~~has been claiming~~ has claimed
2 ~~have been dying~~ died
3 have been making ✓ ('have made' is also possible)
4 ~~have been producing~~ 've (have) produced
5 ~~have been awarding~~ awarded
6 have been looking ✓ ('have looked' and 'looked' are also possible)
7 have also been exploring ✓ ('have also explored' and 'also explored' are also possible)
8 ~~has been making~~ has / have made / made

b
1 ~~has been investing~~ invested
2 ~~has been announcing~~ has announced
3 has been increasing ✓ ('has increased' is also possible)
4 has been running ✓ ('has run' is also possible)
5 has been neglecting ✓ ('has neglected' is also possible)
6 has been cutting ✓ ('has cut' is also possible)
7 ~~have been finding~~ have found
8 have been planning ✓ ('have planned' is also possible)
9 ~~have been speaking~~ spoke
10 ~~have also been writing~~ have also written / also wrote

UNIT 7

7.1

1 a had only been working ('had only worked' is also possible)
b had finally worked
2 a had carried
b had been carrying ('had carried' is also possible)
3 a had applied
b had been applying ('had applied' is also possible)
4 a had flown
b had been flying

7.2

1 had been trying ('had tried' is also possible)
2 had visited
3 had cost
4 had been writing ('had written'is also possible)
5 had been worrying ('had worried' is also possible)
6 had arrived
7 had always believed
8 had been talking

The past continuous is more likely in 8 (We were talking ...).

7.3

1 ✓
2 had been taken
3 ✓ (Note that 'What happened?' is also possible)
4 had just heard
5 ✓
6 had been fishing
7 ✓
8 hadn't wanted
9 ✓
10 had collapsed

UNIT 8

8.1

The most likely verbs and tenses are given.

2 got / arrived
3 feel / am feeling (Present simple and present continuous have a similar meaning here.)
4 go
5 know
6 spent
7 texted
8 was waiting
9 got
10 felt / was feeling (Past simple and past continuous have a similar meaning here.)

11 got
12 enjoys / is enjoying (Present simple and present continuous have a similar meaning here, although the present continuous may suggest that she is not living in Adelaide permanently.)
13 is looking
14 seems
15 doesn't get on / isn't getting on (Present simple and present continuous have a similar meaning here, although the present continuous suggests that this is a temporary problem.)
16 complain / are constantly complaining (Note the word order.)
17 is starting
18 asked
19 am looking
20 hear / heard (Present simple and past simple have a similar meaning here.)

8.2

The most likely tenses are given.

2 said ('has said' is also possible, but less likely here)
3 heard / had heard
4 returned / had returned
5 came / had come
6 was / had been
7 left
8 appointed
9 finished
10 have won
11 accused
12 has disappointed
13 has spent

8.3

1 'Has he had' or 'Has he been having' are more likely
2 ✓
3 thought / had thought
4 has worked / has been working
5 had been trying
6 did you go
7 heard
8 ✓ ('went' is also possible)
9 ✓ ('checked' is also possible)
10 have said / said
11 ✓ ('have given' is also possible)
12 have told ('told' is also possible)

UNIT 9

9.1

2 ✓ (prediction based on opinion / past experience)
3 ✓ (decision made at moment of speaking)
4 ~~Will you take up~~ Are you going to take up (prediction based on present evidence)
5 ✓ (prediction based on opinion / past experience)
6 ~~'ll be~~ 's going to be (decision already made)
7 ~~'ll have~~ 're going to have (prediction based on present evidence)
8 ~~'ll sell~~ 're going to sell (prediction based on present evidence)
9 ~~'ll cut~~ 'm going to cut (decision already made)
10 ~~'ll be sick~~ 's going to be sick (prediction based on present evidence); 'll feel ✓ (prediction based on opinion / past experience)
11 ~~'ll leave~~ 'm going to leave (decision already made); will you tell ✓ (*or* 'are you going to tell'; asking about something planned); 'll try ✓ (decision made at moment of speaking)
12 ~~'ll have~~ 'm going to have (decision already made); ~~'ll see~~ 're going to see (decision already made); 'll sort out ✓ (decision made at moment of speaking)
13 ✓ (decision made at moment of speaking)
14 ✓ (decision made at moment of speaking)
15 ✓ (prediction based on opinion / past experience)
16 ~~'ll build~~ 'm going to build (decision already made)

9.2

Example verbs are given

2 're going to plant (main clause action does not depend on action in the *if*-clause)
3 'll hurt / 're going to hurt (conditional – negative)
4 will … buy (request)
5 will start / stop (logical consequence)
6 'm going to see (main clause action does not depend on action in the *if*-clause)
7 'll be sacked / 's going to be sacked (conditional – negative)
8 'll hear (ability)

UNIT 10

10.1

1 get (fixed event; 'will get' is also possible)
2 will look after (less routine arrangement)
3 rains (with 'in case')
4 will give out (less routine arrangement)
5 goes (fixed event; 'will go' is also possible)
6 starts (fixed event; 'will start' is also possible)
7 stops (with 'provided')
8 change (with 'what if')
9 will miss (prediction)
10 lend (with 'unless')
11 play (or 'plays') (fixed event;'will play' is also possible)
12 will accept (prediction)
13 want (with 'supposing')
14 read (with 'by the time')

10.2

1 (c) ~~is leaving~~ (prediction perhaps based on opinion, experience or present evidence). 'Will leave' and 'is going to leave' have a similar meaning here.
2 (a) ~~will buy~~ (planned future event). 'I'm going to buy' suggests an intention without a definite arrangement; 'I'm buying' suggests a definite arrangement – perhaps the speaker has bought the car and is simply picking it up next week.
3 (b) ~~are going to pick~~; (c) ~~are picking~~ (offer; decision made at moment of speaking)
4 (a) ~~will drive~~ (planned future event). 'I'm going to drive' suggests a personal intention; 'I'm driving' suggests a more definite arrangement – perhaps the speaker has been told to go there by their employer.
5 (c) ~~is cutting~~ (permanent future situation). 'Will cut' and 'is going to cut' have a similar meaning here.
6 (b) ~~am going to call~~; (c) ~~am calling~~ (promise; decision made at time of speaking)
7 (a) ~~will serve~~ (planned future event). As the present continuous for the future suggests a definite arrangement, using 'I am serving lunch' in this context suggests '… and I am not changing what I plan to do', perhaps showing some irritation or annoyance.
8 (c) ~~are starving~~ (no control over predicted event). 'Will starve' and 'are going to starve' have a similar meaning here. However, as 'will' is often used to talk about future facts, it may express more certainty in this context.

10.3

1

1 is joining ✓ joins ✗ (will join ✓ is going to join ✓)
2 are liking ✗ like ✗ (will like ✓ are going to like ✓)
3 is coming ✓ comes ✓ (will come ✓ [but present continuous, present simple or' be going to' are more natural here] is going to come ✓)
4 is giving ✗ gives ✗ (will give ✓ is going to give ✗)

2

1 is / are sacking ✓ sack ✗ (will sack ✓ [but present continuous or 'be going to' are more natural here] is / are going to sack ✓)

2 are closing ✗ close ✓ (will close ✗ are going to close ✗)
3 are building ✓ build ✗ (will build ✓ [but present continuous or 'be going to' are more natural here] are going to build ✓)
4 are seeing ✗ see ✗ (will see ✓ are going to see ✗)

UNIT 11

11.1

1 a will be leaving ('will leave' is also possible)
  b will leave
2 a Will you be working ('Will you work' is also possible)
  b 'll work
3 a won't be using ('won't use' is also possible)
  b won't use
4 a 'll (will) give
  b will be giving ('will give' is also possible)
5 a won't move
  b will be moving ('will move' is also possible)

11.2

2 If the company is making a profit by the end of the year then we will have achieved the objective we set ourselves when we took over.
3 In two years' time Morneau will have been acting for 50 years, and shows no sign of retiring from the theatre. ('will have acted' is also possible)
4 I am confident that I will have finished the report before the end of the week.
5 This book on Proust is really difficult. On Saturday I will have been reading it for a month, and I'm still only half way.
6 As delegates who arrived early will have been discovering, there have been some late changes to the conference programme. ('will have discovered' is also possible)

11.3

1 will have closed
2 will be enjoying
3 will be leaving
4 will be arriving
5 will have been
6 will have been planning
7 won't be spending
8 will be keeping
9 will all be going

UNIT 12

12.1

1 is to be staged ('will be staged' is also possible)
2 will stop
3 is to merge / is to be merged ('will merge' or 'will be merged' are also possible)
4 will rise
5 is to be replaced ('will be replaced' is also possible)
6 is to retire; is to be succeeded ('will retire' and 'will be succeeded' are also possible)
7 will become
8 are to receive ('will receive' is also possible)
9 are to be created ('will be created' is also possible)
10 will increase

12.2

1 are to have (see section B)
2 is to start / is about to start (A/C)
3 wins (B)
4 enjoy (B)
5 'm just about to go (C)
6 recovers (B)
7 is to keep (B)
8 is to resign / is about to resign (C) ('is about to resign' emphasises that he will resign very soon)
9 are about to get (C)
10 is to be improved (B)

UNIT 13

13.1

3 due to return
4 sure to provide
5 set to launch
6 on the verge of becoming
7 on the point of signing
8 sure to face
9 due to undergo
10 on the verge of quitting
11 set to make
12 on the brink of going

13.2

2 propose / 'm proposing to deal
3 expect / 're expecting to finish
4 aim / 'm aiming to study
5 resolves to give up
6 guarantee to find
7 intend / 'm intending to move

13.3

1 will
2 shan't / won't ('won't' is more natural)
3 will
4 shall / will
5 won't

UNIT 14

14.1

1 was going to do
2 will be
3 ✓
4 would have shown
5 ✓ ('was to be announced' is also possible)
6 is about to start
7 ✓
8 was supposed; was about to ask
9 ✓ ('am going to see' is also possible)
10 is to be used
11 ✓ ('were meeting' is also possible)
12 would cause

Past or present tense forms are possible in 5, 9 and 11.

14.2

1	a	6	b
2	b	7	a
3	a	8	a
4	b	9	b
5	a	10	a

UNIT 15

15.1

1 can (A: before passive)
2 were able to (B: single past achievement)
3 could / were able to (A)
4 Could you (B: with 'understand' 'could' is more natural)
5 can't (A: 'know how to')
6 can (A: happening as speaking)
7 were able to (B: single past achievement)
8 could hardly (B: with 'hardly 'could' is more natural)
9 could (B: with 'smell' 'could' is more natural)
10 Can you / Are you able to (A)
11 can (A: before passive)
12 was able to (B: single past achievement)
13 couldn't (B: negative sentence; 'couldn't' is more natural)
14 was able to (B: single past achievement)

15.2

a

1 can
2 couldn't
3 can
4 can't
5 couldn't / weren't allowed to
6 can't
7 were allowed to

b

1 can
2 wasn't allowed to / couldn't
3 was allowed to
4 could
5 could
6 can't
7 was allowed to

UNIT 16

16.1

1 will spend
2 had
3 would exercise
4 found
5 will cause
6 would rarely sit
7 will know
8 will probably be / would probably be

16.2

1 ✗ used to ✓ (changed past state)
2 ✓ ('used to' is also possible)
3 ✗ used to ✓ (changed past state)
4 ✓ ('would' is not possible) (changed past state)
5 ✓ ('would' is also possible)
6 ✗ met ✓ (number of times specified)

16.3

1 will have watched
2 would have approved
3 would have hurt
4 will have heard
5 would have preferred
6 will / would have noticed
7 would have bought

16.4

Example answers

1 B: Well, if you ***will*** drive everywhere instead of walking, I'm not surprised.
2 B: Well, if you ***will*** spend so much time online, I'm not surprised.
3 B: Well, if you ***will*** wear a thick jumper when it's 30 degrees, it's not surprising.

UNIT 17

17.1

1 might (more likely than 'may')
2 may
3 Are you likely to ... (possible answer; 'Might you ...' would be rather formal)
4 might (more likely than 'may')
5 Could (possible answer; 'Might' would be rather formal)
6 may

17.2

1 might have enjoyed (E: possible event in the past)
2 might have been trying (E: possible activity that went on over a period of time)
3 might be coming (E: possible event in the future)
4 might require (C: typically the case in the past)
5 may be moving (E: possible event in the future)
6 may have improved (E: possible event in the future)
7 might be imprisoned (C: typically the case in the past)
8 may have been exaggerating (E: possible activity that went on over a period of time)
9 might be punished (C: typically the case in the past; passive)
10 may have told (E: possible event in the past)

17.3

Possible answers

1 ... at least he's in tune.
2 ... it's never broken down.
3 ... she has a very wide vocabulary.
5 You may / might not agree with him, ...
6 She may / might not express her feelings openly, ...
7 It may / might not sound very exciting, ...

UNIT 18

18.1

1 must have found
2 must be
3 must be starting ('must be going to start' and 'must start' are also possible)
4 must have had to work ('must have worked' is also possible)
5 must have changed
6 must have to show
7 must be taking ('must have taken' is also possible)
8 must be

18.2

2 Hannah rarely has to be asked to tidy her room.
3 Have we got to hand in the homework tomorrow? ('Do we have to ...' is also possible)
4 I didn't have to go to the hospital after all.
5 Did Ben have to go alone?
6 Adam sometimes has to start work at 6:30. ('Adam has sometimes got to start work ...' is also possible)
7 The college has to be extended to accommodate the growing number of students. ('has got to be extended' is also possible, but less likely in a formal context)
8 We may / might have to cancel our holiday because my mother is ill.

18.3

1 ✓
2 ~~always have got to pull~~ always have to pull
3 ~~Have you to bang~~ Do you have to bang ('Must you bang ...' is also possible but less likely)
4 ✓
5 ~~must have to squeeze~~ must have had to squeeze / must have squeezed
6 ~~must leave~~ must have left
7 ✓
8 ~~mustn't wait~~ didn't have to wait
9 ~~must be disturbed~~ must have been disturbed
10 ~~I've to get~~ I've got to get / I have to get (Note that some people use 'I've to get' in informal language, but others think this is incorrect.)
11 ✓
12 ~~may must get~~ may have to get
13 ~~I've to go~~ I must go / I have to go / I've got to go
14 ~~must get~~ must be getting
15 ✓
16 ~~have to get~~ must get (more likely)

The three common expressions with 'must' are 'I must say ...', 'I must admit ...' (both used to emphasise the following point), and 'needs must' (meaning if something is necessary I will do it, even though I may not want to).

UNIT 19

19.1

1 I'll give you a lift to the station so you needn't worry / bother about booking a taxi.
2 The questions are in the book so you needn't bother to copy them down.
3 All the windows have screens so you needn't panic / worry about being bitten by mosquitoes.
4 Our software provides full computer security so you needn't concern yourself with viruses.
5 The new tax laws don't come into force until next year so you needn't change the details on the form.

19.2

2 We need only (*or* We only need ...) look at the rainfall figures to see the seriousness of the problem. (*less formally* We only need to look at ...)
3 With such a lead in the opinion polls the Democrats need hardly bother (*or* ... the Democrats hardly need bother) campaigning before the election. (*less formally* ... the Democrats hardly need to bother campaigning ...)
4 No one need know who paid the ransom to the kidnappers. (*less formally* No one needs to know who paid ...)
5 After such a huge lottery win, he need never work again. (*less formally* ... he never needs to work again.)

19.3

1 don't need to
2 needn't / don't need to

3 needn't / don't need to
4 don't need to
5 needn't / don't need to
6 don't need to

19.4

1 You needn't worry …
2 Do we need to make … *is more likely*
3 … needn't be a problem …
4 ✓
5 I need hardly tell you …, *or less formally* I hardly need (to) tell you …
6 some people would prefer 'needn't' in this context (see C)
7 ✓
8 … needn't mean …

UNIT 20

20.1

1 should / ought to win (should / ought to have won *is also possible*)
2 should I put (*more likely than* … ought I to put …; should I have put *is also possible*)
3 should / ought to have arrived (should / ought to arrive *is also possible*)
4 should be sent (*more likely than* ought to be sent)
5 should be removed (*more likely than* ought to be removed)
6 should / ought to wear
7 should / ought to have resigned
8 Should we answer (*more likely than* Ought we to answer …; Should we have answered *is also possible*)
9 should go (ought to *is not possible*)
10 should / ought to be (should / ought to have been *is also possible*)

20.2

1 should *or* must; 'must' gives a stronger recommendation
2 must
3 must
4 should *or* must; 'must' gives stronger advice and is perhaps more likely than 'should' in this context
5 should *or* must; 'must' gives a stronger recommendation
6 must

(2, 3 and 6 include logical conclusions, so we use 'must' not 'should')

20.3

1 ~~should~~ must
2 ✓
3 ~~shall~~ should / ought to
4 ~~shouldn't~~ 'd better not
5 ~~'d better~~ should / ought to
6 ~~had better not~~ shouldn't / ought not to be
7 ✓
8 ✓
9 ✓
10 ~~had better~~ should / ought to

UNIT 21

21.1

1 (to be)	6 to be
2 to be	7 to be
3 to be	8 to be
4 (to be)	9 (to be)
5 (to be)	10 (to be)

21.2

1 get
2 became
3 become (more likely than 'get' in a formal context)
4 become
5 get
6 get (more likely than 'become' in an informal context)
7 became
8 got

21.3

2 went dead	6 came to like
3 went red	7 go blind
4 get to know	8 went bust
5 get tired	

21.4

1 go wrong
2 seemed to be awake
3 ✓
4 seemed to be taking
5 hadn't got dressed
6 ✓ ('be ill' would also be possible)
7 went missing
8 to get worried
9 becoming obvious
10 ✓

UNIT 22

22.1

2 She was offered a second-hand bicycle. / A second-hand bicycle was offered (to) her.
3 Improvements have been proposed to the developers.
4 Some interesting changes were suggested to me.
5 He was awarded a prize. / A prize was awarded to him.
6 The President's arrival will be announced to the waiting journalists.
7 The password had been mentioned to the thieves.
8 I have been lent some skis. / Some skis have been lent to me.
9 I am being sent a lot of spam emails. / A lot of spam emails are being sent to me.
10 The changes are going to be explained to the students.

22.2

2 introduced; I was introduced to Mrs Rossi by Tony at his birthday party. (*or* … Mrs Rossi at Tony's birthday party.)
3 seen; Has Chris been seen (by anyone) this morning?
4 (have) appointed; Sven Larsen has been appointed (*or* was appointed) Regional Sales Director for Scandinavia.
5 will demonstrate; I am certain that Sarah's suitability as company director will be demonstrated to those who still have any doubt.
6 declared (*or* have declared); Alan Watson was declared (*or* has been declared) winner of the election after a recount.

22.3

2 The product was phased out (by the company) over a period of three years.
3 No passive
4 Many people have been deprived of the right to vote (by the decision).
5 No passive
6 No passive
7 The last two items were held over (by the chairperson) until the next committee meeting.
8 Walkers were prevented from crossing the field after it was fenced off (by the farmer).

UNIT 23

23.1

2 denied being involved
3 was left holding
4 remembered being bitten
5 avoided being taken
6 was observed hiding
7 was sent tumbling
8 faced being expelled
9 was found wandering
10 resented being given

23.2

2 Emil and Laura could be heard arguing next door.
3 Ollie hated being teased by the other children.
4 The burglar was observed entering the museum through a window.
5 The pop concert is expected to attract over 20,000 people.
6 She didn't mind being criticised.
7 I was required to complete two copies of the customs declaration.
8 Mrs Dee was caught shoplifting.

23.3

2 Omar hopes to be selected by the team captain. (different meaning)
3 Kathy arranged to be taken to the station by Alastair. (different meaning)
4 Galdos has come to be recognised as one of Spain's greatest novelists by critics. (corresponding meaning)
5 Holidaymakers continue to be attracted to the south coast. (corresponding meaning)

6 The Finance Minister has agreed to be interviewed by Harris. (different meaning)

UNIT 24

24.1

2 The main stadium has been designed to accommodate many different sports.
3 The temporary stands will be taken down after the Games.
4 The basketball arena will have been completed by the end of May.
5 The rowing competition is being held on the River Nene.
6 The athletics track had been completed (or was completed) only a year after the city got the Olympics.
7 The handball venue was being used as a warehouse until a year ago.
8 The badminton arena should have been finished by now.

24.2

2 The appointment of a new managing director will be made next week.
3 Accusations of corruption in the local council have been made. / Accusations of corruption have been made against the local council.
4 The demolition of the building was completed in only two days.
5 The presentation of the trophy will be made after the speeches.
6 Resistance from local residents to the proposed new industrial area will certainly be expected.

24.3

2 is (being) ruled (or more naturally 'is now (being) ruled')
3 are disappearing / have disappeared
4 fear
5 is estimated / has been estimated
6 will be turned into
7 is using / has used / has been using
8 to be abandoned
9 be affected
10 expect / are expecting
11 are (being) destroyed

UNIT 25

25.1

1 agreed
2 proposed / shown
3 hoped / explained
4 decided
5 explained
6 established / revealed
7 intended
8 planned
9 assumed / thought
10 discovered

25.2

2 ✗
3 It has been discovered that there is water on Mars.
4 It is believed that terrorists are operating in Berlin.
5 It is expected that the moon astronauts will return (to Earth) today.
6 It has been revealed that ex-President Julius is / was a spy.
7 ✗
8 It is said that the King is making a good recovery.
9 It has been established that a restaurant is / was the source of a food poisoning outbreak.
10 ✗

25.3

2 It is not thought that the fault is serious. (*or* It is thought that the fault is not serious.) / The fault is not thought to be serious.
3 It is expected that it will take several weeks to correct the fault. (*or* It is expected that the fault will take several weeks to correct.) / The fault is expected to take several weeks to correct.
4 It has been decided to postpone the next rocket launch.
5 It is suggested that the next launch should take place in May.

UNIT 26

26.1

1 whom
2 Which
3 Which
4 Which
5 Whom / Who ('Whom' is very formal)
6 Who
7 Which / Who
8 Who

26.2

1 are
2 teaches (whether or not the expected answer is one person or two)
3 is
4 makes
5 are / is
6 has

26.3

2 What + d
3 What / How + b
4 How + h
5 What + j
6 How + a *or* g
7 How + e *or* i
8 What + f
9 What / How + c
10 What + e *or* i

26.4

1 Whose
2 ✓
3 whose
4 Who lives *is more likely*
5 Who's
6 ✓ (*or less formally* Whose travels in Nepal did Liam Wilson write a book about?)
7 Which *is more likely*
8 Which *is more likely*
9 To whose address?
10 ✓ (What have *is also possible*)

UNIT 27

27.1

Possible answers are given

2 Didn't you get my email saying I'd be on holiday?
3 Couldn't you get a babysitter?
4 But weren't you supposed to do that last night?
5 Can't you leave it outside?
6 Wouldn't you rather go by plane?

27.2

2 Haven't you any interest in maths at all? (*or* Don't you have any interest in maths at all?) Have you no interest in maths at all? (*or* Do you have no interest in maths at all?)
3 Couldn't you find anywhere else to sleep? Could you find nowhere else to sleep?
4 Can't you remember anything about the accident? Can you remember nothing about the accident?
5 Why don't I ever do well in exams? Why do I never do well in exams?
6 Isn't there anybody you can ask for help? Is there nobody you can ask for help?

27.3

2 He's leaving when? / He's doing what? / He's what?
3 He'll be away for how long? / He'll what?
4 It'll cost how much? / It'll what?
5 He's sold (his) what? / He's done what? / He's what?
6 He's going climbing where? / He's doing what? / He's what?

27.4

1 ~~do you not~~ Why don't you (C)
2 Who do you expect ~~that~~ will read your blog? (F)
3 ✓ (F)
4 ~~Was not~~ Wasn't (D)
5 ✓ (C)
6 What did you say ~~that~~ is in these biscuits? (F)
7 ✓ (F)
8 ~~did not~~ didn't (C)

UNIT 28

28.1

2 answered (the phone)
3 eat (dinner)
4 thanked Val
5 washed (herself)
6 brushed her hair
7 changed (her clothes)
8 put on some makeup
9 drove (her car)
10 reached their house
11 waved (her hand)
12 parked (her car)
13 cooking (dinner)
14 to pick some flowers
15 studying (French)
16 mention her
17 introduce you
18 enjoyed the evening
19 afford it
20 wash up (the dishes)
21 invite Val and Tom

28.2

2 … culminated in the discovery of penicillin.
3 … differentiate between fantasy and reality.
4 … specialises in seafood.
5 … inflicted a surprise defeat on …
6 … attributed his success to …
7 … mistook the black car for …
8 … based her new novel on …

28.3

Example adjectives are given

2 satisfied; She declared herself to be satisfied with the result. / She declared that she was / is satisfied with the result.
3 inedible; They considered the food to be inedible. / They considered that the food was / is inedible.
4 reliable; I have always found him to be reliable. / I have always found that he was / is reliable.
5 happy; We believed her to be happy at school. / We believed that she was / is happy at school.

UNIT 29

29.1

In some cases other tenses are possible

2 I have to choose his clothes for him.
3 Can you take this present for / to her?
4 … pass it to me …
5 … we sold all the carpets to him as well. ('… we offered all the carpets to him …' is also possible)
6 He teaches sports to disabled children.
7 Can you read these instructions to / for me, please?
8 Jane posted the letter for me … ('Jane took the letter for me …' is also possible)
9 I offered my old bike to him …
10 Can you save some dinner for me, please?

29.2

1 He kindly collected some library books for me.
2 He admitted his error to his colleagues.
3 ✓
4 Can I ask you a favour?
5 A special ticket allows (people) entry to all the museums in the city.
6 ✓

29.3

2 his sister to me; me her photograph / her photograph to me
3 the problem to our teacher; us another half hour
4 him a paper aeroplane / a paper aeroplane for him; his broken car for him; him three bedtime stories / three bedtime stories to (*or* for) him
5 you a fortune; me the money / the money to me
6 Ben a drink / a drink for Ben; the glass to him / him the glass

UNIT 30

30.1

2 We don't approve of the developer's locating the factory so close to houses.
3 ✗
4 ✗ (not a verb of [dis]liking or thinking)
5 It is difficult to imagine his accepting the decision without any objection.
6 No one in the crowd that day will forget Ashe's fighting so hard to win the match.
7 I remember their arguing a great deal when they were children.
8 ✗ (not a verb of [dis]liking or thinking)

30.2

2 approve of children wearing
3 end by summarising
4 discouraged me from going
5 rely on Sophie turning up
6 adapt to living / adapt to dealing with life

30.3

1 burst (a single, short event)
2 watching (the context suggests that Carl was being watched before he saw the watcher; in other words, he didn't see the whole of the event)
3 sting ('stinging' is also possible, but this would suggest that the wasp stung several times)
4 feeding (this refers to a repeated event)

30.4

2 + e The new course is intended to help **people (to)** understand modern art.
3 + a Scientists hope the new drug will help **(them) (to)** prevent hay fever.
4 + f We didn't agree with the decision, but we didn't dare **(to)** protest against it.
5 + d When Ethan arrives, have **him** wait outside my office.
6 + c The dial on the left lets **you** control the speed of the fan.

UNIT 31

31.1

1 a told b threatened
2 a offered b allowed
3 a managed b persuaded
4 a encouraged b agreed
5 a reminded b pretended
6 a hoped b advised

31.2

a

When I advertised **for** a website designer for the business, Greta got the job. But I've now learnt that you can't rely **on** Greta to do anything. I waited ages **for** her to come up with some initial ideas for the site, and then I had to keep on **at** her to do any more work on it. Finally, she said she couldn't do it after all.

b

Managers of the National Electricity Company have appealed **to** workers to end their strike, and have called **on** the government to intervene in the dispute. The Energy Minister said that he has arranged **for** employers and employees to meet next week, and he prevailed **on** strikers to return to work in the meantime.

31.3

1 agreed not to tell
2 are / were thought to have escaped
3 don't recall seeing / don't recall having seen (similar meanings)
4 denies / denied having received *or* denies / denied receiving (similar meanings)
5 asked not to be named
6 didn't feel like walking
7 seems to have disappeared
8 are / were believed to have arrived

UNIT 32

32.1

The most likely reporting verbs are given in the answers, but others are possible.

2 'Why don't we stop for a coffee?' she suggested.
3 'All right, Georgia, it was me,' he confessed.

4 'My novel is more exciting than a Dan Brown thriller,' she boasted.
5 'I always carry two umbrellas with me because I'm always losing them,' explained Lena. / … Lena explained.
6 'Oh, no, it's raining again,' grumbled Matt. / … Matt grumbled.
7 'Good morning, Miss Novak,' chorused the children. / … the children chorused.
8 'Have I done the right thing?' I wondered.

32.2
2 threatened not to repay
3 didn't feel – could (*more likely than* He felt that he couldn't ask his parents to help him again.)
4 insisted – wasn't (*or* hadn't been)
5 announced – wasn't going
6 didn't expect – to be (*more likely than* He expected his mother not to be angry.)
7 didn't think – would (*more likely than* She thought Adam wouldn't mind waiting.)
8 promised – wouldn't

32.3
1 'how I heard about the job' is also possible
2 what my long-term career plans were / what were my long-term career plans
3 how many languages I spoke / speak
4 where I (had) learnt / learned Chinese
5 if / whether I could use a spreadsheet
6 if / whether I had organised international conferences before
7 if / whether I would be willing to live overseas for periods of time
8 when I can / could start work

UNIT 33

33.1
1 advised
2 assured / promised
3 warned
4 inform / teach
5 have shown
6 has reassured / has advised
7 promised

33.2
2 ✗
3 The judge thought his explanation to be unconvincing.
4 I expected her plans to fail.
5 ✗
6 Lucas acknowledged his chances of winning the race to be slim.
7 We found the rugby supporters to be very well behaved.
8 ✗

33.3
Likely answers are given
1 complained to
2 complained to; mentioned to; announced to
3 joked with; announced to; mentioned to
4 announced to
5 requires of
6 disagreed with
7 mention to

33.4
Possible necessary objects are given in bold
1 has warned that they
2 explained to employees that
3 confessed to her audience that
4 denied that management
5 replied that an announcement
6 reassured **employees / them** that
7 went on to complain that government help
8 demanded of ministers that ('demanded that ministers provide' would also be possible and less formal)
9 asked of staff that ('asked staff to continue' would also be possible and less formal)
10 reassured **staff / them** that

Note that alternatives without' that' (1 has warned they, 2 explained to employees, etc.) are grammatical, but less likely in a formal written context.

UNIT 34

34.1
Added objects are in bold
2 + j He took my hands and showed **me** *how / where* to hold the golf club properly.
3 + g I explained carefully so that the students understood *what* they had to do in the test.
4 + i Anna was new in the office and I had to keep reminding **her** *who* everyone was.
5 + b I saw Sarah leave the building, but I didn't notice *where* she went after that.
6 + e When I saw Hugo alone at the party I wondered *why* Helen wasn't with him.
7 + h As we walked over the hills the guide warned **us** *where / when* the path was dangerous.
8 + a After I'd dismantled the motor I couldn't remember *how* to fit the parts back together.
9 + f To win a prize you had to guess *how* many sweets were in the jar.
10 + c As the guests came in Diego told **them** *where* to put their coats.

34.2
1 debating
2 discuss
3 considering
4 choose
5 decide

34.3
The villagers warned **me** what the conditions were like at higher altitudes, and advised **me** to take enough food for a week. There was some discussion through the day as **to** whether the snow would arrive before my descent from the mountain, but I never imagined how hard the conditions would be. In the morning they showed me (**the way / how**: *one of these must be deleted*) to get to the track up the mountain.
When the snow started falling it was very light, and I couldn't decide ~~if~~ **whether** to carry on or go back down. Soon, however, I couldn't see where to go.
I wondered ~~if~~ **whether** to retrace my steps and try to find the track again, but by the time I decided ~~whether~~ **that** I should go back, the track had disappeared. As the snow got heavier I began to realise ~~whether~~ **that** my life was in danger. Fortunately, my years in the Andes had taught **me** what to do in extreme conditions. I knew that there was a shepherd's hut somewhere on this side of the mountain that I could shelter in, but I didn't know ~~that~~ **whether** it was nearby or miles away.

UNIT 35

35.1
2 She alleged that Markus had stolen / stole jewellery from her house.
3 She estimated that the vase was ('is' is also possible) around 250 years old.
4 She repeated that she had already seen the film.
5 She conceded that perhaps she treated / had treated Lara unkindly.
6 She recalled that Wilma's great-grandmother was / had been from Spain.

35.2
1 have solved
2 states
3 has
4 understand
5 looks
6 is / was

35.3
1 When I mentioned to Nokes that he **had been seen ✓** (*or* **was seen**) in a local shop last Monday, he protested that he ~~is~~ **was** at home all day. He swears that he ~~didn't own~~ **doesn't own** a blue Ford Focus. He claimed that he **had been ✓** (*or* **went**) to the paint factory two weeks ago to look for work. Nokes alleges that he **is** ✓ a good friend of Jamie Barnes. He

insisted that he **didn't telephone** ✓ (*or* **hadn't telephoned**) Barnes last Monday morning. When I pointed out to Nokes that a large quantity of paint **had been found** ✓ (*or* **was found**) in his house, he replied that he ~~is storing~~ **had been storing** (*or* **was storing**) it for a friend.

2 At the beginning of the interview I reminded Barnes that he **is** ✓ (*or* **was**) entitled to have a lawyer present. He denied that he **knew** ✓ (*or* **knows**) anyone by the name of Daniel Nokes. Barnes confirmed that he ~~is~~ **had been** (*or* **was**) in the area of the paint factory last Monday, but said that he ~~is visiting~~ **was visiting** (*or* **had been visiting**) his mother. He admitted that he ~~is walking~~ **was walking** (*or* **had been walking**) along New Street at around ten. He maintains that he ~~was~~ **is** a very honest person and would never be involved in anything illegal.

UNIT 36

36.1

The most likely answers are given. Possible objects are given in bold.

2 He agreed to collect Declan from school.
3 He ordered **us** to be quiet.
4 He urged **me** to stay for a few more days.
5 He vowed to fight the ban on smoking in public places.
6 He expected / hoped to see Olivia at the party.
7 He asked **me** to lend him ten pounds. (*or* He asked to borrow ten pounds.)
8 He called on **the government** to do more to help the homeless.
9 He hoped / expected to avoid the heavy traffic (by leaving early).

36.2

1 ~~suggested~~ promised
2 ✓
3 ~~intended~~ said / promised
4 ~~insisted~~ expected
5 ~~demanded~~ ordered
6 ~~wanted~~ hoped
7 ✓
8 ~~offered~~ proposed / ordered

36.3

Example answers

2 … reducing bus and train fares.
3 … seeing it.
4 … buying a guide book.
5 … going to the doctor.
6 … building it to the east of the city.
7 … doing more exercise.
8 … going for a long walk.

The verb 'propose' can be followed by a **to-infinitive** without an object (see A). For example:

2 To encourage people to use public transport the council proposed to reduce bus and train fares.
6 The city urgently needs a new airport, and the government proposes to build it to the east of the city.

UNIT 37

37.1

1 will
2 may / might
3 can
4 would
5 couldn't
6 can / could
7 will / would

37.2

2 She promised that she wouldn't be late …
3 He suggested that we could go to Paris for the weekend …
4 She guaranteed that she could get me there in good time …
5 He insisted that he would pay for the meal …

Sentences 2 and 4 have alternatives with a *to*-infinitive clause:

2 She promised not to be late…
4 She guaranteed to get us there in good time…

37.3

2 (that) she would be there this time.
3 had to be in the city centre by one ('must be' is also possible, but less natural)
4 asked where we should meet
5 mustn't forget to bring my student discount card

37.4

2 She said that I could / can travel with them.
3 She said that she wouldn't answer his questions.
4 She said that Karl would / should / ought to be back soon.
5 She said that she may / might / could have to move to Milan.
6 She said that she couldn't / wouldn't accept that Jason is / was dishonest.
7 She said that Maria would / will be disappointed if we leave / left without seeing her.

UNIT 38

38.1

2 He failed to address the question / issue of who would / should pay for the repairs to the building.
3 I was delighted to get an invitation to spend the holidays with them in Scotland.
4 I think it was Aristotle who made the observation that there's no such thing as bad publicity.
5 Amazingly the police accepted Rudi's explanation that he had taken the wallet by mistake.
6 On the webinar they debated the issue / question of whether assisted suicide should be a criminal offence.
7 The letter from the company gave a final warning that I should pay the bill by the end of the week. / … to pay the bill by the end of the week.
8 The government has broken its promise to reduce the rate of income tax. / … that it would reduce the rate of income tax.
9 The positive reaction to my work gave me considerable encouragement to take up photography as a career.
10 Waiting passengers were angry when they heard the announcement that the flight was cancelled. (*or* … had been cancelled).

38.2

2 There has been a great deal of argument as to how to define poverty.
3 There have been months of speculation as to whether President Malik would stand again.
4 Scientists might come to a / some conclusion as to what their results imply.
5 There is still no definite explanation as to why the dinosaurs disappeared.

38.3

1 unsure whether *or* not certain whether *are also possible*
2 dismissive of
3 adamant that
4 unsure how / not certain how
5 angry that / apologetic that
6 apologetic about
7 not certain when / unsure when
8 abusive to / towards
9 complimentary about
10 agreed that / adamant that

UNIT 39

39.1

The most likely answers are given

2 Lee urged that Mara Bianchi should be promoted to export manager.
3 Alice recommended that a sales representative should be sent to South Africa.
4 Alice reported that the Delaware Bridge project should be completed by August next year.
5 Simon insisted that work schedules should be kept to.
6 Simon instructed that all monthly reports should be sent to him directly.

7 Alina suggested that web conferencing should be used for meetings to save money on air fares.
8 Alina declared that the company's head office should remain in London.
9 Nathan agreed that the company should sponsor the European chess league for the next three years.
10 Nathan announced that in future all claims for travel expenses should be made in US dollars.

39.2

2	Yes	7	Yes
3	Yes	8	No
4	No	9	No
5	Yes	10	No
6	Yes		

39.3

Possible adjectives are given in these answers

2 I am shocked that Kristina should behave so badly.
3 I am astounded that anyone should vote for him.
4 It is urgent that he should return home immediately.
5 I am amused that he should take his appearance so seriously.
6 I am upset that they should think I had cheated them.
7 It is appalling that they should be allowed to go free.
8 It is imperative that we should act now to avoid war.

UNIT 40

40.1

2 ~~*is*~~ are
3 ~~*remain*~~ remains
4 ✓
5 ~~*is*~~ are
6 ~~*let*~~ lets
7 ✓
8 ~~*are*~~ is
9 ~~*are*~~ is
10 ~~*have*~~ has
11 ✓
12 ~~*is*~~ are
13 ~~*add*~~ adds

40.2

2 university refuse / refuses
3 audience … is (A singular verb form is more likely here as the focus is on the audience as a whole rather than individual members.)
4 orchestra perform / performs
5 jury includes (A singular verb form is used here as 'include' focuses on the group as a whole rather than individual members.)
6 class have (A plural verb form is used as this is something the individuals did, emphasised by the use of 'all'.)
7 press presents / present
8 The United Nations has / have

40.3

1 ~~come~~ comes
2 ✓
3 ~~report~~ reports
4 ~~are~~ is
5 ✓
6 ✓
7 ~~have~~ has
8 ~~are~~ is
9 ✓ ('… need to be kept …' is also possible)
10 ~~are~~ is

UNIT 41

41.1

1
b his early paintings remains / remain
c the food tastes
d Dr Jones's acquaintances knows

2
a vegetarians is expected
b medicines relieve
c victims … exceeds
d museums in the capital charge

3
a the pieces lasts / last
b player tries
c the cars are / is tested
d these factors influence/influences

41.2

1 are; wants
2 think; has (more likely than 'have' in this formal context)
3 has / have; has
4 claim; constitutes (more likely than 'constitute' as 'the wreck of the ship and its cargo' constitute together, as a single item, a danger)
5 is / are (we use 'is' if we think of 'sausages and chips' as a single item); have; are / 's

UNIT 42

42.1

1 ✓ ('are' is also possible)
2 ✓
3 have
4 ✓ ('were' is also possible)
5 go
6 are
7 ✓ ('has' is also possible)
8 are
9 say

42.2

1 (singular) is
2 (plural) are
3 (singular) is
4 (singular) has
5 (singular) is
6 (plural) provide / offer

42.3

1 have; have; shop / shops
2 is ('are' is also possible, but less likely); expect / expects
3 is; blames / blame
4 was ('were' is also possible, but less likely); has / have
5 admit / admits; were; was
6 were; have
7 shows; is; believe
8 have; says / say; are

UNIT 43

43.1

1 a ✓
b a computer programmer
c a film star
2 a ✓
b girls' school
c the car door
d a cut on the / her head
3 a ✓
b ✓
c a bottle of milk
d a packet of biscuits
e some toothpaste
f ✓
4 a ✓
b songs about pollution ('pollution songs' is not a well-known class of songs)
5 a tool shed
b spiders' webs
6 a armchair
b ✓
c the 500-piece jigsaw puzzle
d glasses case

43.2

1 cover up
2 broken out
3 stopping over
4 get together
5 stopover (related to 3)
6 get-together (4)
7 cover-up (1)
8 outbreak (2)

43.3

2 middle-of-the-road
3 round-the-clock
4 step-by-step
5 once-in-a-lifetime
6 down-to-earth
7 man / woman-in-the-street (*an alternative is* 'man or woman in the street', usually without hyphens)
8 larger-than-life

UNIT 44

44.1

1 an
2 a
3 an
4 a
5 a ('MiG' is said /mɪg/)
6 an
7 an
8 a
9 an
10 a
11 a
12 an
13 an
14 a

44.2

1 ~~one~~ a
2 ✓
3 ~~a~~ one
4 ~~one~~ an
5 ✓
6 ~~one~~ a
7 ~~one~~ a ('one' would imply 'one and no more'; 'a' is more likely if this is a more general invitation to 'have some cake')
8 ✓ ('one' implies 'one and only one')
9 ✓ (both 'one' and 'a' are possible)
10 ~~one~~ a
11 ~~one~~ a ('one' would emphasise the number and seems less likely than 'a' in this context)
12 ✓ (both 'one' and 'a' are possible)
13 ~~a~~ one
14 ~~one~~ a
15 ~~a~~ one
16 ✓ (both 'one' and 'a' are possible)

44.3

1 one / a
2 one
3 one
4 one / an
5 a
6 one
7 one / a
8 an
9 one
10 one
11 one / a
12 A

UNIT 45

45.1

1 a the world b a world
2 a a bright future b the future
3 a the past b a past
4 a a deserted beach
b the beach ('a beach' is also possible here, meaning a particular but unspecified beach)

45.2

1 a customer
2 the individual / an individual (similar meaning)
3 the car
4 The television
5 the smoker

45.3

2 pleasure
3 a sound
4 grammar
5 iron
6 Sound
7 a real pleasure
8 a grammar
9 an iron
10 conversation

UNIT 46

46.1

1 an author
2 ~~the~~ a / – minister
3 a Mac
4 Not the George Clooney
5 a Van Gogh
6 ✓
7 the Nielsens
8 ~~the~~ a / – Usain Bolt

46.2

1 a / the / – ('a' suggests that there are a number of marketing advisers; 'the' or '–' indicate that there is only one)
2 the / –
3 the / –
4 the / – (in journalism)
5 –
6 – ; –
7 –
8 A / –

46.3

1 the
2 (the)
3 (the)
4 the
5 (the)
6 (the)
7 the
8 the

46.4

1 this / a
2 –
3 – ('this' would be unlikely here as the paint is not the topic of what comes next)
4 the / –
5 a / –
6 a
7 the
8 a / this ('this' introduces the woman as the focus of the next part of the story)
9 the / –
10 the / –

UNIT 47

47.1

1 a Children (a general reference; specific children are not referred to)
b the children (a specific reference, probably to my/our children)
2 a the agriculture (a reference to the agriculture in a specific area)
b agriculture (a general reference)
3 a islands (reference to islands generally)
b The islands (reference to a specific group of islands)
4 a the holidays (specific reference; the holidays that are coming soon)
b Holidays (a general reference to holidays in this part of the world)
5 a rain (a general reference)
b the rain (reference to a specific, understood period of rain)
6 a the money (reference to a specific, understood sum of money)
b money (an observation on the effect of money generally)
7 a Parents (= a general reference)
b The parents (a specific reference to particular parents)
8 a the fire (reference to a specific fire)
b fire (a general reference)

47.2

1 – ('all afternoon' is more likely than 'all the afternoon')
2 a
3 the
4 the
5 the
6 –
7 the
8 –
9 the / – ('the winter' might imply 'the coming winter'. However, both 'winter' and 'the winter' might be a generalisation meaning 'any winter')
10 a

47.3

1 an email
2 by car / by air
3 the air
4 the post / an email
5 by post / by email
6 the car
7 by email
8 by air

UNIT 48

48.1

1 some books
2 ~~some~~
3 ~~some~~
4 ✓
5 Some sports
6 ✓
7 ~~some~~
8 Some children

48.2

Suggested answers are given

2 Some 30% of all city buses have been found to be unsafe.
3 An unexploded bomb has been found some five miles from the centre of Newham.
4 Some 25% of electricity will come from wind energy by 2025.
5 Some 200 jobs are to be lost at the Encon steelworks.

48.3

Suggested answers are given

2 He's probably out with some girlfriend or other.
3 Maybe I lent it to some student in my geography class.
4 I think it's in some travel agent's in the High Street.
5 Perhaps she's got to finish some report or other.

48.4

1 any
2 any / some ('any' suggests that I could eat none of the food; 'some' implies that I was able to eat some but not all of it)
3 anything
4 someone ('positive' meaning)
5 anything / something ('anything' suggests that he said that he did nothing at all wrong; 'something' suggests that he has been accused of a particular wrongdoing but denied this)
6 anyone
7 any
8 any
9 Some (= not all)
10 anyone / someone ('anyone' suggests that I don't want to lend it to any person; 'someone' suggests that I may have a particular person in mind (perhaps they have asked me to lend it to them))

UNIT 49

49.1

2 … no one heard …
3 Not a drop …
4 … no point …
5 … nowhere else …
6 … none of the hotels …
7 … never going to get …
8 … nothing wrong …

49.2

1 There aren't any in the cupboard.
4 … there wasn't any point in protesting.
5 … he didn't have anywhere else to go.
7 Isn't he ever going to get a job? (*or* Is he ever going to get a job?)
8 … they couldn't find anything wrong with her.

49.3

1 are no jobs
2 are no trains or buses
3 no seatbelts
4 was no spare tyre
5 ✓
6 ✓
7 are no trees
8 was no swimming pool
9 was no television
10 ✓
11 was no reply
12 ✓
13 was no choice

49.4

Possible answers

2 Mr Carlson didn't want to sell the painting, and no amount of money / persuading could make him change his mind.
3 I sent job applications to over a hundred companies, but not one of them invited me for an interview.
4 Smallpox used to be common all over the world but since 1978 not one case of the disease has been recorded.
5 The floor had dirty black marks all over it, and no amount of polishing could get it clean.

49.5

1 No problem. / No bother.
2 No wonder.
3 No chance. / No way.
4 No idea.
5 No comment.

UNIT 50

50.1

Suggested corrections/improvements are given

1 Lola's had ~~many~~ **a lot of** (more usual than 'many' in conversation) problems with her back for ~~a lot of~~ **many** years. She's having an operation next week and she won't be back at work for ~~a good deal of~~ a **good many** weeks afterwards.
2 A: There's bound to be ~~much~~ **a lot of / lots of** traffic on the way to the station. Perhaps we should leave now.
B: No, there's plenty **of** time left, and at this time of day ~~many~~ **a lot of / lots of** people will already be at work.
3 ~~Many~~ **A lot of / Lots of** (more usual than 'many' in conversation) **people** think that hedgehogs are very rare nowadays, but when I was in Wales I saw ~~many~~ **a lot / lots** (more usual than 'many' in conversation).
4 ~~A lot~~ **Many** have claimed that Professor Dowman's study on current attitudes to politics is flawed. One criticism is that ~~much~~ **far** too many people questioned in the survey were under 18.
5 ~~A lot of~~ **Much** research has been conducted on the effects of diet on health, with ~~a lot of~~ **many** studies focusing on the link between fat intake and heart disease. However, ~~a lot~~ **much** remains to be done. ('much' and 'many' are preferred in a written academic context).
6 While it is true that ~~a lot of~~ **many** thousands of jobs were lost with the decline of the northern coal and steel industries, ~~a lot of~~ **many** advantages have also followed. ~~Much~~ **Far** too many cases of lung disease were recorded in the region, but with lower levels of pollution the number has declined. In addition, a ~~great deal of~~ **a great many** hi-tech companies have moved in to take advantage of the newly available workforce.

50.2

2 many a sunny afternoon
3 Many a ship
4 its / the many golf courses
5 my many emails
6 his many expeditions ('many an expedition' is also possible)
7 Many a teacher
8 the many coffee shops

50.3

1 plenty of ('a lot of' is also possible)
2 A lot of (not 'plenty of')
3 a lot of (not 'plenty of')
4 a lot of (not 'plenty of')
5 plenty of ('a lot of' is also possible)

UNIT 51

51.1

1 were all
2 can all
3 had all
4 are all
5 All the children *or* The children all (both are possible)
6 all been

51.2

1 The whole process
2 Whole areas of the country
3 The whole trip
4 all of the towns
5 all of the pages
6 all the building / the whole building ('all the building' suggests that we see the building as being made up of parts (a number of rooms, for example); 'the whole building' would be more likely in a formal context)
7 The whole room

51.3

1 every
2 each
3 every
4 each / every
5 each
6 every
7 each / every
8 each
9 Every / Each
10 every

(In 4, 7, and 9 'each' emphasises that we are thinking of the places / children / households separately; 'every' suggests something like 'all of'.)

51.4

1 Every so often
2 ✓
3 every few weeks
4 ✓ ('all Friday' is possible in an informal context; 'the whole of Friday' would also be possible here)
5 each of them
6 not all the food usually gets eaten
7 Not all of my brothers always come
8 Neil and his family were all on holiday
9 the rest of us all had a great time
10 ✓ ('all evening' would also be possible)

UNIT 52

52.1

1 few ('a few' would mean that a small number of people would disagree. It would be more likely after 'but …' than 'and …')
2 Little
3 few
4 the few / a few
5 A little
6 The few / What few
7 a little
8 a few
9 a few
10 the little / what little

52.2

Most likely changes are given

1 '… a bit of TV …' (more likely in this informal context)
2 … there are only a few left *or*… there aren't many left.
3 … there isn't much more … *or*… there's not much more …
4 … not many like that … *or* … only a few like that …
5 … has had few female politicians …
6 … exchanged few words …
7 … a little more confident …
8 There seems to be little prospect …

52.3

Possible answers

1 Fewer students had a part-time job in 2000 than now. ('Less students …' would also be acceptable for some people) Less (*or* Fewer) than 10% of female students had a part-time job in 2000.
2 Male students spend less money than female students on books. Students spend less on books now than they did in 2000.
3 Less (or Fewer) than 10% of female students walk to lectures now. Fewer students walk to lectures now than in 1980. ('Less students …' would also be acceptable for some people)
4 Male students spend less time online now than female students.

Surprising results might be:

Female students now spend no less than 20% of their income on books.
Female students spend no less than 24 hours a week online.

UNIT 53

53.1

The relative pronoun can be omitted in 1, 3, 4, 7 and 10.

53.2

1 ('that' or '–' are more likely in an informal context)
2 Eva's father, who is over 80, has just come back from a skiing holiday.
3 The problems faced by the company, which I'll look at in detail in a moment, are being resolved. (some people would use 'that' as an alternative)
4 She was greatly influenced by her father, who / whom she adored. ('whom' is formal)
5 He pointed to the stairs which / that led down to the cellar.
6 These drugs, which are used to treat stomach ulcers, have been withdrawn from sale. (some people would use 'that' as an alternative)
7 The singer, who was recovering from flu, had to cancel her concert.
8 The minister talked about the plans for tax reform that / which / – he will reveal next month. ('which' is more likely in a formal context)
9 I have two older sisters whom / who / that / – I love very much. ('whom' is very formal)

53.3

1 'which' is possible, but less likely than 'that' or '–'
2 'whom' seems rather formal here and less likely than 'who', 'that', or '–'
3 ✓ 'that I can' is also possible
4 … much that can …
5 ~~whom~~ who
6 ~~which~~ 'that' or '–'
7 The boy who took …
8 'which' is possible, but less likely than 'that' or '–'
9 'which' is possible, but less likely than 'that'
10 'which' is possible, but less likely than 'that' or '–'

UNIT 54

54.1

2 + a The newspaper is owned by the Mears group, whose chairperson is Miss Jiu Kim.
3 + f Parents whose children are between four and six are being asked to take part in the survey.
4 + b Children whose diets contain high levels of protein do better in examinations.
5 + e My aunt, whose first job was filling shelves in a supermarket, is now CEO of a department store.
6 + c I enjoy growing plants whose flowers are attractive to bees.

54.2

Example answers

2 A widow is a woman whose husband has died and who has not remarried.
3 An actuary is a person whose job is to decide how much insurance companies should charge their customers.
4 A furnace is a container in which things are melted or burnt.
5 A gazebo is a small garden building in which people can sit to enjoy the view.
6 Polo is a sport in which horse riders hit a ball using hammers with long handles.

54.3

1 the moment when
2 an agreement whereby
3 the area where
4 the reason why
5 a method whereby
6 a condition where

54.4

1 ~~whatever~~ whoever
2 ~~that~~ what
3 ✓
4 ~~which~~ whatever (or 'what')
5 ~~whichever~~ whatever
6 ✓ (or 'no relative pronoun' or 'which')
7 ~~what~~ that
8 ~~which~~ whichever / whatever

UNIT 55

55.1

2 He was the uncle of Anne Boleyn, after whose execution in 1536 he lost power.
3 It is her unmarried name by which she is better known.
4 Mr Wang, across whose land the road will be built, is very unhappy about the plans.
5 The election result, about which there can be no doubt, is a great disappointment.
6 The building from which Marcus emerged was little more than a ruin.
7 It is a medieval palace, in whose tower the king hid during the civil war.
8 I am grateful to Aarav Basu, from whose book on the history of the bicycle this information comes.

55.2

2 Until 1914 the pound sterling was the currency in / with which most world trade was conducted.
3 They have changed the date on / by which the furniture is to be delivered.
4 Pasteurisation was discovered by the French chemist Louis Pasteur, after whom it was named.
5 He was persuaded to stay in England by Charles Dickens, to whom he had shown his novel.
6 There are a number of safety procedures of which you should be aware.
7 Details are in the instruction manual with which the printer was supplied.
8 Ms Park was left the money by her former husband, from whom she was divorced in 2005.

55.3

2 Until 1914 the pound sterling was the currency which / that most world trade was conducted in.
3 They have changed the date which / that / – the furniture is to be delivered on / by.
4 Pasteurisation was discovered by the French chemist Louis Pasteur, who it was named after.
5 He was persuaded to stay in England by Charles Dickens, who he had shown his novel to.
6 There are number of safety procedures which / that / – you should be aware of.
7 Details are in the instruction manual which / that / – the printer was supplied with.
8 Ms Park was left the money by her former husband, who she was divorced from in 2005.

55.4

1 The house which the thieves broke into …
2 ✓
3 … first of which …
4 The party, which I've been looking forward to all week …
5 ✓
6 … both of which …
7 … part of which …
8 … all of whom …

UNIT 56

56.1

The most likely answers are given

2 I went on an IT training course with my colleague Mateo.
3 Rubella, or German measles, is still a common childhood disease in many countries.
4 Four kilos of Beluga caviar, among the most expensive foods in the world, has been ordered for the reception.
5 One of the most popular modern writers for children is the Australian John Marsden.
6 Tonya's father, and (her) trainer for the last ten years, was in the crowd to watch her victory.
7 Dr Sofia Lopez, head of Downlands Hospital, has criticised government plans to cut health funding.
8 Klaus Schmidt, the German 10,000 metres record holder and current European champion, is running in the Stockholm Marathon. (*or* Klaus Schmidt, the current European champion and (the) German 10,000 metres record holder, …)

56.2

2 + d The two countries having land borders with the USA, namely / that is Mexico and Canada, have complained to the President about the new customs regulations.
3 + a The three most popular pets in Britain, namely / that is cats, dogs and rabbits, are found in 25% of households.
4 + f The capital of Estonia, namely / that is Tallinn, is situated on the Gulf of Finland.
5 + b The largest island in the world, namely / that is Greenland, covers over 2 million square kilometres.
6 + c The 'consumers' of education, namely / that is students, should have ways of complaining about poor teaching.

56.3

2 educated; I went to a reunion for students who were educated in the physics department during the 1990s.
3 being told off; As my aunt told me what she thought, I felt like a schoolboy who was being told off by his headteacher.
4 saying; There is a sign on the gate which says 'Entry forbidden'.
5 introduced; Across the river were some of the deer which were introduced into the park in the 19th century.
6 flowing; Rivers which flow into the Baltic Sea are much cleaner now than ten years ago.
7 being printed; The booklets which are being printed as we speak will be on sale later this afternoon.
8 needing; Anyone who needs further information can see me in my office.

UNIT 57

57.1

The most likely answers are given

2 + e She's in the photograph on the piano.
3 + b I plan to cut down the tree in the back garden
4 + a There's a team of people in green shirts.
5 + d We took the footpath by / along the canal.
6 + i The children can't get over the fence around the pool.
7 + g Go along the lane between the houses.
8 + j Nico's a boy with a quick temper.
9 + f Follow the main road from Paris to Lyons.
10 + h She's a teacher from New Zealand.

57.2

2 She's in the photograph which is on the piano.
3 I plan to cut down the tree which is in the back garden.
4 There's a team of people who have / are wearing green shirts.
5 We took the footpath which runs / goes by / along the canal.
6 The children can't get over the fence which is around the pool.
7 Go along the lane which runs between the houses.
8 Nico's a boy who has a quick temper.
9 Follow the main road which runs / goes from Paris to Lyons.
10 She's a teacher who is / comes from New Zealand.

57.3

Possible answers are given with some alternatives

2 Teachers (who work / working) at Queen's College in the city centre, who went on strike last week, have appointed Kristina Borg, the head of English, as their spokesperson.
3 Marge Scott, who has died aged 95, was the first woman (to be) educated at Marston College in south Wales. / Marge Scott, the first woman (to be) educated at Marston College in south Wales, has died aged 95.
4 The conference (held) in Singapore, which approved the world trade agreement drawn up by European and Asian states, has now ended.
5 A book on gardening, *All about Plants*, that / which Anna wanted to borrow, wasn't available in the library. / A book on gardening called *All about Plants* that / which Anna wanted to borrow wasn't available in the library.

6 A painting found in a second-hand shop by Lara Gruber, an antique dealer from Austria, is thought to be by J.M.W. Turner, the British landscape artist. (*or*… by the British landscape artist J.M.W. Turner.)

57.4

1 The sentence could mean: (i) that a man was wearing a grey suit – he was talking; (ii) (the ridiculous) that a man was talking with a grey suit. To remove the ambiguity the sentence should be: A man (who was) wearing a grey suit was talking. / A man in a grey suit was talking.

2 The sentence could mean: (i) that the lorry was carrying thousands of stolen cigarettes – it was stopped by a police officer; (ii) (the ridiculous) that the police officer was carrying thousands of stolen cigarettes at the time s/he stopped the lorry. To remove the ambiguity the sentence should be: A lorry (which was) carrying thousands of stolen cigarettes was stopped by a police officer.

3 The sentence could mean: (i) that I am going to discuss the matter with my parents; (ii) that I am going to decorate the room and my parents will help decorate it with me; (iii) (the ridiculous) that I am going to use my parents as decoration in the room! To remove the ambiguity the sentence should be: I discussed with my parents my plan to decorate the room. (to mean [i]) *or* I discussed my plan to decorate the room with the help of my parents (to mean [ii]).

UNIT 58

58.1

2 Dressed (*or* Being dressed) all in black, she was almost invisible in the starless night.
3 Not having a credit card, I found it difficult to book an airline ticket online.
4 Being unemployed, Antonio spent a lot of time filling in job application forms.
5 Walking quickly, I soon caught up with her.
6 Built of wood (*or* Being built of wood …), the house was clearly a fire risk.
7 Having been told off the day before for arriving late, I was eager to catch the bus in good time.
8 Not knowing where the theatre was, she asked for directions at the hotel reception.
9 Being a nurse, she knew what to do after the accident.
10 Having spent his childhood in Oslo, he knew the city well.

58.2

1 D (first implied subject = 'I'; second subject = 'a car') Waiting for the bus, I was splashed all over by a car that went through a puddle. / While I was waiting for the bus, a car went through a puddle and splashed water all over me.
2 S (subject in both clauses = 'Rashid')
3 S (subject in both clauses = 'Suzanne')
4 D (first implied subject 'we'; second subject = 'the town') Looking down from the hill, we could see the town spread out before us towards the coast. / As we looked down from the hill, we could see the town spread out before us towards the coast.
5 D (first implied subject = 'I'; second subject = 'the boat') I was feeling rather sick as the boat ploughed through the huge waves.
6 S (subject in both clauses = 'the plant')

58.3

1 Not wishing to boast …
2 Pretending not to notice …
3 Determined not to be beaten …
4 Not feeling well …
5 Not bothering to put on his coat …
6 Trying not to cry …

58.4

2 + c Looking over my shoulder, I could see Ida running after me.
3 + f Walking through the tunnel, I banged my head on the low roof.
4 + a Having waited six weeks for the washing machine to be delivered, I decided to cancel the order.
5 + g Having suffered from depression myself as a teenager, I could understand how Nathan was feeling.
6 + h Having parked / Parking the car about a kilometre from the stadium, I walked the rest of the way.
7 + b Having reached / Reaching my mid-thirties, I felt I needed to change my life.
8 + e Having learnt some Swahili as a child, I was able to understand most of what she said.

UNIT 59

59.1

2 While being interviewed …
3 Before taking …
4 While welcoming …
5 Since being overthrown … (*or* After being overthrown …)
6 Through working … (*or* After working …)
7 Before being sold …
8 After leaving …

59.2

2 + a By giving up sugar, she soon began to lose weight.
3 + e In turning down the job, she gave up the possibility of a huge salary. ('By turning down' is also possible. However, 'In turning down' focuses on the consequence of the action and so is perhaps more likely here.)
4 + b By moving to a smaller flat, she saved over a hundred pounds a month. ('In moving …' is also possible. However, 'By moving …'focuses on the method used to save money.)
5 + f On entering the classroom, she was surprised when all the children stood up.
6 + c In criticising her father, she knew that she might offend him. ('By criticising' is also possible. However, 'In criticising' focuses on the consequence of the action and so is perhaps more likely here.)

59.3

1 With Maryam having flu, we couldn't go on holiday.
2 Without having more information, I won't be able to advise you.
3 Without realising it, he had solved the problem.
4 With time running out before the train left, I couldn't wait for Andrei any longer.

59.4

(1) Although from a poor background, Paula Regis gained a place at Southam University. (2) Always fascinated by the stars, she took a first degree in astrophysics. (3) Once at university she also became interested in student politics and, (4) popular with her fellow students, was elected University President in her second year. This didn't distract her from her studies, however, and (5) while in the final year of her degree, she won the International Young Scientist of the Year award for her work on star classification. (6) When asked what was (*or* When asked about …) the secret of her success (*or* When asked what the secret of her success was …) she said, 'Just hard work and a little luck.' (7) Determined to continue her research, she has recently begun work on her PhD.

UNIT 60

60.1

2 prepared (herself)
3 prides itself on
4 occupied themselves with / by ('with' and 'by' could be omitted: 'occupied themselves playing computer games')

5 adapt (yourself)
6 trouble himself about / with
7 dress (herself)
8 absent himself from

60.2
1 me
2 myself
3 us
4 them
5 yourself
6 himself ('him' is also possible if ' he' and 'him' refer to different people)
7 herself ('her' is also possible if ' she' and 'her' refer to different people)
8 me

60.3
1 got ourselves vaccinated / got vaccinated
2 ✓
3 had themselves checked
4 he'd caught hepatitis himself
5 ✓ (however, some people think this is incorrect and would use 'Jan and I')
6 to tear himself away
7 we're going to occupy ourselves
8 they can't reach it themselves

UNIT 61

61.1
1 ~~ones~~ some
2 ✓
3 ~~ones~~ some
4 … mint ~~one~~ … / … some mint …
5 ✓
6 ✓
7 ~~ones~~ one
8 ~~ones~~ some

61.2
1 ones
2 ones (Some people would avoid this use of 'ones' to refer to people.)
3 No
4 one
5 No ('ones' would be unlikely here, referring to a group of people)
6 ones
7 one
8 No
9 No
10 No ('your ones' is possible, but some people avoid it. 'Are these yours?' is much more likely)

61.3
3 (ones) Note that some people think that 'those ones' is incorrect.
4 (one)
5 ✓
6 (one)
7 ✓
8 (ones)
9 (ones)
10 (one)

61.4
Possible answers
1 … one who knew the way.
2 … ones you have to drive to.
3 … one is the burning of fossil fuels.
4 … ones are small and lightweight

UNIT 62

62.1
2 'I doubt it' is also possible.
3 I hope so.
4 I suppose so.
5 I think so.
6 Yes, I hear (that) she is. ('So I hear' is also possible; see E)
7 I guess so.
8 He says so.
9 I promise (that) I will.
10 I'm sure (that) you will.

62.2
1 suppose not / don't suppose so
2 don't think so / think not ('think not' would be rather formal)
3 suspect not / don't suspect so
4 doesn't appear so / appears not
5 didn't say so

62.3
2 Yes, they are.
3 Yes, it has. / So it has.
4 Yes, you did.

62.4
Possible answers
2 So I understand.
3 So I gather.
4 So it appears.
5 So he tells me.

UNIT 63

63.1
2 She was asked to teach more classes, and was happy to do so.
3 My French hosts gave me snails to eat, but I did so very reluctantly.
4 The company wanted to build a dam on the site, but they were prevented from doing so by local opposition.
5 All EU countries agreed to implement the new regulations on recycling plastic, but so far only Finland and Austria have done so.
6 The water freezes in the cracks in rocks, and as it does so it expands.

63.2
1 do so
2 do (not 'do so'; habitual action)
3 doing so
4 do (not 'do so'; 'enjoy' refers to a state)
5 does so
6 do (not 'do so'; 'smell' refers to a state)
7 do (not 'do so'; habitual action)
8 did so

63.3
2 such research
3 such claims / such a claim
4 such a project
5 such destruction
6 such tactics

63.4
Example answers
2 … into research of this kind
3 … claims like this (*or* these) / a claim like this.
4 … this kind of project …
5 … this sort of destruction …
6 … these tactics …

UNIT 64

64.1
2 Yes, we should ~~have booked tickets in advance.~~ / Yes, we should have ~~booked tickets in advance.~~
3 Yes, we will ~~be staying in Brazil permanently.~~ / Yes, we will be ~~staying in Brazil permanently.~~
4 Yes, I'm sure they will ~~have been taken by now.~~ / Yes, I'm sure they will have ~~been taken by now.~~ / Yes, I'm sure they will have been ~~taken by now.~~
5 No, I haven't ~~had dinner yet.~~
6 Yes, I am ~~going to Katalin's party.~~
7 Yes, I would ~~have missed the train.~~ / Yes, I would have ~~missed the train.~~
8 No, I can't ~~see him anywhere.~~
9 No, he couldn't ~~have been looking.~~ *or* No, he couldn't have ~~been looking~~. / No, he couldn't have been ~~looking.~~

64.2
2 do
3 has
4 do
5 (do)
6 hasn't / doesn't
7 is
8 have (done) / did
9 have / do
10 (be)

64.3
2 might / would (be)
3 might / should (be)
4 should (be)
5 might / would be
6 should (be) / would
7 would / might be
8 would / might be

UNIT 65

65.1
2 used to
3 pretended to be
4 used to be
5 claimed to

6 pretended to / claimed to
7 expected it to be
8 expected to

65.2

1 opportunity (to)
2 hated to
3 refused (to)
4 choose to
5 determined (to)
6 deserved to
7 idea (to)
8 delighted (to)
9 prefer to
10 afford to

65.3

1 … if you'd like to (*or* … if you like)
2 ✓ (*or* … you'd like to.)
3 … she doesn't want to.
4 ✓ (*or* … if she'd like.)
5 ✓ (*or* … where I want to.)
6 … if you don't want to. (However, 'if you don't want' is sometimes used in colloquial speech)
7 ✓ (*or* … if they want to.)
8 … I'd like to very much.
9 … you like. (*or* you'd like to)
10 … so I didn't like to.

UNIT 66

66.1

Suggested corrections are given

2 a **lone** figure / a figure walking **alone**
3 ✓
4 a **happy / cheerful** person / a person who was always **glad** and smiling
5 his **sleeping** daughter / his daughter, who was **asleep**
6 **frightened** passengers / passengers on board who are **afraid**
7 ✓
8 a **similar** age
9 ✓
10 The girls, who were sorry for their behaviour, apologised to their teacher. / The girls apologised to their teacher because they were sorry for their behaviour.

66.2

1 a an utter / inevitable
  b inevitable.
2 a unsafe ('domestic' would only be possible here if we wanted to emphasise that the equipment was for use in the home (i.e. domestic) rather than another kind of equipment)
  b domestic / unsafe
3 a educational / entertaining
  b educational / entertaining
4 a serious
  b serious / underlying
5 a legal / stupid
  b legal / stupid

66.3

1 all the people concerned
2 As the minister responsible
3 the opposite effect.
4 a responsible adult.
5 the only available room / the only room available
6 the apparent approval
7 and concerned parents
8 financial advice available

UNIT 67

67.1

The most likely answers are given

1 almost / practically complete
2 mainly cotton
3 absolutely excellent
4 very clear
5 completely illegal
6 very popular
7 an almost permanent
8 very attractive
9 exclusively / mainly male
10 very visible

67.2

Suggested answers:

2 I'd be incredibly upset.
3 I'd be rather angry.
4 I'd be a bit embarrassed.
5 I'd be extremely annoyed.

67.3

Suggested corrections are given, but others are possible

1 extremely old
2 ✓
3 absolutely useless
4 very happy
5 'reasonably unique' is unlikely; more likely is, for example, 'almost unique'
6 ✓
7 ✓
8 quite small
9 perfectly comfortable
10 ✓
11 reasonably quiet
12 virtually impossible
13 ✓
14 a really terrible
15 simply awful
16 ✓

67.4

1 ~~fairly~~ / really
2 really / fairly (both correct)
3 ~~fairly~~ / really
4 pretty / very (both correct)
5 ~~very~~ / pretty
6 pretty / ~~very~~
7 really / ~~fairly~~
8 really / very (both correct)
9 pretty / ~~very~~
10 fairly / pretty (both correct)

UNIT 68

68.1

The most likely answers are given

2 very late
3 very critical
4 a straight
5 false
6 a critical
7 late
8 original
9 very straight
10 very false

68.2

2 a highly technical
  b technical
3 a very human
  b human
4 a largely academic
  b academic
5 a private
  b an intensely private
6 a diplomatic
  b an extremely diplomatic

68.3

Possible answers are given

2 … nice and quiet
3 … lovely and soft
4 … nice and juicy
5 … good and ready

UNIT 69

69.1

2 … the problems identified. / the identified problems.
3 Interested visitors …
4 … the sheet provided.
5 … with flights included.
6 … the resulting publicity / the publicity resulting …
7 … any remaining cheese. / any cheese remaining.

69.2

Example answers

2 The amount of added sugar in dark chocolate is less than that found in white chocolate.
3 Organic oranges contain 30% more vitamin C than those grown conventionally.
4 Cars today are much more fuel-efficient than those manufactured in 1990.
5 The President's salary is 25 times higher than that earned by the average citizen.

69.3
2 well-resourced
3 nerve-wracking
4 far-reaching

69.4
2 were wide-ranging
3 is clean-shaven
4 eye-catching

UNIT 70

70.1
1 to reduce
2 to cheat / cheating
3 knowing
4 to leave
5 to underestimate / underestimating
6 to open / opening
7 talking
8 to resign / resigning
9 to panic
10 turning

70.2
1 stupid going / stupid to go
2 confident that he wouldn't get lost
3 ✓
4 guilty shopping
5 was concerned to learn
6 ✓
7 ✓
8 busy drinking
9 was sorry to (have) upset me / was sorry that he'd upset me ('was sorry for upsetting me' is also possible)
10 wasn't prepared to admit
11 ✓

70.3
2 It was wonderful to hear such a magnificent performance.
3 It was mean of you to eat all the cake and not leave any for me.
4 It was unreasonable of them to complain about the exam results.
5 It was awkward to get the top off the jar. (*or* … to get the top of the jar off.; *informally* … getting the top off the jar.)
6 It was simple to put up the shelves.
7 It was unprofessional of him to criticise the headteacher in front of the staff.
8 It was kind of you to give birthday presents to the children.

70.4
Possible answers are given
2 It made me furious listening to his lies.
3 It made me sad that we wouldn't be working together again.
4 It made me ashamed to learn how badly we treated immigrants in the 1950s.
5 It made me nervous hearing the dentist's drill as I sat in the waiting room.

UNIT 71

71.1
1 repeatedly
2 in / with despair ('despairingly' is also possible)
3 in / with anticipation
4 reputedly
5 disappointedly
6 in a relaxed way / manner / fashion
7 determinedly
8 in / with satisfaction ('in a satisfied way / manner / fashion' are also possible)
9 in an organised way / manner / fashion
10 agitatedly

71.2
1 a most
b mostly
2 a short
b shortly
3 a directly
b direct
4 a wide
b widely
5 a highly
b high

71.3
1 ✓
2 … to me in a friendly way / manner / fashion.
3 ✓ (*or* … fine …)
4 … flatly refused.
5 ✓ ('… very clear' is also possible in informal contexts)
6 … in a cowardly way / manner / fashion …
7 … justly renowned.
8 … slowly turned …
9 'thinly' is grammatically correct, but some people would use 'thin' in informal contexts
10 … loudly applauded …

UNIT 72

72.1
1 more scared
2 deeper *or* more deep (for emphasis)
3 more pretty
4 stronger
5 more naughty
6 harder
7 truer *or* more true (for emphasis)
8 longer

72.2
2 ✓ ('more dirty' would also be possible)
3 ~~recenter~~ more recent
4 ~~excitinger~~ more exciting
5 ✓ ('wealthier' would also be possible)
6 ✓ ('more unique' is used to suggest that some people have particularly individual characteristics)
7 ~~complexer~~ more complex
8 ✓ ('more clever' would also be possible)
9 ~~powerfuler~~ more powerful
10 ~~alerter~~ more alert

72.3
'the' can be left out in 2, 4 and 5.

72.4
1 in
2 of
3 of
4 in *or* of (both are possible)
5 in

UNIT 73

73.1
2 The Downtown Hotel is not such a pleasant place to stay as the Strand Hotel. / The Downtown Hotel is not as pleasant a place to stay as the Strand Hotel.
3 The President's address to the nation is as important a speech as he is ever likely to make in his career.
4 It wasn't such a big problem as I first thought. / It wasn't as big a problem as I first thought.
5 Theresa's dog is as ferocious an animal as I've ever seen.
6 She's not such a fluent Greek speaker as she claims to be. / She's not as fluent a Greek speaker as she claims to be.

73.2
1 as many as
2 as few as
3 as much as
4 As many as
5 as little as
6 as few as
7 as little as
8 as much as

73.3
2 + a Her handwriting was so untidy as to be nearly illegible.
3 + e The bookcase was so heavy as to be almost impossible to move.
4 + c The CD was so badly scratched as to be unplayable.
5 + f The plot of the novel was so complicated as to be completely incomprehensible.
6 + b The difference between the results was so small as to be insignificant.

73.4
1 How serious an injury
2 *or* as serious as
3 bad enough to
4 not as fit as
5 not such a good player as / not as good a player as
6 go so far as to say
7 sufficiently well / well enough
8 as speedy a recovery as possible

UNIT 74

74.1

1 I expect Catalina to win the race **easily**.
2 He regretted missing the concert **greatly**. / He **greatly** regretted missing the concert.
3 I **secretly** hated playing the piano ... (more likely than 'I hated playing the piano secretly, although my parents thought I loved it.' This would mean that my parents thought I loved playing the piano secretly.)
4 He **calmly** started to walk across ... / He started to walk **calmly** across ...
5 She **kindly** offered to do the work.
6 Bruno **hurriedly** finished speaking and sat down. / Bruno finished speaking **hurriedly** and sat down.
7 I **simply** don't remember putting it down.
8 We look forward to hearing from you **soon**.
9 They **deliberately** tried to ignore me. / They tried to ignore me **deliberately**.
10 I don't pretend to understand the instructions **completely**.

74.2

1 around Switzerland in July (place + time)
2 a car at the airport (object + adverbial)
3 south towards the lakes (place [adverb] + place [prepositional phrase])
4 for a week in a beautiful cottage belonging to some friends of Kim's mother (time + place [long adverbial])
5 early at about six o'clock (time [adverb] + time [prepositional phrase])
6 briefly in the village where Kim had spent some time when she was a student (time + place [long adverbial])
7 carefully on the narrow winding roads (manner + place)
8 the train home (object + adverb)
9 ourselves enormously in Switzerland (object + manner + place)
10 there before too long (place + time)

74.3

2 ✓ *or* Next, vigorously beat the eggs in a small bowl. (Both of these are more likely than 'Next, beat the eggs in a small bowl vigorously').
3 I thought I'd securely locked the luggage. / I thought I'd locked the luggage securely.
4 I stopped playing tennis regularly ... (more likely)
5 ✓ *or* Lee was beaten easily in the final. / Lee was beaten in the final easily.
6 He always brings sandwiches from home.
7 No, they moved away last year.
8 The local residents welcomed warmly the decision ... *or* The local residents warmly welcomed the decision ...
9 ✓

UNIT 75

75.1

2 a I was brought up to earn money **honestly** ...
b **Honestly**, I'm perfectly capable of putting up the shelf myself.
3 a she admitted **frankly** ...
b **Frankly**, I went to sleep during his lecture ...
4 a **Seriously**, I don't know what I'd have done ...
b I tried to speak **seriously** to him ...
5 a **Clearly**, he wants me to take the job.
b I'd had very little sleep and was having difficulty thinking **clearly**.
6 a **Plainly**, he was feeling ill at ease.
b She always dressed **plainly** ...

75.2

1 ~~enormously~~ / significantly
2 ~~from time to time~~ / rarely
3 easily / ~~scarcely~~
4 almost / ~~by an hour~~
5 often / ~~on many occasions~~
6 ~~hardly ever~~ / every week
7 ~~greatly~~ / rarely
8 ~~nearly~~ / entirely

75.3

1 [1] & [3]
2 [1] & [3]
3 [2]
4 [1] & [3]
5 [2] & [3]
6 [1] & [2]

UNIT 76

76.1

2 ... and out jumped Daniel.
3 Outside the door stood two small children.
4 In the park the boys were playing cricket, despite the muddy conditions. (no inversion)
5 Around her neck hung a jade necklace.
6 ... and up the tree it climbed. (no inversion)
7 ... and in marched a delegation from the striking workers.
8 ... away swam the fish.
9 ... in the corner was a very old grandfather clock.
10 In the office Lea found (no inversion) it difficult to concentrate, but at home she worked (no inversion) more efficiently.

76.2

2 ... last week I had a holiday. (subject–verb inversion is not possible: 'last week' is an adverb of time indicating a period; does not take inversion [see **C**])
3 ... first came a welcoming address by the head of the organising team.
4 ... at no time were members of the public in danger.
5 No change; the adverb 'daily' can't go in front position.
6 ... seldom can a politician have changed his views so quickly as Beckett.
7 ... next came a blizzard, preventing us from leaving the hut.
8 ... by next Friday we'll be in Japan. (subject–verb inversion is not possible: 'by next Friday' is an adverb of time indicating a definite point; does not take inversion [see **C**])
9 No change; the adverb 'hourly' can't go in front position.
10 ... hardly ever did I hear him raise his voice in anger.

76.3

1 I play squash twice a week / twice a week I play squash
2 your salary will be paid monthly
3 ✓
4 ✓
5 Around the town she drove / She drove around the town; in a side street she spotted the place / she spotted the place in a side street
6 across the room it flew / it flew across the room

UNIT 77

77.1

1 ~~very~~ / ~~much~~ / very much
2 ~~very~~ / much / very much
3 very / ~~much~~ / very much
4 ~~very~~ / much / very much
5 ~~very~~ / ~~much~~ / very much
6 ~~very~~ / much / very much
7 very / ~~much~~ / ~~very much~~
8 very / ~~much~~ / very much
9 ~~very~~ / ~~much~~ / very much
10 ~~very~~ / much / very much

77.2

1 too
2 very / too
3 very
4 very
5 very / too
6 too
7 very
8 too

77.3

1 ... and he **even** offered ...
2 I will **only** be ...
3 ... and **even** the smallest donation can make ...
4 ... he has **even** asked Ann ...
5 **Only** Louis knew ...
6 ... I **only** cook ...

UNIT 78

78.1

A number of positions for these adverbs are possible, depending on the wider context and the particular emphasis that the speaker / writer wants to give. The first answer below gives perhaps the most likely position in many contexts, and then alternatives.

2 ... **Presumably**, the idea is to welcome visitors from other countries. / The idea, **presumably**, is to welcome ... / The idea is, **presumably**, to welcome ... / ... other countries, **presumably**.
3 The builders **generously** agreed to plant new trees to replace the ones they had dug up. / **Generously**, the builders agreed ... / The builders agreed **generously** to plant...
4 Most people **rightly** believe that the prisoners should be released. / **Rightly**, most people ... / Most people believe, **rightly**, that ...
5 **Obviously**, she knew more about the robbery than she told the police. / She **obviously** knew ... / ... told the police, **obviously**.
6 He **carelessly** broke the window when he was painting. / **Carelessly**, he broke ...
7 She **bravely** picked up the spider and put it outside. / **Bravely**, she picked up... / She picked up the spider **bravely** ...
8 **Interestingly**, the road didn't appear on the satnav.

78.2

2 ... outwardly she looked remarkably calm.
3 ... environmentally it is no longer the problem it once was.
4 ... industrially it is relatively undeveloped.
5 ... visually the performance was stunning.
6 ... financially we'd be much better off if we moved there.
7 ... politically he claims to be a socialist.
8 ... technically she could be sent to prison.

78.3

Suggested answers are given

2 **In geological terms**, limestone is a relatively new rock.
3 The building is similar to the opera house in Milan **in terms of architecture**.
4 **From a grammatical point of view** the essay was well written, but its style was inappropriate.
5 The election was clearly rigged and the result is a severe blow to the country **as far as democracy is concerned**.

UNIT 79

79.1

1 as / when ('when' emphasises a direct connection between kicking the ball and falling over – it suggests that kicking the ball caused her to then fall over; 'as' suggests 'at the same time as' – kicking and falling happened simultaneously)
2 When (more likely than 'While ...'; talking about a period of our lives)
3 When
4 While / As
5 while / when ('as' could mean 'because' here)
6 when
7 As / When
8 as
9 while / as
10 As / When ('When' suggests 'By the time the paint is dry'; 'As' emphasises a continuous change during the period it is drying)

79.2

1 ~~As~~ When
2 ~~When~~ While / As
3 ~~while~~ when
4 ✓
5 ~~While~~ When / As (= 'because')
6 ~~as~~ when

79.3

1 until
2 Before / Until
3 before / until
4 before
5 Before / Until
6 until
7 before / until
8 until

79.4

Possible answers are given

2 ... than he broke his arm.
3 ... when it rang again.
4 ... than / when it was time to start work again.
5 ... before members of the audience started to criticise her.
6 ... when the engine cut out.

UNIT 80

80.1

2 + b Andrea agreed to book tickets for us all **as** it was her idea to go to the theatre.
3 + a **Seeing as** it's your birthday, I'll buy you lunch.
4 + h **Because** I'm trying to lose weight I've given up dairy products.
5 + d We were recommended to buy the textbook second-hand **since** a new copy would be very expensive.
6 + c **As** the guest lecturer was late, Dr Gomez spoke about his research instead.
7 + e I suggested we all go on holiday together **seeing that** we get on so well.
8 + g You should never walk under a ladder **because** it's supposed to be unlucky.

80.2

2 ... due to lack of interest.
3 ... due to / owing to its central location.
4 ... due to human error.
5 ... due to / owing to heavy cloud.
6 ... because of the bright sunlight.
7 ... because his mobile was switched off.
8 ... because of local opposition.
9 ... because of his age.
10 ... because there was a fly in it.

80.3

2 I couldn't hear what Isabella was saying with the noise. / With the noise, I couldn't hear what Isabella was saying. / I couldn't hear what Isabella was saying for the noise.
3 With her father (being) in hospital, Olivia went to stay with her aunt. / Olivia went to stay with her aunt, with her father (being) in hospital.
4 With all the exercise I was doing I felt a lot fitter. / I felt a lot fitter with all the exercise I was doing. / I felt a lot fitter for all the exercise I was doing.
5 With the train drivers on strike tomorrow, I don't think I'll go to town after all. / I don't think I'll go to town after all, with the train drivers on strike tomorrow.

UNIT 81

81.1

2 + h He packed his suitcase with the books at the bottom **so as not to / in order not to** crush his clothes.
3 + a Bus fares in the city were being cut **so as to / in order to** encourage people to use public transport.
4 + f We crept quietly towards the deer **so as not to / in order not to** frighten them away.
5 + c I walked around the outside of the field **so as not to / in order not to** damage the growing crops.
6 + b We put up a fence **so as to / in order to** prevent people walking across the grass.
7 + g She looked down at the book in front of her **so as to / in order to** avoid his gaze.
8 + e The roadworks were carried out at night **so as not to / in order not to** disrupt traffic too much.

81.2

2 ✗
3 ✓
4 ✗
5 ✗
6 ✓
7 ✓
8 ✗

81.3

2 ... nobody would know it was there.
3 ... mosquitoes couldn't get in.
4 ... it won't take up a lot of computer memory.
5 ... we could see the view over the city.
6 ... it will receive the new channels.

81.4

Suggested answers are given

2 The meeting room is designed in such a way that everyone's voice can be heard without the use of microphones. / ... in such a way as to allow everyone's voice to be heard without the use of microphones.
3 The website is organised in such a way that it is easy to navigate. / ... in such a way as to be easy to navigate.
4 If the dial is rotated in such a way that the number 1 is at the top, the valve opens. / ... in such a way as to locate the number 1 at the top, the valve opens.

UNIT 82

82.1

2 + b Frightened though / as she was, she forced herself to pick up the snake.
3 + e Scarce though / as food became, they always found enough to share with me.
4 + c Experienced though / as the climbers were, they had never faced such severe conditions before.
5 + a Confusing though / as the instructions first appeared, they were very useful when I looked at them in detail.
6 + h Disgusting though / as it looked, it was actually quite tasty.
7 + f Confident though / as she felt, she knew the examination would not be easy.
8 + d Successful though / as their new products have proved, the company is still in financial difficulties.

82.2

2 In spite of being much younger than the others, he was the most outstanding rider in the team.
3 In spite of eating a big lunch, he had a three-course meal in the evening.
4 In spite of his fear, he allowed the huge spider to be placed in his hands.
5 In spite of her obvious intelligence, she finds it difficult to express her ideas in writing.
6 In spite of her illness, she went on a walking holiday in Nepal.

2 Despite the fact that he was much younger than the others, he was the most outstanding rider in the team.
3 Despite the fact that he ate / had eaten a big lunch, he had a three-course meal in the evening.
4 Despite the fact that he was frightened, he allowed the huge spider to be placed in his hands.
5 Despite the fact that she is obviously intelligent, she finds it difficult to express her ideas in writing.
6 Despite the fact that she was ill, she went on a walking holiday in Nepal.

82.3

1 even though
2 even if
3 Even if
4 Even though
5 even though
6 even if
7 Even though
8 even if

82.4

2 Whereas a decade ago only 5% of students dropped out of college, the figure today is 25%.
3 While the temperature is below freezing, it actually feels quite warm when the sun is out.
4 While the cost of rail travel has increased, the number of train passengers has grown.
5 Whereas I've always wanted to visit Australia, I've never had any wish to go to Canada.

UNIT 83

83.1

Suggested answers are given

2 ... give me a call. / ... take it back to the shop.
3 ... tell him I want to see him. / ... ask him to come and see me.
4 If you see any large, hairy spiders in the grass ... / If you come across any snakes on your walk ...
5 If you're ever in Birmingham ... / If you ever need any more advice ...
6 If you're coming by bus ... / If you don't want to walk far to the shops ...

83.2

1 The present perfect suggests 'if you previously studied *Macbeth* ...'; the present simple suggests 'if you study *Macbeth* in the future, then you will (get to) know ...'.
2 leave / have left; meet. The present perfect and the present simple have a similar meaning.
3 break / have broken; have to. The present perfect suggests that you may have broken it (perhaps I think you have); the present simple may be a warning or threat about a possible future event.
4 doesn't arrive / hasn't arrived; give. The present perfect and the present simple have a similar meaning.
5 haven't filled in / don't fill in; need. The present perfect suggests 'if you previously filled in an application form'; the present simple may imply 'If you don't fill in an application form now, you will need to do so ...'.
6 don't help / haven't helped; go. The present perfect and the present simple have a similar meaning.

83.3

1 belonged
2 ✓
3 liked
4 doubted
5 ✓
6 understood

83.4

2 If it were not for his anxiety over Carla, his happiness would have been complete.
3 Were it not for the intervention of the government (*or* ... for (the) government intervention / intervening ...), the strike would probably still be going on.
4 Had it not been for the arrival of the police (*or* ... for the police arriving ...), the fight could have got out of hand.
5 But for the sound of birds singing, everything was quiet.
6 If it was not / were not for the United Nations, there would have been far more wars in the last 50 years.
7 If it had not been for the roadworks we would have been here two hours ago.

UNIT 84

84.1

2 Had you not been absent from school on Friday, you would know what you have to do for homework.
3 Were Clare's friends still living in Brussels, she would have been able to stay with them. (*or* Were her friends still living in Brussels, Clare would ...)
4 Were the workers prepared to accept a wage cut, the factory would not have had to shut down.
5 Should the financial performance of the company not improve in the near future, we shall have to reduce the number of employees.
6 Had the salary been higher, I might have considered taking the job.

84.2

1 ✗ If I press this button ...
2 ✓
3 ✓
4 ✗ If the disease is untreated ... (*or* ... goes untreated ...)

5 ✓
6 ✗ If you complain about me …
7 ✓

84.3
1 If I happen to see Georgia when I'm in Rome …
2 ✗
3 … if you happen to live nearby.
4 ✗
5 If you happen to be in the south of Spain next week, …

84.4
Possible answers are given using the notes
2 … overcome with a great weariness.
3 … trying to imagine what it contained.
4 … to agree with everything Julia said. (*or* … agreeing with …)
5 … it had been reversed into a wall.

UNIT 85

85.1
2 + d Were the government to increase university fees, there would be an outcry from students.
3 + a Were anyone to lean against the window, the glass would certainly break.
4 + c Were I not already busy in August, I would gladly accept your invitation.
5 + b Were you to see the conditions in which the refugees are living, you would be horrified.

85.2
Possible sentences are given
2 Imagine you were to inherit a million dollars.
3 Suppose your parents were to tell you they were emigrating to Canada.
4 Supposing Spain were to win the World Cup.
5 Imagine the population of Britain were all Buddhist.

85.3
2 even if it were
3 even if she were
4 as if I were
5 as if she were
6 even if I were
7 as if it were
8 even if they were

85.4
Possible answers
2 I'd sooner she were going with friends.
3 B: Well, if only it were as easy as that.
4 I know you haven't got much time, but if I were you I'd have breakfast before you leave.
5 Wearing odd shoes to school was embarrassing and I'd rather it were forgotten by my classmates.
6 I'm very fond of Paul, but I wish he were not so critical of his employees.

UNIT 86

86.1
2 + d Unless alternative sources of funding are found, the research will not be able to continue.
3 + c Unless the roads have changed in that part of town, I'm sure I'll be able to find my way there.
4 + a Unless the weather starts improving soon, the farmers will lose their crops.
5 + e Unless it's ridiculously expensive, I think I'll buy that painting.
6 + f Unless you have been unemployed for six months, you are not entitled to state benefit.

86.2
2 ✓ 'If the infection isn't treated' is also possible.
3 If he wasn't
4 ✓ 'if you don't have' is also possible.
5 if Anya doesn't pass
6 If you don't get
7 ✓ 'if they don't get' is also possible.
8 if Louise isn't at home
9 ✓ 'if they can't prove' is also possible.
10 if she wasn't

86.3
1 if / whether
2 whether
3 whether
4 if / whether
5 whether (*or informally* 'if')
6 whether
7 if / whether
8 if / whether
9 whether
10 if / whether
11 whether
12 if / whether

UNIT 87

87.1
2 A small boy was kicking a ball against a wall; otherwise, the street was deserted.
3 I couldn't remember meeting him before, yet his face seemed familiar.
4 A mass evacuation of islanders is taking place. Meanwhile, the volcano continues to erupt.
5 A: Why don't you like that new French restaurant? B: For one thing, it's too expensive.
6 Ingrid came down with flu while we were on holiday.
7 My landlady didn't mind me having parties in my room as long as the rent was paid on time.
8 One way of getting rid of weeds is to dig them out. Alternatively, you could poison them.

87.2
1 Nevertheless
2 while
3 even though
4 Even so
5 Instead
6 whereas
7 so
8 Meanwhile
9 while
10 Before
11 unless
12 At that time

87.3
Example answers are given
2 However hard you might exercise, it is difficult to lose weight without cutting down on the amount you eat.
3 However much we enjoy being together, it is important to spend some time apart.
4 Professor Malcolm is always happy to spend time with his students, however busy he might be.
5 However many times I see the Eiffel Tower, it never fails to impress me.
6 Some people never seem content, however much money they have / however rich they are.

UNIT 88

88.1
1 across
2 across / over
3 over
4 across / over
5 across
6 across
7 across
8 over

88.2
1 along / through
2 Across
3 through
4 across / over
5 over ('all over' is more likely than 'all across' or 'all through')
6 along

88.3
1 under
2 ✓ ('under' is also possible)
3 below
4 over
5 ✓ ('over' is also possible)
6 over
7 under
8 ✓ ('above' is also possible)

88.4
1 c under the weather = ill
2 d below the belt = cruel or unfair
3 b under her belt = successfully completed

4 e under a cloud = with some people's disapproval
5 f over the top = extreme behaviour; indicating disapproval
6 a over and above = in addition to

UNIT 89

89.1

1 between
2 among
3 between
4 between
5 among
6 between
7 among
8 among
9 between

89.2

2 between / among the pupils
3 between amateur
4 among teenagers
5 between / among his remaining relatives
6 among its clients
7 between intake of refined sugar
8 between cooking
9 among my closest friends
10 between the striking dockers

89.3

1 among
2 among
3 between
4 among
5 between
6 between
7 among
8 between
9 among
10 between

UNIT 90

90.1

1 ✓
2 ✗
3 ✗
4 ✓
5 ✗
6 ✗
7 ✓
8 ✓
9 ✗
10 ✓
11 ✗
12 ✓

90.2

1 a by
b until ('until' would also be possible in (a). It would mean, however, that up to the time dinner was served I was hungry, and then when it was served (but before I ate it) I was not. Perhaps the food was so unappetising that I couldn't face eating it; 'by' in (a) simply means that I was hungry when dinner was served)
2 a until
b by
3 a by
b until
4 a Until
b By ('By' would also be possible in [a])
5 a by
b until
6 a by
b until

90.3

1 Over / During
2 So far
3 Until now
4 so far
5 until now
6 during
7 until
8 by

UNIT 91

91.1

1 except
2 except / except for
3 except
4 except for (in informal contexts); more formally, 'but for' is possible
5 except
6 except / except for (in informal contexts)
7 except / except for
8 except / except for (in informal contexts)
9 except for (in informal contexts); more formally, 'but for' is also possible
10 except / except for
11 except
12 except

91.2

1 ~~besides~~ except for
2 Besides ✓
3 ~~except for~~ besides
4 ~~Except for~~ Besides
5 ~~besides~~ except (for)
6 except for ✓

91.3

2 + a But for the interruptions caused by the bad weather, the building would have been completed by now.
3 + c But for the supply of food and medicines by the charity (*or* But for the food and medicines supplied by the charity ...), many more people would have died in the famine.
4 + f But for the shelter provided by the trees, the wind would have caused even more damage to the house.
5 + b But for the threat of sanctions by the EU (*or* But for the sanctions threatened by the EU ...), human rights would not have improved in the country.
6 + d But for the loan from the bank (*or* But for the loan the bank gave me ... / ... given to me by the bank ...), I would not have been able to set up my business.

UNIT 92

92.1

1 ~~of~~ / ~~for~~ / about
2 ~~after~~ / about / ~~for~~
3 ~~about~~ / ~~for~~ / with
4 ~~of~~ / ~~with~~ / on
5 for / ~~after~~ / ~~about~~
6 for / ~~on~~ / ~~with~~
7 of / about / ~~on~~

92.2

1 for
2 of / about
3 with (note that 'to' would also be possible)
4 for
5 about
6 on / about
7 of ('about' is unlikely in this formal context)
8 about
9 with
10 of
11 about
12 about
13 about
14 on ('about' is also possible but less natural here)

92.3

1 acted on = did what someone else advised or suggested; acted for = represented (usually a professional person such as a lawyer or accountant)
2 thinking ... about = concentrating on; think of = asking about an opinion
3 have called on = have formally asked him to do it; called for = demanded
4 worked for = was employed by; works with computers = uses computers a lot in her work
5 counting on = depending on; counts for little = is of little value

UNIT 93

93.1

2 there has been an improvement in her condition
3 takes (great / a lot of) pride in
4 give / offers / provides advice on
5 cruelty to
6 had a long / lengthy discussion about / on
7 have a vaccination against typhoid / have a typhoid vaccination
8 had a significant influence on
9 There is a lack of affordable housing in the city. / The city has a lack of affordable housing.
10 a ban on fireworks

93.2

2 sign of stopping
3 decision to allow
4 reason to worry
5 risk of transmitting
6 ability to remember
7 failure to protect
8 cost of buying

9 possibility of getting
10 unwillingness to acknowledge

93.3

Likely verbs are given

2 of seeing
3 to take
4 to retire / of retiring
5 of taking / to take
6 of dancing

UNIT 94

94.1

1 intransitive; no noun / pronoun needed
2 … look it up … (a noun or pronoun is necessary)
3 … help (you) out … (a noun or pronoun is possible)
4 … tidy (things) up … (a noun or pronoun is possible)
5 intransitive; no noun / pronoun needed

94.2

1 ∧ out
2 ∧ about ∧
3 up ∧
4 ∧ out ∧
5 ∧ up ∧
6 ∧ away

94.3

2 left her name out / left out her name
3 shut the thing up
4 make my mind up / make up my mind
5 got down the general ideas / got the general ideas down
6 hear me out

94.4

1 ~~ordering about everyone~~ ordering everyone about
2 ~~provide their children for~~ provide for their children
3 ~~let in me on the secret~~ let me in on the secret
4 ~~called motorists on~~ called on motorists
5 ✓
6 ~~took up Emre on~~ took Emre up on
7 ✓
8 ✓
9 ~~looked Mr Gao up to~~ looked up to Mr Gao

UNIT 95

95.1

3 Is there something bothering you?
4 There was a barrier across the road.
6 There remains the problem of what to do with nuclear waste.
8 There is supposed to be a video on the website, but it doesn't work.
9 There was no petrol available anywhere in the city.
10 Is there anyone who / that can help me?
11 There are some general rules (which / that) you can follow.
12 There used to be an art gallery around here.

(Sentences with 'There …' are unlikely in 2, 5, and 7 because the subjects have a definite or specific meaning, indicated by 'Your', 'The', and 'My'.)

95.2

1 are
2 are
3 is
4 is
5 are
6 is
7 are
8 is

95.3

The most likely sentences are given.

2 + c There's a cake in the kitchen (that / which) I've made especially for your birthday.
3 + h There was never any doubt (that) Bruno would get the job.
4 + a There have been suggestions (that) an election will be held next month.
5 + f There aren't many people alive today who / that haven't watched TV.
6 + g There are still some old houses in the village that / which don't have electricity.
7 + d There was absolutely nothing (that) I could do to prevent him falling.
8 + b There are few people in the company who / that are harder-working than Kristin.

95.4

2 There being no further business, the meeting closed at 12:30.
3 There being no doctor available, the patients were sent home.
4 There being inadequate facilities at the hotel, the conference was relocated to a nearby university.

UNIT 96

96.1

2 It was unsettling how he stared straight at me.
3 ✓ (However, in spoken English we might say 'It was surprising, Francesco's excellent exam result'.)
4 It is an advantage in the job to be a qualified driver.
5 ✓ (However, in spoken English we might say 'It's quite radical, her proposal'.)
6 It is highly unusual to put carpet on walls.
7 ✓ (However, in spoken English we might say 'It's a Ferrari, Robin's new car'.)
8 It is hard finding a good plumber these days. (*or* It is hard to find …)

96.2

The most likely answers are given

2 … it astonished me to discover (that) she was also a successful novelist.
3 … it hurts (me) to pedal my bicycle. / … it has hurt (me) to pedal my bicycle.
4 … it struck me (that) he was jealous.
5 … it concerned me to hear (that) he was offended. (*or* … it upset me …)
6 … it didn't bother him (that) everyone could see in.
7 … it upset me (that) she hadn't even told me when she was going away. (*or* … it concerned me …)
8 … it doesn't do to criticise them too much.
9 … it scared me to see (that) they were carrying knives.
10 … it pays to plan your journey ahead.

96.3

Example answers are given

2 It takes a lot of hard work to build your own house.
3 It takes a considerable amount of courage to make a speech in front of a group of strangers.
4 It takes patience and a lot of time to explain the rules of cricket to someone who doesn't know the game.
5 It takes bravery to stand up to a bully.
6 It takes a lot of organisation to be a good administrator.
7 It takes a great deal of time to learn to speak a foreign language well.

UNIT 97

97.1

2 find it
3 discover ('find' would also be possible)
4 owe it
5 remember
6 enjoy it
7 prefer it
8 leave it
9 predict
10 consider it

97.2

2 I see it as part of my role to significantly reduce Rexco's carbon footprint in / over the next five years.
3 I accept it as a necessary evil that some people may be made redundant in the next year.
4 I view it as important for relations with the workforce to make available information about / on managers' salaries.
5 I regard it as unacceptable for a modern company to exclude the workforce from major decision making.

6 I take it as a fundamental principle of the company that suppliers of raw materials should be given a fair price for their products.

97.3

2 there's no hope / chance
3 It's no secret
4 It's no good / use *or* There's no point
5 there's no reason
6 there's no alternative / choice
7 It's no longer
8 there's no denying / question

UNIT 98

98.1

2 … it was to cheer her up that I booked a holiday in Amsterdam.
3 … it's because I've got so much work to do that I can't come.
4 … it was somewhere in there that / where I lost it.
5 … it was only by studying very hard that she improved her Spanish.
6 … it is to my family that I dedicate this thesis.

98.2

2 No, what I hope is that they will be put into a public art gallery.
3 No, what annoyed me was that she didn't apologise.
4 No, what I meant was that she could borrow it until I needed it again.
6 No, what I did was (to) put some oil and soy sauce on it and grill it.
7 No, what I did was (to) give her some money towards it.
8 No, what I did was (to) hire a car and drive all the way.

98.3

Suggested answers

2 I don't know if she's free, but somebody who / that might be able to help is Petra. (*or* … but Petra is somebody who / that might be able to help.)
3 In fact the place where / that I grew up is between this village and the next. (*or* … the place that I grew up in …)
4 I suppose the time when I lived in Australia was when I was happiest.

UNIT 99

99.1

1 (in a narrative 'down comes' is also possible; see Unit 2)
2 along comes
3 up go
4 back / away / off he went
5 out / in came (*or* comes)
6 along / up came (*or* comes)
7 off / away she went (*or* goes)

99.2

2 + h Should you not wish to receive further information about our products, click on the box below.
3 + a Were the plane ever (to be) built, it would cut the journey time from New York to Tokyo by four hours.
4 + g Should the ice hockey team win again today, it will be their tenth consecutive victory.
5 + d Were I (to be) offered the job, I would have no hesitation in accepting.
6 + i Had a car been coming the other way, I might have been seriously injured.
7 + f Had there been a referendum on the issue, it is unlikely that the electorate would have supported the government.
8 + b Should you not be able to afford the SXL3, there are less expensive models in the range.
9 + e Were Charles Dickens (to be) alive today, he would be writing novels about the homeless in London.

99.3

Example sentences

(i)
Europeans spend less of their income on recreation today than do Americans.
Americans spent less of their income on housing in 1970 than did Europeans.
(ii)
Europeans spent less of their income on recreation than on housing in 1970, as is the case today.
Americans spend more of their income on food and drink than on recreation today, as was the case in 1970.

99.4

2 Kamal went to Oxford University, as did his sister.
3 People in poorer countries consume a far smaller proportion of the earth's resources than do those in developed nations.
4 He is a much better teacher now than he was five years ago. (no inversion with a pronoun as subject)
5 Dan is a keen golfer, as is his wife.

UNIT 100

100.1

2 At no time was the public (ever) in any danger.
3 Only with close friends and family did he feel entirely relaxed.
4 Only if the pitch is frozen will the match be cancelled.
5 Little did I know then that Carmen and I would be married one day.
6 Barely had he entered the water when it became clear he couldn't swim.
7 On no account are you to light the fire if you are alone in the house. / On no account should / must you …
8 Not for one moment was there any rivalry between the three brothers.
9 Not only was I wet through, I was freezing cold.
10 Only once had I ever climbed this high before. / Only once before had I ever climbed this high.
11 Hardly had the audience taken their seats when the conductor stepped onto the stage.
12 Only in the last few years has he been acknowledged to be a great author.

100.2

Possible answers

2 … was the strength of the earthquake …
3 … is her dominance in the sport …
4 … alike were the twins …
5 … complicated was the equation …
6 … boring was the lesson …

100.3

Corrections are given in the underlined sections

The people of Sawston were evacuated yesterday as forest fires headed towards the town. Such was the heat of the oncoming inferno that trees more than 100 metres ahead began to smoulder. Only once in recent years, during 2004, has a town of this size (*inversion is likely in this written context*) had to be evacuated because of forest fires. A fleet of coaches and lorries arrived in the town in the early morning. Into these vehicles climbed the sick and elderly (*inversion is likely in this written context*), before they headed off to safety across the river. Residents with cars left by mid morning, as did all non-essential police officers.
Hardly had the evacuation been completed when the wind changed direction and it became clear that the fire would leave Sawston untouched. Soon after that complaints were heard from some residents. 'At no time did the fires pose a real threat,' said one local man. 'I didn't want to leave my home, and nor did most of my neighbours.' So upset are some elderly residents that they are threatening to complain to their MP. But Chief Fire Officer Jones replied, 'Had we not taken this action, lives would have been put at risk. Only when the fires have moved well away from the town will residents be allowed to return to their homes.'

Key to Study planner

Tenses

1.1	B
1.2	D
1.3	C
1.4	A, B
1.5	C
1.6	A
1.7	D
1.8	B
1.9	A, C
1.10	C
1.11	A
1.12	B
1.13	B, D
1.14	C
1.15	B, C

The future

2.1	C
2.2	D
2.3	B, D
2.4	A, D
2.5	C
2.6	B
2.7	A
2.8	D
2.9	B, C
2.10	C, D
2.11	C

Modals and semi-modals

3.1	C
3.2	B
3.3	A
3.4	D
3.5	C, D
3.6	B, D
3.7	B
3.8	C
3.9	A, C
3.10	B, C
3.11	D
3.12	A

Linking verbs, passives, questions

4.1	C, D
4.2	B
4.3	A, C
4.4	B, C
4.5	B
4.6	C
4.7	A, D
4.8	D
4.9	B
4.10	C

Verb complementation: what follows verbs

5.1	D
5.2	A, B
5.3	C
5.4	B
5.5	C, D
5.6	A
5.7	A

Reporting

6.1	C
6.2	A
6.3	D
6.4	B
6.5	B, D
6.6	A
6.7	C
6.8	B, D
6.9	B, C
6.10	A, C

Nouns

7.1	B
7.2	B, D
7.3	C
7.4	A, D
7.5	A, C
7.6	B, D
7.7	A, D
7.8	D
7.9	A

Articles, determiners and quantifiers

8.1	B
8.2	C
8.3	A
8.4	B
8.5	A, D
8.6	C
8.7	D
8.8	A, C
8.9	B
8.10	B, D
8.11	A
8.12	C
8.13	D
8.14	B
8.15	A, C
8.16	A
8.17	B
8.18	B
8.19	D
8.20	B

Relative clauses and other types of clause

9.1	D
9.2	A, B
9.3	B, C, D
9.4	B
9.5	C, D
9.6	A, C
9.7	A
9.8	B
9.9	C
9.10	B

Pronouns, substitution and leaving out words

10.1	D
10.2	B, D
10.3	C, D
10.4	A, B
10.5	C, D
10.6	B
10.7	C, D
10.8	D
10.9	A, B, D
10.10	A

Adjectives and adverbs

11.1	B
11.2	B, C
11.3	A, C
11.4	D
11.5	C
11.6	A
11.7	A, C, D
11.8	B
11.9	C
11.10	B (in informal speech only), C, D
11.11	A
11.12	A (in informal speech only), B, C
11.13	D
11.14	A, B
11.15	C
11.16	A, C
11.17	A, D
11.18	B, C

Adverbial clauses and conjunctions

12.1	B
12.2	A
12.3	A
12.4	C, D
12.5	A, D
12.6	B, C
12.7	A, D
12.8	B, D
12.9	C
12.10	C, D
12.11	B
12.12	A, D
12.13	A, B, C
12.14	A

Prepositions

13.1	A
13.2	D
13.3	A, B
13.4	A, D
13.5	B, C
13.6	A
13.7	C

Organising information

14.1	B
14.2	C
14.3	B
14.4	B, D
14.5	A
14.6	B, C

Key to Additional exercises

1

1 b 'm not promising / don't promise / didn't promise
2 a was reading / read
b read
3 a were expecting / expected
b are expecting / expect
4 a owns (or 'own')
b owned / owns
5 a 'm considering / was considering / considered
b consider
6 a tells / told
b tell / told
7 a phoned
b was phoning / phoned
8 a 's always putting / puts
b 's constantly putting / puts
9 a prefer
b preferred
10 a weighs
b was weighing

2

1	a + (i) *or* (ii)	b + (ii)	
2	a + (ii)	b + (i)	
3	a + (i) *or* (ii)	b + (i)	
4	a + (ii)	b + (i)	
5	a + (i) *or* (ii)	b + (ii)	
6	a + (i)	b + (ii)	
7	a + (i)	b + (ii)	
8	a + (ii)		

b + (i) (b + (ii) is also correct grammatically, but it is unlikely to be used; it suggests that it is difficult to get good pasta in Italy, which is, of course, not the case!)

3

1 'had discussed' is also possible, but less likely as the duration of the discussions is emphasised
2 His condition **had improved** considerably when I saw him in hospital last night. ('improved' would be unlikely as it would suggest that his condition improved *because* I saw him last night)
3 It was announced that the Toulouse train **had been delayed** by ten minutes. ('was delayed' is also possible with a similar meaning)
4 Thomas **had been dieting** for a month when he came to stay with us, and we noticed immediately that he had already lost a lot of weight.
5 Victoria **had been expected to win** comfortably, but she finished third. ('was expected' is also possible with a similar meaning)
6 When I reversed the car out of the garage, I **damaged** the rear number plate.
7 Andrei **was promoted** last week.
8 The tax authorities **had been investigating** Rentpool for a number of months when they arrested the chairman. ('had investigated' is also possible, but less likely as the duration of the investigation is emphasised)
9 The Minister **angered** her colleagues when she criticised them during her speech yesterday.
10 Emilia **had already suggested** that the money should be spent on new tablet computers for the school.

4

A
1 ✓ ('you'll' is also possible)
2 I'll (= 'I will' or 'I shall')
B
1 I'm going to build / I'm building
2 I'll give
C
1 Will / Are you going to be able to /Are you able to
2 we're going to have / we're having
3 I'll
4 ✓
D
1 is going (more likely than 'is going to go')
2 isn't (is not) coming / isn't (is not) going to come / won't come
3 we'll see / we're going to see
4 ✓
E
1 I'm taking / I'm going to take / I'll take
2 ✓
3 more likely is 'It's at 4:15' as this is part of a timetable
4 It'll take
5 'we're going to have' is more likely
6 'I'll stay' is more likely if the decision is made at the moment of speaking

5

1 ought to have asked; would have been
2 should; 'd better
3 won't; can't; used to
4 can't; must have
5 mustn't; can
6 wouldn't; needn't have worried
7 should; would
8 should; may
9 must; could
10 will be able to; might
11 couldn't; didn't have to
12 don't need to; can

6

The agent (after 'by ...') is given only where it is likely to be included. Where it might either be included or left out, it is written in brackets.

A **The Prime Minister is being encouraged** to sack the Environment Minister, Maria Long, after **it was revealed** that she had received payments from a major oil company. However, in a statement today, the Prime Minister said: '**I am told** (by my advisors) / **I am advised** that Mrs Long **was paid** the money (by the company) [*Note the word order*: not '... *by the company the money* ...'] before she joined the government. I have no intention of dismissing her.'

B A tropical storm has caused severe flooding in the city of Chittagong in southern Bangladesh. Although **there are understood to be** (*or* **it is understood that there are / have been**) no casualties, **many thousands of people have been made homeless** (by the floods), and **the damage to property is estimated** as running into millions of dollars.

C Protesters have continued to block the construction of the new ring road by tying themselves to trees along the proposed route. (Police say that) **The protesters have been given** two days to leave the area or **they will be arrested** (by the police).

D Conservation groups have demanded that the nuclear power station should **be closed down** (by the government) after a report which said that unacceptable levels of radiation **have been found** (by investigators) in the local area.

E The Commissioner of the Dublin police force has revealed that a death threat **has been received** (by the police) against the life of President Nabon, who is visiting the capital this weekend. He says that **the threat is being taken** very seriously. **It is expected** that security levels will be increased during the President's visit.

F A man **was found** injured on a Scottish hillside this morning. **It is thought** that he fell while coming down a hillside in bad weather. **He is being treated** in hospital for leg and head injuries. [*We can assume that medical staff would treat him in hospital, so there is no need to mention the agent here.*] **He was reported** missing last night when he failed to return home after a day's walking.

G And now football. **There is expected to be** (*or* **It is expected that there will be**) a record crowd at tonight's match between Barcelona and Real Madrid. **It is reported** that **the Barcelona players will be given** a huge financial bonus (by the club) if they win and **it has even been suggested** that **they might be paid** as much as €50,000 each (by the club).

7

1 on paying
2 by asking
3 his saying / him saying
4 appointed
5 count
6 at me to tidy
7 to visit
8 wearing children's clothes / children's clothes
9 their cat
10 forcing
11 her wearing / wearing
12 to appear
13 let
14 to hearing
15 entitle her to
16 waited for
17 noticed a man take
18 invited
19 tell / telling
20 looking
21 talked
22 to living
23 me from using

8

2 We were disappointed with Karen's decision not to go to university next year. / … Karen's decision that she wouldn't go / wasn't going / isn't going to university next year.
3 Considerable media attention has been focused on Professor Adams's prediction that the Earth will / would pass through the tail of a comet within the next five years.
4 The company has carried out its threat to dismiss the strikers / … that it would dismiss the strikers (if they didn't return to work).
5 Nicky decided to follow her boss's advice that she should delegate more of her work to her secretary. / … her boss's advice to delegate more of her work to her secretary.
6 Jason didn't turn up until eleven, despite his promise to pick me up at ten. / … his promise that he would pick me up at ten.
7 I wasn't surprised by Rob's conclusion that Professor Jones doesn't know what he is talking about. / … Rob's conclusion that Professor Jones didn't know what he was talking about.
8 We decided to ignore Dan's complaint that his dinner was cold.
9 I was astonished by their refusal to negotiate over the ownership of the land.
10 The Health Minister has issued a warning to keep small children indoors until pollution levels have decreased. / … a warning that small children should be kept indoors until pollution levels have decreased.
11 I was surprised by her confession that she has / had never used a computer before.
12 When I asked Zeb where Bethany was, his reply was that he didn't know.

9

1 wants
2 are
3 live
4 points
5 prefer / prefers
6 love / loves (although a plural verb is more grammatical)
7 claim
8 go
9 comes
10 is / are
11 is / are
12 shuts
13 suspect
14 are
15 appears
16 are
17 is / are (although a plural is preferred in formal contexts)
18 plan / plans
19 is
20 provides (more likely than 'provide' in this formal context)
21 get / gets
22 is
23 speak / speaks
24 has / have
25 are
26 have
27 has
28 isn't
29 are
30 is

10

1 a a /one (informally, we could also say '… for the week')
  b a / one
  c one ('one' can complete all three sentences)
2 a A / The; b a; c an (a / an)
3 a the / –; b the; c The (the)
4 a the / –; b some / –; c – (–)
5 a the / –; b some / –; c some / – (–)
6 a – / Some; b –; c – (–)
7 a The / An; b the; c the (the)
8 a The / A;
  b a / one (informally, we could also say '… for the night …');
  c a (a)
9 a the / –; b –; c – (–)
10 a a / –; b a; c a (a)

11

2 Carla's restaurant, which serves a range of Mediterranean dishes, is very good value. (some people would use 'that' as an alternative to 'which')
3 The New Zealand rugby team, all of whose members weigh over 100 kilos, are clear favourites to win the match.
4 Chloe brought home a kitten (which / that) she'd found in the park.
5 The story is about a teenage boy whose ambition is to become an astronaut.
6 Paul has got a job with Empirico, whose main product is electric light bulbs.
7 Politicians should give more consideration to the working people (who / that / whom) they represent.
8 Among the group of people was Professor Fischer, who / whom I had last seen in Munich 20 years earlier.
9 I live on a small road which / that leads down to the river.
10 Monet's earlier paintings, many of which have never been seen in the USA before, are in a new exhibition in New York.
11 Ian McIver, whose first job was selling vegetables in a market, has become managing director of Europe's largest food retailer.
12 Kaspar has a new girlfriend who / that works in the library.
13 My Volkswagen Golf, which I bought in 2006, is a very reliable car. (some people would use 'that' as an alternative to 'which')
14 Bronwen Brookes, after whom the Brookes art gallery is named, will be present at its official opening. / Bronwen Brookes, who(m) the Brookes gallery is named after, will …

12

1 did
2 doing so / so doing
3 promised he would
4 appears so
5 do

6 have / have done
7 didn't want to
8 do ('do so' is unlikely in this informal context)
9 doubt that he will
10 don't suppose so / suppose not
11 want to / want
12 has
13 such a dilemma
14 do
15 afford to
16 expect so
17 suspect not
18 hope not
19 might have / might
20 told me so
21 determined to / determined
22 to be
23 guess not
24 might do / might be

13

Suggested improvements are given

a *Every so often* I leave work *early* (✓) (or I leave work *early every so often*) and go to a performance in the local concert hall. It's very close to my office in the building *opposite*. *Usually* (✓) they are *rather* good, but yesterday's, given by a singer and pianist, was a *total* (✓) disaster. The singer began to sing *with wonderful control*. But when the pianist started to play, it sounded awful. At first I thought he was playing *badly*, but then it became obvious that the piano was *completely* out of tune. They stopped and discussed the problem *briefly* (*or* … and *briefly* discussed the problem). *Clearly*, they couldn't continue (*or* They *clearly* couldn't continue), and they left the stage *unhappily* (✓). *Naturally* (✓), all the people *present* felt sorry for them. I'm sure the person *responsible* for tuning the piano will be severely reprimanded.

b I was *just* going out to work this morning when the postman pushed a letter *through my letterbox*. It was from Mara, who writes *from time to time* (✓). The letter said that she has to come to Bristol to visit her uncle, *who is unwell*. She is one of his few *remaining* (✓) relatives. She wants us to meet and asked if I could suggest a *possible* time. Well, I haven't seen her *for a couple of years*, so I was really pleased. We *first* (✓) met at university. We have *similar* interests (*or Our* interests *are alike*), so we *always* find a lot to talk about. The photos *included* in the letter showed that she hadn't changed since I *last* (✓) saw her. I spent so long reading the letter that I was *nearly* late for work.

14

3 + b Johan must weigh over 120 kilos, whereas his wife is really small. / Whereas Johan must weigh over 120 kilos, his wife is really small. / His wife is really small, whereas Johan must weigh over 120 kilos. / Whereas his wife is really small, Johan must weigh over 120 kilos.

4 + j There had been a lot of publicity about the meeting. Even so, only about 100 people attended.

5 + e I can't afford a coat like that. Besides, I don't like the style.

6 + h I'm determined to finish the report tonight, even if I have to stay at work until midnight. / Even if I have to stay at work until midnight I'm determined to finish the report.

7 + g Make sure you catch the last bus at 11:00. Otherwise, you'll have to walk all the way from the station.

8 + a Although I found the film boring, I stayed until the end. / I found the film boring, although I stayed until the end.

9 + i She hid the letter between the pages of a book so that her husband would never find it. / So that her husband would never find it, she hid the letter between the pages of a book.

10 + c In order to prepare for the marathon, I've been running about 200 kilometres a week. / I've been running about 200 kilometres a week in order to prepare for the marathon.

15

1 … although I know that you *approve* **of** it.
2 There seems to be little *likelihood* **of** Williamson winning Wimbledon because of her *inability* **to** play well on grass tennis courts.
3 Our plan is to *split* the organisation **up** into a number of small units. (*or* '*split* **up** the organisation into'. Note that 'split the organisation into' [without 'up'] is also possible.) This will improve our *prospects* **of** competing with more specialised companies.
4 I *ran* **into / across** Danny in town the other day. He *asked* **for** your email address, so he'll probably by in touch with you.
5 Jack takes great *pride* **in** never *throwing* anything **away** ('throwing away anything' is also possible, but less likely).
6 Although Professor Martinez *knows* a great deal **about** meteorology, even he can't *account* **for** the unusual weather we have been having over the last few weeks.
7 There has been a great *improvement* **in** the behaviour of children in the school. This has *resulted* **from** the headteacher's *idea* **of** involving them in decision-making.
8 Even though Charlotte didn't *act* **on** my advice and follow a career in medicine, I'm full of *admiration* **for** her *determination* **to** train to be a vet.

16

2 Only if an official complaint is made will the police investigate the matter further.
3 So complicated were the instructions, …
4 Had we known how ill Rob was, …
5 Such was the strength of the wind that … (*or* So strong was the wind that …)
6 Seldom did she regret her lack of formal education, …
7 Only in an emergency should you phone for an ambulance. (*or* Only if there is an emergency should you phone for an ambulance.)
8 Not for one moment was there any / a disagreement between us.
9 Were it not for financial assistance from the government, …
10 Hardly had they finished eating before a waiter started to clear away the plates.
11 Under no circumstances should children be allowed into the room without adult supervision.
12 Should the bridge ever be built, …

Index of grammatical items

Index of grammatical items

Index of lexical items